MYTH AND METHOD

MYTH AND METHOD

EDITED BY
LAURIE L. PATTON
AND
WENDY DONIGER

UNIVERSITY PRESS OF VIRGINIA
CHARLOTTESVILLE AND LONDON

THE UNIVERSITY PRESS OF VIRGINIA
© 1996 by the Rector and Visitors
of the University of Virginia

First published 1996

⊗ The paper used in this publication meets the minimum
requirements of the American National Standard for Information
Sciences—Permanence of Paper for Printed Library Material,
ANSI Z39.48-1984.

Library of Congress Cataloging-in-Publication Data

Myth and method / edited by Laurie L. Patton and Wendy Doniger.
    p.   cm. — (Studies in religion and culture)
    Includes bibliographical references and index.
    ISBN 0-8139-1656-9 (cloth : alk. paper). — ISBN 0-8139-1657-7
(paper : alk. paper)
    1. Myth—Study and teaching—Methodology. 2. Mythology—
Study and teaching—Methodology. I. Patton, Laurie L., 1961– .
II. Doniger, Wendy. III. Series: Studies in religion and culture
(Charlottesville, Va.)
BL304.M85 1996
291.1'3'01—dc20   96-14672
                                            CIP

Printed in the United States of America

CONTENTS

CONTENTS

PREFACE

The editing of this volume has been a delightful exercise in continuity, even confluence of interests and conversations. Half of the idea developed after a panel, "Myth and Method in a Post-Eliadean Age," given in November 1991 at the American Academy of Religion. Anthony Yu, Lawrence Sullivan, and David Miller, among many others, provided excellent response and critique to the four panelists both during and after the AAR, and Diane Apostolos-Cappadona shepherded the first initial queries about publication of the papers through to fruition. Early in 1992, Wendy Doniger's discussion of the life and work of Joseph Campbell was published in the New York Times Book Review, and she received several responses to the piece, asking about the future study of mythology. We decided in late 1992 to join forces. In the course of conversation and correspondence, we found that several scholars, young and old, had written, or were in the process of writing, pieces that wrestled with the legacy of their own masters in the study of mythology, and the pieces of the volume naturally fell into place.

Cathie Brettschneider at the University Press of Virginia has been a patient and cheerful editorial witness to all the shapes that the volume has taken over the course of the last four years. Evelyn Krueger and Carol Brener at Bard College have provided enormous assistance with the preparation of the final manuscript, providing expert and patient proofreading, formatting, and copyediting help. Leesa Stanion has provided her always-expert help with indexing.

MYTH AND METHOD

LAURIE L. PATTON AND
WENDY DONIGER

INTRODUCTION

Talking to the Ancestors

IN THE FIRST essay of this volume, Mary Douglas makes a plea for the contextualization of mythic narrative. Such contextualization involves real risks; it might mean that, properly situated, some myths no longer look like myths, but rather like verbal games, proverbs, and so on. She goes on to give the example of Little Red Riding Hood. In the French villages in which the Red Riding Hood stories were told, there was a detail omitted from the Grimm version: the wolf asks the girl whether she will choose the path of pins or the path of needles on her way to her grandmother's house. Yvonne Verdier's work among village women in rural Burgundy shows that the stages of a woman's life were distinguished by the symbolism of pins and needles.[1] According to this schema, a woman progresses from the life of frivolous courtship (symbolized by the pins); to the life of serious adult work (symbolized by the needles, and the attendant sexual symbolism of the threading of a needle); to the grandmother's house, where the grandmother is too old to thread the needle. The Little Red Riding Hood tale, placed in context, shows that "it is a joke, but at the same time it is not a joke that little girls will always grow up to go into their grandmother's houses and consume the substance of their mothers' mothers" (45). As Douglas further remarks, "With all of this the cohort of young girls must be taught that they will advance to take over the reproductive roles of their seniors" (44). Such narratives as these, taken in their social context, are quite open and straightforward about the nature and price of generational change.

But scholars of such narratives are not so deft at handling the passage of time. In recent decades, the historical study of mythology has undergone a massive shift in emphasis and structure. As

in many other disciplines, the hope for an elegant master theory
has atrophied. Those twentieth-century thinkers who have attempted such a theory—Frazer, Jung, Freud, Lévi-Strauss, Eliade,
among others—have kept the customary authority of intellectual
ancestors, but their powers of persuasion have lessened. To use
the language of Red Riding Hood, grandmother's house has been
reached, and the process of change is well under way.

This volume reflects the ambivalence that scholars of the present generation feel toward both sets of their ancestors, the creators of the myths and the creators of the methods. Both of these
have been at times regarded with the respect due to those from
whom one has inherited much that is precious. The creators of
the myths are like grandmothers out of whose houses, in the
sense of "Out of Africa," we have taken rich texts—myths regarded by scholars of the earlier generation, such as Eliade, as the
solution to the abyss of contemporary spiritual poverty, and by
some scholars of the present generation, such as Bruce Lincoln,
as a tool for the subversion of dominant paradigms. The creators
of the theories are also like grandmothers (Jane Ellen Harrison
being one of the very few mythologists who actually has the appropriate chromosomes) out of whose houses we have taken the
original theories through which we have learned to understand
the myths.

But to the present generation of mythologists some of these
ancestors look more like wolves than grandmothers. The creators
of the myths, whatever chromosomes they may have had, have
long been denigrated by traditional folklorists as "old wives."[2]
Now they have come to be denigrated by more recent students of
myth, particularly but not only the proponents of Marx and
Freud, feminists, and disenfranchised groups, as perpetrators of
imprisoning stereotypes and archetypes. And the creators of the
theories are damned both for championing those reactionary
myths and for failing to notice the truly important things about
them, often the negative effects they have on actual social conditions. This present generation of scholars therefore wants to take
mythology "out of grandmother's house" in a very different
sense—they want to get out of the house before they are eaten by
the wolf.

This leaves the mythologist not only with the challenge of
building a new house—creating frameworks more adequate to recent shifts in theoretical perspective—but also with the problem
of how, if at all, to incorporate the voices of her intellectual ances-

tors ("The better to eat you with, my dear"). Another myth told in this volume, this one from first-century-B.C.E. India, relates the fate of Śyāvāśva and his father Arcanānas. Śyāvāśva is a dejected Vedic poet; he has not been able to win the hand of the daughter of a king for whom he and his father have been performing sacrifices. He has been unsuccessful because the king and his wife feel he is unsuitable; he has not had a vision of the gods, and thus become a full-fledged ṛṣi, or seer of Vedic verses. The Vedic storm gods, the Maruts, suddenly appear in his path, with their golden breastplates. The young poet is dumbfounded, and instead of praising them with eloquent verses, he asks, bluntly, "Who are you?" His father Arcanānas is painfully aware of his son's error and, the story implies, reminds him of it. Once he is reminded of his rudeness, Śyāvāśva sings the appropriate verses to the gods, and thus becomes a full-fledged ṛṣi able to marry the king's daughter.

The story of Śyāvāśva is yet another example of myth's straightforward approach to the question of generational change, and a good reminder to scholars as well. Mythologists' inheritance presents them with a double task: just as Śyāvāśva followed his father as an apprentice, they have followed the guidance of scholars like F. Max Müller, Georges Dumézil, Carl Gustav Jung, Claude Lévi-Strauss, and Mircea Eliade. And thus they are also "nudged" by such forebears, as Śyāvāśva was nudged by Arcanānas, when they are presented with material that can be as confounding as was the sudden appearance of the Maruts to the young poet. Intellectual forebears are reminders of familiar and helpful modes of response that can help move a scholarly puzzle toward a successful outcome.

On the other hand, as soon as Arcanānas pushed his son toward the "appropriate" response, he had, as a father, begun the process of his own replacement. While intellectual ancestors play a large role, mythologists must be vigilant about the ways in which such guides are inherently faulty, based on the limited vision and experience of the ones who made them. Put in another way, those "nudges" and reminders, while they must be acknowledged, also produce entirely new formulations, as did Śyāvāśva's praise of the Maruts. The mythologist must ask what entirely new agendas are possible, now that no single "grand unified theory" is vividly present.

What new formulations are possible without the grander vision? At first glance, the limitations of structuralist, morphological, or anthropological paradigms leave the historical study of mythology in an odd, and seemingly not very creative, position. Late twentieth-century discourse on myth finds itself positioned between two temptations—academic arcanity and blatant commercialization. Responding to the legitimate critiques of deconstruction and the new historicism, scholars can bind themselves ever closer to their texts and ethnographies, emerging only occasionally to suggest timidly some possible new meanings. Or scholars can take the other extreme—wresting mythic narratives from their political, historical, and cultural contexts in order to make unfounded comparisons and to market new forms of enlightenment to unsuspecting consumers.

There are, however, several possibilities for a methodological middle course between the twin demons of reductive contextualization and acontextual mystification, and it is the purpose of this volume to explore some of them. It is composed of four sections, each of which deals with the questions of context and comparison from a different angle. The first part, "Bricolage in a New Key: Myth, Method, and Intellectual History," places theories of myths within their own nineteenth- and twentieth-century contexts. Each article examines the cultural agendas at stake in the construction of the discipline of mythology, thus opening up an entirely new and fruitful field of inquiry in intellectual history. The second, "The Dilemma of the Two-Headed Scholar: Myth and Comparison," explores the ways in which comparison might still be used as a helpful heuristic tool. Taking seriously recent critiques of global attempts at comparison, the articles explore more historically grounded ways in which connections and links can be made between traditions. The third part, "A Historicism without Structure and a Structuralism without History: Myth and Cultural Traditions," attempts to show the ways in which cultural history and mythic narrative mutually form each another. While the essays argue for contextual specificity in the study of narrative, they also show the ways in which myths themselves act as templates in history, shaping and mediating cultural change. The final part, "Continuities and Interruptions: Myth, Art, and Literature," addresses the themes of continuity and rupture of myth within various forms of artistic creation. These essays show that works which explicitly juxtapose elements of "myth" and "art" call into question the autonomous nature of both discourses.

Thus, while its focus is on the textual, historical study of my-

thology, the organization of this volume, like the study of myth
in general, includes a number of different disciplines. An attempt
to include a representative from every field that deals with myth
has seemed quixotic and impractical. Instead, it is our hope that
the volume acts as a kind of companion piece to works that attempt a kind of historical overview of the study of myth, such
as those of Perce Cohen, Thomas E. Lawson, Robert Segal, Alan
Dundes, and William G. Doty, and the more recent specialized
studies of myth within particular areas and traditions, all too numerous to mention here.[3]

More central to the purposes of the volume is the involvement
of scholars from several generations in fields primarily influenced
by the great thinkers on myth, who therefore must struggle all
the more fervently with the burden of their ancestral heritage.
While the essays of the volume are written primarily by historians of religion, the book also incorporates many of the fields that
historians of religion must engage: anthropology, folklore, religion and literature, and art history. There are, as a result, any
number of disciplinary perspectives that are not directly addressed in this volume, or are addressed less vigorously than others: semiotics, performance theory, the study of gender and the
body, to name just a few. Those deficiencies are real, and perhaps
unavoidable, given the limitations of size, scope, and purpose of
the volume.

Moreover, as one reader commented, the emphasis of the volume seems to lean toward political and economic correctives to
theories about myth. This, we think, is no accident; for it is precisely in those arenas that the myriad recent debates about the
ancestors (and their related political and economic involvements)
have been most vehement. Also not surprisingly, such debates
have tended to focus most heavily on the questions of comparison
and context, the two recurrent themes of this volume. As they
struggle with the grandly systematizing standards of their for-
bears, current students of mythology are anxious about the relative value of comparative work, and about the claim that
comparative work is by nature dismissive of context—particularly economic and political context.

Myth, Method, and Intellectual History

The volume begins with a series of essays in intellectual history,
tracing the struggle between context and abstraction in the very

earliest years of the theory of myth. Scholars of the last decade
have frequently observed the ways in which these theories of
myths take on the properties of their objects of study. The study
of myth has involved the recasting and reinterpreting of narratives in such a way that scholars of myth cannot avoid becoming
mythmakers themselves, deeply implicated in the narrative project, and not by any means the outsiders that they may present
themselves to be. Just as there is no original telling of a myth, so
too there is no telling of a myth (even in the context of theory)
that does not change the narrative—whether it be through media,
context, content, or a combination of the three.

Such an insight involves two possible responses. The first is
that, in the light of such heavy scholarly complicity in the act of
mythmaking itself, one should give up the study of mythology
altogether, dissolving it into the "solution" of other fields and
methodologies, such as history, sociology, or philology. The other
response is to accept gratefully the charge of perpetuating the
mythical (subversive and suspect as that activity may be) within
the confines of contemporary academic life.[4]

There is, however, a third possible response—a kind of combination of these two: while one can accept the fact that theory is
part and parcel of the mythical project, one does not have to jettison such theory as a vital piece of intellectual history. One can
retell the theory as one would retell a myth, only this time adding
its political and intellectual contexts to show the fuller, and indeed more vibrant, conceptual picture. Like the tellers of myths
themselves, the makers of theories of myth construct and deconstruct cultural values, and the historian of theory, like the mythologist, must give a full account of how this is done. The history of theory, then, can be viewed as a kind of bricolage in a
new key, where what is combined is not the narrative, ritual, and
artistic debris of the storytellers but the cultural and intellectual
texts and contexts of the theorists. The task of the historian of
theory becomes to decide which cultural and intellectual contexts were opposed to others, which were relevant and why. Such
an approach is an accounting for what Ivan Strenski calls "cultural strategies" embedded within theory.

All three essays in the first section of this volume proceed with
this new kind of intellectual history. Mary Douglas's "Children
Consumed and Child Cannibals: Robertson Smith's Attack on
the Science of Mythology," argues that one pays a price in interpretive rigor when one constructs a theory of myth without refer-

ence to practice. Douglas begins by referring to the early criticisms of the German idealist school of comparative mythology, led by Danish theologian Gronbech, who accused the early mythologists of constructing an acontextual, mythic past for the German people which suited their present tastes. Robertson Smith continued the critique by asserting the centrality of institutions and practices, as opposed to creedal elements in the study of myth. Understanding myth solely as a function of belief can lead to a lopsidedly exclusive emphasis upon theological semantics, narratives about deities, and the like. In the light of this practice-centered critique of early schools of mythology, Douglas goes on to discuss the most "scandalous" of the cases of myths: the practice of children being eaten by parents and parents being eaten by children. Ranging from the Moloch stories in the Hebrew Bible to Little Red Riding Hood, Douglas shows the importance of ritual context in each case, whether it be the practice of sacrificial rites in Canaan and Israel, or women's initiation rituals in nineteenth-century France, where the Little Red Riding Hood stories were first collected. As Douglas puts it, the stories have been forcibly narrativized, and by "being endowed with a modest equivalence with those of ancient Greek gods or the Teutonic sagas—even by the mere fact of having been collected as stories—they have been laid open to misunderstanding" (45).

The second essay, Ivan Strenski's "The Rise of Ritual and the Hegemony of Myth: Sylvain Lévi, the Durkheimians, and Max Müller," continues the focus on the myth-ritual debate of the late nineteenth and early twentieth century. It shows the development of the little-studied controversy between the ritualist school of early Indian religions, promoted by Sylvain Lévi, and the mythophilic interpretation, promoted by Max Müller. Lévi's influence on Marcel Mauss, and Mauss's influence in turn on the Durkheimian school, led to the categories of "myth" and "ritual" with which we still often think about religions today. More importantly for Strenski's arguments, these intellectual positions had meanings beyond the bounds of scholarship: they were part of cultural strategies with a great deal more at stake than the description of particular Brahmanical texts. Lévi, as an observant and politically attentive Jew, saw a great deal of threat to the status of Jews in Europe in Müller's Aryanist program, which privileged myth over ritual. As Strenski writes, "While Müller was Aryanist and early on had the reputation of being anti-Semitic, the Durkheimians were cosmopolitan and non-exclusive; where

Müller saw Romantic individualism and mystic rapture, the Durkheimians looked to the Enlightenment fellowship and co-operation; where Müller saw society as formed by its language, myths, philosophy, and poetry, the Durkheimans saw society forming modes of literary, linguistic, and poetic expression; where Müller saw myth and philosophy, the Durkheimians saw ritual and concrete human relations" (69).

Finally, in "Does Myth Have a Future?," Robert Segal takes a closer look at the ways in which theorists have struggled to determine whether myth has a future as a powerful form of discourse within twentieth-century Western culture. Segal focuses on the theorists who have defended myth as integral to Western culture and have grappled directly with the challenge that the explanatory power of science poses to the explanatory power of myth: E. B. Tylor, Mircea Eliade, Rudolph Bultmann, Hans Jonas, and C. G. Jung. Segal's concern is similar to Strenski's in that he explores the cultural commitments of particular authors—in this case the degree to which they are committed to saving myth for twentieth-century culture.

Segal begins by discussing how Tylor, in insisting upon dignifying myth as a form of explanation, also dooms it to be a lesser form of explanation than science, thus depriving it of a future in modern culture. He goes on to show how Eliade can be read as allowing the explanatory function of myth to stand, but additionally crediting myth with several nonexplanatory functions, such as justification and regeneration. While Segal is dubious about these claims, he exposes Eliade's attempts to give myth an alternative function beyond the ken of science. Segal goes on to examine the work of Rudolph Bultmann, whose response is to eschew the explanatory function of myth altogether in favor of a more expressive, existential function, indicative of the "universal human condition." Bultmann's student, Hans Jonas, takes this perspective one step further and sees the potential for myths (particularly Gnostic myths of alienation from the world) to be translatable into a structural model for an inner personal process. The most hopeful model for myth, however, is personified in Jung. Jung's view of myth does not simply translate it into an idiom acceptable to modern culture but shows how myth serves a powerful function and meaning for the unconscious, whether modern or ancient.

The work of all three authors, then, shows theories of myth woven into larger patterns of cultural strategies. Antimythic theories can have a great deal to do with the survival of particular peoples, such as the Jews in late nineteenth- and early twentieth-century Europe. Theories about particular myths, such as that of the Gnostics, can be an attempt to revivify culture through a kind of mythic translation, such as that of the Jungian "modern man." Thus, the bricolage of theory and context creates yet another field of vision, yielding larger and most intriguing insights into the role that the construction of mythology as a discipline has played in debating the very purpose of culture itself.

Myth and Comparison

The second part wrestles with the question of the comparative endeavor. From a number of different perspectives, the comparative study of mythology has come upon hard times. Like Marcel Detienne's "two-headed Greek" (and our own two-headed grandmother and wolf), caught between the philosophically rational and the scandalously fabulous, the comparative scholar must possess the two heads of the particular and the general, the different and the similar.[5] The metaphor of two-headedness is tragically apt. Unlike the head-switching humans and animals so prevalent in Indian myths, it seems that these two-headed creatures cannot merge their two heads. The head of the particular and the head of the general are frequently seen as impossible to reconcile—able only to turn and blink at each other in shock, dismay, or disbelief.

Part, though not all, of the problem is that the "similar" has come to be the scandal: since J. Z. Smith's excellent and influential essay "In Comparison a Magic Dwells," scholars have come to see that many of their comparative moves are based on gossamerlike structures of flimsy identification.[6] The challenge Smith's and other such work poses is whether the similar can have constructive value in comparison and, if so, how we might configure its relationship to the different.[7]

The two essays of this section attempt some responses to such perplexing questions, each wrestling with the legacies of the more scandalous forefathers of the present era—Mircea Eliade and Georges Dumézil. In "Maximyths and Minimyths and Political Points of View," Wendy Doniger argues that comparative work needs to retain the power of historical specificity as well as the power of the individual to avoid falling into the scandal of the same, which can be a facilely affirmative harmony of reductionist schools of comparative mythology. She goes on to argue for a cross-cultural, rather than universalist approach; instead of assuming certain continuities from the top down about broad concepts such as sacrifice, the High gods, and the like, comparativists might assume certain continuities from the bottom up, such as particular narrative details concerning the body, desire, procreation. Thus the hermeneutic value of constructing two kinds of mythic models: (1) a *minimyth*, which isolates within a group of myths a core that no culture would find foreign but that still retains some instrinsic meaning; and (2) a *maximyth*, which creates a kind of international collage in which each culture could find something of its own, and beyond that, find many other things that it had never yet dreamt of (116–18).

For Doniger, these elements provide a larger shared core of meaning to which myth refers, but which can never be located because they are purely theoretical constructs, like proto-Indo-European verbs. It is the implied spider in the web—a crucial but ultimately hypothetical reference point that helps mythologists solve relationships between myths. Following Carlo Ginzburg, Doniger goes on to show the ways in which this model makes possible a way of viewing divergent sexual and political interpretations of myths with the same internal structural characteristics.[8]

In his article, "Dumézil, the Indo-Europeans, and the Third Function," Cristiano Grottanelli begins from a very specific problem of comparative Indo-European mythology. It is one that Bruce Lincoln, in his work *Myth, Cosmos and Society*, raises as well: the continuing inattention to the third function in the tripartite schema of Indo-European society and narratives.[9] The problem of the missing third function acts as a reminder that even the best of comparative methods can leave out something crucial in their schema. Comparative studies sensitive to the concerns of cultural and historical specificity can be structurally (and, some would argue, ideologically) flawed. Grottanelli goes on to expose some of the traces of the third function, particularly the ways in which Indo-European myths and rituals more frequently show the third function serving the second and acknowledge its service as indispensable, for all that its station remains inferior (136).

Further, Grottanelli shows the various mythic episodes where twins, symbolic of the third function, contribute in a material way (cooking, forging weapons, etc.) to the hero's cosmic battle against a treacherous monster. Grottanelli also notes exceptions to the traditional hierarchical pattern and shows how the October

Equus rituals of ancient Rome present the second warrior function as subservient to the third.

In "The Madness in the Method, or a Plea for Projective Inversion in Myth," Alan Dundes tackles the problem of Freud, Jung, and universality from a folklorist's point of view. Dundes begins by taking nonfolklorists to task for their sloppy definitions of myth. Myth should minimumly involve a narrative; in addition, myth should be distinguished from legend in that myth involves a story of how the world and humankind came into being, and from folktale in that myth is not explicitly fictitious as folktale is.

Dundes goes on to emphasize that folklorists continue to use the motific index for good reason. A cursory glance at such an index will reveal that no motif is universal. The implications of the limited distribution of any of the world's inventory of myths should give pause to all mythologists who espouse universalist or psychic unity theories, including those implied, if not explicitly engaged, by literary theorists. Building on this critique, he then inverts the received wisdom that Jung (and not Freud) is a better tool to analyze myths from different cultural sources. On the contrary, Freudian theory can be used in myth analysis because it is possible to reconcile some of Freudian theory with cultural relativism. With Jungian archetypes, there is no place for the intervention of cultural difference, whereas one can add the dimension of culture to the Freudian notions of symbolism displacement, condensation, and projection.

Dundes then gives an example of how one particular Freudian category, that of projective inversion, has not only elucidated tales and legends but can also helpfully illuminate myths. Using the two creation myths of Genesis as his material, he goes on to show the ways in which this strictly Freudian category of projective inversion, used in a strictly folkloric manner, can add further depth and dimension to the traditional feminist interpretation of both Genesis creation myths.

All of these articles approach comparison not from the level of the universal, not from the level of the piecemeal, but from somewhere in between. All argue (one from a discipline of history of religions, the second from within the discipline of Indo-European studies, and the third from the discipline of folklore) that comparison can still help us to solve particular questions. All of the essays argue that similarities between myths should not be ignored simply because such similarities have been treated with various forms of universalist grandiosity in the past. On the contrary, similarities should be treated with even more caution and care precisely because they are so problematic, even dangerous, when interpreted wrongly. For Doniger, similarity can be productively used to illuminate divergent political interpretation; for Grottanelli, similarity can further enlighten the thorny problem of the third function; and for Dundes, similarity can and should be used as folklorists have been doing for decades—as a motific starting point from which to examine psychological dynamics within a particular mythological tradition. Thus Doniger, Grottanelli, and Dundes encourage mythologists to come to terms honestly and responsibly with similarity, even in, and perhaps because of, the valuable postmodern emphasis upon *différance.*

Myth and Cultural Traditions

The third section deals with the social, political, and economic entailments in the study of myth. The call to historicize the study of religion has been made repeatedly in the last decade; the move away from "pattern," "morphology" and similar categories has been virtually universal. The import for such a call in the study of mythology is a challenge, as Bruce Lincoln puts it in his essay, to study "where the stories come from, what it is they reveal, and whose interests they serve" (163). Accompanying this move are varying approaches to what it means to historicize mythologies. Although there are an infinite number of variations, one might broadly speak of three different trends in the discussion. The first element involves placing theorists in their intellectual and political contexts, as the articles in the first section of this book attempt to do. A second strand involves a move away from phenomenology of religion and calls for more attention to empirical perspectives. A third strand, allied with area studies, involves a broadly Marxist socioeconomic view that makes a call to "particularize" in order to respect the individual agency and character of the people who are under study. All of these approaches are also broadly concerned with relations of power (variously defined) within particular religious traditions.[10]

To put it another way, these responses comprise the particularizing, deconstructive impetus of the new historicism. As William Doty observes, "To deconstruct the mythic text would be . . . to expose the structures by which it works, lay out the possible future alternatives to which its gestures might lead, to show how its expression is molded by its cultural contexts, including the ways in which its mythemes and its languages are grounded in its cultural worldview."[11] Excellent work of this kind is beginning to emerge in many different fields;[12] much of the spirit of such historical perspectives is present in the essays presented in this section.

However, there is a difference in the ways in which these articles approach their topic. They take seriously Ioan Culianu's warning that we risk having a "historicism without structure and a structuralism without history."[13] With this view in mind, they all argue for a two-way perspective: in arguing for the fact that cultural history shapes myth, one cannot lose sight of the fact that myth shapes cultural history. As Kay Warren puts it in her work, The Symbolism of Subordination, one must be "centrally concerned with understanding how people use narratives to inform and justify social arrangements and how social arrangements and actions shape cultural meanings."[14]

In exposing a myth to be culturally constructed, one risks ignoring the fact that culture can be mythically constructed—and mythically constructed in a variety of different ways. This approach joins the recent critique of the "cultural model" by some students of religion, such as Pascal Boyer. Culture by itself cannot be an adequate explanatory phenomenon for certain forms of social behavior, such as ritual. Rather than being a single, coherent worldview, cultural forms consist of multiple, negotiated world views, many of which are mediated through myths.

It is important to be very clear here: this approach is not to reify myth as some kind of ahistorical force to which one can only make a kind of weak, quasi-mystical appeal. Instead, it is designed to show the ways in which narrative structures are appealed to as agents of religious change in spite of, perhaps even because of, their very aura of unchangeability. Myths have an "always-already-given" quality to them that make them powerful mediators of cultural transition.[15] Myths provide familiar frames within which all sorts of religious, social and economic change can take place.

In his "Mythic Narrative and Cultural Diversity in American Society," Bruce Lincoln begins with a discussion of the film Avalon, in which the Krichinsky clan narrates the arrival of the ancestor, Sam Krichinsky, on American soil. Lincoln goes on to offer a more general outline of American mythology that involves a transformative (in both positive and negative senses) voyage; a discovery of the land; and finally, an encounter with the previous inhabitants of the land—those who may possess older and better claims to the land.

Beyond this general outline, Lincoln argues, all manner of relations are possible—both with the land and with its predecessors. The narratives of the European immigrants of the sixteenth through the eighteenth centuries about indigenous people of the Americas tended to depict the predecessors as savages, heathens and obstacles to be cleared; these narratives were very different from the story of the nineteenth- and early twentieth-century European Americans about their Yankee predecessors, whose manners and customs they strove to assimilate (169). Different yet again are those African-Americans whose initial encounter with their predecessors involved their oppression as slaves and with whom the only possible relations besides slavery were evasion, defiance, or outwitting. Thus such tales tend to be those of tricksters and outlaws, which celebrate strategies of resistance. Lincoln ends by showing the ways in which the more specific myths become, the more coherent and cohesive is the group whose historic experience, focal values, and sense of social identity are encoded within and transmitted through that story (170).

Francisca Bantly, in her article, "Archetypes of Selves: A Study of the Chinese Mytho-Historical Consciousness," boldly argues that myth should be identified with an ontologically creative function, mediated through the archetype, rather than a specific narrative genre. This revival of the word *archetype* (another term scandalous to much of contemporary discourse) is not constructed outside of history but through history; China's myths are readily apparent in its historical consciousness. Bantly goes on to show how Jiang Qing, twentieth-century member of the Gang of Four, used the figures of the third-century-B.C.E. empress Lu Zhi and the late seventh-century-C.E. empress Wu Zetian as models of self-identity in her own political struggles.

Bantly shows thus not only what cultural forces were at work in shaping the mythical, archetypal self of Jiang Qing but also that myths were quite powerful forces in her own choices as a political actor: as Bantly puts it, this ostensibly modern woman "was compelled to instantiate herself in the mythical rather than the historical mode" (188). The question as to whether these empresses were "authentic existential guides" for Jiang Qing becomes moot, because her personal and political, and thus mythical, identities were intertwined. Bantly concludes by suggesting that archetypes, as she defines them, may well be one of the ways in which a modern, historical being can negotiate her way through history.

In Laurie Patton's essay, "Myth and Money: The Exchange of Words and Wealth in Vedic Commentary," she begins by analyzing the two problematic ways in which myths about money have been analyzed in Western scholarship: the first, that of an overly "materialist" reading that opposes itself to the symbolic, and the second, that of an overly "symbolic" reading that tends to paint languages of exchange with a mystical hue. She then suggests that the anthropological analyses of Nancy Munn, in which acts of exchange are seen as expression of relative value, is a helpful model to engage in analyzing these myths. She goes on to show a particular instance of this problem in myths about *dānastuti*, or praise of wealth, in Vedic commentary. Traditional Indology has viewed the words of praise as "symbolic" and the wealth given in exchange for those words as "material." By looking both at Vedic hymns themselves and sacrificial ritual materials, she shows that words are seen as important objects and agents of exchange, things to be crafted and welded like any material, such as iron or wood.

She then goes on to show the historical shift in attitude toward these relative values as it is expressed in later Vedic literature. While the earlier Vedic texts show a fluidity of exchange between words and wealth as forms of currency, the commentaries on the later narratives are more rigidly codified. The stories they tell allow a king to give wealth but not to utter words in praise of that wealth—such praise being the exclusive prerogative of Brahmin priests. The relationship between the production of material wealth and the production of language as a form of social authority and prestige is geared no longer toward the performance of sacrifice but rather toward the fulfillment of *varṇa* (class) ideals. In examining this Vedic case in which money is an explicit concern, she makes a larger argument about the way in which myths can be read as statements of relative value, and how such values change over time.

All three articles show the ways in which myths interact with cultural history. Indeed, it is clear that history contributes a great deal to the substance and form of mythmaking, whether it be in the differing American myths of the journey and encounter with predecessors, in the twentieth-century construction of the empress as the archetypal self or in the reshaping of the Vedic ideal of exchange into the classical Brahminical ideal.

Conversely, all argue that myth has an enduring viability that can also accommodate, indeed provide the best template for, a change in modes of expression. The mythic template can negotiate the narrative of the seventeenth-century European immigrant to that of the twentieth-century one. It can change the historical archetype of the ruthless seventh-century empress to that of the intelligent, populist leader of the Gang of Four; and it can reshape the narrative of the Vedic poet who sees his words as a form of exchangeable labor to that of the Brahmin priest who competes in status with the king whose wealth he has won.

Myth, Art and Literature

The final set of essays deals with the study of myth as it pushes the boundaries in the field of the historical study of religion and takes a place in the interstices between the fields of religion, art, and literature. In his essay Eric Ziolkowski cites the various recent writings on literature's relationships to myth. He himself begins with six such relationships: express retelling of a myth, specific allusions and motifs, reproduction of a mythic plot structure, the recurrence of universal archetypes, the creation of new myths within literature, and combining the process of literary creation. Other systems, with varying numbers of possible relationships included within the lists, are elaborated by Marcelino Penuelas, E. W. Herd, Lillian Feder, and William Doty.[16] While the lists would change in the context of art history, given the different media, they would be analogously exhausting. The point is that the relationship—the distinct difference between myth and the artistic creation—is infinitely difficult to define and to circumscribe.

Anyone concerned with the relationship between myth and the artistic process (and indeed, all of the essays in this section of the volume are so concerned), must grapple simultaneously with the questions of continuity and difference. Whether myth is "integrated," "camouflaged," "survives," or is "recreated" within the artistic process, interpreters often posit some sense of myth's continuity of meaning or form. As we shall see in the example of the Gilgamesh Epic below, the interpretive process itself may assume a kind of modernist, literary continuity in meaning to the mythic text when an equally compelling case could be made that no such continuity exists. At the same time, in order to identify clearly mythic elements in a work, interpreters also frequently articulate some distance, some distinct difference between the genres of mythic presentation and the modern genres of artistic presentation—whether those differences are those of form, function, or historical context. Accordingly, to dwell in the interstices of myth and art is to be both constructive and deconstructive at the same time.

The constructive aspect of such criticism is not, and cannot be, the search for the lost origin or the universal archetype. As William K. Doty remarks of Eric Gould's work, we must focus rather upon the statement, the archetype, and its network of interpretation-signification: "Once we have discerned an archetypal pattern, we have yet to analyze how a particular author incorporates it and gives it the unique shaping it has within the work."[17] A pattern of continuity must be particularized not only within a tradition but also within a work of art itself.

Yet those very claims to uniqueness in a work of art are also intriguingly problematic when it also incorporates myth. The presence of myth within literature or art, and the critics' tracing of it, is a deconstructive act in that it can interrupt the seamless unfolding of a work. Even if myth is brilliantly and uniquely reconfigured in a work of art (as, for example, Apostolos-Cappadona claims in her study of Picasso), those reconfigurations become windows upon the choices and historical situation of the artist. As Doty continues: "We are left, then, with the insight of contemporary linguistics that meanings are made possible by a system of differences, by systematic choices between possible alternatives, not by individual willing or disclosures from an utterly transcendent authority."[18] In this respect, the presence of myth in art follows a deconstructive, not a syllogistic logic.

All of these essays are involved with the continuous and the interruptive power of myth within art. Eric Ziolkowski, in his "Sancho Panza and Nemi's Priest: Reflections on the Relationship between Myth and Literature," analyzes ten motifs that occur in the Barataria episode of Cervantes's *Don Quixote* and also within Frazer's gargantuan work of myth criticism, *The Golden Bough*. *Quixote* has been traditionally interpreted as parodying the *mythos* of Christ's life and suffering. Readers of the *Golden Bough* are struck by the ways in which the execution of temporary kings, as shown in the rituals of mock kingship of the carnival in medieval Italy, are associated with Christian themes, such as the Eucharist and the Passion. Both authors, Ziolkowski asserts, were influenced by the Christ *mythos* as expressed through the Roman Catholic and carnival traditions. The same tradition of carnivalesque myth and ritual that provided Cervantes with the structure and theme for the episode of Barataria furnished Frazer with data to support his own theories in comparative religion.

Ziolkowski's work focuses on the continuities between the Christ *mythos* and the carnival tradition, boldly juxtaposing theory of myth and literature in a fashion similar to the approaches of the authors in the first section on method. Just as one might treat Müller, Jung, or Jonas as mythmakers in their own right, so too Frazer's interpretive text is treated in the same way as Cervantes's literary text, with startling results. In this sense Ziolkowski interrupts the usual pattern of showing the survival of myth in literature, and instead shows the equal influence of myth in both theory and literature.

Benjamin Caleb Ray's essay, "The Gilgamesh Epic: Myth and Meaning," takes up the interpretation of the *Gilgamesh* from the perspective of postmodern literary theory. After reviewing the different readings of Assyriologists, comparative religionists, and scholars of comparative literature, he argues that a close reading of the text does not uphold any interpretation definitively—that each is a partial reading which can make no claim to absolute authority. Following Stanley Fish and others, Ray argues that the aesthetic richness of the text is to be found precisely in its openness to so many different readings and that "the story is a never-ending one that thrusts the burden of its interpretation back upon its readers to ponder again and again" (304).

Ray goes on to analyze the various scenes in the story as particular moments of perspective on life and death. For example, Ray departs from other earlier readings in arguing that Gilgamesh's words of praise for the city of Uruk after his return from the otherworld are deliberately inconclusive. In this characteristic, they are far more continuous with other texts in the Babylonian Wisdom literature, such as the *Dialogue of Pessimism* and the *Theodicy,* both of which present seriously ambivalent views of the meaning of life. Thus, the Gilgamesh epic joins these other texts in calling its readers to question conventional wisdom and think for themselves. Ray concludes by questioning historicist readings (old or new) that impose a single ideological value on a text like *Gilgamesh,* which seems to provide multiple points of view in its own right. Such a historicist perspective, Ray argues, deprives literature of any genuine countercultural point of view and refuses to take seriously the value of different readings. To put it in the terms of continuity and interruption, one might say that interruptions do not need to be discovered by the postmodern reader but in fact can be contained within the text itself.

In "Picasso's Guernica as Mythic Iconoclasm: An Eliadean Interpretation of the Myth of Modern Art," Diane Apostolos-Cappadona examines a less well known aspect of Eliadean thought: his writing on the "breakdown of traditional symbols and images" and the need for their destruction. In his painting *Guernica,* Picasso intertwines the three mythological motifs of the heroic sacrificial death: the classical Greek myth of the minotaur, the Spanish national ritual of the bullfight, and the Christian theology of sacrificial death and lamentation in the crucifixion of Jesus Christ. However, these images are nontraditionally imagined—that is to say, they are abstract and representational.

The mythic iconoclasm that Apostolos-Cappadona proposes is an understanding that one must annihilate in order to recreate, and she asserts that an element fundamental to Picasso's mythic iconoclasm is societal as well as artistic: the painting stands as a commentary on the very possibility of voluntary sacrificial death and begins the "brutality and darkness" of the involuntary sacrificial death—a war with no honor. Thus, one arrives at the cultural significance of the annihilation of traditional forms. In her study of Picasso's reconfiguration of meaning, Apostolos-Cappadona suggests that "iconoclasm is an appropriate artistic mode for the retrieval and reinterpretation of a culture's fundamental mythology" (347). The study of mythic elements in *Guernica* implies, then, both a continuity and a rupture, and an interpretive lens that takes both modalities into account.

The final essay, Marc Epstein's "Harnessing the Dragon: A Mythos Transformed in Medieval Jewish Literature and Art," reintroduces the theme of myth and Jewish identity briefly discussed by Strenski in the earlier section, but this time dealing directly with the role of myth in the Jewish tradition—specifically the figure of the dragon in medieval Jewish literature and art. Epstein begins by asserting that one should not jettison the nineteenth-century observation that mythic strata are transformed in the biblical and rabbinic tradition. Rather, one should discard the chauvinistic hierarchy (of ethical monotheism over mythical paganism) that their manner of presentation implies. Further, he argues against the idea of a universal core of myth and offers in-

stead the idea of an "indigenous archetype"—in the case of the
dragon, a literal translation of the term *nahash hakadmoni*, and
a reclamation of an entire range of indigenously Jewish understandings of terms associated with primality, paradigm, and prototype.

Epstein then examines the figure of the dragon in Talmudic and
Midrashic heritage and goes on to focus on the continuities and
ruptures of this figure in medieval Jewish commentary and art. In
his interpretation Epstein focuses on the ambiguity of the dragon
figure: in rabbinic sources, it is depicted at once as God's subject
and a symbol of demonic power. The medieval dragon, as exemplified in the writings of Donnolo and Eleazar, is associated with
the biblical dragon but is further expanded into a cosmological
locus on a grand scale—the great twisted serpent upon which
hung the fate of the universe, as determined by the constellations. In Eleazar, the dragon is explicitly associated with the divine throne, mirroring the earthly serpent on Solomon's throne.
Finally, in his analysis of the medieval iconographic tradition, Epstein shows that the images of the dragon are not merely decorative but may represent a conquered threat to faith, Torah, and
even divinity formerly posed by this figure. In illuminations from
the duke of Sussex Pentateuch and fourteenth-century Ashkenazic manuscripts, this serpent is domesticated, declawed—acknowledged to exist but clearly depicted as a servant.

Epstein shows us several alternations between rupture and continuity through his analysis of the changing ways in which the
dragon figure has been harnessed and yet then breaks free. The
rabbinic tradition does not entirely contain him, and, despite the
"cold peace" which is struck in the late middle ages with his
more threatening side, that threatening side continues to be present, never fully domesticated. Moreover, the universal archetype
of the dragon is interrupted by the particularity of the Jewish tradition; a tradition-specific study shows the compromises struck
in theological debate and evident in particular artistic and literary depictions.

All the essays in this section show that, whatever the continuities in pattern or content, the presence of mythological elements
in a work of art or literature also implies the opposite of continuity. If one reads mythic elements correctly, one cannot help but
see the ways in which they break down the ontological movement
of the work toward autonomous meaning—by reminding one of
the necessary reconfigurations of narrative and image that are en-

tailed. That reconfiguration might occur within a single text, as it does in the epic of Gilgamesh, or over a longer period of multiple interpretations over time, as it does with the figure of the dragon in Jewish traditions. Moreover, readings of such mythic elements also remind one of the choices and alternatives made within particular social and historical contexts—whether it be Babylon of the second millennium B.C.E., the twentieth-century Spanish Civil War, the medieval Italian carnival, or the Jewish scholasticism of fourteenth-century Europe.

Comparison and Context: Outlining the Tensions

The volume is timely in the comparative study of religion because it does not simply provide "examples" of the adequacy or inadequacy of the category of myth from various cultural contexts. Rather, it focuses on two central, related themes being debated in a number of different disciplines that deal with myth: the issues of comparison and context. With the help of studies in many different cultural arenas, it attempts to develop new, integrative approaches to myth and yet deliberately avoids the attempt at a unified theory.

For instance, in the spirit of charting the middle course between over- and undercontextualization, we have attempted to strike a balance between an exclusive focus on method and an exclusive focus on area studies. It is our assumption that the very best of methodological discussions (such as that of Grottanelli on the Indo-European third function, or Ziolkowski on the role of myth and literature) push the scholar of myth to reconsider the particular cultural contexts from which a narrative tradition emerged. Moreover, the very best of area studies (such as that of Bantly on myth and history in China) push the scholar out of the details of a particular cultural tradition into a reconsideration of larger questions of theory. A scholar's involvement in the particulars of cultural context should transform her method as well.

Relatedly, the volume keeps the term *myth* itself in a particular kind of tension. Some of the essays, such as those of Douglas, Lincoln, and Patton, engage criticisms of the term in all of its persistently universalist connotations: the sacred and the profane, the symbolic and the concrete, binary opposition, *axis mundi*, the "Center of the World," and the like. The authors do

not simply engage in the by-now familiar critique that mythologists have focused on the static, ahistorical systematization of
narrative material. As will be discussed more fully below, they
also show particular ways in which particular myths are illu-
mined in particular social and ritual contexts—nineteenth-
century France, fourth-century-B.C.E. India, twentieth-century
Philadelphia.

Some of the authors, such as Segal, Strenski, and Ziolkowski,
expose the multiple influences and arguments involved in the
very definition of the term. In revealing such influences, they also
show the ways in which certain definitions of myth have affected
the course of Western intellectual history—whether it be in the
study of Gnosticism, the study of ritual, or the study of literature.
Other authors, such as Doniger, Bantly, Grottanelli, Epstein, and
Apostolos-Cappadona, begin to reexamine and reconstruct the
use of the term in several of the myriad intellectual contexts in
which it is now used—the study of history in China, the criticism
of medieval and modern art, the field of comparative Indo-
European mythologies. These authors argue that scholars must
take care that the old dichotomies implied by the term *myth* not
simply be replaced by a whole new set—historical-ahistorical,
identical-differentiated, and social-aesthetic. Thus, throughout
the volume, the term *myth* will neither be defended uncritically
nor eschewed summarily. Rather, attempts at new formulations
of the term will provide productive criticism of established thinking where necessary and allow the sediment (or "nudges") from
such thinking to remain where helpful.

There are significant ways in which the essays in this volume
nudge at each other as well. Certain tensions, already present
within the various aspects of the study of myth, are played out in
the differing perspectives of the authors. Dundes, for instance,
argues for a clean, folkloristically rigorous narrative definition of
myth; moreover, he argues that scholars who have ignored this
distinction (and many in the volume have done exactly that) do
so at their own definitional peril. In contrast, Bantly challenges
precisely the assumption that the mythical must also be narrative
in her exposition of Jiang Qing. Ziolkowski, true to the spirit of
the volume, veers somewhere in between; he does not argue for a
mythical archetype in literature but for closer attention to the
parallels between the narrative structures *about* myths in *Don
Quixote*, and the narrative structures *about* myths in the
Golden Bough.

Perhaps a deeper tension lies in the various authors' attitudes toward theory itself. Some, such as Dundes, Grottanelli, Epstein, and Apostolos-Cappadona, would argue that there is still much to be learned from the masters, only that it must be ferreted out and applied in new and intriguing ways. Freud may have been wrong about the neurotic basis of all religion, Dumézil about the prevalence of the first two functions, Jung about the universality of the archetype, and Eliade about the transhistorical value of the morphological approach to the study of religion. But Freud can still teach us about projective inversion, Dumézil about the third function in Indo-European studies, Jung about culturally specific archetypes, and Eliade about the iconoclastic role of the artist.

Strenski, Douglas, Segal, and Ziolkowski imply strongly that such an approach is anachronistic at best. In various ways they show that the era of simple application of theory to myth (as if theory were by nature different from myth) is over. All who juxtapose the construction of myth theory with the construction of myth narrative muddy the traditional separation between the two. Douglas and Strenski show that by emphasizing theories of myth at the expense of those of ritual, late twentieth-century Müllerians were creating other metamyths. Douglas argues that such theorists created a metamyth about "story" itself, whereby tales taken from their appropriate ritual context were "forcibly narrativized," and, in order to be treated at all, had to be endowed with an equivalence to the ancient Greek gods. Strenski argues that, while debating about early India, early myth theorists also created a metamyth about the secondary status of European Jews, who were ritually, not narratively, oriented. Finally, Segal demonstrates that, by attempting to create a place for myth in relationship to science, Jonas and Jung perpetuated a twentieth-century form of a gnostic metamyth.

On yet another level others in this volume raise concerns about the critique of myth theorists themselves. Doniger worries about the creation of a new myth of *différance*, in which the important cognitive and analytical value of similarities between stories is all too summarily eschewed. In a related way, Laurie Patton's essay implies that, while the simple economic interpretation of mythological traditions can lead to fruitful understandings of the money behind the myth, one also risks losing an understanding of the mythical value of money. So, too, Ray argues explicitly that the new historicism can, in its own insistence upon the particularity of cultural perspective, effectively erase the possibility of genuinely multiple understandings of a mythological tradition.

In confronting these tensions, then, the contributors provide both an outline of the most troubling questions in the field and a number of possible responses to them. Like "second order" versions of the narratives of Red Riding Hood and Śyāvaśva, which grapple in their own eloquent ways with the ancestral legacy, the authors attempt an honest balance between continuity and rupture as the study of mythology undergoes generational change. They suggest a number of ways in which we might be able to judge whether the creator of a myth or a method is more like a nourishing grandmother or a devouring wolf.

Notes

1. Verdier, "Le Petit Chaperon Rouge dans la Tradition Orale," 31–56.
2. Warner, *From the Beast to the Blonde.*
3. Cohen, "Theories of Myth," 337–53. Lawson, "The Explanation of Myth and Myth as Explanation," 445–70. Segal, "In Defense of Mythology," 3–49. Dundes, ed., *Sacred Narrative.* Doty, *Mythography.*
4. Indeed, the recent work of two authors of this volume represent those two possible responses: Strenski, in his *Four Theories of Myth in the Twentieth Century,* sees theory of myth as an idiosyncratic oddity, a function of twentieth-century political life. Doniger (O'Flaherty), on the other hand, in her *Other Peoples' Myths,* argues that the scholar participates in what she terms a "roundhouse" of myths, whereby each telling in each new context acts as a kind of "track-switching," and the transformation of narratives is inevitable.
5. Detienne, *The Creation of Mythology,* 103–23.
6. Smith, "In Comparison a Magic Dwells," 19–35.
7. For the more historical articulation of this view, see G. Widengren, "La methode comparative," 161–72. See also "Some Remarks on the Methods of the Phenomenology of Religions," 250–60. Also see Baird's *Category Formation and the History of Religions* and his *Methodological Issues in the Study of Religion.* For Eliade in particular, see Dudley, "Mircea Eliade," 345–59; Alles, "Wach, Eliade, and the Critique from Totality," 108–38; Ariel Glucklich, "Images and Symbols in the Phenomenology of *Dharma,*" 259–85, among many others.
8. Ginzburg, *Ecstasies.*
9. Lincoln, *Myth, Cosmos, and Society,* 141–71.
10. More central to this topic, see McCalla's "The Importance of Recent Historiography for the Study of Religious Thought," 167–79, and Luther Martin's reply, 167–79. Also see Rollman, "From Baur to Wrede," 443–54. McNeill's "Mythistory, or Truth, Myth, History and Historians," 1–10; Penner's excellent book, *Impasse and Resolution;* Lawson's "Dispatches from the Methodological Wars," 261–65; and earlier, Ferro-Luzzi, "Strand versus Structure in the Theory of Myth," 437–58. Boyer's *Tradition as Truth and Communication* also gives a critique of the anthropological notion that a unified idea of "culture" can account for certain forms of social behavior, such as ritual.
11. *Mythography,* 236.
12. Many of these works seem to be emerging from the field of Central and South American Studies. Goldin and Rosenbaum's "Culture and History," 110–32, and Warren's *Symbolism of Subordination* are both excellent examples. Also see Bricker's *The Indian Christ, the Indian King.*
13. Culianu, "Review of Carlo Ginzburg's *Ecstasies.*"

14. Warren, *Symbolism of Subordination*, 20.
15. Here I am influenced by the thinking of White, *The Content of the Form*, 3, 14–16.
16. Penuelas, *Mito, literatura y realidad*. Herd, "Myth Criticism," 69–77. Feder, *Ancient Myth in Modern Poetry*. Doty, *Mythography*, 215–48.
17. Ibid., 243.
18. Ibid.

Works Cited

Alles, Gregory. "Wach, Eliade, and the Critique from Totality," *Numen* 35 (1988): 108–38.

Baird, R. D. *Category Formation and the History of Religions*. The Hague: Mouton, 1971.

——. *Methodological Issues in the Study of Religion*. Chico, Calif.: New Horizons Press, 1975.

Boyer, Pascal. *Tradition as Truth and Communication: A Cognitive Description of Traditional Discourse*. Cambridge: Cambridge University Press, 1990.

Bricker, Victoria. *The Indian Christ, the Indian King: The Historical Substrata of Maya Myth and Ritual*. Austin: University of Texas Press, 1981.

Cohen, Perce. "Theories of Myth." *Man*, n.s. 4, no. 3 (1969): 337–53.

Culianu, Ioan. "Review of Carlo Ginzburg's *Ecstasies*," *Times Literary Supplement*, December 15, 1989.

Detienne, Marcel. *The Creation of Mythology*. Translated by Margaret Cook. Chicago: University of Chicago Press, 1986.

Doty, William G. *Mythography: The Study of Myths and Rituals*. Tuscaloosa: University of Alabama Press, 1986.

Dudley, Guilford. "Mircea Eliade: Anti-Historian of Religions." *Journal of the American Academy of Religion* 44 (1976): 345–59.

Dundes, Alan, ed. *Sacred Narrative: Readings in the Theory of Myth*. Berkeley: University of California Press, 1984.

Feder, Lillian. *Ancient Myth in Modern Poetry*. Princeton: Princeton University Press, 1971.

Ferro-Luzzi, Gabriella. "Strand versus Structure in the Theory of Myth." *Anthropos* 78, no. 3–4 (1983): 437–58.

Ginzburg, Carlo. *Ecstasies: Deciphering the Witches' Sabbath*. Translated by Raymond Rosenthal. New York: Pantheon Books, 1991.

Glucklich, Ariel. "Images and Symbols in the Phenomenology of *Dharma*." *History of Religions* 29 (1990): 259–85.

Goldin, Liliana, and Brenda Rosenbaum. "Culture and History: Subregional Variation among the Maya." *Society for Comparative Study of Society and History* (1993): 110–32

Herd, E. W. "Myth Criticism: Limitations and Possibilities." *Mosaic* 2, no. 3 (1969): 69–77.

Lawson, Thomas E. "The Explanation of Myth and Myth as Explanation." *Journal of the American Academy of Religion* 66 (1978): 445–70.

———. "Dispatches from the Methodological Wars." *Numen* 38 (1991): 261–65;

Lincoln, Bruce. *Myth, Cosmos, and Society.* Cambridge: Harvard University Press, 1986.

McCalla, Arthur. "The Importance of Recent Historiography for the Study of Religious Thought." *Method and Theory in the Study of Religion* 2 (1990): 167–79.

McNeill, William. "Mythistory, or Truth, Myth, History and Historians." *American Historical Review* 91 (1986): 1–10.

O'Flaherty, Wendy Doniger. *Other Peoples' Myths.* New York: Macmillan, 1988.

Penner, Hans. *Impasse and Resolution: A Critique of the Study of Religion.* New York: Peter Lang, 1989.

Penuelas, Marcelino. *Mito, literatura y realidad.* Madrid: Gredos, 1965.

Rollman, Hans. "From Baur to Wrede: The Quest for a Historical Method." *Studies in Religion* 17 (1988): 443–54.

Segal, Robert E. "In Defense of Mythology: The History of Modern Theories of Myth." *Annals of Scholarship* 1, no. 1 (1980): 3–49.

Smith, Jonathan Z. "In Comparison a Magic Dwells." In *Imagining Religion.* Chicago: University of Chicago Press, 1982, 19–35.

Strenski, Ivan. *Four Theories of Myth in the Twentieth Century.* Iowa City: University of Iowa Press, 1987.

Verdier, Yvonne. "Le Petit Chaperon Rouge dans la Tradition Orale." *Le Débat* 3:31–56, 1980.

Warner, Marina. *From the Beast to the Blonde: On Fairy Tales and Their Tellers.* London: Chatto and Windus, 1994.

Warren, Kay. *Symbolism of Subordination.* Austin: University of Texas Press, 1989.

White, Hayden. *The Content of the Form: Narrative Discourse and Historical Representation.* Baltimore: Johns Hopkins University Press, 1987.

Widengren, Geo. "La methode comparative: Entre philologie et phenomenologie." *Numen* 18 (1971): 161–72.

———. "Some Remarks on the Methods of the Phenomenology of Religions." In *Acta Universitatis Upsaliensis 17;* Universitet och Forskingen, 250–60.

PART I

BRICOLAGE IN A NEW KEY: MYTH, METHOD, AND INTELLECTUAL HISTORY

MARY DOUGLAS

CHILDREN CONSUMED AND
CHILD CANNIBALS:
ROBERTSON SMITH'S
ATTACK ON THE SCIENCE
OF MYTHOLOGY

Nineteenth-Century Mythology

A HUNDRED YEARS ago Max Müller gave the Gifford lectures
on mythology.[1] He was heir to the Enlightenment presumption
that mythology would replace religion and become the queen of
the humanities. In some ways he was right. It is true that by reflections on mythology Western thinkers have tried to be self-
reflexive. As both Grottanelli (in his study of Dumézil), and Doniger (in her study of Eliade) suggest elsewhere in this volume, how
well or how badly mythology succeeds in opening a window on
our past, on other civilizations, on the origins and nature of religion and language is another matter.

From the article on mythology in the 1773 *Encyclopaedia Britannica* we know that the encyclopedists expected the myths of
early times to be filled with fantasy and gross excesses, as befitted
their origins in the most ignorant and superstitious stages of civilization. To refined, nineteenth-century classicists, the frivolous,
lustful behavior of the Greek deities, and particularly the stories
about gods swallowing children and vomiting them up, were an
embarrassment. This embarrassment was an admitted problem
for Max Müller, who claimed to be proud that the philological
movement had found ways to exonerate our mythologizing forebears. The new philological science of mythology could recognize

dignity in even the crudest adventures of the gods by connecting
up the Indo-European groups of cultures. The classicists at first
found it hard to accept that the Greek myths they so revered had
affinity with Sanskritic myths of early India. Trying to persuade
them that the news was good, Müller wrote: "And this lesson that
there was continuity connecting the first crude, barbarous attempts at expressing whether in wood, stone, or words, the first
nascent ideas of divine powers, with the more recent creations of
the poetry of Homer and the art of Phidias, was surely a lesson
worth learning." Max Müller himself was to say of those inspiring
early days: "These things were new to us, like a new revelation,
like a new history of the world. . . . We saw in language a bond
that held all the prominent nations of the world together more
closely than blood and brain. . . . It was an age of discovery and of
conquest, almost a crusading age for the recovery of the sacred
cradle of our race, and every new word that could be proved to
have been uttered by the as-yet-undivided Aryan family was like
discovering an old uninjured window in the ruins of an ancient
cathedral, through which we knew our ancestors had once gazed
at the world without and at the world above."[2]

Over the last one hundred years, Müller has been subjected to
a stream of ridicule. Though we now find him wrong about many
things, he was not, however, so wrong about the unity of the Mediterranean cultures and those of India or about the etymological
affinity of names of gods and goddesses. He was far from wrong
in his idea that the problem of civilization is to control instruments of knowledge. He was brilliantly prescient in his treatment
of speech as the central instrument of knowledge. It was he who
alerted us systematically to its tendency to concretize, to ob-
struct meanings by getting stuck, and its resulting tendency to
deceive. His account of speech gave him an early critique of objectivity. Though he ascribed all the weaknesses of language to the
remote past, we still find its weaknesses interfering with our efforts to interpret.

Where he was wrong was in tying too closely and exclusively
the bond of common origin around Aryan cultures. One result
was to separate Greek civilization from Semitic influences, thus
making the culture of Greece into a miracle separate from the
cultures of Phoenicia and Egypt. Another consequence was to
have made the study of the Bible origins more isolated than it
should be. The culture of early Israel is treated as so distinctively
separate from Egypt and Africa that it sounds sacrilegious to be

placing it in a perspective of Africanist mythology, which is what I must do, as an Africanist.

Müller's mythology was also the object of biting political criticism. The Danish theologian Grönbech could have meant Müller's scientific movement in mythology when he wrote against Grimm:

> In their histories Schelling and his eager disciples drew a picture of sentimental inhabitants of ancient India and Greece who to a disturbing degree suggest benevolent despots and their duly appointed clergymen, clergymen who felt quite as much at home when cultivating potatoes as when expounding the catechism. . . . According to the philosophers the old myths which seemed to be naughty stories about the loves of Zeus, were *realiter* profound symbols for the truths of natural science. In other words, when Zeus is said to commit bigamy, it is because Zeus is the sun and the earth is a goddess, and when earth proffers herself to the blessed rays of the sun she casts a long shadow into space, which forms of course a second goddess. And behold, everything offensive has been blown away! In such pedantic visions Schelling and his disciples discovered a natural theology which was as unrealistically poetic and as prosaic *à la petite bourgeoisie* as the time required.[3]

Grönbech was right in that the new science of mythology found a mythic past for the German peoples that suited their present tastes and related their heroes directly to the heroes of ancient Greece. Furthermore, in doing so mythology became a key idea in the transformation of German culture:

> Germany had lost touch with its past in the unhappy era after the religious wars. The best men in Germany were constantly perturbed because their people lacked the feeling of stability which gave to England and to France self-assurance in intellectual work, and men like Lessing, Herder, and Goethe devoted their lives to the development of a German culture. Grimm had found the solution to the problem: a bridge could be constructed which led directly to the glorious Middle Ages; the planks of the bridge would be the common people. . . . So Grimm gave Germany what it needed: a relation to the past. His fatherland acquired a German god who fuses with Odin and Thor and reveals himself quite as fully in the old myths as in the Old Testament.[4]

Grönbech's political critique can be contextualized and turned against himself. His dislike of the German Romantics can partly be connected with the historic relations between Denmark and Germany. The same effort of political self-justification inspires to some extent the study of myths and legends, in any time and place, even today. Michael Herzfeld's study of contemporary Greek folklore shows that behind all the disinterested activity of research into the Greek mythological past lies a deliberate assertion of cultural continuity. Classical Greece belongs to the modern Greeks now freed from Turkish yoke. Mythology is their ticket of entry to a European community from which dominion by an Oriental despot had for centuries excluded them. Mythology enables them to say to the rest of Europe: "We not only share your beloved cultural origins, but they actually belong to us, they are ours more than they ever can be yours; we are the direct descendants of these mythic heroes."[5] Glorification of the brigands and their assimilation to Homeric heroes combined with research into folklorist survivals of rituals of Adonis and Orpheus make the political point.

Folklorist activity in contemporary Eastern Europe has the same uses: it draws the political alignments with and against Soviet rulers according to whether the language, agricultural and culinary implements, or songs, show Romance or Slavic influences. This exercise runs right down the middle of a traditional road that sees the task of anthropology to be the unveiling of hidden motives, the ripping off of disguises. Herzfeld is saying, along with other Greek anthropologists, that folklore is not what it seems. These folklorists, who seem to be full of disinterested piety and devotion to their ancestral heritage, have their motives exposed: they are actually promoting their own ends; their interest in folklore and mythology is merely an expression of their political commitment.

In this criticism there is the unstated, spurious notion that mythologists and folklorists ought to be disinterested: they should have no axes to grind; their analyses should be pure vehicles of unbiased truth. The same applies to the mythmakers. Myths are narratives that carry important meanings for the community in which they are narrated. What else should the mythmakers do? Where else are they supposed to be if not aligned on important issues in their own place and time? And by what lesser motives should they have been inspired? And likewise for the myth analyts and folklorists: why should they give up their time to trivial things? Their interpretations matter to them as do the myths to the mythmakers. We do not take Grönbech's criticism as fully deserved, but at the same time we note that mythology is an effective vehicle of political justification.

An Antimythology Lobby

In the very same year that Max Müller's Gifford lectures came out, William Robertson Smith was delivering the Burnett Lectures in Aberdeen (1888–91) on "The Primitive Religions of the Semitic Peoples, Viewed in Relation to Other Ancient Religions." The ensuing book, *The Religion of the Semites*, was a strong counterblast to Müller. But given the isolation of academic departments, it was not an attack to which Müller needed to pay much attention because it did not deal with Aryan languages or Aryan myths. The general theory of mythology that Robertson Smith announced ought to have been devastatingly destructive for mythology as it was understood at the time. For one thing, Robertson Smith was teaching the heresy that mythology is not very important. He even said that the study of myth is incapable of revealing the thoughts or the religions of our ancestors, and he went so far as to say that myths do not in themselves carry very much meaning.

Though this counterblast was heard by Durkheim and applied by him to the study of religion, practically it made no difference to mythologists.[6] They pursued their studies as if it had never sounded. Robertson Smith was inveighing against an overintellectual idea of religion whose perniciousness is only now beginning to be understood.[7] He pointed out the distortion that comes from looking at religion from the side of creed, assuming that religious duties flow from the dogmatic truths, instead of, as he said, the other way round. He said in his first lecture:

> The antique religions had for the most part no creed; they consisted entirely of institutions and practices. No doubt men will not habitually allow certain practices without attaching a meaning to them; but as a rule we find that while the practice was rigorously fixed, the meaning attached to it was extremely vague, and the same rite was explained by different people in different ways, without any question of orthodoxy or heterodoxy arising in consequence.

In all the antique religions, mythology takes the place of dogma;
that is, the sacred lore of priests and people, so far as it does not
consist of mere rules for the performance of religious acts, assumes
the form of stories about the gods. . . . But, strictly speaking, this
mythology was no essential part of ancient religion. The myths
connected with individual sanctuaries and ceremonies were merely
part of the apparatus of the worship; they served to excite the fancy
and sustain the interest of the worshipper; but he was often offered
a choice of several accounts of the same thing, and, provided that
he fulfilled the ritual with accuracy, no one cared what he believed
about its origin.

There can be no doubt that in the study of ancient religions we
must begin, not with myth, but with ritual and traditional usage. . . . There can be no doubt that, in the later stages of ancient
religions, mythology acquired an increased importance. In the
struggle of heathenism with skepticism on the one hand, and
Christianity on the other, the supporters of the old traditional religion were driven to search for ideas of a modern cast, which they
could represent as the true inner meaning of the traditional rites.
To this end they laid hold of the old myths, and applied to them
an allegorical system of interpretation. Myth interpreted by the aid
of allegory became the favorite means of infusing a new significance into ancient forms. But the theories thus developed are the
falsest of guides as to the original meaning of the old religions. . . .
the myth apart from the ritual affords only a doubtful and slippery
kind of evidence.[8]

These strong words might have demoted the study of mythology
from its glorious first place in comparative religion. The mythologists might well have been discredited by the accusation of "arbitrary allegorical theories." Indeed, we can still ask why
mythology is so weak on its own methodology, and still answer
that it surely would have become more self-critical had it not
been shored up by the political commitments mentioned by
Grönbech above. This essay discusses the anarchy that reigns in
the study of mythology when Robertson Smith's views are not
accepted and the methods that would have to be adopted to do
justice to his theories about dogma and practice.

Kronus and Moloch

What is a myth, anyway? Wendy O'Flaherty distinguishes myth from other stories by the criterion that myth is essentially a collective product, and anonymous: its authors are unknown.[9] This simple definition, which to many will seem too inclusive, at least distinguishes myth from signed fictions and from historical archives. It postulates nothing about the truth or untruth of the story: an anonymous, collectively produced story can still be true or false. It does not draw a distinction between myth and folklore. She further adds that a myth is a story about things held to be important by the myth tellers. The definition so improved includes sacred stories of the founders of cults. By implication, she invites us to include the Bible insofar as it is a sacred book and collectively written in that the authors' signatures are inferred from the style of the text. The Bible will here be counted sufficiently like myth for some comparisons to be drawn without offense.

We can explore this issue of belief and reality by asking whether the worshippers of the Baals really sacrificed their children as burnt offerings on the altar. The Israelites probably believed that they did. That was their collective myth. But do we therefore believe it? And was the myth important, or as Robertson Smith taught, unimportant? In the Bible the Israelites are presented as believing that the Canaanites sacrificed children to their gods. It was evidently an important issue, whether the composers and editors themselves believed it to be true or not.

Max Müller regarded the Greek myths of child-eating as the most vulgar and most difficult to beautify. Therefore they would be the ones that, if he could interpret them edifyingly, would be the most telling for the success of his theory, so he kept reverting to the theme of gods swallowing their young.[10] "What can be in our days the interest of mythology? What is it to us that Kronus ... swallowed his children, Hestia, Demeter, Pluton and Poseidon, as soon as they were born? ... Why should we listen to such horrors as that Tantalus killed his own son, boiled him, and placed him before the Gods to eat? ... Can we imagine anything more silly, more savage, more senseless to engage our thoughts, even for a single moment?"[11] Müller resisted the popular idea that a reminiscence of ancient cannibalism explained the story of Kronus eating his children. It would not have suited his wish

to present a beautiful vision of the innocent childhood of humanity. A better explanation for his purposes was that Kronus was a
personified god of time, so that if "the word for time originally
meant night, would not the whole myth of Kronus, both in his
swallowing up the bright gods and giving them up again, become
transparent."[12] "Even the swallowing and vomiting stories, which
are supposed to be proofs of a primitive Greek barbarism and cannibalism, appear in Egyptian mythology without leaving in any
doubt their original meaning. Anubis swallows his own father,
Osiris, i.e. the sun has disappeared in the dark."[13] As to there being no doubt about the original meaning, E. B. Tylor ridiculed
Max Müller's nature myths: how absurd to interpret Red Riding
Hood as the rosy goddess of dawn.[14] Dumézil refuted them both,
assimilating Red Riding Hood to Nantosuelta, a fertility goddess
of the ancient Gauls, on the strength of the pot of butter that she
carries, and the wolf with a Gallic god who is represented with a
wolfskin over his shoulders.[15] He could be right: without a
method, there is no way of deciding that any interpretation is
wrong. Without a method the whole world of myth thrown open
by Max Müller is subject to arbitrary use and ridicule and deserves Robertson Smith's strictures. Red Riding Hood has of recent years become the focus of a vast industry of comment, but
in all that I have read I find only one scholar trying to use the
methodology that would recommend itself to anthropologists following in the tracks of Robertson Smith and Yvonne Verdier, of
whom more below.

It may seem absurd to bother with these outmoded and discredited ideas. Claude Lévi-Strauss has demolished such wild and
vague pretensions and given us the method of structuralism.[16] But
this has nothing to say for historicity. Structuralist method does
not help us to decide whether Moloch's child sacrifices were a
true or a false myth. Structuralist method on its own cannot evaluate the truth or falsity of the beliefs or the rightness of any given
reading. The bare text is no guarantee of its own interpretation
and hardly to be taken as evidence of anything. What we think a
story means is underdetermined. The question is what other kind
of evidence can be brought in to reinforce interpretation. One
answer, and the one I prefer, will be on the lines of Robertson
Smith's advice to interpret institutions first, and myths after. Anthropologists vary it slightly by interpreting institutions and
myths together, the myth as a verbal part of the institution it
belongs to, as well as a commentary upon it.

Problems of Credibility

First let us expand the range of examples. In Central Africa to this day there are traditional myths about child-eating ogres, some male, some female.[17] There are also contemporary myths, widely believed, about white men who go round at night in lorries picking up any little black children they can find and taking them off to be butchered and eaten. If anyone questions the validity of the myth, they are given what seems to be compelling circumstantial evidence. Go to any European hotel and see for yourself the vast quantities of meat served there regularly, grilled or stewed or in sausages. How else but by cooking their fellow humans can such an extravagant carnivorous cuisine be maintained? I will take this contemporary African example as a springboard for comparisons with Moloch. We Europeans no more believe in our own cannibalism than we believe in medieval Christian allegations that the Jews performed ritual human sacrifice.

In the Bible the frantic prohibitions on worshipping foreign gods recall the African myth of white child-eating monsters. Over and over again, along with the other abominations of the false religions, the habit of offering children to Moloch is denounced.[18] It is not just something horrible that foreigners do; it is a temptation to which Israelites keep succumbing, just as they also tend to other vicious practices (sexual and gastronomic) associated with the foreign cults. The combination of these vices is too like the blood libel that has been used to blacken the name of the Jews in Christian history: sacrifice of children, temple prostitution, sodomy, all connected with bowing down to graven images. The wary anthropologist suspects that perhaps the foreign religion has not been accurately portrayed by its enemies. In the same way that we question the accuracy of the African myth of white men consuming black children, we are entitled to cast doubt on the Baals' demands for child sacrifice. Both cases could be treated as false propaganda against powerful neighbors in fifth-century B.C.E. Israel, or Western European colonists in twentieth-century Africa.

Comparing the credibility of Moloch worship with the credibility of tales about cannibalism may seem an unwarranted digression. Moloch worshippers are not accused of cannibalism, but there is an analogy. The fervid imagination of nineteenth-century Bible scholars had suggested a vast oven shaped as a flaming mouth bordered with fangs into which babies were thrust. The Moloch myth was not about consumption of human flesh for food; it was about children being consumed.

Skepticism about cannibalism is fueled by sophisticated studies of the fantasies of cannibalism.[19] Further systematic doubt has been thrown over the whole topic by William Arens. His book *The Man-eating Myth* examines the reports of cannibalism and finds little reliable evidence.[20] A panel of the American Anthropology Association was devoted to the question. Polynesian and Melanesian specialists gave very specific, positive evidence to refute Arens's general skepticism.[21] The upshot is that it is not possible to dismiss the idea that in some cultures people do expect to eat other people, and do it. However, the rest of the evidence goes against the credibility of biblical assertions about Canaanite child sacrifice. Cannibalism as reported by anthropologists involves eating enemies or slaves. Sometimes cannibalism is practiced as a last resort to ward off death by starvation, in cases that correspond to the imprecations in Deuteronomy. Being done without ceremony and a prescribed ritual, this practice is different again from the accusations against Moloch worshippers. In short, wherever cannibalism is instituted ceremonially, detailed prescriptions govern who can eat what. There is no doubt that cannibalism has been practiced. We cannot dismiss the evidence of myths about anthropophagy on those grounds.

But notice a significant difference: unlike known cases of cannibalism, Moloch worshippers were thought to offer, not slaves, or prisoners of war, or senior kinsmen, but their own children. The sacrifice implied a desperate bargain. The sacrificer offered the most treasured possession in expectation of a miraculous rescue (as when the bad king of Moab so outraged the Israelites by burning his son before a battle that they withdrew from the field). To an Africanist anthropologist the idea that people should ever offer up their own children as a sacrifice is almost unimaginable, because African cultures make such a point of protecting progeny. But notice again that the notion is not unimaginable to Africans, who commonly believe that their relatives are cannibal sorcerers in league with outside enemies who bargain with one another over the lives of their own children or sister's children. In other words, it is credible as an accusation. But this raises the same problem, because the anthropologists are already skeptical about the existence of sorcery. And, finally, to muddle the credibility issue even more, child sacrifice as well as cannibalism is certainly practiced in other parts of the world. For instance, among the Aztecs there was a touching ceremonial for drowning girl babies in fertility rites.[22] These children were evidently sacrificed to the lake spirit. Infanticide, and especially female infanticide, is not unthinkable anywhere in the world, and we should not lightly dismiss the possibility that the destruction of unwanted children was sacralized in the ancient Near East.

So human sacrifice is known and infant sacrifice is known. What is not credible is that at the dawn of human history everyone practiced it and that gradually by processes of moral evolution some people came to abandon the practice, leaving the others stranded on the sands of human progress, still doing the outmoded, barbarous thing. This has been a very hardy misconception. Bible students have been so obsessed with trying to work out where the Israelites stood on the ethical evolutionary ladder compared with Canaanites and Phoenicians that the weaknesses in the evidence that this barbarous usage was ever in practice among Israel's neighbors have hardly been challenged. The center of interest has been when and how the Israelite culture rose above that primitive level of savagery.[23] Some Bible scholars are impressed with archaeological findings of cats walled up in foundations of buildings or with bodies of children buried under floors.[24] This is not acceptable evidence, however. The people of southern Zaire, the Lele, who practiced human sacrifice in the form of killing slaves to be buried with their chiefs, also had the practice of burying the corpses of young babies under the floor of the home. This was intended to comfort the bereaved mother with the theory that it would make it easier for the spirit of the child to find its way back to her in a new pregnancy. In this case at least, an archaeologist finding infant skeletons in excavations of houses would be quite wrong to interpret their remains as evidence of child sacrifice. Even the evidence from Carthage seems dubious in the absence of other information than bones and pots.[25]

The Genre Question

Anthropological criticism cannot solve the questions that divide Bible scholars, but it can help by placing the issue in the context of Robertson Smith's teaching. A myth cannot be interpreted without the context in which it is told. Who tells it? To whom? On what occasion? What sort of ceremonial is it used to explain? In more contemporary terms, Robertson Smith required the mythologist to assess the *genre* to which the myth belongs. And it would not be a matter of the mythologist assigning the story to a genre created by the outside civilization: the question of whether this is what we would call a myth or what we would call a bedtime story does not arise. It is sufficient to know whether in the composition the artist we call the mythmaker expected the tale to be told to children by nurses and mothers at bedtime or to be respectfully recited at a major rite or told to neophytes to explain a major rite. We shall try to circumvent the bristling problems of credibility of the Moloch stories in the Bible by demonstrating how this method is applied to a nursery tale. The advantage of considering the story of Red Riding Hood is that it points up the kind of information that would have to be gathered to make the equivalent kind of sense of the Bible stories. The information may be unattainable, but the method still stands as the only sensible way to approach mythology.

Our children hear a story about a little girl who takes butter and cakes to her grandmother; on the way she meets a wolf who asks where she is going and runs ahead to kill and to eat the old lady. Disguised as the grandmother he gets into her bed before the little girl arrives. An innocent conversation takes place: What big eyes you have, Grandmama! What big ears you have, Grandmama! and when she says What big teeth! the wolf jumps out of bed and is just about to devour her when a woodcutter turns up in time to save the child, kill the wolf, and rescue the grandmother. However, our children get a bowdlerized version. According to the most frequently recorded form of the original tale, both the wolf and the little girl eat parts of the grandmother.[26] Learning this was for me a shock. How could the story about that sweet child have anything to do with her drinking bowls of her own grandmother's blood? Or eating her grandmother's sexual organs and breasts? It is even more of a shock than discovering that none of the original versions describes her hood as red. Admittedly, the child does not know that the soup the wolf gives her is made from her grandmother's blood. She is an unwitting cannibal. Though our versions make the wolf into a child-eating monster, in fact, according to Yvonne Verdier's interpretation based on an analysis of all the French versions, his role is quite incidental and unimportant.

Following Lévi-Strauss's teaching, we now know that some myths may be read as inverted structures. This news ought to have delighted Max Müller. The tales that we try to interpret in

terms of people's institutions often turn out to be not elaborations upon real life, past or present, but inside-out and upside-
down versions of daily practice. So viewed, instead of being taken
seriously as evidence of primitive human sacrifice or cannibalism, as Müller ardently denied, tales of cannibal gods have to be
read as presenting exactly the opposite of normal divine behavior.
But what is the right way up, and how are we to know whether
to read the story the right way up or upside down? Is Red Riding
Hood to be taken as an inversion of everyday behavior or the
norm? Was Moloch an inversion of Canaanite behavior? Or were
the Canaanites portrayed to the people of Israel as inverted wor-
shipers? Is the message that false gods consume children and the
true God of Israel protects children? Fortunately, the rules of
structural analysis are clear. But they cannot be applied without
the full context of everyday behavior. To recognize an inversion
of reality, we need to follow Robertson Smith's advice and study
the normal institutions.

A quotation about Southern Bantu cannibal tales illustrates
how to do it. In these stories,

> first cannibals are contrasted implicitly with the good ancestral
> spirits, who protect people and foster human health and fertility.
> Second, cannibals are directly contrasted to human beings. Unlike
> man, who lives in settlements, the cannibal lives in a cave in the
> bush, like a wild animal. The cannibal hunts human beings (whom
> he calls "game" [gibier]) and cooks human meat together with ani-
> mal meat. The cannibal is also very large and very hairy, unlike
> normal people, and more like an animal. He or she often has one
> huge leg or toe, and one-leggedness is a characteristic of intermedi-
> aries between man and the spirits in bantu lore. . . . Ancestor spirits
> may live in the sky or below the ground, and may intervene in the
> form of snakes or birds. . . . When people escape from cannibals,
> they often do so disguised as birds or snakes.[27]

Clearly the Bantu ogres are not like normal human beings: they
are inversions, like ancestors, but in the other direction, toward
land animals instead of toward birds. So what about Red Riding
Hood? Is the story about her eating her grandmother meant to
portray normal circumstances, or is it an upside-down, inside-out
version of human life? Yvonne Verdier paying particular attention
to the cannibal meal, faces the problem and argues that there is
nothing in Red Riding Hood to indicate signs of myth inversion.[28]

Arrivée chez sa grand-mère, la petite fille est invitée par le loup à
se restaurer; ou bien c'est elle qui, d'entrée, declare qu'elle a faim,
puis soif (puis sommeil). Il lui dit de prendre de la viande dans le
placard, ou le coffre, ou l'armoire, et de se servir un verre de vin.
La scène est intime, domestique, le loup dans son lit la regarde
s'affairer: elle fait tous les gestes de préparation du repas, sort les
ingredients, allume le feu, remue les casseroles. . . . Rappelons les
gestes du loup. Il arrive, tue la grand-mère, la dévore en partie, la
saigne, met le sang de coté dans une bouteille, un verre, un plat,
une terrine, une écuelle, un assiette, un bol, et reserve la chaire—
c'est le terme employé -qu'il range comme des provisions dans le
coffre, l'armoire ou le placard. Dans une version c'est la tête qu'il
met sur un assiette.[29]

Except for the presence of the wolf, this is definitely not an inverted version of everyday comportment. The girl is conducting
herself as any young housewife would in a normal kitchen. That
being so, how is the story to be interpreted? Was life so rough
that little girls really attacked their grandmothers in nineteenth-
century France?

Robert Darnton, a historian who has paid attention to these
Mother Goose stories, has suggested that Red Riding Hood belongs in the genre of French trickster stories. Making a general
comparison between German and French folktales, he finds more
cunning and humor on the French side, more numbskull Simple
Simon types of heroes on the German side, dealing with more
terror and fantasy. Since he finds that the central feature of this
story is that Red Riding Hood cheats the wolf at the end, he adds
it to his category of French folktales that extol roguery. "Peasants
of early, modern France inhabited a world of stepmothers and
orphans, inexorable unbending toil, and of brutal emotions,
both raw and repressed . . . lives really were nasty, brutish and
short[30]. . . . If the world is cruel, the village nasty, and mankind
infested with rogues, what is one to do? Roguery runs through the
whole corpus of French tales." Does this mean that the German
peasantry at the same time were enjoying a more comfortable
life? The historian would have quite a hard time justifying the
implications of this interpretation based on experience of
roguery.[31]

Anthropologists are not allowed to make a free selection from
the text. Deciding what is the key feature of a story is a technical

matter bristling with difficulty. Accounting for everything that is in the story is an impossible rule to fulfill, but the effort to respect it is a great protection against errors of omission. All the original versions of Red Riding Hood have got something about her choice of routes to her grandmother's house; will she take the way of pins or the way of needles. This is omitted in our versions. They are also full of sexual reference. An interpretation that omits these elements is arbitrary. In the original versions the conversation between the wolf and the little girl is laced with racy innuendo: he asks her to get into bed with him, and she complies. Her surprised remarks on how she finds her grandmother's body changed ("How big . . .! How hairy . . .! How strong . . .!) and his lewdly double-edged answers are not at all the kind of talk that the nannies who used to reign in our nurseries would approve.

The Feminine Order

When the wolf meets the girl (and the language suggests we should be imagining a girl approaching puberty), he asks her which way she is going to her grandmother's house. Will she take the path of needles or the path of pins? Different versions put different answers into her mouth. The answer she gives does not matter. The important thing is the mention of the two paths. Peasant women in nineteenth-century France, when these stories were collected, had an informal system of age classes. The stages of a woman's life were distinguished by the symbolism of pins and needles. Pins are easy to use but make only temporary fastenings; needles are employed with skill and perseverance, and make permanent ties. Putting a thread through the eye of a needle has a simple sexual connotation. Needles are for adult women, pins for courting girls who receive pins as gifts from their admirers or throw pins into the wishing well. The choice between pins and needles is in all the versions before Perrault and Grimm tidied them up to be suitable for our nurseries. Any interpretation that omits that detail is suspect.

The mention of pins and needles would alert the listener to expect a story referring to sex and to the sequence of roles that the female child will go through in her life. As the sequence is punctuated by girls' initiation ceremonies, we have found the context for applying Robertson Smith's rules. After puberty the young girl goes with her cohort to another village to spend a happy winter season with the dressmaker. Living together away

from home for the first time the girls form the solidary ties that
will last through their lives. After the period of seclusion, their
homecoming in the spring has its own ceremonious implications.
They are esteemed now to be the right age to enjoy the frivolous
period of pins, courtship, and temporary attachments. After the
giddy May festivities they mature to womanhood, marriage, and
the serious work of needles. Finally they will grow too old to be
able to thread a needle, like the grandmother. By omitting the
wolf's question about pins or needles, the versions we have received have lost the main cue for interpreting the stories.

According to Yvonne Verdier, who conducted field research
among the old women in the village of Minot in Burgundy, the
succession of roles in the feminine world is the known backdrop
to a range of Mother Goose stories about blood, sex, and rivalry
between generations of women.[32] Not just the roles but beliefs
about female physiology are necessary background for interpretation. Unlike men, whose bodies are set on a steady course
through life, alienated from the cycles of nature, those women
know that their bodies swing them between reason and emotion
on a monthly program in harmony with the seasons of the year.
The women's physiological month reproduces in small nature's
whole year. The days of menstruation correspond to the month
of May, when nature swings into a state of fermentation, birthing,
hatching, budding, mushrooming in rich profusion. Knowing the
reality of this connection between their bodily cycles and those
of nature, women impose upon themselves a prohibition during
their own monthly period of fermentation on doing work that
could contaminate other fermentation processes: so menstruat-
ing women avoid touching wine vessels or going into the wine
cellar, or touching pork in brine, lest by contagion it ferments and
turns bad. These are responsibilities of women that demonstrate
their close affinity to nature; their work is giving birth, feeding,
washing, and caring for the body. With all of this the cohort of
young girls must also be taught that they will advance to take
over the reproductive roles of their seniors.

The Mother Goose stories provide an informal backdrop to the
seasonal and life-cycle rituals, that for the girls culminate in
the May Day celebrations. The actual arrangements for training
the girls and for ordaining their place in the social order are supported by the rituals of first communion and marriage, a liturgy
for which the stories, if that is what they are, provide ad hoc commentaries. No direct narrative meaning justifies the stories of

Sleeping Beauty or Red Riding Hood. To ask what the stories mean as stories hardly makes sense. They have some entertainment value, but that is because of the reference to well-known rituals and statuses. Their meaning lies in the play upon the current pattern of roles and upon their inherent conflicts and tensions. It is a joke, and at the same time it is not a joke but true, that little girls will always grow up to go into their grandmothers' houses and consume the substance of their mothers' mothers.

Puzzles Raised by Narrativization

Folktales have been wrongly assimilated to our own idea of narrative. By being treated as tales, and by being endowed with a modest equivalence with the legends of ancient Greek gods and the Teutonic sagas—even by the mere fact of having been collected as stories—they have been laid open to misunderstanding and forcibly narrativized. Verdier considers folktales to be more like a genre of little proverbs, games, lampoons, limericks, joke moral lessons. In her view they never were full-blown stories with beginnings, middles, and ends but have been forced by folklorists into the narrative genre. It is doubtful whether there is any other genre in our culture that corresponds to such little bits and pieces. Scraps of songs and sayings, a salacious commentary upon the feminine order, they are too fragile to bear by themselves the freight of meaning with which they are credited. Without knowing the context of action and institutions, there is no way to interpret the stories, and when the context is given, they are not so much stories as little verbal rituals.

Even now a very large element is missing. The stories, as Verdier interprets them, are about and for women who live in villages strictly divided into male and female spheres. Her book, about such a village, has practically nothing to say about the men. They appear only as shadowy background figures, utterly dependent on women who bring them into the world as babies and see them out of it when women prepare their corpses for burial. In the women's culture, women are at the center of the universe, the men at the periphery. Women are in tune with nature and the seasons and have cosmic responsibilities. In a real sense they have created a world that reverses the world of men, not merely at the level of the domestic house, but through their association with the phases of the moon and the cycle of vegetation.

In the opposite world of men there are male life-cycle rituals, which are coarser than the coarsest of the versions of Red Riding Hood. The style in itself marks the difference between male and female spheres. In the village of Minot the annual pig killings were the occasion of hilarious scatologic rites that left the little boys in no doubt about their future sexual roles. Stories about the female child appropriating the sexual parts of the grandmother are matched on the male side by the pantomime of filling the little boys' pockets with pigs' testicles. The contrast between the medium of instruction is striking. If we thought that the original stories of the little girl's cannibal feast and the titillating scene of her in bed with the wolf were crude, they are much more refined than the counterpart lessons for the boys. The medium speaks for the domestic scope of the woman compared with the men's work of the farm and with animals. The feminine version is only verbal; the masculine version is a vulgar mime. The little girl politely drinks the blood and eats the meat which she has cooked over the fire and served in bowls and dishes taken out of cupboards. Her lesson is just a bit of a story: The little boy is chased around the farmyard, with bleeding pig's entrails thrown at him and real pig's innards on his head and in his clothes. The vigor and realism of the teaching of sex roles in the evocation of the respective scenes of work all a far cry from the desiccated sex instruction in our schools. Yvonne Verdier herself has commented in the article cited on the defeminization of modern culture that has made it so difficult to think about femininity at all, and so has made it difficult to recognize these stories as teaching about gender.

The lesson for the would-be mythologist or folklorist is that the story is a comment on something that is currently happening. Before mythology developed as a science about words, this is what all the mythlike stories would have been. When a myth seems to be an inverted version of another myth, two fields of action will always be self-defined by reference to each other. In the cannibal-ogre tales of the Southern Bantu the two fields would have been the profane life of humans, where cattle are raised to be eaten, contrasted with the sacred life of the ancestral spirits to whom humans offer animal sacrifice. As humans are contrasted with spirits, so ogres are contrasted with both. The actions on which the tales are commenting are sacrificial actions, offerings of slain domestic animals to ancestors: the ancestors protect humans, the ogres eat them. The ogre stories also have their scatologic side: in some of the stories children enter the body of the ogre through his anus and voyage around inside him. Detailing the indecent topology of internal organs which they encounter contributes to the entertainment value of the tales and makes the same point as the graded difference in physicality in the treatment of boys and girls in Minot.[33] Ancestors are spiritual beings. Ogres are gross, material creatures, equipped with extralarge animal parts. Girls are sheltered, protected from the real rough stuff of life, which boys cannot but confront.

Conclusion

To cite further African exemplars, Pierre Smith has argued well that for there to be mythology at all, or ritual at all, the culture will be formed around some grand central act, that "ensnares the mind" and so integrates the different forms of life.[34] He illustrated this with the great rituals of the Swazi king's enthronement ceremonies. Historically the idea of "ensnaring" would mean the process of standardization by which various free or spontaneous rituals are trapped by the attraction of the central act and reformed as variants of it designed upon the same basic analogies according to categories of thought that pick up and amplify the grand analogy. For the women's culture in Minot the grand acts to ensnare the mind were giving birth and burial, celebrated by the christenings, marriages, and funerals in which women played a central role. More private events underpinning the whole system were their own personal arrivals at puberty, their menstrual cycle, pregnancy and menopause, their physical model for themselves and for the cycle of nature.

Yvonne Verdier's austerely minimalist approach, with its close attention to the everyday construction of cultural categories, stands in the forefront of new movements in mythology. Her work converges in sympathy with the line of interpretation exemplified by Jean-Louis Durand in his *Sacrifice et Labour en Grèce Ancienne,* in which he relates the myths and pictures of the gods to the agricultural work of the worshippers.[35]

In reading the Bible as myth the first task is to recognize the snare for the mind, the great central act by which the culture knows and renews itself. For the Israelite culture the center is held in sacrificial rites, which are drawn by their calendrical placings to match and comment upon each other, each with metonymic reference to the whole. The stories about Israelites and Canaanites sacrificing their children to Moloch have to be seen

as inversions of the normal pattern. The Canaanite gods present
the opposite of the Israelite God. Their demand for sacrificed children seems to be structurally like the cannibalism attributed to
white men in Africa, making a total contrast between insiders
and outsiders. Red Riding Hood devouring her grandmother is
part of an internal contrast, between men and women, and between women of different generations within the one society.
Again, for another contrast between nursery tales or nonsacred
fireside stories, the Red Riding Hood stories do not accuse: they
teach, with laughter. The Moloch stories accuse and could be
used politically against defectors. These are the kinds of differences that emerge when literature is analyzed with due regard
for context.

Though the examples are about children eating or being eaten,
or being offered in sacrifice, the theme is a demonstration of Robertson Smith's revolutionary teaching. I have tried to show what
kind of information needs to be gathered to make a serious context for interpretating "other people's myths." At the same time
I have tried to introduce a branch of anthropological criticism to
mythologists who still, a hundred years later, like to gather up the
materials of so-called myths from here and there and anywhere,
without regard to sources or to how or why the stories were told,
to say nothing of how and why they have been preserved or collected.

Notes

A version of this argument was given in Edinburgh in the Gifford Lectures, 1989,
Claims on God. A French version was offered at the Maison des Sciences de
l'Homme as a tribute to the memory of Yvonne Verdier, who had recently and
tragically died: 1989 "Les Ogres, Mangeurs d'Enfants: Kronos, Moloch, le Loup et
le Petit Chaperon Rouge; à la mémoire de notre bien regretté collègue, Yvonne
Verdier." I am grateful to J.-P. Durant for invaluable help.

1. Müller, *Natural Religion, Physical Religion, Theosophy or Psychological
   Religion, Contributions to the Science of Mythology.*
2. Müller, *Contributions to the Science of Mythology,* 1:x.
3. Grönbech, "The New Germany," 114–19.
4. Ibid., 119.
5. Herzfeld, *Ours Once More.*
6. Durkheim saluted Robertson Smith in "Sur les systèmes religieux des sociétés inferieres," 90–91, quoted in Lukes, *Emile Durkheim,* 238.
7. Lindbeck, *The Nature of Doctrine, Religion and Theology.*
8. Smith, *The Religion of the Semites,* 16, 17, 18, 19.
9. O'Flaherty, *Other Peoples' Myths.*
10. Müller, *Contributions to the Science of Mythology,* 302. When he first saw

that *theos, deva,* and *deus* were part of a whole family of words derived from the root *div* or *dyu,* he said near the end of his career that he had felt before "a new revelation, like a new history of the world. . . . It was an age of discovery and of conquest, almost a crusading age for the recovery of the sacred cradle of our race, and every new word that could be proved to have been uttered by the as yet undivided Aryan family was like discovering an old, uninjured window in the ruins of an ancient cathedral, through which we knew our ancestors had once gazed."

11. Müller, *Introduction to the Science of Religion,* 335.
12. Müller, *Contributions to the Science of Mythology,* 13.
13. Ibid., 166–67.
14. Tylor, *Primitive Culture.*
15. Dumézil, *Le Festin d'Immortalité,* 189 f.; Verdier, "Le Petit Chaperon," 51.
16. Lévi-Strauss, "The Structural Study of Myth," 428–44, and a subsequent series, *Mythologies.*
17. Paulme, *La Mère Dévorante.*
18. Leviticus 18:21; 2 Kings 23:10; Jeremiah 32:35.
19. Pouillon, *Destins du Cannibalisme.*
20. Arens, *The Man-eating Myth.*
21. Brown and Tuzin, *The Ethnography of Cannibalism.*
22. Fournier, "Les larmes fécondes de la mort Aztèque," 107–27.
23. Heider, *The Cult of Molek.*
24. Maccoby, *The Sacred Executioner,* chap. 2.
25. Stager and Wolff, "Child Sacrifice at Carthage," 31–51.
26. Verdier, "Le Petit Chaperon Rouge," 31–56.
27. Kuper, *South Africa and the Anthropologist,* 170.
28. Verdier, "Le Petit Chaperon Rouge," 31–36.
29. Ibid., 41.
30. Darnton, *The Great Cat Massacre,* 29.
31. Ibid., 55.
32. Verdier, *Façons de Dire, Façons de Faire.*
33. My debt to Anita Jacobson Widding in this adaptation of Paul Ricoeur's analysis of levels of discourse will be clear to anyone who has read the essay "The Shadow as an Expression of Individuality in Congolese Conceptions of Personhood." Ricoeur, "The model of the text."
34. Smith, "Aspects of the Organization of Rites," 103–28.
35. Durand, *Sacrifice et Labour en Grèce Ancienne.*

Works Cited

Arens, William. *The Man-eating Myth: Anthropology and Anthropophagy.* London: Oxford University Press, 1979.

Brown, Paula, and Donald Tuzin, eds. *The Ethnography of Cannibalism.* Washington, D.C.: Society for Psychological Anthropology, 1983.

Darnton, Robert. *The Great Cat Massacre and Other Episodes in French Cultural History.* New York: Basic Books, 1984.

Dumézil, George. *Le Festin d'Immortalité.* Paris: Librairie Orientaliste, 1924.

Durand, Jean-Louis. *Sacrifice et Labour en Grèce Ancienne, Essai d'Anthropologie Religieuse.* Paris: Editions La Découverte/Ecole Français de Rome, 1986.

Durkheim, Emile. "Sur les systèmes religieux des sociétés inférieres." *L'anne Sociologique* 12 (1913): 90–91.

Fournier, Dominique. "Les larmes fécondes de la mort Aztèque." *Lieux d'Enfance: L'enfant et l'eau* 13 (Jan.–Mar. 1988): 107–27.

Grönbech, W. "The New Germany" [original in Danish 1922]. *Religious Currents*. Lawrence: University of Kansas Press, 1964, 114–19.

Heider, George. *The Cult of Molek, a Reassessment.* Sheffield, England: JSOT Press, 1985.

Herzfeld, Michael. *Ours Once More: Folklore, Ideology, and the Making of Modern Greece.* New York: Pella Publishing, 1986.

Kuper, Adam. *South Africa and the Anthropologist.* London: Routledge and Kegan Paul, 1987.

Lévi-Strauss, Claude. "The Structural Study of Myth." *Journal of American Folklore,* 1955.

——. *Mythologies.*

Lindbeck, G. A. *The Nature of Doctrine, Religion and Theology in a Postliberal Age.* Philadelphia: Westminster Press, 1984.

Lukes, Steven. *Emile Durkheim: His Life and Work, A Historical and Critical Study.* London: Allen Lane, Penguin Press, 1973.

Maccoby, Hyman. *The Sacred Executioner: Human Sacrifice and the Legacy of Guilt.* London: Thames and Hudson, 1982.

Müller, Max. *Introduction to the Science of Religion.* London and New York: Longmans Green, 1873.

——. *Natural Religion.* London and New York: Longmans Green, 1888.

——. *Physical Religion.* London and New York: Longmans Green, 1890.

——. *Theosophy, or, Psychological Religion the Gifford Lectures.* London and New York: Longmans Green, 1893.

——. *Contributions to the Science of Mythology.* London and New York: Longmans Green, 1897.

——. *Theosophy or Psychological Religion.*

O'Flaherty, Wendy. *Other People's Myths; The Cave of Echoes.* New York: Macmillan, 1988.

Paulme, Denise. *La Mère Dévorante: Essai sur la morphologie des contes Africains.* Paris: Gallimard, 1972.

Pouillon, Jean. "Destins du Cannibalisme." *Nouvelle Revue de Psychanalyse,* 6. Paris: Gallimard, 1972.

Ricoeur, Paul. "The Shadow as an Expression of Individuality in Congolese Conceptions of Personhood." *Personhood and Agency: The Experience of Self and Other in African Cultures.* Edited by Michael Jackson and Ivan Arp. Sweden: Acta Universitatis Upsaliensis, 1990.

———. "The Model of the Text: Meaningful Action Considered as Text." *Interpretive Social Science.* Edited by P. Rabinow and W. Sullivan. Berkeley: University of California Press, 1979.

Robertson Smith, William. *The Religion of the Semites, the Fundamental Institutions.* Edinburgh: Black, 1889. 2d ed., New York: Schocken Books, 1972.

Smith, Pierre. "Aspects of the Organization of Rites." In *Between Belief and Transgression: Structuralist Essays in Religion, History and Myth.* Edited by Michel Izard and Pierre Smith. Chicago: University of Chicago Press, 1979.

Stager, Lawrence E., and Samuel R. Wolff. "Child Sacrifice at Carthage— Religious Rite or Population Control?" *Biblical Archaeology Review,* 1984.

Tylor, Edward. *Primitive Culture.* London: J. Murray, 1873.

Verdier, Yvonne. *Façons de Dire, Façons de Faire: La Laveuse, la Couturière, la Cuisinière.* Paris: Gallimard, 1979.

———. "Le Petit Chaperon Rouge dans la Tradition Orale." *Le Débat,* 1980.

IVAN STRENSKI

THE RISE OF RITUAL AND THE HEGEMONY OF MYTH SYLVAIN LÉVI, THE DURKHEIMIANS, AND MAX MÜLLER

Items

"DURING THE 1930s, Georges Bataille, a former student of Marcel Mauss, the pornographer, philosopher, and eventual head curator of the Bibliothèque Nationale, campaigned to establish the Place de la Concorde for a revival of ritual animal sacrifice in Paris."[1]

"Two other offspring of the original Durkheimian *équipe*, the Africanists, Marcel Griaule and Michel Leiris peer at us from a photograph catching their likeness. Outfitted in standard issue pith helmets, newly pressed khaki shorts and smart knee socks, they are the image of the typical 'scientific' ethnographers of the 1930's. Sons of the bourgeoisie, they stand stiffly at attention before a mud walled shrine. As a condition of their entry into the sanctuary, they prepare to sacrifice a chicken at the Kono altar at Kemeni, on the 6th of September 1931."[2]

Myth, Religion, and Ritualism

While many of us might draw short of the ritual and sacrificial practice of these wild men of religious studies, we need little intellectual persuasion to accept that ritual is a genuine part of religion. Along with myth, belief, social organization, ethics, experience, and art, rituals are "good to think." They are perennial foci of the study of religion and society at large.[3] Such attitudes are, however, relatively recent in the study of religion, and even to this day often a cause of discomfort. Mary Douglas, both in her essay in this volume and in other works, and Victor Turner, to name just two of our more influential contemporaries, devoted much of the effort of their mature work to establishing the claims of ritualism in one form or another.[4] Thanks to them, some investigators have gone even further, arguing that religious life is shaped or caused by rituals; others indeed have closed the gap with Bataille, Griaule, and company and seek to promote a revival of ritual life. For them it is not enough that rituals are "good to think"; rituals must be "good to do" as well.

Ritual has not always been received so kindly; intellectual and cultural obstacles to its study, appreciation, and practice have been numerous.[5] In this essay I want to discuss a historical case of how ritualism in the study of religion overcame impediments erected to it by the hegemony of the idea of the special relation of myth to religion. This hegemony has persisted even to the present day, where it has ridden the backs of the modern leaders of religious studies: Joseph Campbell, Eliade, and Lévi-Strauss.[6] Several essays in this volume struggle (in both positive and negative directions) with just such an inheritance, particularly the essays by Doniger, Ziolkowski, Bantly, Segal, and Apostolos-Cappadona. In a sense our contemporaries have served to prolong the priorities of the nineteenth-century founders of religious studies like Friedrich Max Müller. He slighted ritual and preferred to mark myth, however "diseased" a thing it might be, for the honor of being closer to the essence of religion than, for example, ritual.

Despite the prestige of Max Müller, the early part of this century saw the first challenges to the hegemony of myth—a challenge made in the name of ritual. In this discussion I want to understand how these first breaks in mythophilic and antiritualist sensibility were made by those teachers of the Batailles, Griaules, and Leirises, those two members of the original Durkheimian nucleus, Henri Hubert and Marcel Mauss.

I am not however claiming that Hubert and Mauss (and Durkheim as well) would have lined up, chickens in hand, behind Bataille and those other fellows of transgression. Although Durkheim made much of the importance of myth in his analysis of religion, it is hard to know precisely how to read this enthusiasm in light of countervailing tendencies of Durkheim's thought.[7] Despite their support of methodological ritualism, the Durkheimians always remained aloof from ritual even while being patrons of its modern-day study.

This essay will explore some of the cultural and intellectual conditions that made it possible for the original members of the Durkheimian *équipe* to become the (diffident) ritualists that they were. The Durkheimians continued, for example, the thrust of an anti-Aryanist cultural polemic aimed at the influence of the work of Müller.[8] This polemic was in part a protest against Müller's assertion, however nuanced, of the importance of myth. In this the Durkheimians were not original. As Robert Alun Jones has powerfully argued, we must point to the widely accepted influence of William Robertson Smith.[9] I think, however, that this story needs to be filled out by showing how Durkheimian ritualism was occasioned by the antimythological—and anti-Aryanist—approach of Müller's French ritualist critics. This line of criticism began with the Sanskritist Abel Bergaigne and was continued by the great Indologist Sylvain Lévi. He, in turn, taught its lessons to his own student and Durkheim's successor as head of the Durkheimian group, Marcel Mauss.

Four Kinds of Ritualism

In speaking about scholarly attitudes to ritual, what I have also referred to as *ritualism*, we run the risk of conflating at least four distinct senses of the term. I want to sort them out from one from another so that we can be clear on what people really believed about the value of ritual. These senses include ritualism in the causal (or constitutive), methodological, practical, and perennial uses.

Thus, first, when we accept, like the early Durkheimians, that ritual is central to the *nature* of religion, we are saying that the very existence of religion depends on the existence of rituals. For convenience sake, let me term this simply *causal*, or *constitutive*, ritualism. In its most perfect form, such ritualists will go so far, for example, as to say not only that rituals make or *cause* religions but that religion essentially and simply *is constituted* by a set of rituals.

Second, given at least some form of causal or constitutive ritualism, we therefore assume that the *study* of religion ought to include the serious *study* of ritual. Let me call this *methodological* ritualism. This sort of ritualism takes the form of recommending the study of ritual as a way to understand the nature of religion. One recommends the study of ritual because ritual either *is* religion or is a key *causal* or *constitutive* factor accounting for its existence. Once again the early Durkheimians stand out as exemplifying this position.

Third are those like Bataille or some of our contemporaries, such as Karen McCarthy Brown and Tom F. Driver, but unlike the Durkheimians, who draw certain practical religious conclusions from these positions for the sake of their personal lives.[10] They are the *practical* ritualists, since they hold that participating in, even creating, rituals is a good thing.

Four, practical ritualists, in turn, also often hold that we *ought* to participate in ritual because it is essential to human nature and *perennial* in human culture. But one should immediately add that perennial ritualism does not require one's being a practical ritualist. For example, some nonpractical causal or constitutive ritualists may also be perennialists simply because they feel that rituals have a place in any sort of society irrespective of its so-called stage of development or degree of religiosity. Rituals are a perennial facet of life, even if I personally may not care to practice them. This last position, I shall refer to as *ritualist perennialism*.

Ritualist Clusters: The Probable and Improbable

Although the stories of the rise of any of these senses of ritualism would be interesting to trace, for the present discussion I want to account for the historical rise of *causal, constitutive* and *methodological* ritualisms. I do so because they prepared the way for the full-blown practical and perennial ritualisms of our own day. What is more, for the purposes of this volume, these are the very senses of ritualism that arose in historical conflict with the prestige of myth. How was it that we actually—historically—came to think about religion as constituted or caused by ritual instead of myth, and why do we believe it worthwhile studying religion by studying ritual even in preference to studying myth?

Now, having registered my intention to focus this discussion along the lines of methodological and theoretical lines, I will be the first to admit that it is not always possible *in fact* to separate matters of method and theory from other domains. Often enough attitudes about one sort of ritualism cluster with others; conclusions about one sort of ritualism may be drawn from holding or rejecting another. Indeed, they typically are. Here we can cite, for example, the relatively obvious conclusion that if one believes ritual *constitutes* religion, then one would doubtless adopt *methodological* ritualism in studying it. Thus, oftentimes causal, constitutive, and methodological ritualism cluster in the thought of a single individual or school of thought. Less obvious, but more interesting from the viewpoint of historical and social analysis, are the various possible historical clusterings of ideology or religious commitment with causal, constitutive, and methodological ritualist positions. What conclusions, for instance, might be anticipated about the methodological views of an investigator or about the theory of the ritual (or nonritual) nature of religion from the fact of religious practice?

Religion and Myth: When
Antiritualism Was in Flower

A classic instance of such a cluster is to be found among the liberal Protestant founders of religious studies in France. There, the occurrence of rituals was considered ipso facto evidence of a "religion" having fallen into "superstition." To translate, if a religion were found to be constituted by rituals, this was deemed sufficient evidence that the religion had degenerated into something base, such as a superstition so called. Rituals were sure signs of corruption, signs that where magic now was, religion used to be. Real religion may have had to do with purity of heart, philosophical ideas, or profound inner experience, but certainly not with ritual. As a result, the methods used to study religion excluded the study of ritual: methodological antiritualism thus clustered with constitutive antiritualism.

In Durkheim's France, a prime exponent of this antiritualism typical among the liberal religious thinkers of the day was Albert Réville, the doyen of the Ecole Pratique des Hautes Etudes, Fifth Section. Réville felt that ritual could not be the heart of religion because all cultural or embodied forms of religion were examples of what he (and others) called "religious materialism." Rituals were nothing more than examples of the "need to make use of religious forms, as if they were indispensable receptacles of the divine reality."[11] Interestingly enough, Réville is equally hard on the Anglican liturgical reformers of the mid-nineteenth century, saying that ritual "enjoins participation in its mysterious ceremonies as necessary for the salvation of souls."[12] As such, rituals were "always more or less superstitious."[13] A really religious person will inform their sensibility with a religious "spiritualism," which originates in a "more elevated moral and religious sense."[14]

Réville's antiritualism was well grounded in the peculiar history of French Protestantism. Yet he was joined in his views by liberal Protestants from different national traditions as well—notably by his friend the great student of myth Friedrich Max Müller (1823–1900). I am suggesting that we can read Durkheim's position on ritual as a point at least partly made against such opponents of ritualism as Réville and Müller. Durkheim himself was concerned both to refute the naturism that Réville and Müller shared, and to refute their antiritual views of religion and in doing so to place ritual at the center of understanding religion.[15] Let me now turn to the powerfully influential figure of Friedrich Max Müller, who, Richard Dorson says, "reoriented all previous thinking about the origin of myths" with the publication in 1856 of his "Comparative Mythology."[16]

Max Müller, Myth, and Religion-as-Such

In the heyday of the celebration of German folklore, language, and literature, myth was naturally enough a favored category of cultural expression.[17] This was true for Friedrich Max Müller, even if myth, in turn, was for him both a derived feature of language ("only a dialect, an ancient form of language") and, moreover, something that was symptomatic of a "linguistic breakdown."[18] This of course is the well-known theory of myth as a "disease of language."[19] Müller accordingly says that "mythology is inevitable, it is an inherent necessity of language, if we recognize in language the outward form and manifestation of thought; it is in fact the dark shadow which language throws on thought, and which can never disappear till language becomes altogether commensurate with thought, and which it never will."[20] Müller's belief in the importance of myth is thus secondary to his even deeper conviction of the overriding importance of language in culture. If a people's language should change, said Müller, its social arrangements would follow suit.[21]

Typical of the idealism and romanticism of his generation of young German intellectuals, Müller's own religion reinforced such a view. His personal piety tended toward pantheism, and he, like others of his class, much admired Vedanta philosophy.[22] His religious sensibilities were accordingly cast in terms of a romantic nature mysticism.[23] After describing the nature worship of the Vedas, Müller rhetorically asks: "And are we so different from them?" In contemplating nature, "do we not feel the overwhelming pressure of the Infinite . . . from which no one can escape who has eyes to see and ears to hear?"[24]

Such statements meant that Müller had considerable appreciation and sympathy for religions that even he considered low on the evolutionary scale. Müller ranked the original nature religion of the ancients, what he called "Physical Religion," lower than the "Philosophical Religion" of his own day, but he nonetheless seemed to indulge some nostalgia for it. Physical Religion, like the Vedas, may display certain "childish" features, but at the same time, it represented an approximation of the absolute.[25] The Vedas were, for instance, revelation in their own way. Despite their childish sacrificial, ritual, and priestly character, was not their polytheism more precisely a "henotheism," and thus a way station on the road to monotheism or monism?[26] A Physical Religion like the Vedas thus exemplified a vital progressive stage in the history of religions. And for Müller, the "real history of man is the history of religions: the wonderful ways by which the different families of the human race advanced toward a truer knowledge and a deeper love of God."[27] Müller's willingness to see what for him were the "precious stones . . . hidden" in the "rubbish" of the highly ritualistic Physical Religion put distance between him and some of the other liberal Protestant students of religion of his day.

As for the relation of myth to religion, Müller was considerably more ambiguous. This ambiguity of Müller's was also something Durkheim exploited to raise himself up as the new champion of the essential religiousness of myth—even though he was himself confused about the place of myth in religion.[28] This ambiguity arises partly from Müller's own intellectual confusions—due to his simultaneous attachment to a theory of natural religion and to a historicist tendency to stress cultural distinctiveness.[29] But Müller's confusions need not detain us here. We can head directly to the matter of Müller's attachment to natural religion.[30]

For Müller, "religion" meant two things: in the descriptive

sense, it meant the many different historical religions studied by anthropologists, historians, philologists, and others; in the normative sense, it stood for *real* religion, religion in its true essence. This "real" religion can be called "religion-as-such," although it has also gone by the name "natural religion." For Müller, this real and essential religion cannot change, even if the history of religions is a history of change. Real, natural religion is the "deepest" root of the many religions that come and go over the course of the ages.[31] Accordingly, the many religions were at best "sects if not corruptions" of the original religious natural impulse of humanity.[32]

Müller often jumps back and forth between descriptive historical and normative uses of the term *religion*, making it difficult to know the reference of his language about religion at any given time. Müller can say, for instance, that myths *arose* from religion-as-such, and thus that religion (in the historical sense) cannot be equated with myth.[33] To explain this paradox, we need to see that for him the religions were those mélanges of cult, myth, and practice; but religion-as-such was the perfectly spiritual activity of the "perception of the Infinite," later modified to include the moral element.[34] This notion of religion-as-such refers to something that existed "before" sacrifice, ritual, and myth, and thus was not something that could be equated with myth.[35]

It is the dissociation of myth from this *normative* sense of religion in Müller's writing that drew Durkheim's attack. In his critique of Müller, Durkheim tells us that he will have none of the "abstract and philosophic" thinking about religious notions such as God, which result from the dismissal of myth from the really religious domain.[36] Durkheim is of course only partly correct, since he has in effect attacked Müller for not giving myth its due as part of religion-*as-such*. But insofar as the *religions* are concerned, Müller is quite pleased to declare, as we have seen, that religion and myth are integral to one another.

Thus, when it came to the Greeks, Müller could say, on the one hand, that he did not believe that the *Iliad* was their "Bible."[37] But this did not stop him from turning around and declaring in the very same lecture that "although mythology was not religion in our sense of the word . . . yet I would not deny altogether that in a certain sense the mythology of the Greeks belonged to their religion."[38] Indeed, as he says in the same lecture, myth was "the religion of the ancient world."[39] This identification of religion and myth was the cornerstone of his reading of the Vedas, which, for

Müller, are "the real theogony of the Aryan races."[40] Further affirming the perennial religious value of that great trove of myth and the love of his scholarly life, the Vedas, Müller said that in the Vedas "we get one step nearer to that distant source of religious thought and language which has fed the different national streams of Persia, Greece, Rome and Germany, and we begin to see clearly that 'there is no religion without God,' or as St. Augustine expressed it, that 'there is no false religion which does not contain some elements of truth.'"[41]

Thus, for Müller myth did not succeed in capturing the high-flown abstract truth of the philosophical religion-as-such that he preferred, but nonetheless the many ancient religions were often constituted by myth. Proper piety therefore presupposed a special reverence for myth and, at least in consequence, a playing down of the value of ritual.

Müller and Aryanism

Müller's spirituality was driven in part by a Romantic German nationalist cultural politics that emphasized the overriding importance of the folkish and homegrown.[42] These traditions, broadly inhospitable to ritual and institutional religious life as they were, shaped Müller's spirituality along the mystical lines of individualistic communion with the God who dwelled in all things.[43] In turn, they shaped Müller's sensibility to such a point that for him it was simply taken for granted that, despite its flaws, myth was a primary and essential element in the makeup of genuine archaic religion.

As a young man, Max Müller went to Berlin to study languages and philosophy. As an educated German of his generation as well as the son of one of Schubert's chief librettists, the Romantic poet Wilhelm Müller, Max Müller had already come prepared by the popular Romantic culture of Indianism and Aryanism.[44] In Berlin he was able to develop these tendencies academically and in tandem through Oriental studies and comparative historical linguistics. As an admirer of Schlegel, for instance, he came under the influence of such pieces of early theoretical glorification of India as *Über die Sprache und Weisheit der Indier* (1808). Müller also trained under the Indo-Europeanist Franz Bopp.

Müller was thus already a kind of religious idealist in that he saw what one might call intellectual and literary things as primary religious data. Beyond the spiritual ambience he assumed as a child of the German Romantic movement, Müller gained an even more sophisticated appreciation of myth from his formal association in Berlin with F. W. J. Schelling, the first real philosopher of myth.[45] Müller was especially taken with Schelling's attempts to rehabilitate myth in the manner of Herder and the German Romantics in general. Over against the universalizing and iconoclastic tendencies of the Enlightenment, the German Romantics felt that myths captured the spirit of the peoples who originated them. That the folk elements of a culture represented something noble about the "soul" of the nation spoke directly to Müller's rising sense of German cultural nationalism. Myths embodied a kind of folk wisdom, indeed, an ancient philosophy that despite its simple folk origins expressed the essence of the self-conception of national groupings—like the Germans.[46]

Although Müller felt that Schelling's knowledge of the religions of India was inadequate and misguided, he nonetheless became a devotee of the great philosopher of myth, crediting him with having "opened" up his mind to the possibilities of a systematic study of religion, myth, and philosophy.[47] Indeed, Müller fancied himself Schelling's successor, but now argued that a more thorough study of the Vedas than Schelling could manage would fulfill the promise of the philosopher's program. Indeed, to Müller's mind the study of the Vedas was fundamental to accomplishing Schelling's life project. Like his philosophical mentor, Müller's study of the Vedas was for him only a means to an end, namely, a philosophy of mythology and religion. In his expert philological hands, this new philosophical scheme would be based on more trustworthy materials than those on which Schelling had been able to build his earlier philosophy of religion and mythology.[48] As a result of this engagement in Schelling's philosophical project, Müller's feelings against ritual gained philosophical depth.

Both philosophic and Orientalist lines of inquiry fed Müller's lifelong fascination with the so-called Aryans. In his quest for the religion of the ancient Aryans, Müller lined up with other scholars of his inclination, notably J. G. Frazer.[49] He, along with others, was struck with a sense of the significance of the relationships among the Indo-European languages. Müller in fact was the person who applied the term *Aryan* to designate that group of peoples who spoke original Indo-European, feeling that such a term was more appropriate than the cumbersome, then current alternative, Indo-Germanic.[50] In Müller's view, ancient Aryan myths, such as the Vedas, held the key to the ancient wisdom of the Aryans. In some real sense, then, this ancient Vedic wisdom lay at the root of Western culture and German national identity. "We are by nature Aryan, not Semitic," Müller said in 1865.[51]

Max Müller's belief in the special place of myth in Vedic religion was thus in effect part of a deeper theological and sociological idealism, linked with Aryanist cultural ideology. When he encountered the Vedas, Max Müller felt that he had fulfilled his own German Romantic longings and the promise of his deistic liberal Protestant religious rearing at the same time. In the Vedic myths he felt that he had made contact with a pure, primordial contemplative nature religion, which, as the "bible of the Aryans," was at the same time the primordial religious lore of his beloved Germany. Mrs. Max Müller said of her husband that his "'highest object was to discover reason in all the un-reason of mythology, and thus to vindicate the character of our ancestors, however distant.'"[52]

Because of their mythic qualities and because they seemed to be truly archaic, and thus closer to the natural religion of the dawn of humanity, the Vedas held pride of place for Müller. As such, they should be recognized as coequal in cultural stature with the biblical traditions and literature of the ancient Hebrews. Now, of course, they were even more important because they were the sources of a properly European (read "Aryan") cultural heritage. In the Vedas, Müller saw a record of the religion of a pre-European golden age. They provided a direct route into a profound philosophy, the primordial wisdom of the human race, and, in particular, into what he believed to be the mother race of the West—the Aryans.

It does not seem, however, as if this affection for the ideals of the Aryans as revealed in the Vedas moved Müller to embrace Schopenhauer's religious and cultural radicalism. The philosopher felt that Christianity should be revived by finding in the Vedas a new Aryan "old" testament to replace its relatively inferior Semitic heritage.[53] Citing Schopenhauer with apparent approval, Max Müller records the philosopher's delight in reading the Upanishads: "oh how thoroughly is the mind washed clean of all early engrafted Jewish superstitions, and of all philosophy that cringes before those superstitions!"[54] Müller's thought thus pushes in the radical direction laid out by Schopenhauer, even if he does not go as far as the philosopher. Müller's way consisted in denying *any* single religion privileges before the truth by granting all religions an equal share of the truth: "We share in the same truth, and we are exposed to the same errors, whether we are Aryan or Semitic or Egyptian in language and thought."[55] For Müller the Vedas and other scriptures as revelation ranked right alongside the Bible.[56]

But despite his differences with Schopenhauer, suspicions of anti-Semitism dogged Müller during his life. In truth, Müller's responsibility for fostering anti-Semitism and racism in this manner is somewhat problematic. As early as 1865, even while asserting the Aryan nature of European peoples, he lavishly praised the Jews for having a history that was the "one oasis in that vast desert of ancient Asiatic history."[57] After 1871 Müller seemed repelled by the nationalist implications of Aryanism, confessing as much to none other than Ernest Renan. Léon Poliakov, certainly no friend of anti-Semitism, seems persuaded of Müller's sincerity in refusing to identify race and language—even if he calls Müller's retraction of earlier Aryanism "timid."[58] Müller opposed the German nationalist Aryanists: Indo-European philology had nothing to do with race; there is no such thing as an Aryan skull! Despite his affection for the ancient Aryans, Müller himself was not an Aryanist supremacist. But with the genie out of the bottle, not even Max Müller could control "Maxmüllerism." It took on a life of its own and influenced the racist dimension of the thought of such disciples of Müller's as the American John Fiske.[59]

Getting Serious about Ritual:
Robertson Smith and Durkheim

The most substantial break with the approach identified with Max Müller came with the work of the Durkheimians.[60] They, it is claimed, inaugurated our modern methodological, causal, and constitutive ritualism.[61] Yet the fact remains that the place of Robertson Smith and the Durkheimians in aiding and abetting ritualism remains puzzling and improbable. In both cases, the Durkheimians and Robertson Smith were men of liberal modernist, and thus antiperennialist and *practical* antiritualist, temperament. Their religious orientations—both Robertson Smith's Calvinism and the liberal or free-thinking Judaism of the Durkheimians—gave them every reason *not* to press ritualist trends in the study of religion. Indeed, we have already seen how Durkheim

attacks Müller for not giving a significant role to myth in identifying the nature of religion. Yet the upshot of the work of Durkheim (and Robertson Smith through him) was to achieve just this
turn toward the study of ritual. How is it, then, that they began a
trend toward causal, constitutive, and methodological ritualism
when they neither practiced rituals nor thought that they had un-
qualified perennial value? Let us look at Robertson Smith first.

Robertson Smith, Antiritualist

It is imprecise to credit Robertson Smith with advocating the un-
qualified primacy of ritual in religion. Indeed, he opposed such an
affirmation of ritual in religious life. To be precise, we should say
that only in his views of *primitive* and non-Christian religions
was Robertson Smith a ritualist, and then only in causal, constitutive, and methodological senses. Robertson Smith saw ritualist
religions as lower on the evolutionary scale than the religions of
morality, which he thought his own brand of Calvinist Christianity represented.[62] Unhappily for truth's sake, Robertson Smith felt
that all of these primitive and non-Christian religions were thus
caused and constituted by ritual and that therefore to understand
primitive religion we needed to be methodological ritualists.

But when it came to what was for him "real" religion (to Christianity) or to practical and perennial ritualism, Robertson Smith
turned his back on religious ritual: "A ritual system must always
remain materialistic, even if its materialism is disguised under
the cloak of mysticism."[63] Leaving no role for ritual in the "real"
religiosity of his own faith, Robertson Smith proclaims that the
"real living power . . . in Christianity is *moral*. . . . personal Christianity is not a play of subjectivities, but moral converse with God
practically dominating the life."[64] We should also note how at the
same time Robertson Smith's ironic approval of ritual in "primitive" religion drew upon the anti-Judaism and anti-Catholicism
of his teacher, Paul Lagarde. The rabbinic Jewish and Roman
Catholic ritualism of his own day, Lagarde felt, exemplified the
common libel of the period—the "dessication" of a religious life
dominated by rituals.

Even in 1875, when Robertson Smith seemed to move toward
a position granting considerable importance to liturgy, he stepped
back from the brink. For while it is true that Robertson Smith
thought that liturgy was important, it mattered only because it
depended upon individual psychological states of personal piety

and moral rectitude. On the ritualist side, Robertson Smith thus says that "the church is not a fellowship of Christian love which requires no unity of organization—but a fellowship of worship" and that "church fellowship has a molding and up-building power on those who take part in it."[65] But then putting ritual into dependent status, he undercuts his own utterance: in Robertson Smith's view, this "common worship of many individuals" is only an "expression in intelligible form of their common relation of faith towards God."[66] Ritual again comes second to the inner condition of the Christian soul. This likewise fits with his Reformation view earlier expressed in the same essay that "the effectual factor in the sacraments is not the outward sign, but the word of promise signified. [Thus] all participation in the benefits purchased by Christ is to be gained in converse with God, in hearkening continually to His Word."[67]

Such revelations about Robertson Smith may surprise those associating him with the celebration of the communion enjoyed during the "jolly feast," which was for him ancient Hebrew sacrificial religion. But a closer look sheds light on the truth of Robertson Smith's rejection of the view that religion in its essence is constituted by rituals. While it is true that Robertson Smith was initially fond of the communion aspects of sacrifice among aboriginal Hebrews, this attraction gave way to outright and thinly veiled disapproval. In Robertson Smith's eyes, after the primitive Hebrew period, sacrifice became dominated by the ideas of bribery or gift. Like the rest of ritual life, sacrificial rituals are "materialistic" and thus true indicators of the barbaric and uncivilized cultures producing them.[68]

Thus, Robertson Smith's ritualism (causal, constitutive, and methodological) is confined to the narrow area of human life where, in his eyes, the religious spirit has not yet realized its own nature.

The Durkheimians as Diffident Ritualists: Their Confused Causal and Methodological Ritualism

At first glance, the original Durkheimian group did not seem to differ greatly from the standard set by Robertson Smith for the study of religion by way of its rituals. Their ritualism was no more practical in terms of their own (lack of) religious behavior than was Robertson Smith's. Unlike Robertson Smith's Lutheran teacher Albrecht Ritschl, for instance, they certainly did not intentionally promote anything remotely approaching his programs of liturgical reform.[69] Yet the Durkheimian position on the perennial value and role of ritual is more positive and nuanced than Robertson Smith's, even if this may mean it is only more confused.

The Durkheimians tended to believe that human life, and religion included in it, is everywhere and always, and thus perennially, ritualist, even if they kept aloof from religious ritual themselves. Thus, the Durkheimians talk about the positive value of the *practice* of certain everyday rituals. In contemporary society, these would be such events as the celebration of Bastille Day, various civic rites,[70] or indeed whatever is required to stir the community into a state of creative "effervescence." It is granted that some of these modern rites may be best interpreted as "vestigial" rituals, impoverished forms of religious ritual life typically found in full flower in traditional society.[71] But another reading of the Durkheimians indicates that they felt that all societies needed their moments of effervescence in order to rise above the emotional and moral mediocrity that Durkheim lamented in his own day.[72]

Perhaps the first student of the Durkheimians to take their approval of ritual seriously was a Protestant student of Hubert's, Philippe de Félice (1880–1964). About the same time that Bataille, Griaule, and Leiris were making their own moves in the direction of practical ritualism, Félice had written a rather popular and broad defence of ritualism called *Poisons sacrés; Ivresses divines* (1936).[73] There, he repeatedly lavishes credit on what he claims that Hubert had taught him about religion.[74] Félice records the many ways the religions of the world cultivated ritually induced religious raptures, accompanied often by inebriants like beer and other more exotic drugs. It is a "general human phenomenon" fundamental to religion, he tells us in matter-of-fact tones.[75] Moreover these ancient practices of quaffing "nectars" and "ambrosias" can be found also in the writings of the Church Fathers; they are even continued, Félice suggests, in the fervent expressive language of the mystics. A basic "need" exists, says he, "to transcend the self, which imposes itself upon human beings." We "desire to enter into the source of the immense river, where people, since their existence, have sought to refresh their souls."[76] Rituals were instrumental in achieving these states of transcendence.

Thus, rituals were not just appropriate to unevolved societies but even to those organized along rational lines. In this sense the Durkheimians might be said, unlike Robertson Smith, to be at least partial perennial ritualists.

In taking this line, Durkheim was committed to the view that evolution was continuous and in a way cumulative. The past was not in all respects effaced in the passage of time; it continued to live in its transformations. Durkheim here reminds one of Freud, who argued that the child lives in the adult and is never lost in the course of human maturation. Working at the social level, Durkheim argued that ritual practices were concrete primitive practices that would later develop into abstract moral judgments.[77] Ritual sacrifice continues into our day as civic sacrifice or altruism—as the "elementary form" of moral practice. The ritual realm grows into the moral by a kind of organic historical evolution.

The Durkheimians were also more positive about myth than those of other political and ideological persuasions—even though they shared Robertson Smith's causal, constitutive, and methodological ritualism. On the matter of the relation of ritual and myth or belief, for instance, the Durkheimians held that they were causally interdependent, albeit often in the form of a somewhat asymmetrical interdependence.[78] Ritual, taken as society made visible, had a certain causal priority to myth or beliefs. In his 1887 review of Guyau, Durkheim announced what amounts to an appreciation of the causal priority of ritual. There he says that "cult is religion become visible and tangible; like religion, it is based on a sociological relationship, formed as an exchange of services."[79] Making clear the causal priority of ritual to myth some years later, Henri Hubert colorfully says: "Myths are social products; it is in the rituals that society is visible, present or necessarily involved. The mythological imagination dances on the threshing floor trodden by rituals, and it is there that one might grasp it."[80] This reflects the Durkheimian view that rituals were somehow closer to the bedrock of social reality: they were the "*sine qua non* of the maintenance of society."[81] In another place Hubert says, "First of all, as for a ritual, it implies by definition, the collaboration of the entire society in which it takes place. The rite carries in itself the idea of its efficacy and reason for its observance. Secondly, every religious act puts the *sacred things* into action."[82]

Briefly, this is what is at stake. Against the antiritualist position of Jewish and Protestant liberals, Hubert and Mauss adopt a *causal* or *constitutive* ritualism. Religion *is* its rituals, not just its beliefs or even morality. Ritual is the locus of the positive power of the sacred that injects effervescence, energy, and power into people, and because of which people are religious at all. Thus, sacrifice is for them what *makes* (things) *sacred*, as the root meaning of *sacrificium* testifies. It even creates the gods. Sacrifice performs a positive function of creating the religious life of people. The Durkheimians say all this, of course, because as we noted in relation to the Durkheimian critique of the antiritualism of Albert Réville, ritual *is* religion in social form, and thus ritual *is* "religion made visible and tangible."[83]

Having said this, however, we should not overlook the confusions to which the Durkheimians were prone. Hubert's brilliant metaphor, for example, also served as a recipe for a relation of interdependence with myth that the Durkheimians were apparently unable to describe or explain unambiguously. In "Individual and Collective Representations" (1898), Durkheim qualifies the rule of ritual causal priority.[84] He says that once myths get launched, so to speak, they become causally independent of any rituals previously related to them. Thus, in certain contexts the Durkheimians saw myths affecting the shape of rituals, thus making them worthy of study, virtually, in and of themselves— or at least as causally prior to rituals. They indeed take this line in *Sacrifice* in beginning their discussion of the sacrifice of the god. There they explain at the very heart of the book that "our main efforts will be especially directed toward determining the considerable part that *mythology* has played in this development."[85]

Yet while the Durkheimians wanted to admit that myths could *acquire* autonomy, they always seemed to want to keep their feet on the ground by asserting that flesh-and-blood social realities (like ritual) were the primary realities.[86] We can confirm this when we attend to the range of things they studied. There, we see how the balance tips in favor of ritual: sacrifice draws their attention in both Hubert and Mauss's *mémoire*, and in Durkheim's great classic, prayer as an "oral rite" becomes the focus of Mauss's doctoral dissertation. The guiding methodological principle here is that ritual is a way society manifests itself, thus making it available to empirical study.[87] In the end, then, although the Durkheimians wanted to have it both ways, in the balance between ritual and myth, ritual proves "more equal" than myth.

The Cultural Strategies of Durkheimian Ritualism

But from the point of view of their membership in the secular, liberal, and modernist culture of the day, how did the Durkheimians find themselves uncharacteristically embracing ritualism as much as they did? Why did not they turn out more like other cultural and religious liberals, such as their contemporaries Albert Réville, William Robertson Smith, or Salomon Reinach? Part of the answer is bound up in the subtle cultural strategies of the Durkheimian group.

We already know how Max Müller's preference for myth was embedded in a whole network of cultural strategies. The same is true about the evolution of the Durkheimians' ritualist positions. Where Müller was Aryanist and early on had acquired the reputation of being anti-Semitic, the Durkheimians were cosmopolitan and nonexclusive; where Müller saw Romantic individualism and mystic rapture, the Durkheimians looked to Enlightenment fellowship and cooperation; where Müller saw society as formed by its language, myths, philosophy, and poetry, the Durkheimians saw society actively forming modes of literary, linguistic, and poetic expression; where Müller saw myth and philosophy, the Durkheimians saw ritual and concrete human relations.

But the Durkheimians were not original in reaching out for ritual; they owed their ritualism to the direct influence of Mauss's mentor in Indic studies, the Jewish scholar Sylvain Lévi.[88] Sylvain Lévi's ritualism was in turn hammered out in opposition to Max Müller's mythophilic interpretation of the Vedas—and perhaps invoked by the anti-Semitic cultural strategies it furthered. Lévi's ritualism was thus just as thickly nuanced by involvement in a program of cultural strategies as anything Max Müller and the Aryanists had attempted—but from the opposite side of the field.

This fashioning of a ritualist theory of culture began in the field of Indology, in controversies about the nature of the religion and culture of the Vedas, at that time dominated by the work of Max Müller.

Ritual Makes the Gods

The first break in Müller's idealist German Romantic reading of the Vedas came with the assertion by French scholars that the Vedas were not purely and simply "a profound philosophy" and one from which Indian religion degenerated into mindless ritualism.[89] The ritual sacrifice of the succeeding texts such as the *Brāhmaṇas* could not thus be seen as symptomatic of a "long and profound degeneration of religious feeling," as the partisans of the Vedas as Aryan Bible claimed.[90] Sylvain Lévi thus struck at the heart of the theory of religious evolution typical of Robertson Smith, taken over from Wellhausen and the volkish Paul de Lagarde.[91]

Such a devolution from philosophy to ritual made little sense because it was not possible to separate the supposedly philosophic wisdom of the Vedas from practical ritualism. The supposed philosophical activity of the Vedic sages was thus not incompatible with their practical ritualism. Lévi indicated that even the elaborate ritualism of the Brāhmaṇas, for instance, reached its peak among an elite class of brahmins—ritual specialists who were leading philosophers at the same time. Therefore, contrary to the prejudices of religious liberalism, ritualism and philosophy do not mutually exclude each other. Indeed, they coexist under the same conditions. Even the brutal brâhmanical sacrificial system contains a speculative theological core that gives immediate rise to the lofty philosophical speculations of the Upanishads.[92]

But beginning with Bergaigne and continuing with Sylvain Lévi, the French even went further toward recognizing the role of ritual in the earliest stages of Indian religion. The leaders of French Indology taught that Hindu texts would be better read as "smoke" to the "fire" of ritual, indicators of rituals, rather than of philosophical arguments.[93] Once the German bias toward philosophy was eliminated, other readings of the Vedas could emerge. Bergaigne, for instance, believed that the hymns of the Veda needed to be set into the performative context of their settings. Significantly, Max Müller on the other hand felt that the Vedic hymns had only "incidental dramatic value."[94] If they were not philosophy as Max Müller in effect said, then they were myth. But with the growing attention to the performative settings of the Vedic hymns, Bergaigne began to suspect their mythological character as well. In a testimony of intellectual conversion remarkable in the history of science, Bergaigne tells us of being "suddenly stopped on the road leading to Damascus" shortly after an article of his on Vedic mythology, done in the solarist style of Max Müller, went to press. "What was it," Bergaigne asks, "if not the evidence of the texts, or in any case, something which appeared to me to be such, that could have been the reason for the change?"[95] Bergaigne no longer believed: "I ultimately came to recognize that exclusively solar interpretations, just like exclusively meteorological interpretations . . . when they applied to the analysis of the Rigvedic myths, almost always leave behind a liturgical residue, and that this residue . . . is exactly the most important portion from the point of view of the exegesis of the hymns."[96] In the words of the eminent Paul Mus, Bergaigne had started a '"heresy in traditional Indianism" by "showing that one ought above all to interpret the Vedas as explaining a ritual."[97] Thus Bergaigne's rejection of Max Müller's mythophilic reading of the ancient Indian texts led him directly to ritualism.

In Vedic studies, Bergaigne's lead was eagerly taken up by Sylvain Lévi. To Lévi, as to Bergaigne, it was clear that the Vedas were heavily committed to ritual—a trend, Lévi argued, that continued into the Brāhmaṇas.[98] Sylvain Lévi's La Doctrine du sacrifice dans les Brāhmaṇas (1898) in fact argued the position that ritual, not the idea of gods, was the key to the origins of religion found there.[99] Now, in making a causal point about the role of ritual, Lévi thus differs from the methodological approach of William Robertson Smith—to understand primitive religion, we should begin by trying to understand ritual life. For Lévi the issue was rather a constitutive or causal ritualism—an issue about the ritual nature and origins of religion itself, not how to go about studying it. Confirming this, Sylvain Lévi says that the nature of the religion revealed in the Brāhmaṇas is constituted by sacrificial ritual. Thus sacrifice "is God and God par excellence." Further, sacrificial ritual "is the master, the indeterminate god, the infinite, the spirit from which everything comes, dying and being born without cease."[100] Behind the figure of Prajāpati, a major Hindu creation deity, is the sacrificial ritual: "Prajāpati, the sacrifice is the father of the gods . . . and its son."[101] Sylvain Lévi in effect argues what Renou calls the "omnipotence" of ritual, what I have earlier termed causal or constitutive ritualism.[102]

Mauss

Marcel Mauss came to Sylvain Lévi at precisely the moment Bergaigne's ritualism had ripened to its full in the thought of the great Jewish Indologist. Early in his career as Sylvain Lévi's student, Mauss was submitted to an initiation test. He was told to assess the theoretical thrust of a text of which he, at the time, knew nothing. This book turned out to be the locus classicus of Bergaigne's ritualism, *La religion védique*. After three days of intense reading, Mauss returned to Lévi, reporting that he felt that Bergaigne had made his case. And, were Bergaigne correct, Mauss concluded, the major assumptions of Vedic studies would be overturned. Since he had made such a stark and uncompromising judgment on the book, Mauss awaited Lévi's reaction with some apprehension. But naturally Sylvain Lévi was pleased, and Mauss gained the confidence of his future teacher for life.[103]

It is well to recall, however, that things might have gone otherwise. Mauss was at that time very much an idealist philosopher and, thus in theory more likely to be sympathetic to German idealist readings of the Vedas than to the emergent contextual and liturgical interpretations begun by Bergaigne and followed through by Sylvain Lévi. As it happened, the meeting of Mauss and Lévi was to be momentous for the future of Mauss's intellectual development as a partisan of ritualism—something that Mauss recognized in his review of *La Doctrine du sacrifice dans les Brāhmaṇas*. There Mauss recites the lessons of Sylvain Lévi's view of the causal power of rituals, even to the extent that they created the gods themselves.[104]

Sylvain Lévi and the Cultural Meaning of Ritualism

For Lévi, the cause of ritualism had been for some time important to him beyond the academic matters of interpreting religious texts. As an observant and politically attentive Jew, he knew that the mythophilic Aryanist program of Max Müller and his fellows posed special cultural threats to the status of Jews in Europe. Max Müller's interpretation of the Vedas as a body of Aryan, archaic European philosophical wisdom and mythological lore was at its worst a piece of Aryanist (and thus anti-Semitic) ideology. Lévi reacted against the Aryanists by leveling a devastating attack on the supposed superiority of the Vedic religion. The language of the *Ṛg-Veda* was notoriously "barbaric";[105] the very existence of something called a "Vedic society" remained unproved; claims about its archaic character had been refuted by the discovery of the pre-Aryan Indus Valley civilization of Mohenjo-Daro.[106] In sum, the Vedas were far from anything marking a golden age with respect to which later Hindu religion—such as the *Brāhmaṇas*—could be seen to have fallen.

Sylvain Lévi's criticisms also took on existential pertinence because the German Aryanists symbolically identified later, post-Vedic, "degenerate" Hinduism with his own contemporary Talmudic Judaism. This follows the pattern assumed by biblical scholars in Germany, like Lagarde, Wellhausen, and through them William Robertson Smith; they had paired their admiration for long-gone ancient Israel with an equal distaste for "Judaism" proper—Talmudic Judaism.[107] Thus, in terms of symbolic relations, Talmudic Judaism was, for the German Aryanists, like Hinduism in decline *after* the glory of the Vedic period, and before the philosophical renaissance of the Upaniṣadic "reform."

To Sylvain Lévi, the course of Hindu and Jewish religious histories looked different from the picture painted by the Aryanists. While he agreed with them and with Jewish modernists that Jewish religious history ought to be divided along various lines, there were no *stages* of an irreversible historical evolution. What the evolutionists might call "stages" ought rather to be called *aspects* of Jewish religion, and "aspects" in a perennial rhythm of change. He addressed these issues oddly enough in a tract written for the "Ligue des Amis du Sionisme." [108] First, from his perspective as a republican French thinker, he recognized "prophetic" Judaism, doubtless echoing James Darmesteter, as enlightened, universalist, or reformed Judaism.[109] This Judaism "holds out a fraternal hand to humanity to march in concert, anticipating the triumph of justice." Sealing the pact with the Enlightenment, he immediately adds that "French genius with its passion for universal humanity which expresses itself in its classics as well as in the Revolution is the closest relative of this messianic spirit. It is its natural safeguard against sectarians who have never renounced its suppression."[110] But in this tract Sylvain Lévi also speaks as someone confirmed in his own Jewish particularity by the Dreyfus Affair. Without minimizing its difficulties from the viewpoint of "prophetic Judaism," he nonetheless applauds Zionism. He likewise recognizes the value of the "Mosaic" Judaism—that aspect of Judaism contrasting with the "prophetic." It is that moment where Judaism "tends to regroup the chosen people into its ethnic isolation, to multiply the barriers which separate it from the nations."[111] Sylvain Lévi felt both aspects were perennial and, in their own times, desirable for Judaism to encompass.[112]

The Aryanists (although apparently not Max Müller) also

sought to replace the very scriptural heart of Western culture, the Jewish bible, with an "Aryan bible," the Vedas.[113] Alternative Aryan foundations for the religious traditions of the West would then replace those linked with Jewish traditions and religion. Although apparently not a radical Manichean Aryanist like his old professor of philosophy, Schopenhauer, Max Müller's work tended to decenter Judaism from its privileged relation with Christianity.[114] Thus, the radical cultural anti-Semitism of the Aryanist interpreters of the Vedas motivated Sylvain Lévi to undo their entire project. Part and parcel of the Aryanist program was a ritual-hating mythophilia to which Sylvain Lévi reacted by asserting the power of ritual.

The Significance of Durkheimian Ritualism

Bergaigne's methodological ritualism, mediated in this way by his student Sylvain Lévi, passed on to Lévi's student Marcel Mauss. Through the classics of Indological scholarship of Bergaigne, mediated by Sylvain Lévi, Durkheimians like Mauss began taking ritual seriously as a key to the study of religion. Thus, the real historical line followed by the movement to rehabilitate ritual in this century stems from France.[115] One does not need to deny Robertson Smith's possible reinforcing effect on Durkheim (and thus on the Durkheimians) in this regard. From 1895, Durkheim always credited Robertson Smith with certain principal theoretical insights of *The Elementary Forms of the Religious Life*.[116] This polemic line matters materially to the formation of our own sense of the value of ritual because Lévi's critique of Müller's preference for mythological interpretation of the Vedas aided the formation of the sociological approach to religion of the Durkheim school. In its Durkheimian incarnation, Lévi's opposition to Max Müller and myth amounted to an assertion that religion is primarily constituted by ritual, and thus that both religious and social life are founded on concrete human relations rather than merely upon ideas alone.

Notes

1. Clifford, "On Ethnographic Surrealism," 141.
2. Clifford, "Power and Dialogue in Ethnography," 145.
3. Smart, *The Religious Experience of Mankind*, chap. 1.
4. Douglas, "Away from Ritual"; Turner, *The Ritual Process*; Leach, "Ritual," 520–26.

5. Douglas, "Away from Ritual."
6. Cf. Lévi-Strauss, "Structure and Dialectics," 232–41, with Lévi-Strauss, *L'Homme nu.*
7. Durkheim, *The Elementary Forms of the Religious Life,* 100.
8. For a longer treatment of Durkheimian anti-Aryanist argument, see Strenski, "Henri Hubert, Racial Science and Political Myth," 180–201.
9. Jones, "Robertson Smith, Durkheim, and Sacrifice," 184–205.
10. Brown, *Mama Lola*; Driver, *The Magic of Ritual.*
11. Réville, "Contemporaneous Materialism in Religion," 152.
12. Réville, "Evolution in Religion, and Its Results," 243.
13. Réville, "Contemporaneous Materialism in Religion," 151.
14. Ibid., 154.
15. Durkheim, *The Elementary Forms of the Religious Life,* chap. 3.
16. Dorson, *The British Folklorists,* 161; Müller, "Comparative Mythology," 299–451.
17. See my discussion of Liberal Protestantism and deism in my forthcoming book, *Religion/Politics and History in a Time of Sacrifice.*
18. Müller, "Comparative Mythology," 451.
19. Ackerman, *J. G. Frazer,* 76.
20. Müller, "On the Philosophy of Mythology," 590.
21. Müller, *Chips from a German Woodshop,* 24.
22. Voigt, *Max-Müller,* 32.
23. Ackerman, *J. G. Frazer,* 76.
24. Müller, *Natural Religion,* 138.
25. Müller, "On the Vedas," 112.
26. Ibid., 136–37.
27. Ibid., 129.
28. Durkheim, *The Elementary Forms of the Religious Life,* 100.
29. He was, for example, just as torn between theories of cultural decline and theories of evolutionary development (Voigt, *Max-Müller,* 18; Müller, *Natural Religion,* 51–53, 104, 138–53).
30. Byrne, *Natural Religion and the Nature of Religion,* 185–90.
31. Müller, *Natural Religion,* 104.
32. Ibid., 54.
33. Müller, *Physical Religion,* 292–93, 302.
34. Ibid., 294 f.
35. Ibid., 302.
36. Durkheim, *The Elementary Forms of the Religious Life,* 101.
37. Müller, "On the Philosophy of Mythology," 585.
38. Ibid., 586.
39. Ibid., 589.
40. Müller, "Comparative Mythology," 381.
41. Müller, "On the Vedas," 135.
42. Chauduri, *Scholar Extraordinary,* 84.
43. Müller, *My Autobiography,* 294–95; Byrne, *Natural Religion and the Nature of Religion,* 186.
44. Chauduri, *Scholar Extraordinary,* 134.
45. Ibid., 84.
46. Müller, *My Autobiography,* 152.
47. Müller, *Natural Religion,* 17.
48. Ibid., 20.
49. Ackerman, *J. G. Frazer,* 81.
50. Voigt, *Max-Müller,* 5.
51. Müller, "On the Vedas," 112.
52. Quoted in Chauduri, *Scholar Extraordinary,* 364.
53. Poliakov, *The Aryan Myth,* 247.

54. Müller, *Physical Religion*, 36.
55. Ibid., 274.
56. Müller, "On the Vedas," 126; Müller, *Natural Religion*, 51.
57. Müller, "On the Vedas," 113.
58. Poliakov, *The Aryan Myth*, 214.
59. Ibid., 214. For more extensive treatment of Fiske, see Hofstadter, *Social Darwinism in American Thought*.
60. Some would say that it came earlier with Robertson Smith. But Durkheim claimed to have been substantially influenced by Robertson Smith and by reference to the contents of Robertson Smith's classic work *Lectures on the Religion of the Semites* (Jones, "Robertson Smith, Durkheim, and Sacrifice," 184–205).
61. Beidelman, W. *Robertson Smith and the Sociological Study of Religion*, 64–68. See also Leach, "Ritual," 520–26.
62. Smith, *The Religion of the Semites*, 53.
63. Ibid., 440.
64. Robertson Smith, "The Place of Theology in the Work of the Growth of the Church," 317, 324.
65. Ibid., 324, 330.
66. Ibid., 324.
67. Ibid., 319.
68. Smith, *Lectures on the Religion of the Semites*, 440.
69. But see Ranulf's criticism of the Durkheimians as precursors of fascism precisely on this point, as well as Mauss's implicit admission of unintended responsibility (Lukes, *Emile Durkheim*, 338 n. 71).
70. Hubert and Mauss, "Introduction à l'analyse de quelques phénomènes religieux," 17; Pickering, *Durkheim's Sociology of Religion*, part 4.
71. Pickering, *Durkheim's Sociology of Religion*, 350.
72. Durkheim, "Individualism and the Intellectuals," 71–72.
73. Félice, *Poisons sacrés. Ivresses divines.*
74. Ibid., 372.
75. Ibid., 363.
76. Ibid., 317 n. 6.
77. Wallwork, *Durkheim*, 80.
78. Durkheim, *The Elementary Forms of the Religious Life*, 121.
79. Remarkable to say in the light of those critics who attribute Durkheimian sociological ritualism to William Robertson Smith is Durkheim's view expressed in his 1887 review of Jean-Marie Guyau's *L'Irreligion de l'avenir*. It was not until April 1887 that Robertson Smith had been invited to deliver his famous lectures; it was not until October 1888 that he began and October 1891 that he completed his commission. Durkheim reportedly had not read Robertson Smith's *Lectures on the Religion of the Semites*, earlier than the second edition, published in 1894.
80. Hubert, Préface to Czarnowski, *Les Cultes des héros et ses conditions sociales*, xxxix.
81. Pickering, *Durkheim's Sociology of Religion*, 347.
82. Hubert, "Rituel," 247–48.
83. Durkheim, review of Guyau, *L'Irreligion de l'avenir*, 26, also cited in Pickering, *Durkheim's Sociology of Religion*, 326.
84. Durkheim, *Sociology and Philosophy*, 31–32.
85. Hubert and Mauss, *Sacrifice*, 77 (my emphasis). See also Hubert, Préface to Czarnowski; in several places, Hubert asserts the priority of myth to hero rite, for instance on pages lxvii, lxix. See especially Hubert's view that "it is myth which makes the hero, not his death" (lxxxix).
86. Hubert, Préface to Czarnowski, xxxix.
87. Pickering, *Durkheim's Sociology of Religion*, 326.

88. Now although Andrew Lang was probably the first vocal opponent of Max Müller's solarist mythology and mythophilia, we cannot materially link this eclectic virtuoso to any movement to take ritual more seriously than myth, and thus to our own ritualist movements in the study of religion (Reinach, "The Growth of Mythological Study," 437).

89. Mus, "La Mythologie primitive et la pensée de l'Inde," 119. See also Lévi, "Abel Bergaigne et l'indianisme," 7–9. Although he was more concerned about Max Müller's solarist interpretation of myths than his mythological reading of the Vedas, Salomon Reinach identifies our ritualists as the first critics of solarism—"Max Müllerism" as he calls it—as "Barth, Bergaigne and Darmesteter" (Reinach, "The Growth of Mythological Study," 437).

90. Lévi, La Doctrine du sacrifice dans les Brāhmaṇas, 9.

91. Stern, The Politics of Cultural Despair, chap. 1.

92. Lévi, La Doctrine du sacrifice dans les Brāhmaṇas, 10.

93. Mauss, "Sylvain Lévi", 539.

94. Renou, "Sylvain Lévi et son oeuvre scientifique," xv.

95. Bergaigne, Abel Bergaigne's "Vedic Religion", 283.

96. Ibid., 283.

97. Mus, "La Mythologie primitive et la pensée de l'Inde," 119. See also Hubert and Mauss's connection of James Darmesteter to Bergaigne and Sylvain Lévi on vedic texts in Hubert and Mauss, Sacrifice, 64, 370n.

98. Interestingly, Sylvain Lévi's claim that the brahmins practised a violent rite conflicts with early German Romantic views, for example, Herder, that the brahmins were actually remarkably gentle. See Poliakov, The Aryan Myth, 186. Barth is critical of Sylvain Lévi, saying he paints a "blacker" picture of the brahmins than they really were, indeed perhaps even a "caricature" (Barth, review of Lévi, La Doctrine du sacrifice dans les Brāhmaṇas, 91).

99. This is confirmed by Louis Renou, who says that for Lévi "ritual dominates mythology" ("Sylvain Lévi et son oeuvre scientifique," xxiii).

100. Lévi, La Doctrine du sacrifice dans les Brāhmaṇas, chap. 2, noted as well by Mauss in his review of La Doctrine du sacrifice, 293–95, 353. So potent is the sacrificial ritual that even if gods are relevant, those very gods are "born" from sacrificial ritual, are "products" of it (Lévi, La Doctrine du sacrifice dans les Brāhmaṇas, chap. 2), noted as well by Mauss in his review of La Doctrine du sacrifice, 293–95, 353.

101. Lévi, La Doctrine du sacrifice dans les Brāhmaṇas, 27. See also 38, where sacrifice is identified as the life source of the gods; 54, where it is said to save the gods; 76, where the superiority of sacrifice to the gods, in particular, Indra, is asserted.

102. Renou, Préface to La Doctrine, viii. Renou refers specifically to sacrificial ritual.

103. Mauss, "Sylvain Lévi," 537.

104. Mauss, review of Lévi's La Doctrine du sacrifice, 353, originally in L'Année sociologique 3 (1900): 293–95.

105. It should be noted that Friedrich Max Müller too felt that certain features of the narrative in the Vedas were "childish," even if he does not describe the language of the Vedas in this way (Müller, "On the Vedas," 135, 136).

106. Renou, "Sylvain Lévi et son oeuvre scientifique," xxii.

107. The Assumptionist fathers who edited La Croix likewise held Talmudic Judaism in contempt, holding it to be a form of anti-Christianism created in opposition to the new teachings of Jesus. See Sorlin, "La Croix" et les Juifs, 138.

108. Lévi, Une Renaissance juive en Judée.

109. Ibid., 22, and Darmesteter, Les Prophètes d'Israel.

110. Lévi, Une Renaissance juive en Judée, 22.

111. Ibid., 22.
112. Ibid.
113. Lévi, *La Doctrine du sacrifice dans les Brāhmaṇas*, 9.
114. Voigt, *Max-Müller*; 3; Poliakov, *The Aryan Myth*, 247.
115. The French movement included partisans of the "science du Judaïsme" such as James Darmesteter, who as early as 1886 went to India in order to study Oriental languages in their concrete contexts (Monod, "James Darmesteter," 162 f.); also see Darmesteter on the need for religion to be embodied in rituals in his "The Prophets of Israel," 59.
116. Jones, "Robertson Smith, Durkheim, and Sacrifice," 184–205. But see Durkheim's citations to Bergaigne in *The Elementary Forms*, 49–50.

Works Cited

Ackerman, Robert. *J. G. Frazer: His Life and Work*. Cambridge: Cambridge University Press, 1987.

Barth, Albrecht. "Bulletin des religions de l'Inde I: Védisme et ancien Brahmanisme." In *Revue d'histoire des religions* 39 (1899): 60–98.

Beidelman, T. O. *W. Robertson Smith and the Sociological Study of Religion*. Chicago: University of Chicago Press, 1974.

Bergaigne, Abel. *Abel Bergaigne's "Vedic Religion."* Vol. 3 [1878–83]. Translated by V. G. Paranjoti. Delhi: Motilal Banarsidass, 1978.

Brown, Karen McCarthy. *Mama Lola*. Berkeley: University of California Press, 1991.

Byrne, Peter. *Natural Religion and the Nature of Religion*. London: Routledge and Kegan Paul, 1989.

Chauduri, Nirad. *Scholar Extraordinary*. London: Chatto and Windus, 1974.

Clifford, James. "Power and Dialogue in Ethnography: Marcel Griaule's Initiation." In *Observers Observed: Essays on Ethnographic Fieldwork*. Edited by George W. Stocking, Jr. Madison: University of Wisconsin Press, 1983.

———. "On Ethnographic Surrealism." In *The Predicament of Culture*. Cambridge: Harvard University Press, 1988.

Darmesteter, James. *Les Prophètes d'Israel*. Paris: Calmann Lévy, 1892.

———. "The Prophets of Israel." In *Selected Essays of James Darmesteter*. Translated by Helen B. Jastrow. Edited by Morris Jastrow, Jr. Boston: Houghton and Mifflin, 1895.

Dorson, Richard M. *The British Folklorists: A History*. Chicago: University of Chicago Press, 1968.

Douglas, Mary. "Away from Ritual." *Natural Symbols*. New York: Vintage Books, 1973.

Driver, Tom F. *The Magic of Ritual*. San Francisco: Harper and Row, 1991.

Durkheim, Emile. *The Elementary Forms of the Religious Life*. Translated by Joseph W. Swain. New York: Free Press, 1915.

———. *Education, Sociology and Philosophy.* Translated by D. F. Pocock. New York: Free Press, 1974.

———. "Individualism and the Intellectuals" [1898]. In *Durkheim on Religion.* Edited by W. S. F. Pickering. London: Routledge and Kegan Paul, 1975.

———. Review of *L'Irreligion de l'avenir* by Jean-Marie Guyau [1887]. In *Durkheim on Religion.* Edited by W. S. F. Pickering. London: Routledge and Kegan Paul, 1975.

Félice, Philippe de. *Poisons sacrés. Ivresses divines: Essais sur quelques formes inférieures de la mystique.* Paris: Albin Michel, 1936.

Hofstadter, Richard. *Social Darwinism in American Thought.* Boston: Beacon Press, 1955.

Hubert, Henri. Préface to *Les Cultes des héros et ses conditions sociales* by Stefan Czarnowski. Paris: Alcan, 1919.

———. "Rituel." *L'Année sociologique* 5 (1902).

Hubert, Henri, and Marcel Mauss. "Introduction à l'analyse de quelques phénomènes religieux." In *Les Fonctions sociales du sacré.* Vol. 1, Marcel Mauss, *Oeuvres.* Edited by Victor Karady. Paris: Editions de Minuit, 1968.

———. *Sacrifice: Its Nature and Function* [1899]. Translated by W. D. Halls. Chicago: University of Chicago Press, 1964.

Jones, Robert Alun. "Robertson Smith, Durkheim, and Sacrifice: An Historical Context for *The Elementary Forms of the Religious Life.*" *Journal for the History of the Behavioral Sciences* 17 (1981): 184–205

Leach, Edmund. "Ritual." *International Encyclopedia of the Social Sciences.* New York: Macmillan, 1968.

Lévi, Sylvain. *La Doctrine du sacrifice dans les Brāhmaṇas.* Paris: Leroux, 1898.

———. "Abel Bergaigne et l'indianisme" [1890]. *Mémorial Sylvain Lévi.* Edited by Jacques Bacot. Paris: Paul Hartmann, 1937.

———. *Une Renaissance juive en Judée.* Ligue des Amis du Sionisme, Tract no. 5. Paris: Driay-Cahen, 1918.

Lévi-Strauss, Claude. *L'Homme nu.* Paris: Plon, 1971.

———. "Structure and Dialectics" [1956]. *Structural Anthropology.* New York: Basic Books, 1963.

Lukes, Steven. *Emile Durkheim.* New York: Harper and Row, 1972.

Mauss, Marcel. Review of *La Doctrine du sacrifice* by Sylvain Lévi. *L'Année sociologique* 3 (1900); reprint in *Les Fonctions sociales du sacre,* vol. 1, Marcel Mauss, *Oeuvres.* Edited by Victor Karady. Paris: Editions de Minuit, 1968.

———. "Sylvain Lévi" (1935). In *Cohesion sociale et divisions de la soci-*

ologie. Vol. 3, Marcel Mauss, *Oeuvres*. Edited by Victor Karady. Paris: Editions de Minuit, 1969.

Monod, Gabriel. "James Darmesteter." In *Portraits et souvenirs*. Paris: Calmann Lévy, 1897.

Müller, Friedrich Max. *Chips from a German Woodshop*. Vol. 3. New York: Charles Scribner's Sons, 1881.

———. "Comparative Mythology" [1856]. In *Selected Essays on Language, Mythology and Religion*. Vol. 1. London: Longmans, Green, 1881.

———. *My Autobiography: A Fragment*. London: Longmans, Green, 1901.

———. *Natural Religion*. London: Longmans, Green, 1889.

———. "On the Philosophy of Mythology" [1871]. In *Selected Essays on Language, Mythology and Religion*. Vol. 1. London: Longmans, Green, 1881.

———. "On the Vedas or the Sacred Books of the Brahmans" [1865]. In *Selected Essays on Language, Mythology and Religion*. Vol. 2. London: Longmans, Green, 1882.

———. *Physical Religion*. London: Longmans, Green, 1891.

Mus, Paul. "La Mythologie primitive et la pensée de l'Inde." *Bulletin de la Societé Française de Philosophie* 37 (1937): 83–126.

Pickering, W. S. F. *Durkheim's Sociology of Religion*. Part 4. London: Routledge and Kegan Paul, 1984.

Poliakov, Léon. *The Aryan Myth*. New York: New American Library, 1974.

Reinach, Salomon. "The Growth of Mythological Study." *Quarterly Review* 215 (1911): 423–41.

Renou, Louis. Préface to *La Doctrine du sacrifice dans les Brāhmaṇas* [1898], by Sylvain Lévi. 2d ed. Paris: Presses Universitaires de France, 1966.

———. "Sylvain Lévi et son oeuvre scientifique." In *Mémorial Sylvain Lévi*. Edited by Jacques Bacot. Paris: Hartmann, 1937.

Réville, Albert. "Contemporaneous Materialism in Religion: The Sacred Heart." *Theological Review* 44 (1874): 138–56.

———. "Evolution in Religion, and Its Results." *Theological Review* 12 (1875): 230–48.

Robertson Smith, William. *Lectures on the Religion of the Semites*. 2d ed. London: A and C Black, 1894.

———. "The Place of Theology in the Work of the Growth of the Church" [1875]. In *Lectures and Essays of William Robertson Smith*. Edited by J. Sutherland Black and George Chrystal. London: Adam and Charles Black, 1912.

————. *The Religion of the Semites*. Rev. ed. London: A and C Black, 1923.

Smart, Ninian. *The Religious Experience of Mankind* [1968]. 3d ed. New York: Schocken, 1984.

Sorlin, Pierre. *"La Croix" et les Juifs*. Paris: Grasset, 1967.

Stern, Fritz. *The Politics of Cultural Despair*. Berkeley: University of California Press, 1961.

Strenski, Ivan. *Religion/Politics and History in a Time of Sacrifice*. Forthcoming.

————. "Henri Hubert, Racial Science and Political Myth." *Journal of the History of the Behavioral Sciences* 23 (1987); reprint in *Religion in Relation: Theory, Application and Moral Location*. London: Macmillan, 1992.

Turner, Victor. *The Ritual Process*. London: Routledge and Kegan Paul, 1969.

Voigt, Johannes. *Max-Müller: The Man and His Ideas*. Calcutta: Firma K. L. Mukhopadhyay, 1967.

Wallwork, Ernest. *Durkheim: Morality and Milieu*. Cambridge: Harvard University Press, 1972.

ROBERT A. SEGAL

DOES MYTH HAVE A FUTURE?

WHETHER MYTH HAS a future depends on its capacity to meet the challenge posed by modern science. This essay examines the varying responses to that challenge by leading theorists of myth.

As Marcel Detienne and many others have shown, the challenge to myth does not begin in the modern era.[1] It goes back to at least Plato, who rejected Homeric myth as trivial and immoral. The Stoics defended myth against these charges by reinterpreting it as metaphysical and moral allegory.

Modern challenges to myth have been made on intellectual, theological, and political grounds. (In another essay in this volume, Ivan Strenski points out the political challenge to myth made by Durkheimian ritualists at the turn of the century.) The chief modern challenge, however, has come from natural science, which does so well what myth had long been assumed to do: explain the origin and operation of the physical world. Where myth attributes events in the world to the decisions of gods, science ascribes them to impersonal, mechanical processes. To accept the scientific explanation of the world is to render the mythic one both superfluous and outright false—superfluous because superseded by the scientific account, false because incompatible with the scientific one.

Science does not challenge the *origin* of myth. How and why myth arises does not matter. Science challenges the *function* of myth by usurping that function.

The most facile response to the gauntlet thrown down by science has been cavalierly to ignore science. An only slightly less facile response has been to pronounce science itself mythic. A more credible response has accepted science as the reigning explanation of the world and has then either surrendered or regrouped. *Surrendering* means simply replacing myth with science. Myth is here conceded to be an outdated and incorrect explanation of the world. *Regrouping* means altering either the function or the content of myth in order to make myth compatible with science. Myth here becomes other than a (1) literal (2) explanation of the world. Either the function of myth becomes other than explanatory, or the meaning of myth becomes other than literal.

The Surrender of Myth to Science: Tylor

The exemplars of the surrendering response to science are the pioneering anthropologists Edward Tylor and James Frazer. Tylor represents a purer case than Frazer, whose views on the function and meaning of myth are muddled and contradictory.[2] According to Tylor, myth arises and functions solely to explain events in the physical world. Like science, myth serves neither to endorse nor to condemn the world but only to account for it. Myth does not moralize, sanction, or emote. It explains.

Tylor's surrender of myth to science presupposes not only that the exclusive function of myth is explanatory but also that mythic explanations are unscientific. For Tylor, myth is unscientific because it employs personal rather than impersonal causes. Yet Tylor never quite explains why personal causation is unscientific and so why myth must be at odds with science. In light of contemporary science and philosophy of science, none of his likely assumptions is tenable.

(1) Tylor may be objecting to personal causes on the grounds that they are mental—the decisions of immaterial gods—where impersonal causes are material. But Tylor himself contrasts the primitive religious conception of the soul as *material* to the modern, metaphysical conception of it as *immaterial*.[3] From the primitive conception of souls comes the conception of gods, who are therefore material as well: "The lower races are apt to ascribe to spirits in general that kind of ethereal materiality which we have seen they attribute to souls."[4] Even if Tylor assumes that science, in contrast to modern religion, limits itself to material phenomena,[5] so, too, for him does primitive religion. Indeed, he states that "the later metaphysical notion of immateriality could scarcely have conveyed any meaning to a savage."[6]

Tylor's own views aside, most present-day scientists and philosophers of science do not consider mental causes unscientific or inferior.[7] The relationship of the mind to the body remains an open scientific as well as philosophical question. If, then, personal causation is unscientific, the reason cannot be that gods are immaterial entities.

(2) Perhaps Tylor's objection to personal causes is that they are merely imagined where impersonal causes are proved. But Tylor himself considers the postulation of gods a careful inference from primitives' experience of natural phenomena, so that it is unlikely that he is assuming *this* distinction between mythic and scientific explanations. In any case atoms are themselves merely inferred, not observed. Only the purported effects of atoms are directly observed.

(3) Maybe Tylor's objection to personal causes is that they are unpredictable and therefore untestable where impersonal ones are predictable and therefore testable. For example, while it is certain that lightning will cause thunder, it is not certain that the god of thunder will decide to send thunder. But the events that, according to Tylor himself, primitives most want explained are recurrent ones like the daily course of the sun, not irregular ones like thunder. Furthermore, religious explanations, even if given ex post facto rather than in advance, *are* certain: whenever there is thunder, the incontestable cause is the god of thunder.

Moreover, not all mythic explanations take the form that Tylor assumes: attributing events to *decisions* by gods. While thunder may occur because a god chooses to send it, it may also occur because something befalls the god which automatically causes thunder. When Adonis is taken to be the god of vegetation, as Frazer especially assumes him to have been taken, the crops die not because Adonis decides to kill them but because he himself is dead for the third of the year that he spends in Hades with Persephone. Even if Adonis chooses to descend to the underworld, he is not choosing to keep the crops from growing during his stay there. Rather, as he goes, so automatically go the crops. When he resurfaces, so automatically do the crops. The explanation of the course of vegetation is thus mechanical, not deliberative, and is therefore open to prediction.[8]

Finally, not all scientific explanations themselves predict with certainty. Many scientific explanations offer mere probabilities: they state that events will likely, not necessarily, occur. Probabilistic, or inductive, scientific explanations are hardly less scientific than certain, deductive ones. Many contemporary physicists even believe that the ultimate explanations of physics will prove to be merely probabilistic.[9] Writing before the emergence of quantum mechanics, Tylor is likely assuming that scientific explanations are in principle predictable with certainty. If so, he would have to concede this distinction, too, between myth and science.

(4) Tylor may be objecting to personal causes on the grounds that they are teleological where impersonal causes are efficient: gods act not just in response to something but also for some end; atoms behave merely in response to something. But biology was at least partly teleological until Darwin, and science continues to offer teleological explanations of human behavior. Even if science is increasingly explaining human behavior itself mechanistically, most human behavior still gets explained teleologically. The difference between myth and science is that myth explains the *whole world* teleologically. There is no disjunction between the nature of the explanations of human behavior and the nature of the explanations of the behavior of everything else. Indeed, gods for Tylor are postulated on analogy with human beings.

In sum, it is not easy to see how Tylor could defend his conviction that the personal explanations of myth are automatically unscientific and inferior.

Because Tylor nevertheless sees personal explanations as both unscientific and inferior, he takes for granted that the rise of science spells the fall of myth. Yet the rise of science somehow does not also dictate the end of religion. Even though for him religion and myth operate in tandem to explain the world—religion identifies which god causes an event; myth tells how and why that god causes the event—Tylor makes provision for the retention of religion in the wake of science but no provision for the retention of myth. Religion can be transformed in both function and content from an explanation of the world to an espousal of ethics—a view typified by Matthew Arnold—but for some unstated reason myth cannot.

In fact, Tylor rails against those theorists of myth who make myth other than an explanation, including those who turn myth into moral allegory.[10] According to this group of theorists, the myth of Helius, for example, is actually a clever technique for promoting self-discipline: "Helius daily drives his chariot across the sky" means "One should work hard." "Thus the story of Memnon depicts the destinies of rash young men of promise; while Perseus symbolizes war, and when of the three Gorgons he attacks only the mortal one, this means that only practicable wars are to be attempted."[11] For the moral allegorizers, myth is compatible with science both because it is really about human beings rather than about gods and because it says how human beings ought to behave rather than how they do behave. The function of myth becomes normative rather than explanatory, and the meaning of myth becomes symbolic rather than literal.

Tylor denounces the moral allegorizers not because they alter the function or meaning of myth for themselves but because they do so for primitives. For Tylor, to cede the explanatory function of myth is to trivialize myth, and the explanatory function requires a literal reading. He thus says that "the basis on which such (mythic) ideas as these are built is not to be narrowed down to poetic fancy and transformed metaphor. They rest upon a broad philosophy of nature, early and crude indeed, but thoughtful, consistent, and quite really and seriously meant."[12] Tylor assumes that the allegorizers anachronistically project their own incredulity onto primitives. Scarcely taking myth seriously themselves, these theorists cannot imagine that anyone else has ever done so.

It is, then, in the *name* of myth that Tylor *denies* myth a future. For him, to take myth seriously is to take it as an explanation of the world. That that explanation has been vanquished by the scientific one does not, for Tylor, demean it. On the contrary, myth remains a competitor, simply a losing competitor, in the grandest intellectual enterprise.

The Regrouping of Myth in the Wake of Science: Eliade, Bultmann, Jonas, and Jung

As common as the strategy of surrendering myth to science has been, even more popular has been the strategy of regrouping. Conceding to science only the explanatory function and the literal meaning of myth, this strategy seeks alternative functions and meanings beyond the ken of science. Regrouping has taken several forms. One form has been to credit myth with one or more nonexplanatory functions, in which case myth runs askew to science and can therefore coexist with it. The exemplar of this response is Mircea Eliade. A second form of response has been to interpret the meaning of myth symbolically, in which case myth does not even refer to the physical world and so can likewise coexist with science. The exemplars of this response are Rudolf Bultmann and Hans Jonas. The boldest form of response has been to alter both the function and the meaning of myth, so that on neither count does myth compete with science. The exemplars of this two-pronged rejoinder to science are C. G. Jung and Joseph Campbell.

MIRCEA ELIADE

Mircea Eliade does not reject the explanatory function of myth. For him, as for Tylor, myth serves to explain how gods created and control the world: "Myth narrates a sacred history; it relates an event that took place in primordial Time, the fabled time of the 'beginnings.' In other words, myth tells how, through the deeds of Supernatural Beings, a reality came into existence, be it the whole of reality, the Cosmos, or only a fragment of reality."[13]

Indeed, Eliade goes beyond Tylor in crediting myth with explaining not only natural phenomena but also social ones: "Myths, that is, narrate not only the origin of the World, of animals, of plants, and of man, but also all the primordial events in consequence of which man became what he is today—mortal, sexed, organized in a society, obliged to work in order to live, and working in accordance with certain rules."[14]

How, then, does Eliade meet the challenge of science? By proposing functions served by myth in addition to the explanatory one. Myth for Eliade justifies as well as explains phenomena. Myth does not, to be sure, pronounce phenomena good. But it does pronounce them inevitable and in that sense seeks to reconcile humanity to them. For example, myth justifies death less by postulating an afterlife, though Eliade notes myths that do, than by rooting death in an event in primordial time, when the world was still malleable but when any action made permanent whatever it effected. In primordial, or mythic, time the cosmic clay is soft; by subsequent, historical, ordinary time it has hardened. According to myth, human beings die because "a mythical Ancestor stupidly lost immortality, or because a Supernatural Being decided to deprive him of it, or because a certain mythical event left him endowed at once with sexuality and mortality, and so on."[15] Myth makes the present less arbitrary and therefore more tolerable by locating its origin in the hoary rather than the recent past.

Myth for Eliade does more than explain and justify. Above all, it regenerates. To hear, to read, and especially to reenact a myth is magically to return to the time when the myth took place, the time of the origin of whatever phenomenon it explains and justifies: "But since ritual recitation of the cosmogonic myth implies reactualization of that primordial event, it follows that he for whom it is recited is magically projected *in illo tempore*, into the 'beginning of the World'; he becomes contemporary with the cosmogony."[16] In returning one to primordial time, myth reunites one with the gods, for it is then when they are nearest, as the biblical case of "the Lord God['s] walking in the garden in the cool of the day" typifies.[17] That "reunion" reverses the post-lapsarian separation from the gods, a separation that is equivalent to the Fall, and renews one spiritually: "What is involved is, in short, a return to the original time, the therapeutic purpose of which is to begin life once again, a symbolic rebirth."[18] The ultimate payoff of myth is experiential: it is the encounter with divinity.

Clearly, science offers no regenerative or even justificatory function. Science simply explains. Myth, then, has a future: it can do things that science cannot.

But Eliade offers another argument in favor of the future—in fact, the eternality—of myth. Myth not only serves functions that transcend the function served by science; it also serves them for moderns as well as for primitives. Moderns for Eliade fancy themselves scrupulously rational, intellectual, unsentimental, and forward-looking—in short, scientific. Nothing could veer farther from their collective self-image than adherence to myth, which they dismiss as egregiously outdated. Yet even they, according to Eliade, cannot dispense with myth:

> A whole volume could well be written on the myths of modern man, on the mythologies camouflaged in the plays that he enjoys, in the books that he reads. The cinema, that "dream factory," takes over and employs countless mythical motifs—the fight between hero and monster, initiatory combats and ordeals, paradigmatic figures and images (the maiden, the hero, the paradisal landscape, hell, and so on). Even reading includes a mythological function . . . because, through reading, the modern man succeeds in obtaining an "escape from time" comparable to the "emergence from time" effected by myths. Whether modern man "kills" time with a detective story or enters such a foreign temporal universe as is represented by any novel, reading projects him out of his personal duration and incorporates him into other rhythms, makes him live in another "history."[19]

Plays, books, and movies are mythiclike because they reveal the existence of another world alongside the everyday one—a world of extraordinary figures and events akin to those found in earlier, superhuman myths. Furthermore, the actions of those figures account for the present state of the everyday world. Most of all, moderns get so absorbed in plays, books, and movies that they imagine themselves to be back in the world before their eyes. Identifying themselves with the characters of the stories, they experience the same hopes and fears. If, argues Eliade, even self-professed atheists ineluctably have their own myths, then surely myth is panhuman, in which case it has a boundless future.

However appealing, Eliade's dual counterargument to Tylor—that myth serves functions that science cannot duplicate and that even moderns cherish myth—is dubious. First, the nonexplanatory functions of myth depend on the explanatory one, as Eliade himself recognizes in always characterizing myth as at least an explanation. But then myth can serve its other functions only if it can fend off science in serving its explanatory function. How it can do so, Eliade never says. Perhaps he is assuming that the phenomena explained by modern myths are entirely social—for example, the origin of tools, marriage, government, and nationalities—and not at all natural—for example, the origin of the sun and the moon. But *social* science seeks to account for social phenomena, so what is left for myth alone to explain?

Second, modern myths do not return one to the time of the gods. They may not even go backward in time but may instead go forward, as in science fiction, or go sideways, such as to other cultures around the world. Even myths that do move backward rarely go as far back as the time of the gods. They take one back to only "post-primordial" time. These myths may provide escape from the present, but how much renewal can they provide? A hagiographical biography of George Washington may attribute the establishment of twentieth-century American laws and mores to the accomplishments of this larger-than-life hero, but a human being he remains. Reliving the American Revolution might be inspiring, but would it provide cosmic regeneration?

Third, moderns travel back in time only in their imaginations, not in reality. Americans may feel *as if* they are present at the Revolution, but they hardly claim actually to be back there, whisked on a mythic time machine. Once the play, book, movie, or other vehicle is over, so is the myth. One may remember a stirring story long afterward, but as a memory or an inspiration only. As affecting as Eliade's effort to confer a future on myth is, it is unconvincing.

RUDOLF BULTMANN

The second main regrouping response to the challenge of science has come from the existentialist camp: from the New Testament scholar and theologian Rudolf Bultmann and from his onetime student, the philosopher Hans Jonas. Both were students of Martin Heidegger.

For both Bultmann and Jonas, myth does not explain the world—a function left to science. Instead, myth expresses the relationship of human beings to the world. As Bultmann puts it, "The real purpose of myth is not to present an objective picture of the world as it is, but to express man's understanding of himself in the world in which he lives. Myth should be interpreted not cosmologically, but anthropologically, or better still, existentially."[20]

Bultmann acknowledges that, read literally, myth is about the world itself. But unlike Eliade and Tylor, both of whom retain a literal interpretation of myth, Bultmann, together with Jonas, offers a symbolic one. In Bultmann's famous, if excruciatingly confusing, phrase, one must "demythologize" myth, which means not eliminating, or "demythicizing," the mythology but instead extricating the true, existential meaning of that mythology.

Taken literally, myth for Bultmann is exactly as it is for Tylor: a prescientific explanation of the world, an explanation rendered not merely superfluous but plainly false by science. Were myth to harbor no other meaning, Bultmann no less than Tylor would spurn it altogether as primitive.

Demythologized, however, myth ceases to be an explanation at all and becomes an expression—an expression not of the nature of the world but of the nature of the human experience of the world. Myth ceases to be merely primitive and becomes universal. It ceases to be false and becomes true. It becomes a statement of the human condition.

Read literally, the New Testament in particular describes a cosmic battle between good and evil anthropomorphic gods and angels for control of the physical world. These beings intervene not only in the operation of nature, as for Tylor, but also in the lives of human beings. The beneficent beings direct humans to do good; the malevolent ones compel them to do evil. Taken literally, the New Testament describes a prescientific outlook:

> The world is viewed as a three-storied structure, with the earth in the centre, the heaven above, and the underworld beneath. Heaven is the abode of God and of celestial beings—the angels. The underworld is hell, the place of torment. Even the earth is more than the scene of natural, everyday events, of the trivial round and common

task. It is the scene of the supernatural activity of God and his angels on the one hand, and of Satan and his daemons on the other. These supernatural forces intervene in the course of nature and in all that men think and will and do. Miracles are by no means rare. Man is not in control of his own life. Evil spirits may take possession of him. Satan may inspire him with evil thoughts. Alternatively, God may inspire his thought and guide his purposes. He may grant him heavenly visions. He may allow him to hear his word of succour or demand. He may give him the supernatural power of his Spirit.[21]

Demythologized, the New Testament still refers in part to the physical world, but now to a world ruled by a single, nonanthropomorphic, transcendent God. Because God does not act directly in the world and because no evil powers exist, human beings are free rather than controlled like puppets:

Mythology expresses a certain understanding of human existence. It believes that the world and human life have their ground and their limits in a power which is beyond all that we can calculate or control. Mythology speaks about this power inadequately and insufficiently because it speaks about it as if it were a worldly [i.e., physical] power. It [rightly] speaks of gods who represent the power beyond the visible, comprehensible world. [But] it speaks of gods as if they were men and of their actions as human actions. . . . Again, the conception of Satan as ruler over the world expresses a deep insight, namely, the insight that evil is not only to be found here and there in the world, but that all particular evils make up one single power which in the last analysis grows from the very actions of men, which form an atmosphere, a spiritual tradition, which overwhelms every man. The consequences and effects of our sins become a power dominating us, and we cannot free ourselves from them.[22]

Demythologized, God still exists, but Satan does not. Sin becomes one's own doing, and Satan symbolizes only one's own evil inclinations. Damnation refers not to a future place but to a present state of mind, which exists as long as one rejects God. Similarly, salvation refers to one's state of mind once one accepts God. Hell symbolizes despair over the absence of God; heaven, joy in his presence. The eschatology refers not to the coming end of the physical world but to the personal acceptance or rejection of God in one's daily life.

Because a literal interpretation of the New Testament reduces human beings to the pawns of cosmic forces, a literal reading focuses on those forces themselves, which means on the world itself. Because a symbolic interpretation pronounces humanity free, it concentrates on the actions humans choose in response to the world.

Taken literally, myth, as a supernatural explanation of the physical world, is incompatible with science and is therefore unacceptable to moderns:

> Man's knowledge and mastery of the world have advanced to such an extent through science and technology that it is no longer possible for anyone seriously to hold the New Testament view of the world—in fact, there is no one who does. What meaning, for instance, can we attach to such phrases in the creed as "descended into hell" or "ascended into heaven"? We no longer believe in the three-storied universe which the creeds take for granted. . . . No one who is old enough to think for himself supposes that God lives in a local heaven. There is no longer any heaven in the traditional sense of the word. The same applies to hell in the sense of a mythical underworld beneath our feet. . . . Now that the forces and the laws of nature have been discovered, we can no longer believe in spirits, whether good or evil.[23]

Once demythologized, however, myth is compatible with science because it now refers both to the transcendent, nonphysical world and, even more, to humans' experience of the physical one.

Like Eliade, Bultmann urges moderns to accept myth. But where Eliade neglects to show how moderns can accept myth, Bultmann translates myth into existentialist terms in order to make it acceptable. At the same time he justifies his translation not on the pragmatic grounds that otherwise moderns could not accept it but on the grounds that its true meaning *is* existential: "If the truth of the New Testament proclamation is to be preserved, the only way is to demythologize it. But our motive in so doing must not be to make the New Testament relevant to the modern world at all costs. The question is simply whether the New Testament message consists exclusively of mythology, or whether it [itself] actually demands the elimination of myth [at the literal level] if it is to be understood as it is meant to be."[24]

To say that myth is acceptable to scientifically minded moderns is not, however, to say why myth should be accepted. In providing a modern *meaning* of myth, Bultmann provides no modern *function*. What myth does for moderns, Bultmann never says. Perhaps for him the answer is self-evident: myth, and myth alone, serves to reveal the human condition. Bultmann may never go so far as to deem myth untranslatable into nonmythic terms, the way such theorists as Paul Ricoeur and Philip Wheelwright do, but the message translated may for him be contained only in myth. In encouraging moderns to accept the message of myth, Bultmann would thereby be encouraging them to accept myth itself.

But even when demythologized, myth is acceptable to moderns only if the existence of God is. For as a religious existentialist rather than, like Jonas, a secular one, Bultmann takes myth to be preserving the reality of God, simply of a nonphysical god. Bultmann saves myth from science only insofar as moderns can accept even a sophisticated conception, not to mention a specifically Christian conception, of God. Where Eliade saves myth from science by appealing to the existence of distinctively modern myths—myths without gods in them—Bultmann retains an ancient myth with its God. Furthermore, at least Eliade tries to demonstrate that moderns, however avowedly atheistic, actually espouse myth. Bultmann merely leaves myth as something worthy of espousal. He does say that the message of myth need not be conscious: "It goes without saying that this existential self-understanding need not be conscious."[25] But he nowhere establishes that this message is commonly espoused.

HANS JONAS

In proposing a demythologization of the New Testament, Bultmann declares his debt to Hans Jonas, who had already (1934) offered a demythologization of Gnosticism: "A good example of such treatment [i.e., demythologization] is to be found in Hans Jonas's book on Gnosticism. Our task is to produce an existentialist interpretation of . . . the New Testament along similar lines."[26]

Jonas argues that ancient Gnosticism touts the same fundamental view of the human condition as modern existentialism. Both philosophies stress the radical alienation of human beings from the world. Taking the roots of existentialism all the way back to the seventeenth century, Jonas describes Pascal's depiction of the human situation:

> "Cast into the infinite immensity of spaces of which I am ignorant, and which know me not, I am frightened." "Which know me not": more than the overawing infinity of cosmic spaces and times, more than the quantitative disproportion, the insignificance of man as a magnitude in this vastness, it is the "silence," that is, the indifference of this universe to human aspirations . . . which constitutes the utter loneliness of man in the sum of things. As a part of this sum, as an instance of nature, man is only a reed, liable to be crushed at any moment by the forces of an immense and blind universe in which his existence is but a particular blind accident, no less blind than would be the accident of his destruction. As a thinking reed, however, he is no part of the sum, not belonging to it, but radically different, incommensurable: for the *res extensa* does not think, so Descartes had taught, and nature is nothing but *res extensa*—body, matter, external magnitude. If nature crushes the reed, it does so unthinkingly, whereas the reed—man—even while crushed, is aware of being crushed.[27]

While Pascal, unlike Sartre and Camus, is a religious existentialist, his God "is essentially an unknown God, an *agnostos theos*, and is not discernible in the evidence of his creation."[28] The result is human estrangement from God as well as from the world.

For Jonas, ancient Gnosticism presents an outlook as forlorn as that of modern existentialism. For here, too, lies an uncompromising divide between human beings and the world:

> And, like Pascal, he [the Gnostic] is frightened. His solitary otherness, discovering itself in this forlornness, erupts in the feeling of dread. Dread . . . is the self's reaction to the discovery of its situation, actually itself an element in that discovery: it marks the awakening of the inner self from the slumber or intoxication of the world. . . . Becoming aware of itself, the self also discovers that it is not really its own, but is rather the involuntary executor of cosmic designs. Knowledge, *gnosis*, may liberate man from this servitude; but since the *cosmos* is contrary to life and to spirit, the saving knowledge cannot aim at integration into the cosmic whole. . . . For the Gnostics, on the contrary, man's alienation from the world

is to be deepened and brought to a head, for the extrication of the inner self which only thus can gain itself.[29]

The Gnostic and existentialist worldviews are far from identical, as Jonas certainly grants. In Gnosticism one is presently separated from one's true, divine self, which itself is separated from both the true god and the true world. One finds oneself trapped in an alien, material self that is part of an alien world under the control of an alien god. In secular existentialism the true self from which one is separated is the *absence* of any fixed nature or essence. One is presently severed from the true self exactly insofar as one deems one's nature determined by heredity or environment rather than freely created and recreated. There beckons no higher world beyond the present world. And there looms no god of any kind, lower or higher.

In Gnosticism one's false self is not just the body but worldly values. In existentialism one's false self is the role with which one identifies oneself—for example, that of professor, student, lawyer, parent, child, sibling. One has no essence because no god created humanity. In Gnosticism one's true self is consubstantial with the true world: the spark is part of the immaterial world. The alien world is the material world ruled by the Demiurge, the nemesis of the true god. In existentialism the sole world that exists is antithetical to oneself: human consciousness stands over against inert, dead matter, which is amoral rather than demonic. The world is meaningless. It has no essence, or purpose, precisely because no god created it. In Gnosticism one's true self is consubstantial with the true god: the spark is a split-off piece of the godhead, which strives for reunification. In the ideal state one is reunited with the godhead and loses all individual identity. In existentialism belief in any god is false hope and, like the identification of oneself with a single role, is an attempt to avoid responsibility for one's life. It is what Sartre calls "bad faith."

In Gnosticism the state of alienation is temporary. To heed the revelation of the true nature of things from the savior is automatically to begin the process of overcoming that state—a process that culminates in the severance of the spark from the body at death. In existentialism the state of alienation from the world is permanent. It is the human condition. Alienation from one's true self is overcome the moment one recognizes that one has chosen to forge one's present identity. No savior from outside is required for that recognition. No world or god has deceived one. To evade responsibility for one's actions, one has deceived oneself.

Despite these not inconsiderable divergences between ancient Gnosticism and modern existentialism, Jonas demonstrates the even keener similarities. Like Bultmann, Jonas translates ancient myth into contemporary parlance. While Jonas himself is as captivated by the way ancient Gnosticism sheds light on modernity as by the way modernity sheds light on ancient Gnosticism, it is the light that modern existentialism sheds on ancient Gnosticism which gives myth a future.

For Jonas, as for Bultmann, myth, rightly deciphered, refers not to the world but to the experience of the world. Gnostic myths no longer describe the godhead, the emanations, the creator god, or the material world. They now describe the state of alienation from the material world. Gnostic myths no longer explain the origin of the material world from or through the immaterial world. They now describe the way human beings feel toward the material world. Gnostic myths cease to offer any escape from the material world and instead condemn one to life in that world.

More accurately, Jonas, like Bultmann, ignores those aspects of ancient myths that are cosmogonic or eschatological and concentrates on those aspects that are existential. The fact of human alienation from the world, not the source of it or the solution to it, is the demythologized subject of myth. The residue is mere mythology—to be discarded, just like *all* mythology for Tylor.

Yet no more than Bultmann does Jonas offer any alternative function of myth for moderns. At most, myth functions to express the human condition. But Jonas, unlike Bultmann, never makes myth the exclusive bearer of its message. If twentieth-century philosophy provides the key to unlocking the meaning of myth, what part does myth itself play once its own meaning has been unlocked? Where Bultmann fails to make the New Testament palatable to atheistic moderns, Jonas fails to make Gnostic myths necessary for them.

Like Freud and Jung, Jonas labels myth "projection": "To the Gnostic, this fact [about the world] is the subject of revealed knowledge, and it determines gnostic eschatology: *we* may see in it the projection of his basic experience, which thus created for itself its own revelatory truth."[30] "I am convinced that what in the myth, e.g. in the Poimandres and in certain Ophitic systems, is described as an objective, spatial journey of the soul, could eventually transform into the structural model for an innerpersonal process; and I believe that later mysticism in effect represents an internalization of this schema."[31] Yet Jonas is not, strictly, psychologizing myth. He is saying that what especially early Gnosticism presents as a description of the external world comes to be recognized by later Gnostics as the projection onto the world not of the human psyche but of the human experience of the world.[32] The subject of myth for Jonas, as for Bultmann, is no more human nature itself than the world itself. It is the relationship between the two.[33]

C. G. JUNG

C. G. Jung and Joseph Campbell offer the staunchest rejoinder to the death sentence that Tylor pronounces on myth.[34] For they transform both the function and the meaning of myth. Like Eliade, they make the function of myth more—indeed, other—than explanatory. Like Bultmann and Jonas, they make the subject of myth other than the physical world. Because I have discussed Campbell's theory voluminously elsewhere, I will focus here on Jung.[35]

For Jung, myth functions to reveal the existence of the unconscious: "Myths are original revelations of the preconscious [i.e., collective] psyche, involuntary statements about unconscious psychic happenings. . . . Modern psychology treats the products of unconscious fantasy-activity as self-portraits of what is going on in the unconscious, or as statements of the unconscious psyche about itself."[36] Whoever takes myth literally *thinks* that it is revealing the existence of something external like the godhead and immaterial world, but in fact it is revealing the workings of the unconscious.

Myth functions not merely to tell one about the unconscious but actually to open one up to it. Because the unconscious for Jung is inherently unconscious, one can never experience it directly but must experience it via myths and other symbolic manifestations.

Like Jonas, Jung is entranced by ancient Gnosticism because he sees in it an uncanny parallel to the present. Where for Jonas the key similarity is the experience of alienation from *the world*, for Jung the key similarity is the experience of alienation from *oneself*. That alienation is projected onto the world, so that one feels severed from the world, but one is really severed from oneself. The world is the manifestation, not the source, of alienation.

For Jung, late antiquity and the twentieth century are the periods in Western history when human beings have most felt lost, aimless, unfulfilled, incomplete—with traditional myths and religions no longer working and humans consequently being cut off from their unconscious:

> The psychological interest of the present time is an indication that modern man expects something from the psyche which the outer world has not given him: doubtless something which our religion ought to contain, but no longer does contain, at least for modern man. . . . That there is a general interest in these matters cannot be denied. . . . The world has seen nothing like it since the end of the seventeenth century. We can compare it only to the flowering of Gnostic thought in the first and second centuries after Christ. . . . What is striking about these Gnostic systems is that they are based exclusively on the manifestations of the unconscious. . . . The passionate interest in these movements undoubtedly arises from psychic energy which can no longer be invested in obsolete religious forms.[37]

Jung sees Gnostics as the ancient counterparts to moderns—better, to what should be called "twentieth-century moderns." Non-Gnostics are the counterparts to "nineteenth-century moderns." In Jung's history of the psyche, "nineteenth-century moderns" have properly forged independent egos. They have substantially withdrawn their projections from the external world, which they therefore encounter in itself, unfiltered by the unconscious. That demythicized world is composed of trees, not tree gods. In largely withdrawing their projections from the world, nineteenth-century moderns have rightly differentiated themselves from both the world and the unconscious.

Invariably, however, these moderns have not merely separated themselves from their unconscious, for which Jung applauds them, but rejected it altogether. They have thereby pitted themselves—their egos—against their unconscious. Like moderns generally for Eliade, nineteenth-century moderns for Jung consider themselves wholly rational, unemotional, scientific, and atheistic. Religion, through which earlier humanity had realized its unconscious, gets dismissed by them as a prescientific delusion. Marx, Nietzsche, and Freud epitomize nineteenth-century modernity for Jung.

In contrast to nineteenth-century moderns, twentieth-century moderns are conscious of their nonrational side, whether or not of its unconscious source. Like nineteenth-century moderns, twentieth-century ones reject religion as a prescientific relic, but unlike nineteenth-century moderns, they are dissatisfied with a scrupulously rational life and yearn instead for the kind of fulfillment that religion once provided. They seek new, nonprojective outlets to replace the dead, projective ones of religion. They do not, like their psychological predecessors, boast of having transcended the need that religion once satisfied.

In identifying contemporary moderns with twentieth-century persons, Jung deems them not average but distinctive. For him, most persons today are psychologically equivalent either to nineteenth-century moderns, and therefore oblivious to any nonrational needs, or to premoderns, and therefore content with traditional means of fulfilling them. Because contemporary moderns are sensitive both to the existence of nonrational inclinations and to the demise of past means of satisfying them, they comprise a select minority.

Jungian patients are the twentieth-century counterparts to ancient Gnostics, who in turn are the ancient counterparts to Jungian patients: "The spiritual currents of our time have, in fact, a deep affinity with Gnosticism."[38] Like Gnostics, twentieth-century moderns feel alienated from their roots and are seeking to overcome the alienation. Where Gnostics feel severed from the outer world, twentieth-century moderns feel severed from the inner one. They do not, like Gnostics, project their alienation onto the cosmos.

Despite his reference to contemporary "Gnostic systems," Jung, like Jonas, considers Gnosticism an ancient, not a contemporary, phenomenon. Just as Jonas sees existentialism as the present-day *counterpart* to Gnosticism, not the present-day *version* of Gnosticism,[39] so Jung sees analytical psychology. For both, the periods paralleled are unique in human history. States Jonas: "There is one situation, and only one that I know of in the history of Western man, where that [present-day] condition [of alienation] has been realized and lived out with all the vehemence of a cataclysmic event. That is the Gnostic movement."[40] To quote Jung again, "We can compare [the present] only to the flowering of Gnostic thought in the first and second centuries after Christ."[41]

Jung, like Jonas, gives myth a reprieve by translating its meaning into a contemporary idiom. But Jung offers a far more detailed glossary and grammar than Jonas. He makes sense psychologi-

cally of the state of Gnostics not merely upon receipt of the revelation but also both before and after. Jung renders into
psychological lingo the course of Gnostic myths from the pre-
fallen state of the world through the fallen one to the restored
one.[42]

Understood in Jungian terms, Gnostic myths, which either
present or presuppose a cosmogony, describe the development not
of the world but of the human psyche. The godhead symbolizes
the primordial unconscious. It is the source or agent of everything
else. Prior to emanating anything, it lacks nothing. It is whole,
self-sufficient, perfect. The godhead thus symbolizes the unconscious before the emergence of the ego out of it.

The emergence of matter alongside the material godhead symbolizes the beginning, but only the beginning, of the emergence
of the ego out of the unconscious. Inert matter itself does not
symbolize the ego, which requires a reflective entity conscious of
itself as a subject distinct from the external world. The ego fully
emerges not with the creation of either the Demiurge or Primal
Man but only with the creation of individual human beings.

The ego is symbolized not by the spark but by the thinking part
of the human body, the unspecified center of human thoughts and
actions vis-à-vis the external world. The spark, as the link to the
forgotten godhead, symbolizes the unconscious. As long as one
remains unaware of the spark, one remains an unrealized self. As
long as one's values are material, one is merely an ego.

Insofar as a Jungian interpretation of myth is psychological, it
collapses the literal distinction between the outer world and humanity. Both matter and the body symbolize the development of
the ego—raw matter symbolizing the beginning of the process
and the thinking portion of the body the end. Similarly, both the
immaterial godhead and the spark symbolize the unconscious, if
also at opposite stages of development.

The ego in Jungian psychology develops not just alongside the
unconscious but also out of it. Those Gnostic myths in which
matter originates out of the godhead express the dependence of
the ego on the unconscious. Those myths in which matter is pre-
existent and merely comes into contact with the godhead evince
dissociation of the unconscious from the ego and thereby fore-
shadow the problems that dissociation spells.

Non-Gnostics, who for Jung's interpretation should also possess a divine spark, are not only ignorant of their origin and the
origin of the world but also smugly content with the false, ma-

terial nature of both. Their complacency makes them apt counterparts to nineteenth-century moderns. Gnostics have also forgotten the true nature of themselves and the world, but they are
nevertheless dissatisfied with the existing nature of both. Their
dissatisfaction makes them suitable counterparts to twentieth-
century moderns.

If ignorance alone, according to Gnostic tenets, keeps humans
tied to the material world, knowledge frees them from it. Because
humans are ignorant, that knowledge must come from outside
them. Because the powers of the material world are ignorant, too,
that knowledge must come from beyond them as well. It can
come from only the godhead. The dependence of humanity on
the godhead matches the dependence of the ego on the unconscious to reveal itself.

The response of Gnostics to the revelation parallels that of
twentieth-century moderns to their own discovery: gratitude.
The disclosure of a heretofore unknown self and, for Gnostics, of
a heretofore unknown world provides a fulfillment tantamount
to salvation. As Jung says of twentieth-century moderns, "I do
not believe that I am going too far when I say that [twentieth-
century] modern man, in contrast to his nineteenth-century
brother, turns to the psyche with very great expectations, and
does so without reference to any traditional creed but rather with
a view to Gnostic experience."[43]

The response of non-Gnostics to the revelation parallels that
of nineteenth-century moderns to their own discovery: fear. The
disclosure, which applies to non-Gnostics as well as to Gnostics,
shatters the non-Gnostics' vaunted image of both human nature
and the world.

Gnostic myths preach total identification with one's newly discovered divinity. Because that identification symbolizes the
Gnostic's identification with the unconscious, Jungian psychology would consider it no less lopsided and dangerous than the
non-Gnostic's identification with the ego—more precisely, with
ego consciousness, or consciousness of the external world. Jungian psychology would consider both attitudes unbalanced. It
would say that non-Gnostics, like nineteenth-century moderns,
suffer from an exaggerated persona: their ego identifies itself
wholly with the conscious, public personality. But Jungian psychology should equally say that Gnostics, whether or not
twentieth-century moderns, suffer from an exaggerated, or in-
flated, ego, which, conversely, identifies itself wholly with the re-

discovered unconscious. Minimally, the consequence of inflation is excessive pride in the presumed uniqueness of one's unconscious. Maximally, the consequence is outright psychosis, or the dissolution of any consciousness of the external world. The Jungian aim is no more to reject ego consciousness for the unconscious than, like the nineteenth-century aim, to reject the unconscious for ego consciousness. Rather, the aim is to balance the two.

Jung himself idiosyncratically interprets Gnosticism as seeking the equivalent of balance between ego consciousness and the unconscious rather than identification with the unconscious. Unlike Jonas, Jung is so eager to find similarities between ancients and moderns that he misses the differences.[44] But Jung's misinterpretation of Gnosticism does not preclude a more accurate Jungian interpretation of Gnosticism, according to which Gnosticism espouses the equivalent of inflation rather than balance.

By interpreting the Gnostic's permanent return to the godhead as inflationary, Jungian psychology would even be able to make sense of what in Gnostic metaphysics is paradoxical: the creation by an omniscient and omnipotent godhead of a world that the godhead then seeks to destroy. Jungian psychology would make not the creation but the dissolution of the world the mistake. Though it would admittedly thereby be evaluating Gnosticism by its own world-affirming rather than world-rejecting ideal, it would at least be able to make sense of creation. The unconscious, as symbolized by the godhead, would not be erring in creating the ego, as symbolized by the material side of humanity. The unconscious would truly be both omniscient and omnipotent. It is the ego that would be neither: lacking both the knowledge and the will to resist the spell of the unconscious, it would be returning of its own accord to the unconscious, which, to be sure, would be enticing it.

Where Jonas transforms only the meaning of myth, Jung also transforms the function. Jung would say that Gnostic mythology served not just to reveal the unconscious but actually to put Gnostics in touch with it. Jung even deems the Gnostics budding psychologists: "It is clear beyond a doubt that many of the Gnostics were nothing other than psychologists."[45] Jung thus accords Gnostic mythology, and mythology generally, a role as well as a viewpoint that is acceptable to moderns.

Still, Jung does not go as far as Joseph Campbell, who proclaims myth outright indispensable. As valuable for Jung as myth is, religion, art, dream, and the "active imagination" can serve as well—even if he sometimes loosely uses the term *myth* to apply to all of them. For Jung, the functions that myth serve are themselves indispensable, but myth is not itself indispensable to serving them. And in even keener contrast to Campbell, myth for Jung can never substitute for therapy, to which it is only a most helpful adjunct.[46]

Jung ventures beyond Jonas in granting myth a future not only by providing a function as well as a meaning that is acceptable to moderns but also, like Eliade, by uncovering modern as well as ancient myths. Jung does not claim to find modern *Gnostic* myths, but he does claim to find modern myths of other varieties. Because he psychologizes the meaning of all myths, he circumvents Eliade's dilemma that myths acceptable to moderns lack the element necessary for their efficacy: gods. For Jung, gods are merely the symbols that ancient myths used to represent archetypes. Modern myths, using other symbols, are equally efficacious.

Whether the theories of myth discussed are correct is not at issue here. At issue is whether those theories commit themselves to a future for myth. Of the four theories which do—Eliade's, Bultmann's, Jonas's, and Jung's—Jung's theory envisions the brightest future for myth.

Notes

1. See Detienne, *Creation of Mythology,* chaps. 3–5.
2. See Ackerman, *Myth and Ritual School,* 55–60.
3. See Tylor, *Primitive Culture,* 2:41, 85.
4. Ibid., 284.
5. See ibid., 85.
6. Ibid., 41.
7. See, for example, Hempel, *Aspects of Scientific Explanation,* 463–87.
8. On this interpretation of Adonis see my "Adonis: A Greek Eternal Child," 65–68.
9. See Salmon, "Determinism and Indeterminism," 321.
10. See Tylor, *Primitive Culture,* 1:277–78, 408 ff.
11. Ibid., 277.
12. Ibid., 285.
13. Eliade, *Myth and Reality,* 5.
14. Ibid., 11.
15. Ibid., 92.
16. Eliade, *Sacred and Profane,* 82.
17. Gen. 3:8.
18. Eliade, *Sacred and Profane,* 82.

19. Ibid., 205.
20. Bultmann, "New Testament and Mythology," 10.
21. Ibid., 1.
22. Bultmann, *Jesus Christ and Mythology*, 19, 21.
23. Bultmann, "New Testament and Mythology," 4.
24. Ibid., 10.
25. Bultmann, "Bultmann Replies to his Critics," 203.
26. Bultmann, "New Testament and Mythology," 16.
27. Jonas, *Gnostic Religion*, 322.
28. Ibid., 324.
29. Ibid., 329.
30. Ibid., 326–27.
31. Jonas, "Delimitation of the Gnostic Phenomenon," 107.
32. See Jonas, *Gnosis und spätantiker Geist*, 2: pt. 1, 122–70; "Myth and Mysticism."
33. Jonas is not the only philosopher to "update" Gnosticism. The other preeminent figure is the political philosopher Eric Voegelin. Voegelin, however, is interested less in myth than in ideology and, more important, is interested in showing only the Gnostic nature of modernity and not also, like Jonas, the modern nature of Gnosticism. He seeks to show how modern movements like positivism, Marxism, communism, fascism, and psychoanalysis evince what he calls "the Gnostic attitude." See esp. *Science, Politics and Gnosticism* and *New Science of Politics*.
34. One might add Freud to the duo, but Freud hardly sees himself as a defender of myth.
35. See my *Joseph Campbell*.
36. Jung, "Psychology of the Child Archetype," 154–55.
37. Jung, "Spiritual Problem of Modern Man," 83–84.
38. Ibid., 83.
39. See Jonas, *Gnostic Religion*, 320–21.
40. Ibid., 325.
41. Jung, "Spiritual Problem of Modern Man," 84.
42. Jung writes about Gnosticism throughout his corpus. See esp. "Gnostic Symbols of the Self."
43. Jung, "Spiritual Problem of Modern Man," 84.
44. For a criticism of Jung's interpretation of Gnosticism see my introduction to *Gnostic Jung*, 23–27, 31–32.
45. Jung, "Structure and Dynamics of the Self," 222.
46. On the limitations of myth for Jung see my *Joseph Campbell*, 259–62. On Campbell's skewed interpretation of Gnosticism see ibid., 126–27, 134–37.

Works Cited

Ackerman, Robert. *The Myth and Ritual School*. Theorists of Myth Series. Vol. 2. New York: Garland Publishing, 1991.

Bultmann, Rudolf. "New Testament and Mythology" [1941]. In *Kerygma and Myth*. Edited by Hans-Werner Bartsch. Translated by Reginald H. Fuller. London: SPCK, 1953, 1:1–44.

———. "Bultmann Replies to His Critics." In *Kerygma and Myth*. Edited by Hans-Werner Bartsch. Translated by Reginald H. Fuller. London: SPCK, 1953, 1:191–211.

———. *Jesus Christ and Mythology*. New York: Scribners, 1958.

Detienne, Marcel. *The Creation of Mythology.* Translated by Margaret Cook. Chicago: University of Chicago Press, 1986.

Eliade, Mircea. *The Sacred and the Profane* [1959]. Translated by Willard R. Trask. New York: Harvest Books, 1968.

———. *Myth and Reality* [1963]. Translated by Willard R. Trask. New York: Harper Torchbooks, 1968.

Hempel, Carl G. *Aspects of Scientific Explanation and Other Essays in the Philosophy of Science.* New York: Free Press, 1965.

Jonas, Hans. *Gnosis und spätantiker Geist.* Vol. 2, pt. 1. Göttingen: Vandenhoeck & Ruprecht, 1954.

———. *The Gnostic Religion* [1958]. 2d ed. Boston: Beacon, 1963.

———. "Delimitation of the Gnostic Phenomenon—Typological and Historical." In *Le Origini dello Gnosticismo.* Edited by Ugo Bianchi. Supplements to *Numen,* XII. Leiden: Brill, 1967, 90–108.

———. "Myth and Mysticism: A Study of Objectification and Interiorization in Religious Thought." *Journal of Religion* 49 (October 1969): 315–29.

Jung, C. G. "The Psychology of the Child Archetype." In *The Archetypes and the Collective Unconscious.* Collected Works, vol. 9, pt. 1, 2d ed. Edited by Sir Herbert Read and others. Translated by R. F. C. Hull and others. Princeton: Princeton University Press, 1968, 151–81.

———. "Gnostic Symbols of the Self." In *Aion,* Collected Works, vol. 9, pt. 2, 2d ed. Princeton: Princeton University Press, 1968, 184–221.

———. "The Structure and Dynamics of the Self." In *Aion.* Collected Works, vol. 9, pt. 2, 2d ed. Princeton: Princeton University Press, 1968, 222–65.

———. "The Spiritual Problem of Modern Man." In *Civilization in Transition.* Collected Works, vol. 10, 2d ed. Princeton: Princeton University Press, 1970, 74–94.

Salmon, Wesley C. "Determinism and Indeterminism in Modern Science." In *Reason and Responsibility.* Edited by Joel Fineberg. 2d ed. Encino, Calif.: Dickenson, 1971, 316–32.

Segal, Robert A. *Joseph Campbell: An Introduction* [1987]. Rev. ed. New York: New American Library, 1990.

———. "Adonis: A Greek Eternal Child." In *Myth and the Polis.* Edited by Dora C. Pozzi and John M. Wickersham. Ithaca: Cornell University Press, 1991, 64–85.

Segal, Robert A., ed. *The Gnostic Jung.* Princeton: Princeton University Press; London: Routledge, 1992.

Tylor, Edward. *Primitive Culture* [1871] I (Retitled *The Origins of Culture*). 5th ed. New York: Harper Torchbooks, 1958.

———. *Primitive Culture* [1871] II (Retitled *Religion in Primitive Culture*). 5th ed. New York: Harper Torchbooks, 1958.

Voegelin, Eric. *The New Science of Politics.* Chicago: University of Chicago Press, 1952.

———. *Science, Politics and Gnosticism.* Chicago: Regnery Gateway Editions, 1968.

PART II

THE DILEMMA OF THE
TWO-HEADED SCHOLAR:
MYTH AND
COMPARISON

WENDY DONIGER

MINIMYTHS AND MAXIMYTHS AND POLITICAL POINTS OF VIEW

Universalist Problems, Cross-Cultural Solutions

THE TENSION BETWEEN sameness and difference has become a crucial issue for the self-definitions of postmodernism, the age that cannot name itself. Now the mere addition of an *accent aigu* transforms the modest English word into the magic buzz-word for everything that right-thinking (or, as the case may be, left-thinking) men and women care about: *différence* (or, buzzier yet, *différance!*). For postmodernism, sameness is the devil, difference the angel. From Paris the new battle cry rings out: *Vive la différance!* This is one of the many reasons why, in the discipline of the history of religions, universalist comparative studies of the sort that Mircea Eliade once made so popular are now very much *vieux jeux.*

There is, I think, some irony in the fact that the modern comparative study of religion was in large part designed in the fond hope of teaching our own people that Alien religions were like Our Own in many ways, so that we would no longer hate and kill the followers of those religions. A glance at any newspaper should tell us that this goal has yet to be fulfilled in the world at large. But the academic world, having gone beyond this simplistic paradigm, now suffers from a post-postcolonial backlash: in this age of multinationalism, it is politically incorrect to assume that two nations' views are the same in any significant way, for it is regarded as demeaning to the individualism of each, a reflection of the old racist attitude that "all wogs look alike." Thus, for instance, Rolena Adorno has referred to "the process of fixing 'oth-

erness' by grasping onto similarities." This has led to a kind of
hypertrophy of contextual studies. Moreover, in the climate of
anti-Orientalism, it is regarded as imperialist of a scholar to stand
outside (presumably, above) two different cultures and to equate
them.

But historicism when reduced to the absurd (as is too often is)
may lead to problems of infinite regress, for it tends to generate
even smaller foci until it is impossible to generalize even from
one moment to the next; nothing has enough in common with
anything else to be compared with it even for the purpose of illu-
minating its distinctiveness. Eve Sedgwick has made this point
well:

> Every single theoretically or politically interesting project of post-
> war thought has finally had the effect of delegitimating our space
> for asking or thinking in detail about the multiple, unstable ways
> in which people may be like or different from each other. This proj-
> ect is not rendered otiose by any demonstration of how fully people
> may differ also from themselves. Deconstruction, founded as a very
> science of *diffEr(e/a)nce*, has both so fetishized the idea of differ-
> ence and so vaporized its possible embodiments that its most thor-
> oughgoing practitioners are the last people to whom one would
> now look for help in thinking about particular differences.[1]

As a postmodern Eliadean, I am unwilling to close the mythological shop just because it is being picketed by people with
whose views I happen, by and large, to agree. I want to salvage,
for my own use at least, the broad comparative agenda of the Eliadean paradigm, even if I acquiesce, or even participate, in the sav-
aging of certain of its elements. In particular I want to rehabilitate
the element of *différe(a)nce* in comparativism, to show how it
is possible to bring into a single (if not necessarily harmonious)
conversation the genuinely different approaches that several cultures have made to similar human problems.

Clifford Geertz has pointed out both the advantages and the
dangers of the comparative method: "There is a difference between a difference and a dichotomy. The first is a comparison
and it relates; the second is a severance and it isolates. . . . The
dissimilitudes of Morocco and Indonesia do not separate them
into absolute types, the sociological equivalent of natural kinds;
they reflect back and forth upon one another, mutually framing,
reciprocally clarifying."[2]

The argument for comparativism must justify taking things out of context; we must face the implications for the fact that we use other peoples' ideas for our purposes. The political problem inheres in the dissymmetry of power between the appropriating culture and the appropriated. Thus, if Europe has dominated India, it is deemed wrong for a European to make use of an Indian myth. But it seems to me that the usual alternative to appropriating a foreign text (however inadequate or exploitative or projective that appropriation may be) is even worse: ignoring it or scorning it. There are, moreover, useful tests to guard us against projection: anachronism, coherence of explanation, and the like. The European appropriation need not supplant the Indian version; the native voice can be heard even above the academic clamor of the foreign voice. Otherwise, no conversation can take place at all, and we find ourselves trapped in the self-reflexive garden of a deconstructed Wonderland, forever meeting ourselves walking back through the cultural door we were trying to escape from.

The question of the universality of certain myths has been much debated in the history of the history of religions. Indeed, many of the essays in this volume continue the debate with vehemence: there are those who attribute to the scholarly study of myth a sloppy universality (Dundes); a dangerously nationalist one (Strenski); or one that pretends to transcend the claims of rationalist science (Segal). Very different sorts of universality have been claimed by Freud, by Jung, by Claude Lévi-Strauss, by Eliade, even by Joseph Campbell. I would argue that many of the great myths are demonstrably cross-cultural, that is, they occur in more than one culture, but they are not necessarily universal, they may not occur in all cultures. Again, many of the essays in this volume argue the same point with specific case studies, whether they be the literary commonality of Sancho Panza and the priest at Nemi (Ziolkowski), or the political commonality of Jiang Qing and previous empresses of China (Bantly). Claude Lévi-Strauss put it with uncharacteristic naïveté: "How are we going to explain the fact that myths throughout the world are so similar?"[3] And, more subtly: "Mythic stories are, or seem, arbitrary, meaningless, absurd, yet nevertheless they seem to reappear all over the world. A 'fanciful' creation of the mind in one place would be unique—you would not find the same creation in a completely different place. . . . If this represents a basic need for order in the human mind and since, after all, the human mind is only part of the universe, the need probably exists because there is some order in the universe and the universe is not a chaos."⁴ If one did not know that the author of this remarkable credo was the great structuralist, one might have mistaken him, in the dark, for Jung.

Yet even were we to be able to demonstrate that a particular story does in fact occur in every known culture (a task that is theoretically impossible, since stories are being forgotten and cultures created all the time, and in practice unlikely to be achieved even in approximation), the assertion that that story was universal would require us to explain its universality in terms of some universalist theory (Jungian, Freudian, Eliadean, or at least diffusionist), a daunting proposition. On the other hand, to assert that a story occurs cross-culturally is merely to show that its meanings are not bounded by any one particular culture, a far less ambitious task (though no sinecure, either).

I would argue that, although there are few universals (for there are exceptions to almost everything), there are many human experiences that occur in many different cultures, particularly experiences connected with the body, experiences that we might call quasi-universal. Underlying these myths are certain widespread, if not universal, human experiences: the realization that I am separate from my parents, the discovery that I am one sex and not the other, the knowledge that I will die. My own rather cumbersome definition of a myth is: a narrative in which a group finds, over an extended period of time, a shared meaning in certain questions about human life, to which the various proposed answers are usually unsatisfactory in one way or another.⁵ These would be questions such as, Why are we here? What happens to us when we die? Is there a God? Stories about these themes, though inevitably mediated by culture, must needs have *something* in common. As Geertz has argued, "People, as people, are doubtless much the same everywhere. That is what you commit yourself to in calling them people, rather than Egyptians, Buddhists, or speakers of Turkish. But the parts they play, the parts available for them to play, are not."⁶

I would not claim that the most important aspect of a myth consists in the elements of the narrative that it has in common with other myths. But I would claim that those elements are indeed held in common and that this is a useful base from which to proceed to ask questions about differences, differences between men and women storytellers, between Japanese and Hindus, and also between rich and poor, dominant and oppressed.

Some of the questions are quasi-universal, and some of the images are quasi-universal, and the naked outlines of the narrative are more or less quasi-universal, but the shared images and ideas are structured in the narrative in different ways so as to give different answers, and sometimes to ask different questions or to give rise to different images and ideas.

Jungians would argue that the basic theme was always available everywhere, like a kind of underground stream of story flowing everywhere on the planet, and that from time to time, and from continent to continent, a storyteller would sink a well and tap into the stream. They would argue that we're all hotwired (or hardwired) with myths. A. K. Ramanujan used a similar metaphor in referring to the recycling of themes *within a particular culture:* "The cultural area in which *Ramayanas* are endemic has a pool of signifiers (like a gene pool), signifiers that include plots, characters, names, geography, incidents, and relationships. . . . Every author, if one may hazard a metaphor, dips into it and brings out a unique crystallization, a new text with a unique texture and a fresh context."[7] This is a variant of the theory of cultural diffusion.

But accounting for mythological themes that appear in different cultures by assuming that they derive from certain shared human experiences frees us from the obligation of specifying a mechanism (such as Jung's collective unconscious, or, more respectably, historical diffusion) by which a universal theme might be perpetrated. All we need point out is that the same forms do appear in many different places in response to human experiences that appear to be similar on at least one level and that they take on different meanings to the extent that those experiences turn out to be dissimilar on other levels.

There is another charge against universalism that must be answered here. Marina Warner has argued that "the theory of archetypes, which is essentially ahistorical, helps to confirm gender inevitability and to imprison male and female in stock definitions."[8] The archetype is therefore the enemy not only of social change but of social justice: "When history falls away from a subject, we are left with Otherness, and all its power to compact enmity, recharge it and recirculate it. An archetype is a hollow thing, but a dangerous one, a figure or image which through usage has been uncoupled from the circumstances which brought it into being, and goes on spreading false consciousness."[9] But it is by no means the case that what we regard as archetypal, universal, or even natural is immutable or desirable; it is merely *given*. And we can change what is given; indeed it is easier to change it if we acknowledge that it is, in fact, given. "I have seen the enemy, and he is us" is surely true of archetypes. If the great mythic themes are social rather than biological (or psychological), they are not built into the brain and they can be changed. Storytellers may, like Judo wrestlers, use the very weight of archetypes to throw them, and with them to throw the prejudices that have colored them for centuries. Call it deconstruction, call it subversion, or just call it creative storytelling.

The Political Problem of Individualism

One way of avoiding some of the pitfalls of universalism in our approach to cross-cultural variants is to take a middle ground. If we construct a continuum of the individual, the group-culture, and the human race, we might focus on one relatively solid intermediary path between the two extremes: cultural morphology, or the morphology of cultural types. Groups or societies that have the same sorts of structures and practices may tell the same sorts of myths. Perhaps it is best to look for parallels not even with a single culture (where kings are so different from peasants, men from women), let alone across cultures, but between the same sorts of people in different cultures (Chinese peasant women and Indian peasant women).[10] This approach also allows us to acknowledge what the historicizing approach often obscures, that the negative aspects of other people's prejudices are also shared (such as their attitudes to women). Cultural studies, by silencing the cross cultural critique, often backs into another political problem by enshrining injustices such as cliterodectomy.

Nor should we leap from the frying pan of universalism into the fire of another sort of essentialism that results from contextualizing a story in one cultural group; for we may find that the members of the group may approach the story very differently, and it is just as insulting to say that all Japanese (or fin de siècle types) are alike as to say that the Japanese are just like the French. This position, which is in itself both indefensible and politically nefarious, is often assumed in culturally contextualized studies: "Let me tell you how everyone felt in fin de siècle Europe and America." The focus on the middle group, the ethnic and class group, if monolithic, can become racist and offensive, as well as boring. One way to sidestep this problem of difference would be to anchor our cross-cultural paradigms in an investigation of the particular genius of particular tellings of our cross-cultural themes, to focus on the individual and the human on both ends of the spectrum—one story, and then the human race—thus not so much ignoring the problematic cultural generalizations in the middle as leaping over context and culture altogether, never touching down in cultural context at all. (This is rather a different jump over culture from the one posited by Eliade.) This focus balances the move outward, from culture to cross-culture, with a move inward, from culture to the individual author. It argues that *Hamlet* must be read not merely in the context of Elizabethan England (culture, and more particularly history) but as the peculiar insight of one Elizabethan Englishman who was in many ways different from all other Elizabethan Englishmen. By concentrating on the insights from individual stories, we need not assume that all Hindus are alike, or all Jews. Rather, every telling is different, and a telling from one country is as likely to share something with a telling from another as with a telling from elsewhere in the same country.

The focus upon individual genius leads us to a kind of second naïveté: it leads us to posit a sameness based not on any quasi-Jungian universalism but on a kind of pointillism, formed from the individual points of individual authors whose insights transcend their particular moment and speak to us across time and space: individuals who move us on the level of what David Tracy calls the classic.[11] This approach also makes it possible for us to make use of the insights and methods of contemporary literary criticism. We may apply to our individual, if anonymous, myths the literary critics' insights into both the products of popular culture and great works of literature. Though both of these narrative forms do have, as some of our ancient myths do not, known social contexts, the works of popular culture share with many myths the lack of known or individual authors and hence come within the mythologists' camp (and I do mean camp). So, too, the hermeneutics of suspicion that render irrelevant the problem of the intention of the individual author of a great work of literature make that, too, a fair game for mythologists (and I do mean game).

Those who would regard universalism as a colonialist debasement of the integrity of the ethnic unit might also regard such an emphasis upon individual genius as an elitist debasement of the democratic unit. But surely this need not be the case. It is just as foolish to assume that an emphasis on the individual will be élitist as it is to assume that the opposite emphasis, on the entire human race, will be fascist. By searching for our individual geniuses not merely in the bastions of the Western canon but in the neglected byways of oral traditions and rejected heresies, by paying homage to the many Prousts among the Zulus (to respond to Saul Bellow's notorious challenge), one is arguing not for a narrow range of cultural excellence but, on the contrary, for a wider construction of cross-cultural genius. It is also arguing, ultimately, for difference, for that particular flash of difference that is illuminated only by the context of sameness.

Minimyths and Maximyths

We might express what we regard as the same in several different tellings by constructing a kind of nonoccurring metamyth that contains the basic elements from which all possible variants could be created, a theoretical construct that will enable us to look at all the variants at once and ask our various questions simultaneously. If we define the comparative unit of myth on the level of the basic narrative—a sentence, with a subject and a verb—we exclude the adjectives and adverbs that reflect the editorializing and moralizing author. And it is then possible for us to use those basic units to construct two different sorts of nonoccurring metamyths, a minimyth and a maximyth (or a mickey myth; for there is something Mickey Mouse about any attempt to define a myth).

The minimyth only superficially resembles what Joseph Campbell called the monomyth. It is much starker, much more elemental. Geertz's caveat applies well to reductionist comparative studies: "This reversed, dominant and subdominant representation will not do, however. For what one discovers when one looks at Java with Morocco as optic and the other way around is that one is faced not with a collection of abstractable, easily stateable themes (sex, status, boldness, modesty . . .) differently tied into local bundles, the same notes set into different melodies. . . . When ingeniously juxtaposed, these fields can shed a certain amount of light on one another; but they are neither variants of one another nor expressions of some superfield that transcends them both." [12] If it does not aim at this sort of "superfield," what good is the minimyth? It is useful as an armature that defines a group of texts; it is also useful as a source of some basic cross-cultural meanings. Just how interesting those meanings are is determined by the balance that we strike for each myth between, on the one hand, a structure simple enough to accommodate a significant number of variants and, on the other hand, a corpus of detail complex enough to constitute a distinct, unique story. For you can state any myth in a series of forms that can be arranged on a continuum: you can say, "A woman is born, has children, and dies," and it applies to a million stories and hardly tells us anything we do not already know; or you can include all the details of *Anna Karenina*, which is unlike any other story. Depending upon where you draw the line of details, you can argue that the stories are more similar or more different. I choose to make the cut for the minimyth, where they are relatively similar, and to begin by investigating what it is that they share. This is a minimalist construct: its goal is to isolate within a group of myths a core that no culture would find foreign, but a core that still retains some intrinsic meaning.

The Platonic minimyth is the pivot of a kind of Venn diagram of family resemblances. The hermeneutic value of this pivot is that it makes it possible for us to find meanings shared by all the cultures that share the story, meanings over and behind the individual cultural and moral inflections. It makes it possible for us to make a statement that is true of several different versions of a myth but that we wouldn't think of making of any single one alone. It makes it possible for us to outline the borders of the sphere of influence of any particular theme. The neutral myth forms a nonexistent roundhouse in which all known variants can come to rest and out of which we could construct still unknown variants.[13]

The cycle of accordion action between the nonexistent, uninflected, condensed myth and the actually occurring, inflected, expanded myth functions like a condensed soup cube: the soup (a particular variant of the myth) is boiled down to the soup cube, the basic stock (the minimyth), and then cooked up again into all sorts of soups (various detailed myths), and finally into the great narrative bouillabaisse that is the maximyth. So, too, a dream may be transformed into a myth that may then play a part in another dream. The minimyth is not merely a scaffolding on which each culture erects its own myths; it is more like a trampoline, which allows each culture to fly far from it to its own specific cultural meanings. The metameaning may not be explicit or

even conscious; but it is there, latent, and it is what gives the
punch to the manifest meaning that may at first appear to be the
only meaning of any culturally specific retelling.

The minimyth, however, systematically eliminates all the detail that gives the myth its charm and its profundity, if not its
meaning. It threatens to reduce the group of myths to a bland
core that all share, a truly common denominator. We must therefore also formulate a maximyth in order to note the particular
spin that each individual telling (not merely each individual culture) puts on the basic tale, including details that no other telling
has. This is a maximalist construct: its goal is to build up an international multimyth, a collage in which each culture could find
something that was its own and, beyond that, find many other
things that it had never—yet—dreamed of but that might expand
its own particular insight into the shared story. It is inclusivist
not only in the range of details that it incorporates but in the
range of genres from which it mines these themes.

The maximyth makes possible the cross-cultural rather than
universalist approach. The great universalist theories were constructed from the top down, so to speak. That is, they assumed
certain continuities about broad concepts such as sacrifice, or a
High God, or an Oedipal complex; but these continuities necessarily involved cognitive, cultural, and rather arbitrary shared factors that, it seems to me, are the least likely places in which to
find cross-cultural continuities. The method that I am advocating
is, by contrast, constructed from the bottom up. It assumes certain continuities not about overarching human universals but
about particular narrative details concerning the body, sexual desire, procreation, pain, death which, though unable to avoid medi-
ation by culture entirely, are at least *less* culturally mediated, *less*
arbitrary, than the broader conceptual categories of the universal-
ists. Working from the bottom up is one of several reasons for
including many variants in any study of myths. You need a lot of
examples to induce a generalization, for the bottom-up argument
is more numerological than logical, more inductive than deductive: it seeks to persuade by the sheer volume of its data rather
than by the inevitability (or falsifiability) of the sequence of its
assertions.[14] Of course, the maximyth is just as Platonic and ide-
alistic a construction as the minimyth: we could never get all the
details from all the variants, and if we did the result would make
The Golden Bough look like a sound bite. But we can get *enough*
details to make a persuasive argument. I would hope that a reader

of such a study, if asked if he or she believed in comparative mythology, might answer like the man who, when asked if he believed in baptism, replied, "Believe in it? I seen it done."

The Myth with No Point of View

With the help of the metamyth in its two forms, we may hypothesize a non-existent story told with no point of view at all. More precisely, we may hypothesize both a minimyth that minimizes, though it cannot entirely exclude, the expression of any point of view, and a maximyth that suggests, though it cannot entirely encompass, the expression of all points of view. For, in a larger sense, it could be argued (and not just by a structuralist) that any myth is a neutral structure that allows paradoxical meanings to be held in a charged tension. Indeed, we might even single this out as one of the defining characteristics of a myth, in contrast with other sorts of narratives (such as novels): a myth is a narrative that is transparent to a variety of constructions of meaning. This is one of the qualities that allow a myth, unlike other forms of narrative, to be shared by a group (who have various points of view) and to survive through time (through different generations with different points of view). E. M. Forster once made a distinction between story and plot: "The king died and then the queen died" is a story. "The king died and then the queen died of grief" is a plot. A myth is a story, not a plot; but each retelling is a plot.

The minimyth is highly problematic, but as a heuristic device it does provide us with a springboard from which we can vault over several otherwise insuperable hurdles in the comparative enterprise. It enables us to compare as variants of the same basic narrative different versions that embellish that narrative with different points of view. The minimyth sends no explicit message, no explicit moral. Though the word *myth* is often used nowadays to designate an idea (particularly a wrong idea), the one thing a myth most certainly is *not* is an idea. It is a narrative that makes possible any number of ideas but does not commit itself to any single idea. A myth is like a gun for hire, like a mercenary soldier: it can be made to fight for anyone. The myth's attitude to dogma is similar to that of the great Sam Goldwyn, who, when asked why he didn't make movies with messages, replied, "When I want to send a message, I send for Western Union."

But can there be a story with no point of view at all? Yes and no. Behind the narrative is an experience, real or imagined: something has happened, and not once, like a historical event, but many times, like a personal habit. This experience is neutral at least in the sense that it is capable of being interpreted from any number of different points of view. For example, the hypothesis of an unmarked, neutral experience involving a woman, a man, a garden, a tree, a fruit, a snake, and knowledge allows us to understand how the Hebrew Bible could tell that story as it does (an evil snake, forbidden fruit, evil woman, disobedient and destructive knowledge), while other interpretations of that story tell it differently (a benevolent goddess in her form of life-giving serpent and tree, giving the blessing of the fruit of useful knowledge that makes human life possible). This alternative reading of Genesis implies not a Fall but a progression from the Garden of Eden (a place of ignorance and constriction) to the wider world, a place of open possibility, of freedom and knowledge (not to mention the pleasures of sex), the gift of the seductive woman or the satanic snake. This is a Romantic reading which argues that eternal seduction is the price of liberty. Though this reading is often said (usually by feminists) to have existed in the Ancient Near East alongside the biblical text, there is no textual evidence for this assertion.[15] The positive reading of the serpent (though not of the woman) was, however, accepted in the Ophite version of Genesis, in which Yaldabaoth (God) is evil, and the serpent is good. It was further developed by Romantics such as Shelley, who saw a direct parallel between Satan's gift of the fruit and Prometheus' gift of fire—a gift that, like the fruit in Eden, provoked the wrath of the jealous gods and the creation of the first, disastrously seductive woman, Pandora. The fact that these very different constructions of the myth of Genesis are not only possible but attested makes it possible to construct an ideal, Platonic form of the story in which the tree, woman, serpent, and fruit are morally neutral.

Can an uninflected story have meanings? I think so. The building blocks of myths have their own meaning to which other, successive layers of meanings are attracted. The neutral, or uninflected, hypothetical story of Eden already tells us a great deal. It tells us that men and women are opposed as well as attracted, that women rather than men are responsible for change (though we can disagree as to whether the change was good or bad), that women rather than men supply the original food (mother's milk), that food has something to do with sex, that both food and sex have something to do with knowledge, and so forth. But the most basic meaning shared by all variants of any cross-culturally attested story is that the experience reflected in the story is important, that it is so important that several different cultures have selected it (or, if you prefer, constructed it), rather than one of the million other experiences that human beings have, to use as the basis of the story. It is not really a colorless grid but rather a rainbow or a beam of pure light that seems colorless until it is refracted through the prism of a particular culture: many meanings are there, and each culture takes from it some of the meanings rather than others.

Roland Barthes also sees myth as essentially nonpolitical, but whereas I would see myth as *prepolitical,* he sees it as *postpolitical,* as a text from which politics has been extracted: "What the world supplies to myth is an historical reality, defined, even if this goes back quite a while, by the way in which men have produced or used it; and what myth gives in return is a *natural* image of this reality. . . . The world enters language as a dialectical relation between activities, between human actions; it comes out of myth as a harmonious display of essences. A conjuring trick has taken place; it has turned reality inside out, it has emptied it of history and has filled it with nature. . . . *Myth is depoliticized speech.*"[16] And, I would add, each telling keeps the nature but puts the history back into the myth.

The Myth with Points of View

It is not the task of myths to moralize explicitly, but every myth implicitly invites the teller, the listener, the commentator to moralize. And so, inevitably, any particular variant, any telling of a myth does send a message. By choosing to tell one story rather than another, the teller is choosing to make one point rather than another. And, indeed, if we assume, as surely we must, that the myth in its earliest telling was made by a human with opinions about it, there was always a point of view. But we must also admit that the second telling might have expressed a different point of view. If there could be an experience devoid of a telling, it would be possible to say, "This happened," without saying why it happened, or what was the point of it happening. But in actual practice we cannot have access to such an untold experience. Although the experience itself has no ideology, no spin, every telling puts a spin on it—indeed, it puts several different spins on it.

Each time anyone tells the tale there is an inflection in one direction or the other (or both: the snake might be good and evil,

and both the woman and the man might be evil, or neither, or
one or the other). And when we have seen that, we can take another, harder look at the inflected version that we know (in this
case, the Book of Genesis). And then we can notice the text's ambivalence about the tree (there are, after all, *two* trees) and, indeed
about the woman and the fruit, even in the story as it is told in
the Hebrew Bible, a text often alleged (before Mieke Bal) to have
a single point of view ("patriarchal").[17] It may happen that one
telling of a myth states the traditional view and another text subverts it; but far more often in a single myth we find the traditional
view cheek by jowl with a view that subverts it. In many tellings,
different political opinions are simultaneously expressed and
were probably differently perceived by different individuals in the
audience. Indeed, a single telling may have so many points of
view that ultimately the voices may seem to cancel one another
out, and there may seem to be no (single, or even dominant) point
of view. But the text does favor one point of view over all others;
if we cannot decide which one is favored, we must simply admit
that we do not have enough data, or enough discernment, to find
what is in fact there. The political stance of any telling of the
myth is not chaos, not Brownian motion: there is always weight
in one direction or another.

Here again it is useful to recall that our building blocks are not
merely nouns, but nouns plus verbs. A noun, such as *serpent*,
may symbolize so many polarized things—wisdom and evil, rebirth (sloughing) and death (poison), masculinity (the phallus) and
femininity (the coiled power), water (the element of many snakes)
and fire (the flame of its tongue)—indeed, it may symbolize almost anything. But when we add a verb, such as "gives" or
"bites," the meanings of the resulting theme are more circumscribed than the meanings of the noun alone, not only because
the meanings of verbs are inherently far more specific than the
meanings of nouns, but because the meaning of the resulting
theme is constructed in the area in which the two terms intersect, each activating a particular subarea within the larger potential area of meaning of the other insecting term. If a snake is a
symbol, one has to know what it symbolizes in the particular
culture that tells a story about it. But the more verbal theme of
incest or mutilation in a story has a generic meaning that one
learns from any variant of the story, a generic meaning that is
then often further complicated by taking on a particular cultural
meaning as well.

There are many examples of myths that, like the story of the
serpent in the garden, have been used, even within a single culture, to argue for diametrically opposed morals, political theories,
or social codes. One example of such a 180-degree turnabout may
be seen in the American myth of the cowboys and Injuns. The
basic narrative remains stable: the cowboys move west, the
Apaches attack, the cowboys circle the wagons, the Apaches kill
some of the cowboys, the cavalry arrives at the eleventh hour, and
the cowboys massacre all the Apaches. When I was growing up
in the 1940s and 1950s, we saw films with these plots and we
cheered for the good cowboys and booed the evil Injuns. Now we
see the same films (*Dances with Wolves* is a good example), but
we cheer for the good Apaches and boo the evil cowboys. The
same myth, but now a different idea has been attached to it. The
same narrative (in this case, a narrative based upon the undeniable outlines of actual history: the white man did move west, and
many white men and native Americans died in the resulting clash
of cultures), and even the same characters, but a very different
meaning. We might have assumed that the Apaches also told
more or less the same story, and always rooted for the Apaches:
but except for anthropologists, perhaps, no one in Hollywood
cared about those variants of the myth. The change of point of
view was wonderfully demonstrated in a recent television program telling the story from the native American point of view,
entitled, "How the West Was Lost."

Yet another example of a myth that swings both ways, or bats
for both teams, is the Irish antiwar folksong "Johnny, I Hardly
Knew You," which speaks of the returning soldier's disfiguring
mutilations, his leg blown off; this song is then, amazingly, transformed into the American pro-war song "When Johnny Comes
Marching Home" ("And we'll all turn out when Johnny comes
marching home!"). The story is the same: the soldier returns
home from war and is greeted by his mother. But the plot is entirely different: in one he returns in tragedy, in the other, in triumph. On a lighter level, there is the infamous Stan Freberg
comedy routine about Thanksgiving: the turkey was to be the national bird, and the eagle was to be eaten at the Thanksgiving
feast, but someone mixed them up ("What!?! You cooked the turkey!?!!? Our national bird?!?!!!!")

A striking example of a myth that has grafted very different
political meanings onto the basic narrative within the same culture is the Old Norse myth of the Valkyries and the magic ring of

Rhinegold. The myth of the Valkyries already had a richly multivalent set of meanings in the medieval text of the *Nibelungenlied*, to which Wagner added new layers in his cycle of operas known as *The Ring*, and the Nazis in turn reinterpreted both the ancient myth and the Wagnerian variant for their own purposes. The Wagnerian variant took on the status of a true mythic retelling; people still find, and I think will for many generations continue to find, beauty and meaning in it. The Nazi variant lasted far too long, but ultimately it did not succeed as a myth; it is no longer regarded as a valid retelling of the ancient tale. More recently, Francis Ford Coppola used the Wagnerian music of the Valkyries to refer simultaneously to Wagner, the Nazis, and the American forces in Vietnam (not to mention Joseph Conrad), in his film *Apocalypse Now*. Clearly it behooves us to distinguish between the very different uses to which the basic theme has been put, but at the same time we must acknowledge that our understanding of Coppola's film is greatly enhanced by an understanding of the *Nibelungenlied*. To this extent, at least, they are two variants of the same myth.

Bruce Lincoln has explained, with many wonderful examples, some of the ways in which people have used myth for very different sorts of political ends, not only reactionary (which we always knew) but revolutionary (which mythologists have generally failed to note).[18] Myths do not merely reflect the eternal, reactionary archetype or even the present hegemonic Zeitgeist but can subvert the dominant paradigm. As Marina Warner demonstrates, although traditional storytellers, "negotiating the audience's inclination, may well entrench bigotry,"[19] they may also oppose prevaiing prejudice.

Roberto Calasso explains how a myth can twist in this way:

> Myths are made up of actions that include their opposites within themselves. The hero kills the monster, but even as he does so we perceive that the opposite is also true: the monster kills the hero. The hero carries off the princess, yet even as he does we perceive that the opposite is also true: the hero deserts the princess. How can we be sure? The variants tell us. They keep the mythical blood in circulation. But let's imagine that all the variants of a certain myth have been lost, erased by some invisible hand. Would the myth still be the same? Here one arrives at the hairline distinction between myth and every other kind of narrative. Even without its variants, the myth includes its opposite. How do we know? The

knowledge intrinsic in the novel tells us so. The novel, a narrative deprived of variants, attempts to recover them by making the single text to which it is entrusted more dense, more detailed. Thus the action of the novel tends, as though toward its paradise, to the inclusion of its opposite, something the myth possesses as of right.[20]

Revolutionary myths express what David Tracy has called not the status quo but the fluxus quo.[21]

Conclusion: Knowledge, Power, and Difference

Mythology often plays upon the tension between knowledge and power. Since narratives are open-ended, they cannot simply further the political agenda of the weak, or, for that matter, of the strong. The relationship between knowledge and power is complex. Knowledge often results from power, for those in power can force Others to reveal themselves; and power often results from knowledge; knowledge can be used to manipulate, to blackmail, and so forth. Often, however, the dominator does not need to know anything about the objects of domination in order to dominate; power and ignorance may coexist. And ignorance, too, may be powerful, as Eve Sedgwick points out: "Knowledge, after all, is not itself power, although it is the magnetic field of power. Ignorance and opacity collude or compete with knowledge in mobilizing the flows of energy, desire, goods, meanings, persons. . . . The epistemological asymmetry of the laws that govern rape, for instance, privileges at the same time men and ignorance, inasmuch as it matters not at all what the raped woman perceives or wants just so long as the man raping her can claim not to have noticed (ignorance in which male sexuality receives careful education)."[22]

Myths, however, also argue that the knowledge of the weak is their weapon against the strong.[23] Ignorance may bring about the loss of the power to dominate; ignorance of the Other may render the powerful weak. It is even more essential for the weak to understand the powerful, to know their enemies, and to *tell them apart*, as Sedgwick acknowledges: "It was the long, painful realization, *not* that all oppressions are congruent, but that they are *differently* structured and so must intersect in complex embodiments that was the first great heuristic breakthrough of socialist-feminist thought and of the thought of women of color."[24] In

myth, as in life, knowledge, not ignorance, is power, and knowledge of *difference* is the key to both sex and politics. It is also the
key to the analysis of myth.

Notes

Parts of this essay constituted my Surjit Singh Lecture at the Graduate Theological Union, Berkeley, California, on October 31, 1994. Other parts will be incorporated in my forthcoming AAR-ACLS Lectures in 1996.
  I am indebted to David Tracy for the little that I know about postmodernism.

1. Sedgwick, *Epistemology of the Closet*, 23.
2. Geertz, *After the Fact*, 28.
3. Lévi-Strauss, "The Structural Study of Myth," 208.
4. Lévi-Strauss, *Myth and Meaning*, 11.
5. For a fuller discussion of the problems inherent in any definition of myth,
   see O'Flaherty, *Other Peoples' Myths*.
6. Geertz, *After the Fact*, 51.
7. Ramanujan, "Three Hundred Ramayanas," 46.
8. Warner, *From the Beast*, 279.
9. Ibid., 239.
10. Personal communication from Carolyn Bynum, May 1992.
11. Tracy, *The Analogical Imagination*, 102.
12. Geertz, *After the Fact*, 28.
13. For the roundhouse of myths, see O'Flaherty, *Other Peoples' Myths*.
14. For a devastating critique of this "encyclopedic" approach, see Smith,
    "Adde Parvum."
15. Graves, *Adam's Rib*.
16. Barthes, *Mythologies*, 142–43.
17. Bal, *Lethal Love*.
18. Lincoln, *Discourse and the Construction of Society*.
19. Warner, *From the Beast*, 409.
20. Calasso, *The Marriage of Cadmus and Harmony*, 280.
21. David Tracy, private conversation, November 1994.
22. Sedgwick, *Epistemology of the Closet*, 4–5.
23. Scott, *Weapons of the Weak*.
24. Sedgwick, *Epistemology of the Closet*, 33.

Works Cited

Bal, Mieke. *Lethal Love: Feminist Literary Readings of Biblical Love Sto-
    ries*. Bloomington: University of Indiana Press, 1987.

Barthes, Roland. *Mythologies*. Selected and translated from the French
    by Annette Lavers. London: Jonathan Cape, 1972.

Calasso, Roberto. *The Marriage of Cadmus and Harmony*. New York:
    Alfred Knopf, 1993.

Geertz, Clifford. *After the Fact: Two Countries, Four Decades, One An-
    thropologist*. Cambridge: Harvard University Press, 1995.

Graves, Robert. *Adam's Rib, and other Anomalous Elements in the Hebrew Creation Myth.* New York: Thomas Yoseloff, 1958.

Lévi-Strauss, Claude. *Myth and Meaning.* New York: Schocken Books, 1979; reprinted, with a new foreword by Wendy Doniger, 1995.

———. "The Structural Study of Myth." In *Structural Anthropology,* translated by Claire Jacobson and Brooke Grundfest Schoepf. Harmondsworth: Penguin Books, 1963.

Lincoln, Bruce. *Discourse and the Construction of Society.* New York: Oxford University Press, 1989.

O'Flaherty, Wendy Doniger. *Other Peoples' Myths: The Cave of Echoes.* New York: Macmillan, 1988; Chicago, University of Chicago Press, 1995.

Ramanujan, A. K. "Three Hundred Ramayanas: Five Examples and Three Thoughts on Translation," 22–49 of Paula Richman, ed., *Many Ramayanas: The Diversity of Narrative Traditions in South Asia.* Berkeley: University of California Press, 1991.

Scott, James C. *Weapons of the Weak: Everyday Forms of Peasant Resistance.* New Haven and London: Yale University Press, 1985.

Sedgwick, Eve Kosofsky. *Epistemology of the Closet.* Berkeley: University of California Press, 1990.

Smith, Jonathan Z. *"Adde Parvum Parvo Magnus Acervus Erit,"* 240–64 of *Map Is Not Territory.* Leiden: E. J. Brill, 1978.

Tracy, David. *The Analogical Imagination: Christian Theology and the Culture of Pluralism.* New York: Crossroad, 1981.

Warner, Marina. *From the Beast to the Blonde: On Fairy Tales and Their Tellers.* London: Chattos and Windus, 1995.

CRISTIANO GROTTANELLI

DUMÉZIL, THE INDO-EUROPEANS, AND THE THIRD FUNCTION

TOWARD THE END of his life, Georges Dumézil declared that his work as a scholar had consisted of (1) studying the Indo-Europeans as social groups united not only by linguistic affinities but also by a series of common cultural traits derived from a common prehistoric past and a common set of myths, and (2) "discovering" that the main cultural trait of the Indo-Europeans was a trifunctional ideology, in which human (and divine) phenomena were hierarchically classified as belonging to the sphere of sovereignty (first function), war (second function), or production, health, fertility, and wealth (third function). This trifunctional ideology was, according to Dumézil, not only typical of the Indo-Europeans, but exclusive to them.[1]

A discussion of this complex system of historical propositions, based largely on the study of myth, would require many volumes; in this essay I can do no more than mention the main problems it raises. As Doniger has mentioned in her essay in this volume, the comparative problems are manifold. In the specific case of Dumézil, one needs to consider first of all the problem of the Indo-Europeans. Do the linguistic affinities existing between the languages of the Indo-European group also imply profound cultural affinities across millennia and thousands of miles, and, if so, what kind of affinities are these? Again, what historical explanation(s) can be offered for the similarities among the languages (and cultures) in question? Second, one has to consider the trifunctional ideology. Are there consistent traces of that ideology in the cultural heritage of each and every ancient community speaking an Indo-European language? Are such traces lacking in all other cultures? What is the social, economic, and political background of such an ideology? Does such a possible background correspond to the kind of social structure that can be attributed to the age and situation of Indo-European "origins"?

Of course, Dumézil addressed each of these questions either implicitly or explicitly, and each of his answers articulates aspects of his general theory. At the same time, each question may also be answered—indeed *has* also been answered—in many different ways. And each different answer to each question creates problems in accepting the *whole* system reconstructed by Dumézil.

I shall quote only a few examples. To the first group of questions there is an old answer, given in 1939 by N. S. Trubetzkoy, in an article that was republished in 1968 and has received further attention in recent years. According to Trubetzkoy, the Indo-European linguistic uniformity is the result of a convergence—that is, languages of different areas that were not of themselves necessarily connected were "Indo-Europeanized" through contact processes. In his recent reappraisal of the Indo-European problem, Colin Renfrew rejects this solution;[2] but his version of the spread of the Indo-European languages across Europe in Neolithic times leads him to reject Dumézil's theories as well. Most specialists who study Indo-European languages and cultures tend to disagree both with Trubetzkoy and with Renfrew, yet some of the problems they have raised, such as the influence of modern ideologies on the reconstruction of linguistic prehistory or the relationship between linguistic and archaeological knowledge, have not yet been addressed convincingly by their critics.[3]

Dissonant answers have also been offered for the second group of questions. First of all, specialists have often asserted that in *their* field Dumézil's trifunctional ideology is absent or useless. One may cite Gonda for the Indian world, Momigliano for the Roman, Di Donato for the Greek, Philippson for the Germanic.[4] Others have seen different structures as fundamental to Indo-European culture, such as binary ideology or patterns of kinship and marriage.[5] Still others have stressed or modified certain aspects of Dumézil's trifunctional ideology along lines that diverge from those of Dumézil himself.[6] Further, the *specificity* of Indo-European trifunctionalism has been denied, both by scholars who tried to dismiss Dumézil's theory of a trifunctional ideology as an unwarranted fantasy and by those who saw it attested far beyond the limits of the Indo-European world.[7]

Different views also exist regarding the kind of society in which trifunctional ideology originated and flourished. Abaev places it in the transitional period between "primitive" and "class" societies;[8] Renfrew, for his part, sees it as typical of "heroic" chiefdom societies, as opposed to the much simpler and more egalitarian social structures of the Neolithic farmers who were, in his view, responsible for the diffusion of Indo-European languages.[9] These efforts, however, are offset in part by Dumézil's own effort to separate the problem of ideological trifunctionality from that of social organization, thus defending himself from the kind of criticism to which he was subjected by specialists earlier in his career, when he believed there was a necessary correspondence between the ideological trifunctionalism of Indo-European societies and their actual structure. But it is clear that such a separation between ideologies and social forms may not be stretched too far without undermining the very credibility of the ideologies reconstructed. On the other hand, once one begins to look for such a connection, a problem arises, especially in cases like Greece and Rome, where peasants *were* warriors. Moreover, one cannot solve this problem by projecting social tripartition and the distinction between producers and warriors into a reconstructed common past, for this is precisely the stance Dumézil moved *away* from, ever since the late 1940s.[10]

In spite of these difficulties, the data Dumézil unearthed that point toward trifunctionalism in the fields of mythology, ritual, classification, and other cultural productions are impressive and, I believe, were most often correctly interpreted by him. Trifunctionalism is obviously present in many cultures of different historic times among people who spoke languages of the Indo-European family. But, as I have tried to show elsewhere, (1) trifunctionalism is not necessarily transmitted "genetically" within the Indo-European linguistic group; (2) trifunctional modes of classification are present in very different cultural milieus and connected with specific social structures;[11] (3) trifunctionalism is not necessarily a complex ideological system; indeed, it would be better described as a simple mode of thought.[12] Moreover, the most strongly organized form of trifunctional ideology ever produced belongs not to the Indo-European origins, but to the European Middle Ages, and one may suspect that some of the

documents often quoted in support of Indo-European trifunctionalism and some of the modern trifunctional interpretations of
Indo-European lore were both influenced by medieval trifunctionalism.[13] Finally, there are modern modes of trifunctionalism: to
cite but one example, Martin Heidegger clearly used trifunctional
structures in his public address to the students and faculty of the
University of Freiburg in a speech delivered upon his appointment
as rektor in May 1933.[14]

What cannot be accepted, in my opinion, is the projection of
trifunctionalism into prehistoric "Proto-Indo-European" past,
that is, a period difficult to date and to define that is reconstructed hypothetically, as indicated by the asterisks preceding
the lexemes of the fictitious protolanguage of that equally fictitious stage. But it must be noted here that, since the 1950s, Dumézil took care to open his books and essays with discussions of
data and texts from one or more cultures of the Indo-European
linguistic sphere, after which he compared these phenomena, and
only then raised the possibility of their derivation from a common source, without indulging in any detailed hypothetical re-
constructions of a cultural or linguistic nature. The "genetic"
outcome of cultural comparatism is always (or almost always)
present in Dumézil's work, but it is never dwelled upon at length,
let alone described or discussed in detail. On the other hand,
many other Indo-Europeanists, Dumézilian and non-Dumézilian
alike, have been bolder (or less prudent) in reconstructing proto-
societies, protomyths, and "original versions" of myths and
rituals.

As noted above, Dumézil's trifunctional ideology is hierarchical: the first function, by definition, outranks the other two, and
the third function is the lowest, so that the ideology itself may
be seen as a most powerful self-portrait (and self-construction)
of a (relatively simple) class society.[15] Because of this hierarchic
structure and because Dumézil's reaction against Frazer and the
fertility myth schools of the 1920s and 1930s was extremely important in shaping his methodology, the all-important function
of production has received less attention than the other two in
Dumézil's work and has often been forgotten by Dumézilians.[16] I
would thus suggest that were greater attention paid to issues of
production (in its various aspects of agricultural activity and outcome, animal husbandry, and specialized craftsmanship), this
would constitute an important correction to Dumézilian trifunctionalism. While there may be some truth to the observation that

anthropologists and historians of religions became interested in the fertility paradigm around the time chemical fertilizers were discovered, it is also clear that agricultural fertility was of crucial importance to societies long before Mannhardt and Frazer became obsessed by it! Indeed, when one forgets this, or when one tries to study ancient cultures without ancient production or producers, problems inevitably arise.

Although it is fair to say that in Dumézil's work, the third function was less favored than the sovereign and the military, one must acknowledge that he often contributed important insights to the study of the ideology of agricultural fertility and of specialized manufacture. Things have become worse in the last few years, however, for both Dumézilians and non-Dumézilians (such as those critics of Eliade who mysticized third-function deities) have adopted a hypercritical stance toward any interpretation of ancient myth or ritual that is in any way connected with agricultural fertility. The old fashion is thus being reversed, but the attitudes are no less rigid. I shall cite two meaningful examples of this trend.

The first of these comes from the best book I know on the *Rāmāyaṇa*, Daniel Dubuisson's volume of 1986. If I understand correctly, the two main results of Dubuisson's study are his treatment of this epic as a mythic narrative about kingship and his interpretation of the relationship between Rāma and Sītā as a symbol of the relationship between the monarch and his land. Dubuisson is an *élève* of Dumézil's; his important new insights are reached by way of a Dumézilian interpretation of the epic text, involving trifunctionalism and a comparatism that is exclusively Indo-European.

Now, both of Dubuisson's important results I previously reached by way of a totally different comparative endeavor in an article that was published in *History of Religions*.[17] That article offered a comparative study of three ancient narratives: a biblical episode, a Greek myth, and the adventures of Sītā in the *Rāmāyaṇa*: a strange comparison indeed, if envisaged from a Dumézilian point of view, for the three texts (different in length, function, context, and date) belong to cultures that were not all linguistically connected.[18] Yet that study yielded a clear understanding of the royal quality of the *Rāmāyaṇa* (and of course, in different ways, also of the other two traditional narratives), and a view of the Rāma-Sītā relationship as describing at one level the relationship of king and land, in line with a justly famous article of Dubuisson's that dealt with Sītā as a symbol of the fertile earth.[19] I wrote then that in the Indic poem a series of narrative details "suggests that the rejection of the helpless female (i.e., that of Sītā by Rāma) is in reality a rejection of the land" by the king.[20] This theme of the rejection of the earth Dubuisson echoes, taking the very same phrase ("la répudiation de la Terre") for the title of the third chapter of part one of his book.

Dubuisson does not ignore my article; but he quotes it in a way that shows he is unable to use it properly because of his faithfulness to (1) his maître's "genetic" approach to comparison, and (2) a hyper-Dumézilian distrust of interpretations that stress the importance of the third function (a distrust that seems contradicted by his earlier article of 1978!). In the volume's final bibliography, my article is classified among the "Etudes consacrées à différents aspects des civilizations indienne, indo-iranienne et indo-européene," a classification that is easily explained by the fact that in the author's mental taxonomy there is no place for my approach. In the text, Dubuisson writes that Krappe's old theme (or rather, old error) of fertilité céréalière reappears in my article.[21] This is a different classification of my contribution, but still a wrong one, for though I did quote the old "fertility myth interpretations," I insisted upon their dates (1937, 1928, 1931), and concluded that "we cannot accept their basic assumption . . . especially because, though most if not all ancient myths are (also) about agricultural fertility, there is no such thing as a 'fertility myth' stricto sensu, for no myth is only about fertility, and agricultural fertility, being the consequence of social cohesion, is never 'alone.'"[22]

In spite of the obvious correspondences in the result of our work, Dubuisson thus misunderstood my contribution to the study of the Rāmāyaṇa, I think, because he could not see it well through his Dumézilian lenses. First of all, my comparatism was not Indo-European; second, I gave attention to the problem of agricultural fertility; therefore, my proposal had to be seen as an erreur, and as an erreur connected with old ideas on la fertilité céréalière.

In a later article I have developed further the comparative study of mythic narratives in which a powerful male confronts a fecund female, treating their symbolic and ideological implications.[23] Once again, the relationship between Rāma and Sītā has proved meaningful, and once again the comparative spectrum includes important non-Indo-European materials. I think one should go still further toward a general study of myths and rituals involving the relationship between the third function of the Dumézilian series and the other two functions. In particular, the relationship between a king and his land may not be understood without dealing with this problem.

Dumézil was the first to be aware of this, and although he played down the sexual and naturalistic aspect of the Indian royal-horse sacrifice (aśvamedha), it is also true that he correctly interpreted that ritual; his parallel essays on the Roman-horse sacrifice are also an important contribution toward understanding the reciprocal relationships among the three functions as represented in an archaic ritual practice.[24] In this case, he went so far as to note that the ritual representations of the second function were subservient to those of the third.[25]

The opposite may be said of the ritual and mythology of another Roman festival, the Nonae Capratinae, or Caprotinae, also studied by Dumézil, and cited here as a second example of the increasing prejudice against the third function.[26] To examine this, let me quote from Plutarch's *Life of Camillus*, where it is told how the Romans were besieged by their Latin enemies, and

in their perplexity, a handmaiden named Tutula, or, as some call her, Philotis, advised the magistrates to send her to the enemy with some of the most attractive and noble looking handmaidens, all arrayed like free-born brides; she would attend to the rest. The magistrates yielded to her persuasions, chose as many handmaidens as she thought meet for her purpose, arrayed them in fine raiment and gold, and handed them over to the Latins, who were encamped near the city. In the night, the rest of the maidens stole away the enemy's swords, while Tutula, or Philotis, climbed a wild fig-tree of great height, and after spreading out her cloak behind her, held out a lighted torch towards Rome, this being the signal agreed upon between her and the magistrates, though no other citizen knew of it. Hence it was that the soldiers sallied out of the city tumultuously, as the magistrates urged them on, calling out one another's names, and with much ado getting into rank and file. They stormed the entrenchments of the enemy, who were fast asleep and expected nothing of the sort, captured their camp, and slew most of them. This happened on the Nones of what was then called Quintilis, now July, and the festival since held on that day is in remembrance of the exploit. For, to begin with, they run out of the city gate in throngs, calling out many local and common names, such as Gaius, Marcus, Lucius, and the like, in imitation of the way the soldiers once sallied aloud upon each other in their haste. Next, the hand-maidens, in gay attire, run about jesting and joking with the men they meet. They have a mock battle, too, with one another, im-plying that they once took a hand in the struggle with the Latins. And as they feast they sit in the shade of the fig-tree's branches. The day is called "Nonae capratinae," from the wild fig-tree, as they suppose, from which the maid held forth her torch: this goes by the name of *caprificus.* But others say that most of what is said and done at this festival has reference to the fate of Romulus. For on this same day he vanished from sight, outside the city gates, in sudden darkness and tempest, and, as some think, during an eclipse of the sun. The day, they say, is called the "Nonae Capratinae" from the spot where he thus vanished. For the she-goat goes by the name of *capra,* and Romulus vanished from sight while haranguing an assembly of the people at the Goat's Marsh, as has been stated in his *Life.*[27]

In a recent book Jan Bremmer firmly rejects any interpretation of this festival that would see fertility elements in it.[28] He writes that according to Latte "the close connections of Juno with the fig-tree pointed to fertility, since the tree is 'Symbol des Frücht-barkeit'. Although Dumézil is in general less receptive than most of his contemporaries, to the fertility paradigm, which dominated the study of Greek and Roman ritual during the first half of this century, he nevertheless also states: 'Figuier, bouc: l'animal comme le végétal fournissent beaucoup à la symbolique de la sex-ualité'. All these explanations overlook the fact that wild fig-trees do not bear fruit and thus hardly can be symbols of fertility; in addition, they leave most of the ritual totally unexplained. We shall therefore look in a different direction."[29]

Bremmer is right in pointing to the Nonae Capratinae as a festi-val of inversion, whereby, as happened with male servants in the Saturnalia, female slaves temporarily played a dominant role. Yet his too rapid dismissal of the vegetable and animal life present or evoked in the festival, in the name of a rejection of the fertility paradigm, leaves other parts of the ritual totally unexplained, these parts being the caprificus and the capra, surely two mean-ingful symbols. Here again Dumézil is correct in recognizing the importance of the agricultural components of the ritual and myth, though it is true that he does not explain their presence and fails to interpret the festival convincingly.

A way out is offered by Dario Sabbatucci's recent book on Roman religion.[30] Though it bears no fruit, Sabbatucci observes, the wild fig-tree was extremely important in Roman agriculture because it harbored insects that bore pollen to the female flowers of the domestic fig, thus transforming them into fruits (figs). This process—known in Latin as *caprificatio*—was well known in antiquity and was discussed by such authors as Theophrastus, Pliny, and Columella. The caprificus, Sabbatucci adds, is a good symbol for the central theme of the festival, for just as the wild fig-tree (which itself produces no edible fruit) helped the domestic fig-tree produce its fruit, similarly in the mythic etiology and the ritual performance of the Nonae Capratinae, women (who were excluded from public and military life) helped the male members of the community to solve a military crisis of the state, while in turn slave women offered their help to the free women, and took their place in helping the men. Far from being an irrelevant aspect of the festival, the caprificus is the very symbol, the synthetic emblem, of the profound structural meaning of the festival and of the connected narrative. Here, too, though it is "not alone," fertility is significant. And in this specific case, Dumézil was aware of its importance, although he failed to recognize its specific meaning. It would seem, however, that later scholars were less attentive.

We have seen that in the October Equus rituals of ancient Rome the second function was presented as subservient to the third, and we have examined a Roman mythical narrative in which female slaves, together with a symbol of fertility, helped to solve a crisis pertaining to the second function. This last case is an instance of the most frequent situation, where myths and rituals show the third function serving the second, and acknowledge its service to be indispensable, for all that its station remains inferior.

The most interesting example of this symbolic configuration comes in myths where third-function figures help divine or heroic warriors in their fights against chaotic monsters or usurpers. Such myths are endowed with important meanings as second-function myths par excellence and as initiation scenarios;[31] at the same time, as shown also by the parallel Near Eastern mythologies, they are clearly cosmogonic, even when they do not ex-

plicitly deal with the establishment of a macrocosmic order but
with the founding or renewal of a correct social order often based
upon the rule of a legitimate and righteous monarch.[32] In many
cases the craftsmen who aid and abet the warrior god or hero in
such myths are similar to the typical third-function twins de-
tected by Dumézil and Wikander in various mythical traditions
and more recently investigated by Ward and others.[33] Such is the
case, I suggest, of Apollo's victory over the drakaina in Delphi,
and the aid he received from the brothers Trophōnios and
Agamēdēs.[34] Trophōnios and Agamēdēs appear as builders in the
Homeric Hymn to Pythian Apollo, and their names point to the
first as well as to the third function, more specifically to nourishing and healing.[35] The same is also true of the Persian royal hero
Ardashir, who was assisted by the brothers Burz and Burzātur in
his fight against a voracious dragon according to the Pahlavi *Book
of Ardashir*, an epic narrative dated around A.D. 650 by its first
translator. And although Burz and Burzātur have traits that point
to the priestly function, they impersonate cooks in order to enter
the monster's abode, where they kill the dragon (*kirm*, "worm")
by pouring molten metal down its throat.[36]

This last trait is not surprising in a Mazdaean context, but it
acquires a different meaning if we compare Ardashir's assistants
to two other mythical helpers of a heroic serpent slayer, who are
attested to in nineteenth-century Russian folklore. In one of the
folktales collected by A. N. Afanasjev, the hero, Ivan, a figure of
the "third brother" type comparable to the Indo-Iranian T(h)rita,
fights against an anticosmic brood of serpents and is finally saved
by Saints Cosmas and Damian, who are presented as heavenly
smiths and who kill the female serpent by holding its tongue with
red-hot iron tongs and beating upon it with their hammers.[37] It
should further be noted that the brothers Cosmas and Damian are
a popular pair of saints, famous (both in Western and in Eastern
Christianity) as physicians who refused payment from their patients.[38] At least in some cases their cult continued the pagan
worship of the Dioscuri.

To these data we should add a fourth case: the two assistants
who serve Arthur in many medieval texts, Kei (Keu) and Bedwyr
(Bedoer), who were his seneschal and his cupbearer, respectively.
In Wace's *Brut* and in Geoffrey of Monmouth's *Historia Regum
Brittaniae*, these two noble ministers (associated respectively
with food and with drink, like the Zoroastrian "archangels"
Haurvatat and Ameretat) accompany Arthur in his expedition

against the giant of Mont-Saint-Michel; they take no active part
in the fight, but Bedoer cuts off the giant's head after the monster
has been defeated by Arthur.[39] Again, in the medieval Welsh tale
of Culwch and Olwen, the inseparable Kei and Bedwyr take part
in Arthur's expedition to win Olwen for Culwch from her father
the giant Ysbaddaden, and the giant is beheaded at the end of
the story.[40]

These four cases, where twin figures associated with the third
function (craftsmen in two cases, specialists associated with food
and drink in the others) help a hero associated with the second,
differ in many respects, the most notable of which is the specific
way in which each pair assists the warrior. Burz and Burzātur, like
Cosmas and Damian, actually kill the monster; Trophōnios and
Agamēdēs build a structure over its body; and Arthur's two helpers merely follow (although in one case Bedoer does decapitate
the giant after Arthur has killed him). Still, a common pattern is
surely present, and we could compare the relationship between
the two helpers and the victorious hero to the complex relationship between Indra and the Aśvins in Vedic mythology.[41]

In the Shāh Namēh of the Iranian poet Abu'l Qasim Mansur
(Firdusi), dated to the eleventh century A.D., two enemies of the
triple and serpentine usurper Zohāk pave the way for the hero and
legitimate heir to the kingship, Ferīdūn.[42] Like Burz and Burzātur
in the older Book of Ardashir, these two champions (Kermail and
Irmail) possess aspects of the first function, but they also offer
themselves as cooks and butchers to the tyrant, and thus manage
to save lives by sparing many potential victims of the monster's
cannibalistic meals. But in the Shāh Namēh another third-
function figure helps the hero. This is the smith, Kāvēh, who,
having lost two sons to Zohāk, protests publicly, abusing the
monstrous tyrant to his face, and raising his own leather smith's
apron as a banner of resistance.[43] This apron then becomes the
banner that Ferīdūn's army carried in their march against Zohāk,
and the weapon with which Ferīdūn kills the usurper—a huge
mace shaped like a bull's head—was especially fashioned for him
by the smiths who helped him prepare his attack.

In this episode the contribution of the third function to the
hero's cosmic battle against a bloodthirsty monster is offered by
a group of smiths who fashion his special weapon and by a single
craftsman who initiated the rising against the monster. Though
both these patterns are clearly distinct from the motif of the twin
third-function helpers we have dealt with so far, there is for each

of them a rich series of parallels in other narrative traditions, as
in the case of the two special maces fashioned by the craftsman-
god Kothar-wa-Hasis ("Adroit and Cunning") for the storm-god
Baal in the Ugaritic *Baal Epic* (thirteenth century B.C.), before
Baal fought the usurper Mot ("Death").[44] Again, there is the Ken-
ite heroine Jael, a member of a small tribal unit of seminomadic
smiths, who in Judges 3 and 4 is said to have put the Canaanite
war leader Sisera to sleep by giving him milk to drink, then hammered a peg into his skull and presented his body to the Israelite
leader Barak.[45] A comparable case is that of Jehonadab ben Rekab,
who clasped Jehu's hand and climbed into his chariot as that Yah-
wist hero was driving against the idolatrous oppressor Ahab.
Ahab was killed in that coup, and Jehu reigned in his stead, destroyed the foreign gods, and killed their priests.[46] As John Gray
has shown, Jehonadab was not, as is usually stated, the founder
of an ascetic order but the eponymous ancestor and prototype of
a clan of smiths and chariot builders.[47] His alliance with Jehu
against Ahab should be compared to Kāvēh's cooperation with
Ferīdūn in the *Shāh Namēh*.

It may be suggested that the motif of the paired third-function
helpers of the monster-slayer is a specific Indo-Iranian and European (Indo-European?) form of a more general narrative topos of
the third function aiding the second. But some surprising co-
occurrences give us pause. For instance, the theme on Indra's
complex relationship with the third-function twins Nakula and
Sahadeva coexists in the *Mahabhārata* with the tradition that his
amoghā śakti, or "unfailing javelin," was made by the craftsman
god Tvaṣṭṛ (9.17.44). A further motif, involving the beheading of
the enemy by a member of the third function who aids the heroic
warrior, is also found in Vedic traditions, for we are told that Indra
bade a carpenter cut off the three heads of Triśiras, the monster
he had just defeated.[48] This last tradition is most similar to the
episode mentioned above, in which Bedoer beheads the giant defeated by Arthur, but it may also be compared to the roles played
by Burz and Burzātur, Cosmas and Damian, and Jael in their respective narrative contexts. So it may be stated that specific motifs and narrative details are present in different contexts without
any necessary connection with the linguistic classification of the
respective cultures. The Vedic repertoire seems the most complete, but it must be added that in no context has the relationship
between the second and third function been expressed more
clearly than in the Babylonian *Enuma Elish* texts, in which the

warrior-god Marduk is presented as the son of the wise, cunning, and able god Enki (Ea), master of all the crafts, lord of the sweet chthonic waters, and is constantly helped by his father in his fight against the monsters of Chaos.[49]

As we have seen, in the mythical narratives of many Asiatic and European societies third-function figures collaborate in different ways with the second function, the main forms of cooperation being. (1) the administration of food; (2) the production of powerful weapons for the battle against an anticosmic being; (3) the actual killing, or the partial dismembering, of the monster, after it has been defeated by the warrior; (4) the building of a new structure near its remains. Now, all the third-function figures we have encountered so far are in different ways subservient, or at least complementary, to the warrior who in every case is the protagonist of the narrative. This general tendency is, however, not without exceptions, for in some narratives the role played by the third-function figure is more than subsidiary;[50] and in others, although he acts as a warrior, the protagonist is presented as a member of a class of producers.[51]

This last case is actually far from isolated, in light of other traditional narratives like the Roman story of Cincinnatus, or the Irish myth of Lug, in which the valiant warrior (and war leader) is also an agriculturalist or a capable craftsman, and emphatically so. In such cases, although the two different functions remain distinct, they are attributed to one single figure who practices each function in turn and is thus a representative of both: a "producer-warrior." The complex mythic and taxonomic situation of the Iranian Thraītaona, may also be similar, rather than a "mobilisation, dans l'oeuvre combattante, de la troisième fonction par la seconde," as Dumézil would have it.[52] The case of the producer-warrior points up the connection as well as the difference between function and class. For whereas the motif of third-function figure(s) serving the second-function hero well represents ideals and interests of a warrior aristocracy, the producer-warrior and his mythology point to the central role of producers and is thus more open, if not to a democracy of producers, at least to a promotion of some producers through their deeds in war.

All this not only indicates the obvious fact that the third function is important, but also that the three Dumézilian functions may be a useful tool in comparative research in the field of mythology and ritual, provided they are used with the necessary subtlety and freely applied to the full set of available data—outside as well as inside the Indo-European world. For although the excessively rigid application of Dumézilian paradigms can only give rise to misunderstandings, Dumézil's work still contains much that can inspire and help.

What we should learn from Dumézil is his freedom from any preconceived methodological allegiance, his capacity to reconsider fossilized ideas, his ability to criticize and to question even his own apparently most solid achievements—in sum, the readiness that he never lost, to begin all over again when the necessity arose.

Notes

1. See Dumézil, *Entretiens avec Didier Eribon.*
2. Renfrew, *Archaeology and Language;* Ginzburg, *Storia notturna.*
3. Renfrew, *Archaeology and Language;* Trubetzkoy, *Gedanken über das Indogermanenproblem.*
4. Philippson, "Phänomenologie, vergleichende Mythologie und germanische Religionsgeschichte"; Strutynski, "History and Structure in Germanic Mythology"; Gonda, *Triads in the Veda;* Di Donato, *Di Apollon Sonore;* Momigliano, "Georges Dumézil and the Trifunctional Approach to Roman Civilization."
5. Gamkrelidze and Ivanov, *Indoevropejskij jasyk i Indoevropeici;* Oosten, *The War of the Gods.*
6. Lincoln, *Myth, Cosmos and Society.*
7. Brough, "The Tripartite Ideology of the Indo-Europeans"; Abaev, "Le Cheval de Troie"; also Smith, "La forge de l'intelligence"; also Grottanelli, "Temi duméziliani fuori dal mondo indo-europeo;" Crevatin, *Ricerche di antichità indeuropee.*
8. Abaev, "Le Cheval de Troie."
9. Renfrew, *Archaeology and Language.*
10. Dumézil, *Mythe et Eropée III.*
11. Grottanelli, "Temi duméziliani fuori dal mondo indo-europeo."
12. Grottanelli, "Trifunzionalismi bianchi e neri."
13. Duby, *Les trois ordres ou l'imaginaire du féodalisme;* Niccoli, *I sacerdoti, i guerrieri, i contadini;* Grottanelli, "Temi duméziliani fuori dal mondo indo-europeo."
14. Heidegger, *Die Selbstbehauptung der Deutschen Universität—Das Rektorat.* For the implications of this correspondence between Heidegger and Dumézil see Grottanelli, *Ideologie Miti Massacri;* on Dumézil's politics see also Lincoln, *Death, War, and Sacrifice.*
15. Lincoln, *Myth, Cosmos and Society: Indo-European Themes of Creation and Destruction.*
16. Well explored in the medieval and modern forms of trifunctionalism by Niccoli, *I sacerdoti, i guerrieri, i contadini.*
17. Grottanelli, "The King's Grace and the Helpless Woman."
18. The story contained in the Book of Ruth, and the Delphic story of Charila in Plutarch's *Moralia.*
19. Dubuisson, "La déesse chevelue et la reine coiffeuse."
20. Grottanelli, "The King's Grace and the Helpless Woman," 22.
21. Dubuisson, *La légende royale dans l'Inde ancienne.*

22. Grottanelli, "The King's Grace and the Helpless Woman," 19.
23. Grottanelli, "The Story of Deborah and Baraq."
24. Dumézil, La religion romaine archaïque, Fêtes romaines d'été et d'automne.
25. For warriors protect the crops, as shown by the meaning of the formula *ob frugum eventum* in Paul. Fest. 246 L^1-326 L^2.
26. Dumézil, Fêtes romaines d'été et d'automne.
27. Plutarch, Life of Camillus (29); Life (chap. 27).
28. Bremmer and Horsfall, Roman Myth and Mythography.
29. Ibid., 77.
30. Sabbatucci, La religione di Roma antica, 231–35.
31. See Lincoln, "The Indo-European Cattle Raiding Myth"; see also Walcot, "Cattle Raiding, Heroic Tradition and Ritual"; Ivanov and Toporov, "Le mythe indoeuropéen du dieu de l'orage poursuivant le serpent"; Oguibénine, Structure d'un mythe védique; Grottanelli, "Cosmogonia e sacrificio l."; Grottanelli, "L'Inno a Hermes e il Cantico di Deborah"; Lincoln, Priests, Warriors, and Cattle; Varenne, Cosmogonies védiques.
32. See Wakeman, God's Battle with the Monster; Day, God's Conflict with the Dragon.
33. For a bibliography from 1968 to 1982, see Grottanelli, "The Story of Deborah and Baraq."
34. Homeric Hymn to Pythian Apollo, vv. 294–299. On this hymn, see Aloni, L'aedo e i tiranni, and De Martino, Omero agonista in Delo.
35. Benveniste, "La tradition médicale des Indo-européens."
36. Pagliaro, Epica e Romanzo nel Medioevo persiano.
37. A. N. Afanasjev, Antiche Fiabe Russe; Toporov, "Parallels to Ancient Indo-Iranian Social and Mythological Concepts"; and "Avest. Thrita, Thraetaona, dr.ind. Trita i dr. i ich indoevropejskie istoki"; Grottanelli, "Giuseppe nel pozzo, l."; Ajello, "Mec Tigran e il mito del combattimento col Tricefalo."
38. Deubner, Kosmas und Damian.
39. Grisward, Archéologie de l'épopée médiévale, Chp. 8; see also Layamon, Chronicle of Britain.
40. Gantz, The Mabinogion, 134–76.
41. Esp. Mahābhārata 7.84.18, where the Aśvins join Indra in his chariot; cf. Hopkins, Epic Mythology, 124–25; 169.
42. A figure derived from the Zoroastrian Thraītaona and the Indo-Iranian T(h)rita; see Dumézil, Heur et malheur du guerrier; see also Lincoln, "The Indo-European Cattle Raiding Myth."
43. See Christensen, Smeden Kâvâh og det gamle persiske Rigsbanner.
44. See Del Olmo Lete, Mitos y Leyendas de Canaán según la tradición de Ugarit; Xella, "Il dio siriano Kothar."
45. See Soggin, Judges; also Grottanelli, "The Story of Deborah and Baraq."
46. 2 Kings 10.
47. Gray, I and II Kings; Frick, "The Rechabites Reconsidered."
48. Hopkins, Epic Mythology, 131: Mahābhārata 5.9.2f; Ṛg-Veda 10.8.7.
49. On Eriki(Ea), see Bottéro and Kramer, Lorsque les dieux faisaient l'homme, 151–202.
50. E.g., Kāvéh in the Shāh Nameh.
51. E.g., Ivan in the Afanasjev folktale.
52. Dumézil, Heur et malheur du guerrier.

Works Cited

Abaev, V. I. "Le Cheval de Troie: Parallèles caucasiens." Annales, Economies Sociétés Civilisations 18 (1963): 1041–70.

Afanasjev, A. N. *Antiche Fiabe Russe*. Translated by Gigliola Venturi. Torino: Einaudi, 1953.

Ajello, Vincenzo. "Mec Tigran e il mito del combattimento col Tricefalo." *Transcaucasica* 2 (1980): 68–81.

Aloni, Antonio. *L'aedo e i tiranni: ricerche sull'Inno omerico a Apollo*. Filologia e critica, 59. Roma: Edizioni dell'Ateneo, 1989.

Benveniste, Emile. "La tradition médicale des Indo-européens." *Revue de l'histoire des religions* 130 (1945): 5–12.

Bottéro, Jean, and S. N. Kramer. *Lorsque les dieux faisaient l'homme: Mythologie mésopotamienne*. Paris: Gallimard, 1989.

Bremmer, J. N., and N. M. Horsfall. *Roman Myth and Mythography*. University of London: Institute of Classical Studies. Bulletin Supplement 52, 1987.

Brough, J. "The Tripartite Ideology of the Indo-Europeans: An Experiment in Method." *Bulletin of the Society of Oriental and African Studies* 12 (1959): 69–85.

Christensen, Arthur. *Smeden Kâväh og det gamle persiske Rigsbanner*. Copenhagen: A. F. Høst, 1919.

Crevatin, Franco. *Ricerche di antichità indoeuropee*. Trieste: Edizioni LINT, 1979.

Day, John. *God's Conflict with the Dragon: Echoes of a Canaanite Myth in the Old Testament*. Cambridge: Cambridge University Press, 1985.

Del Olmo Lete, Gregorio. *Mitos y Leyendas de Canaán según la tradición de Ugarit*. Madrid: Ediciones Cristiandad, 1981.

De Martino, Francesco. *Omero agonista in Delo*. Antichita classica e cristiana, 22. Brescia: Paideia, 1982.

Deubner, Ludwig. *Kosmas und Damian*. Leipzig and Berlin: B. G. Teubner, 1907.

Di Donato, Riccardo. "*Di Apollon Sonore* e di alcuni suoi antenati: Geoges Dumézil e l'epica greca arcaica." *OPUS* 2 (1983): 401–21.

Dubuisson, Daniel. *La légende royale dans l'Inde ancienne: Rāma et le Rāmāyana*. Paris: Economica, 1986.

―――. "La déesse chevelue et la reine coiffeuse: recherches sur un thème épique de l'Inde ancienne." *Journal Asiatique* (1978): 266.

Duby, Georges. *Les trois ordres ou l'imaginaire du féodalisme*. Paris: Gallimard, 1978.

Dumézil, Georges. *Entretiens avec Didier Eribon*. Paris: Gallimard, 1987.

―――. *Fêtes romaines d'été et d'automne, suivi de dix questions romaines*. Paris: Gallimard, 1976.

―――. *La religion romaine archaïque*. 2d ed. Paris: Payot, 1974.

―――. *Mythe et Epopée III: Histoires romaines*. Paris: Gallimard, 1973.

―――. *Heur et malheur du guerrier*. Paris: P.U.F., 1969.

Frick, F. S. "The Rechabites Reconsidered." *Journal of Biblical Literature* 90 (1971): 279–87.

Gamkrelidze, T. V., and V. V. Ivanov. *Indoevropejskij jasyk i Indoevropeici.* 2 vols. Tbilisi: Izdatel'stvo Tbilisskogo Universiteta, 1984.

Gantz, Jeffrey. Translation and introduction. *The Mabinogion.* Harmondsworth: Penguin Books, 1976.

Geoffrey of Monmouth. *The Historia regum Britannie of Geoffrey of Monmouth.* Cambridge, England, and Dover, N.H.: D. S. Brewer, 1985.

Ginzburg, Carlo. *Storia notturna: Una decifrazione del Sabba.* Torino: Einaudi, 1989.

Gonda, Jan. *Triads in the Veda.* Amsterdam: North Holland Publishing Co., 1976.

Gray, John. *I and II Kings: A Commentary.* 3d. ed. London: SCM Press, 1977.

Grisward, Joel. *Archéologie de l'épopée médiévale.* Paris: Payot, 1981.

Grottanelli, Cristiano. *Ideologie Miti Massacri: Indoeuropei di Georges Dumézil.* Palermo: Sellerio, 1993.

————. "Trifunzionalismi bianchi e neri." *Quaderni linguistici e filologici dell' Università di Macerata* 4 (1989): forthcoming.

————. "The Story of Deborah and Baraq: A Comparative Approach." *Studi e Materiali di Storia delle Religioni* 11 (1987): 365–89.

————. "Yoked Horses, Twins, and the Powerful Lady: India, Greece, Ireland and Elsewhere." *Journal of Indo-European Studies* 14 (1986): 135–52.

————. "Temi duméziliani fuori dal mondo indo-europeo." *OPUS* 2 (1983): 365–89.

————. "The King's Grace and the Helpless Woman: A Comparative Study of the Stories of Ruth, Charila, Sītā." *History of Religions* 22 (1982): 1–24.

————. "L'Inno a Hermes e il Cantico di Deborah: due facce di un tema mitico." *Rivista degli Studi Orientali* 56 (1982): 27–37.

————. "Cosmogonia e sacrificio I: Problemi delle cosmogonie 'rituali' nel RgVeda e nel Vicino Oriente antico." *Studi Storico-Religiosi* 4 (1980): 207–35.

————. "Giuseppe nel pozzo, I: Un antico mitico in Genesi 37:12–24 e in RV I. 105." *Oriens Antiquus* 17 (1978): 107–22.

Heidegger, Martin. *Die Selbstbehauptung der Deutschen Universität— Das Rektorat 1933/34.* Frankfurt am Main: Klostermann, 1983.

Hopkins, E. Washburn. *Epic Mythology.* [1915]. Delhi: Motilal Banarsidas, 1974.

Ivanov, V. V., and V. N. Toporov. "Le mythe indoeuropéen du dieu de l'orage poursuivant le serpent. Reconstruction du schéma." In *Echanges et communications: Mélanges offerts à Claude Lévi-Strauss.* Vol. 1. The Hague: Mouton, 1968, 1180–1206.

Layamon. *Lazamons Brut; or, Chronicle of Britain.* New York: AMS Press, 1970.

Lincoln, Bruce. *Death, War and Sacrifice.* Chicago: University of Chicago Press, 1992.

———. *Myth, Cosmos and Society: Indo-European Themes of Creation and Destruction.* Cambridge: Harvard University Press, 1986.

———. *Priests, Warriors, and Cattle. A Study in the Ecology of Religions.* Berkeley: University of California Press, 1981.

———. "The Indo-European Cattle Raiding Myth." *History of Religions* 16 (1976): 42–65.

Momigliano, Arnaldo. "Georges Dumézil and the Trifunctional Approach to Roman Civilization." *History and Theory* 23 (1984): 312–30.

Niccoli, Ottavia. *I sacerdoti, i guerrieri, i contadini: Storia di un' immagine della società.* Torino: Einaudi, 1979.

Oguibénine, Boris. *Structure d'un mythe védique: Le mythe cosmogonique dans le Rgyeda.* Paris and The Hague: Mouton, 1973.

Oosten, Jarich G. *The War of the Gods: The Social Code in Indo-European Mythology.* London: Routledge and Kegan Paul, 1985.

Pagliaro, Antonino. *Epica e Romanzo nel Medioevo persiano: Due racconti tradotti per la prima volta dal Pahlavi con introduzione e note.* Firenze: Sansoni, 1927.

Philippson, E. A. "Phänomenologie, vergleichende Mythologie und germanische Religionsgeschichte." *PMLA* 77 (1962): 187–93.

Plutarch. *Plutarch's Lives.* Cambridge: Harvard University Press and London: W. Heinemann, 1982–1990.

Renfrew, Colin. *Archaeology and Language: The Puzzle of Indo-European Origins.* London: Jonathan Cape, 1987.

Sabbatucci, Dario. *La religione de roma antica, dal calendario festivo all' ordine cosmico.* Milano: Mondadori, Il Saggiatore, 1988.

Smith, Pierre. "La forge de l'intelligence." *L'Homme* 10 (1970): 5–21.

Soggin, J. A. *Judges: A Commentary.* London: SCM Press, 1981.

Strutynski, Udo. "History and Structure in Germanic Mythology: Some Thoughts on Einar Haugen's Critique to Dumézil." In G. J. Larson, ed., *Myth in Indo-European Antiquity.* Berkeley: University of California Press. 1974, 18–29.

Toporov, V. N. "Avest. Thrita, Thraetaona, dr.ind. Trita i dr. i ich indo-evropejskie istoki." *Annali ca' Foscari* 16 (1977): 41–56.

———. "Parallels to Ancient Indo-Iranian Social and Mythological Concepts." In *Pratidānām. Indian, Iranian, and Indo-European Studies Presented to F. B. J. Kuiper on his 60th Birthday.* The Hague: Mouton (1968): 113–20.

Trubetzkoy, N. S. "Gedanken über das Indogermanenproblem." *Acta Linguistica* 1 (1939): 81–89.

Varenne, Jean. *Cosmogonies védiques.* Paris: Les Belles Lettres, 1982.

Wace. *La partie arthurienne du roman de Brut [de wace].* (Excerpt from a manuscript in Bibliothèque Nationale, 794). Edited by I. D. O. Arnold and M. M. Pelan. Paris: C. Klincksieck, 1962.

Wakeman, Mary K. *God's Battle with the Monster.* Leiden: E. J. Brill, 1973.

Walcot, Peter. "Cattle Raiding, Heroic Tradition and Ritual: The Greek Evidence." *History of Religion* 18 (1979): 326–51.

Williams, Frederick J. *Callimachus: Hymn to Apollo, a Commentary.* Oxford: Clarendon Press and New York: Oxford University Press, 1978.

Xella, Paolo. "Il dio siriano Kothar." In *Magia: Studi di Storia della Religioni in memoria di Raffaela Garossi.* Roma: Bulzoni (1976): 111–24.

ALAN DUNDES

MADNESS IN METHOD
PLUS A PLEA FOR
PROJECTIVE
INVERSION IN MYTH

MYTH AS A form of folk narrative has long fascinated scholars from a variety of academic disciplines including anthropology, classics, literature, philosophy, religion, among others. Yet the study of myth by folklorists tends to be virtually ignored by these would-be mythologists. Consequently, from a folkloristic perspective, most of these academic discussions of "myth" have little or nothing to do with myth in the strict and technical sense of the term. Even in volumes purportedly treating "myth and method" one will find essays treating folktales and legends, rather than myths. There is, of course, nothing inherently wrong with analyzing folktales and legends, or short stories or poems for that matter, but it is truly dismaying to folklorists to see such analyses wantonly labeled discussions of "myth."

The generic distinctions between myth, folktale, and legend have been standard among folklorists for at least two centuries, going back to the publications of the brothers Grimm, who published separate works on each of these genres.[1] For the folklorist, a myth is a sacred narrative explaining how the world and mankind came to be in their present form. Myths and legends (narratives told as true and set in the postcreation era) are different from folktales, which are narratives understood to be fictional, often introduced as such by an opening formula such as "Once upon a time." These generic distinctions are independent of dramatic personae. Thus it is possible to have a myth of the creation of Adam and Eve, but once these individuals are created, one can tell legends of these same individuals. Moreover, it is also possible to have folktales involving Adam and Eve.[2]

If we agree that a myth must minimumly involve a narrative, then we can dismiss all the references to "myth" as a synonym for error or fallacy. In popular as opposed to academic parlance, myth, like the word "folklore," is frequently used in this sense. The phrase "That's just folklore" or "That's a myth" means typically that the previously mentioned subject is an erroneous belief. Such usage is certainly worth noting, but it has nothing to do with the formal definition of myth as employed by folklorists.

Members of other academic disciplines may complain about what they perceive to be the narrowness and specificity of the folkloristic concept of myth. They claim the right to interpret the term "myth" any way they wish, even at the risk of inventing idiosyncratic definitions of the term. This is just fine as an illustration of free speech or poetic license, but such a practice has little to do with scholarship and intellectual rigor. Let me cite one or two examples of what I mean.

Little Red Riding Hood is a standard folktale. It is Aarne-Thompson tale-type 303, The Glutton (Red Riding Hood), and it is almost certainly related to Aarne-Thompson tale-type 123, The Wolf and the Kids, which is the same tale using exclusively animal characters.[3] It has been the subject of numerous analyses as it is quite a fascinating tale. In no way can the story be considered a sacred explanation of how the world or mankind came to be in their present form. Hence it is not a myth. Nor is it told as true. It is a fictional story set in no particular place and time—"Once upon a time" partly signals the timelessness of the plot. As it falls under the rubric of tales of magic (Aarne-Thompson tales 300 to 749), it is a particular kind of folktale, namely, a tale of magic, or fairy tale. (*Fairy tale*, the term of choice in English, is a misnomer inasmuch as fairies rarely if ever appear in fairy tales. Stories involving fairies—and other supernatural creatures—are usually told as true and are consequently legends.) No folklorist would call Little Red Riding Hood a "myth" any more than he or she would call Cinderella a myth. (Cinderella is Aarne-Thompson tale-type 510A, Cinderella.)[4]

Another all too common mislabeling occurs with respect to the story of Oedipus. Classicists, psychoanalysts, and others adamantly insist upon calling the Oedipus story a myth. Yet the story is *not* a sacred narrative offering an explanation of how the world and mankind came to be in their present form. It is the standard folktale, namely, Aarne-Thompson tale-type 931, Oedipus.[5]

One unfortunate result of the sloppiness of literary critics and anthropologists and others in claiming almost any narrative as a "myth" is that folklorists simply cannot trust the titles of books and articles allegedly concerned with the subject of myth. For example, if one examines *Recent Studies in Myths and Literature, 1970–1990*, one finds that more than half the entries have nothing whatever to do with myth in the folkloristic sense.[6] Most of these tend to refer to either themes or patterns, but definitely not myths.

In the absence of a proper myth-type index, folklorists usually refer to myths by motif number. The six volume *Motif-Index of Folk-Literature*, first published in 1932–1936 (second revised edition, 1955–58) employs letter prefixes to indicate motif categories.[7] A motifs are mythological motifs, B motifs are animal motifs, C motifs are taboo motifs, and so on. The system is not airtight and there is obviously overlap, as in the case of a myth involving an animal that breaks a taboo! Nevertheless, the A section of the *Motif-Index* does in effect constitute an inventory of the world's myths. Thus A 710, Creation of the sun, and A 740, Creation of the moon, would refer to narratives treating the origins of those celestial bodies. Folklorists expect fellow professionals to use motif designations when appropriate, and they deem writings amateurish that fail to do so. (The reader may note how many of the essays contained in this volume make use of motif numbers!)

Unlike the tale-type index, wherein all references following a tale-type number are assumed to be cognate—that is, historically or genetically related—the references grouped under a motif rubric may or may not be cognate. Any myth of the origin of death, for example, could in theory be labeled A 1335, Origin of death. Still, one can often get some sense of the geographic distribution of a particular myth (motif) from the *Motif-Index*. While on the subject of geographic distribution of myths, let me point out that even the most cursory examination of the various A motifs clearly demonstrates that *no motif is universal*. To my knowledge, there is not one single myth that is universal, "universal" meaning that it is found among every single people on the face of the earth, past and present. Indeed, myth scholarship clearly and conclusively proves that individual myths have their own particular circumscribed areas of geographical or cultural provenience.

Accordingly, there are Indo-European myths that are *not* found among native North or South American Indians; there are Asian-Amerind myths that are not found in Europe or Africa. So it is one thing to say that all peoples may have some myth allegedly explaining how death came into the world, but *it is not the same myth.* In Africa, for example, the most popular origin-of-death myth, according to Abrahamsson's superb 1951 monograph is "The Message that Failed."[8] This is motif A 1335.1 Origin of death from falsified message. The gist of this myth is that "God sends the chameleon to mankind with the message that they should have eternal life, and the lizard with the message that they must die. The chameleon dawdled on the way, and the lizard arrived first. When she had delivered her message, the matter was settled. The chameleon's message was no longer valid, and death had entered the world."[9]

This is quite different from the standard myth of the origin of death in Oceania. According to Anell's excellent survey, the most common story refers to how "primitive man in a bygone age could rejuvenate himself by changing his skin like a snake. In the usual version it is an old woman who is rejuvenated in this matter and subsequently reappears before her young children (grandchildren). They fail to recognize her in this young woman, however, and cry for their mother (grandmother) until she is forced to resume her old skin. This act, alas, leads to death for all mankind."[10] This is motif A 1335.4 Origin of death when early people put on new skins.

Neither the African perverted-message myth nor the Oceanic skin-renewal myths are to be found among the large corpus of native North American Indian origin-of-death myths.[11] The important theoretical point is that no one origin-of-death myth is found among all peoples. Different peoples have different myths!

The implications of the limited distribution of any of the world's inventory of myths should give pause to all those mythologists who espouse universalist or psychic unity theories. If there really were panhuman Jungian archetypes, then all peoples should in theory have the same myths. They do not! So how is it that dozens of literary scholars find credible the mystical and nonrational concept of Jungian archetypes? Without empirical evidence to support the notion of archetype, it is astounding to folklorists that so many writers on myth continue to advocate such an implausible theory.

It would take too long to demonstrate all the logical (not to say

psychological) flaws in the Jungian archetype, but let me cite just
a few of Jung's own words on the subject. Consider his double talk
on the issue of whether archetypes are "inherited." In a statement
made in August 1957, he said, "It is important to bear in mind
that my concept of the 'archetypes' has been frequently misunderstood as denoting inherited patterns of thought." Note his
clarification: "In reality they belong to the realm of the activities
of the instincts and in that sense they represent inherited forms
of psychic behavior."[12] Actually, in his famous essay "The Psychology of the Child Archetype," Jung's view is less garbled.
Speaking of "impersonal fantasies" "which cannot be reduced to
experiences in the individual's past," Jung maintains that "they
correspond to certain *collective* (and not personal) structural elements of the human psyche in general, and like the morphological elements of the human body, are inherited."[13]

I shall forebear commenting on the blatant ethnocentrism of
Jungian myth theory with its claim that Jesus Christ is an archetype![14] Keep in mind that archetypes are supposed to be panhuman, and as Jung says, "For the archetype, of course, exists a
priori."[15] Since archetypes are panhuman, and since Jesus Christ
is an archetype, then Jesus Christ is presumably part of *all*
people's collective unconscious. What hubris and arrogance in
such an assumption!

The real problem for mythologists comes from the difficulty in
applying Jungian theory to myth texts. The problem stems from
the fact that, according to Jung, archetypes are unknowable.
"Contents of an archetypal character are manifestations of processes in the collective unconscious. Hence they do not refer to
anything that is or has been conscious, but to something essentially unconscious. In the last analysis, therefore, it is impossible
to say what they refer to."[16] If the master of archetypes admits
that it is impossible to ascertain the referents of archetypes, then
how can lesser critics presume to do so? Jung continues, "If, then,
we proceed in accordance with the above principle, there is no
longer any question whether a myth refers to the sun or the
moon, the father or the mother. . . . The ultimate meaning of this
nucleus was never conscious and never will be."[17] I cannot im-
prove on this pessimistic statement. What amazes me is how serious scholars could possibly take this kind of vague approach as a
bona fide means of studying myth. It is vastly different from
Freud's approach to myth, which is utterly opposed to mysticism
and a know-nothing attitude. Freud believes that the unconscious

content of myth (and other forms of folklore) is knowable, and it is precisely the task of the mythologist to decipher that content.

Most folklorists refuse to consider either Jung or Freud when analyzing myth texts. They prefer to avoid dealing with the unconscious content of myths; instead they employ every means possible to avoid confronting that content. Whether it is motifing the texts, or mapping a myth's geographical distribution and guessing at possible paths of diffusion, or deconstructing a text into its structural constituents, any method of myth analysis is preferable to coming to grips with the highly human content of myths.

One reason why Freudian theory can be used in myth analysis (whereas Jungian theory cannot) is that it is possible to reconcile some Freudian theory with cultural relativism. With Jungian pan-human archetypes (Jung refers as follows to them: "the archetype—let us never forget this—is a psychic organ present in all of us")[18] there is no place for the intervention of culture and cultural differences. Archetypes are basically precultural givens. In contrast to the Freudian notions of symbolism, displacement, condensation, and projection, one can add the dimension of culture.

If we assume, for example, that there may be a correlation between patterns of infantile conditioning in a culture with adult-projective systems in that same culture (including folklore, film, literature, and the like), then to the extent that infantile conditioning differs from culture to culture, there could and should be different adult-projective systems. And that is precisely what the empirical data suggest. Different cultures have different myths; and different cultures have different norms of infantile conditioning (with respect to weaning, toilet training, etc.). In any case, a possible correlation between infantile conditioning and adult-projective systems in a given culture is certainly knowable. One can examine infantile conditioning *and* the adult-projective systems in a culture, and either there is a demonstrable correlation or there is not. It is not a question of dealing with something that "was never conscious and never will be."

I should like to indicate very briefly the utility of Freudian theory to the analysis of myth by distinguishing projection from what I call projective inversion. Simple projection, in my view, consists of displacing an individual psychological configuration directly onto another plane or into a different arena. It is roughly analogous to shining a light behind shadow puppets (or the fingers of a hand) to "project" an image or shadow on a wall or screen or other surface. Stellar constellations in the heavens, if perceived as mythological gestalt figures (often involving myths) would be an illustration of simple projection. A human drama is projected to the heavens such that heavenly bodies enact or play out the problems of human bodies here on earth. (Is it just a coincidence that in Western cosmology the earth is situated between the planets Venus [love] and Mars [war]?) Sex and violence are surely earthly or earthy matters.

Perhaps a more striking example of projection in myth is found in the World parents myth. The basic myth is motif A 625 World parents: sky-father and earth-mother as parents of the universe. The sky-father descends upon the earth-mother and begets the world. This is a widespread myth, but it is not universal. Consider motif A 625.1 Heaven-mother–earth-father. The World-parents myth would appear to be a celestial projection of one of the more common forms of human sexual intercourse, a form that also reflects male dominance: man on top, woman on the bottom. But the more interesting projection occurs in motif A 625.2 Raising of the sky. In this widespread myth, a male culture hero (= son) pushes the sky-father upward, off the earth-mother to make room for mankind. Even a non-Freudian ought to be able to see the possible Oedipal implications of that myth.

What I term *projective inversion* differs from straightforward projection inasmuch as a reversal or inversion takes place. The terminology difficulty arises from the fact that it is this latter psychological process that Freud and his followers called "projection." In Freud's terms, the "proposition 'I hate him' becomes transformed by *projection* into another one: 'He *hates* (persecutes) me, which will justify me in hating him.'"[19] An individual's view of hate or dislike, for example, are supposedly projected outward onto the object of hate or dislike. In this way, subject and object exchange places. I think this transformational principle was a brilliant insight and further that it has enormous relevance to the study of myth content. Otto Rank illustrated it beautifully in his classic *The Myth of the Birth of the Hero*.[20] Using Oedipal theory, Rank argues convincingly that sons want to get rid of their fathers (in order to marry their mothers) but as this is a taboo thought, the narrative projection transforms this wish into the invariable attempt by the fathers to get rid of their sons.[21] Inasmuch as the majority of Rank's narrative illustrations come from folktales (such as Oedipus) or legends (such as Romulus and Siegfried), it is clear that the device of projection, or what I prefer to call projective inversion, occurs in narrative genres other than myth. Curiously enough, Rank fails to interpret the detail of the father's refusal to give his daughter to any of her suitors in the same way, instead understanding it literally from the father's perspective (as wishing to retain his daughter for himself). If Rank were consistent (keep in mind that most of the early Freudians did *not* understand women as well as they understood men), he might have realized that the father's keeping his daughter for himself could have been a projective inversion of the daughter's (Electral) wish to keep her father for herself![22] The point here is that I do think there is a critical distinction between straightforward one-to-one projection, as to the heavens, and projective inversion, a distinction that is in many ways analogous to the literal-versus-symbolic approaches to myth. Simple projection would be parallel to a literal approach while projective inversion would be parallel to a symbolic approach.

In a previous study I have sought to utilize projective inversion as a means of explaining the puzzling blood-libel legend in which the Jews were said to murder Christian infants so as to extract their blood to use in making matzohs. Jews are forbidden to eat blood whereas Christians are encouraged to do so, especially via partaking of the Eucharist.[23] I have argued that Christians have displaced any guilt arising from their cannibalistic eating of the blood and body of Jesus Christ through a legend involving projective inversion: by means of this inversion it is no longer Christians eating the blood-body of a Jew (Jesus) but Jews eating the blood-body of a Christian sacrificial victim![24] Let me add that without invoking the transformational principle of projective inversion, the blood-libel legend remains an enigmatic, bizarre, and virtually incomprehensible plot in terms of normal logic. These examples suggest that projective inversion can indeed be applied to the content of tales and legends. The question is, Can projective inversion also illuminate myths?

In the Old Testament there are two distinct creation myths that recount the origin of man. In the first chapter of the Book of Genesis, we find what might be termed the *simultaneous* creation of man and woman. Genesis 1:27 reads: "So God created man in his own image, in the image of God created he him; male and female created he them." Less egalitarian is the myth found in the second chapter of Genesis. First in 2:7 we are told "And the Lord God formed man of the dust of the ground, and breathed into his nostrils the breath of life; and man became a living soul." And then after God planted a garden in Eden, placed man there, instructed man not to eat of the tree of the knowledge of good and evil, and after the man, Adam, named all the animals, then and only then did God begin a totally separate creation of woman. According to Genesis 2:21 and 22: "And the Lord God caused a deep sleep to fall upon Adam, and he slept; and he took one of his ribs, and closed up the flesh instead thereof. And the rib, which the Lord God had taken from man, made he a woman, and brought her unto the man."

The first part of the second myth is a version of motif A 1241. Man made from clay (earth) while the second part is motif A 1275.1 Creation of first woman from man's rib. The second myth clearly implies a *sequential* (as opposed to *simultaneous*) creation inasmuch as man has to be created prior to woman if his rib is to be used in that creative act. Both second-creation myths reflect a strong undeniable male bias. In the first portion we have a typical male creation myth involving the creation of the world or man from feces or fecal substitute (clay, earth, dust). Men trying to compete with women who are apparently magically able to create new life from their bodies have to resort to cloacal creation in order to create new life from *their* inadequate bodies. In the second portion the very order of creation implies social priority: man first, woman second! This male bias is entirely consistent with the notion of a *male* god as creator, and a male savior figure, Noah, who in a re-creation myth builds a male womb (ark) that floats for approximately nine months. (It is noteworthy in this context that Mrs. Noah doesn't even merit having a name!) In Noahian Arkeology, we have an echo or reverberation of the male creation myths of Genesis 1:27, and 2:7, 21–22. All this may be persuasive in the light of feminist ideology, but what about projective inversion? Can it be applied to these two myths of creation or not?

In the second myth, we see an articulation of the male wish to procreate like females. How do females procreate? From their bodies. In biological reality, man comes from woman's body. In the fantasy world of mythical reality, biology is reversed. It is woman who comes from man's body. Moreover, inasmuch as biology dictates that man comes specifically from the woman's genital area, the reversal would logically have woman coming from man's genital area. That is why it is almost certainly the missing bone in man, the *os baculum* that is the likely *fons et origo* of woman. The penis bone is found among a number of animals, a fact no doubt observed by early hunters who slaughtered such animals for food. The first recorders of the biblical narratives would not easily include narratives involving a penis bone and so the euphemistic dodge of substituting a rib bone instead was doubtless employed.[25] There are few texts in print from any culture exemplifying motif A 1263.6 Man created from culture hero's genitals (but the very existence of the motif at all makes this hypothetical interpretation plausible). The inevitable censorship difficulties involved in translating oral tradition into writing or print could account for the dearth of such texts. In the Bible, we know that euphemisms were frequently employed. When Abraham asks his eldest servant to swear an oath, he instructs that servant "Put, I pray thee, thy hand under my thigh" (Genesis 24:2). If one swears by something holy, then it was very likely the male genitals, not the thigh, on which the oath was sworn through placement of the hands. This is signaled even in contemporary times by the words "testify" and "testimony" (from *testes*) and even the word *Testament* itself. In any event, it is the principle of projective inversion that allows us to propose such a hypothetical reading of the second myth of the creation of woman.

Returning now to the first myth, we recall "So God created man in his own image," which would strongly suggest a very anthropomorphic deity fully equipped with ears, eyes, nose, mouth, and so on. If man were created in God's image, then one could logically assume that God must look very much like man does. However, armed with the principle of projective inversion, we can understand that it was not God who created man in his image, but rather man who created God in *his* image! So just as a patriarchal society demanded that normal biology be contravened through myth—by creating a male myth whereby woman was said to come from man's body, so the male invention of a male deity (to justify and fortify a male-oriented society) can be denied or concealed by constructing a male myth whereby it is a male deity who creates males in his image. Myth once created and accepted as dogma or truth is not easily overturned.

The long-term effects of these two instances of male-inspired projective inversions in the form of two separate creation myths in Genesis are indisputable. They constitute in large measure the "sociological charters for belief" (in Malinowski's words) in a male-dominated society.[26] The belief in such a society is bolstered by the assumed existence of a male deity as well as a myth which claims that woman was created secondarily, almost as an afterthought. When fantasy is elevated to the level of myth, it becomes a force to be reckoned with. Thus the principle of projective inversion can add a new dimension to the burgeoning feminist literature on myth. The power and deleterious impact of these two myths in Genesis continue unabated, and it is hard to gauge just how long it will take to undo the social damage and mental anguish of Western women caused directly or indirectly by these two fundamental myths in Genesis.

Notes

1. For a useful delineation of these three genres, see William Bascom, "The Forms of Folklore," 3–20. For further definitions of these genres as well as numerous subgenres, see Laurits Bødker, *Folk Literature (Germanic)*.
2. All tale-type numbers cited come from Aarne and Thompson, *The Types of the Folktale*. For this tale in particular, see Geddes, *Various Children of Eve*.
3. For details, see Dundes, *Little Red Riding Hood: A Casebook*.
4. Dundes, *Cinderella: A Casebook*.
5. Edmunds and Dundes, *Oedipus: A Folklore Casebook*.
6. Accardi et al. *Recent Studies in Myths and Literature 1970–1990*.
7. Thompson, *Motif-Index of Folk-Literature*.
8. Abrahamson, *The Origin of Death: Studies in African Mythology*, 4–34.
9. Ibid., 4.
10. Anell, "The Origin of Death according to the Traditions in Oceania," 1.
11. For surveys of native American origin-of-death myths, see Boas, "The Origin of Death," 486–91, and Dangel, "Mythen vom Ursprung des Todes bei den Indianern Nordamerikas," 341–74.
12. Jung, Preface, in de Laszlo, *Psyche & Symbol*, xvi.
13. Jung, "The Psychology of the Child Archetype," in Jung and Kerényi, *Essays on a Science of Mythology*, 74.
14. Jung, "Aion," in *Psyche & Symbol*, 36.
15. Ibid., 15.
16. Jung, "The Psychology of the Child Archetype," 75.
17. Ibid.
18. Ibid., 79.
19. Freud, "Psycho-Analytic Notes upon an Autobiographical Account of a Case of Paranoia," 449. For representative discussions of "projection," see Bellak, "On the Problems of the Concept of Projection," in Abt and Bellak, *Projective Psychology*, 7–32; and Lindzey, *Projective Techniques and Cross-Cultural Research*, 25–31. Rycroft in his *A Critical Dictionary of Psycho-Analysis*, 125–26, includes both types of projection under the same rubric noting only that "reversal" occurs more frequently.
20. Rank, *The Myth of the Birth of the Hero* was first published in 1909.
21. Ibid., 78.
22. Ibid., 80. For an Electral interpretation, see Dundes, "To Love My Father All: A Psychoanalytical Study of the Folktale Source of *King Lear*," in Dundes, *Interpreting Folklore*, 211–22.
23. Dundes, "The Ritual Murder or Blood Libel Legend," in Dundes, *The Blood Libel Legend: A Casebook in Anti-Semitic Folklore*, 336–76.
24. Ibid., 354–59.

25. Dundes, "Couvade in Genesis," in Dundes, *Parsing through Customs,* 145–66.
26. Malinowski, *Magic, Science and Religion,* 144.

Works Cited

Aarne, Antti, and Stith Thompson. *The Types of the Folktale.* 2d rev. FF Communications no. 184. Helsinki: Academia Scientiarum Fennica, 1961.

Abrahamsson, Hans. *The Origin of Death: Studies in African Mythology, Studia Ethnographica Upsaliensia* 3. Uppsala: Almqvist and Wiksells, 1951.

Abt, Lawrence Edwin, and Leopold Bellak, eds. *Projective Psychology.* New York: Alfred A. Knopf, 1950.

Accardi, Bernard, David J. Charlson, Frank A. Doden, Richard F. Hardin, Sung Ryol Kim, Sonya J. Lancaster, and Michael H. Shaw, comps. *Recent Studies in Myths and Literature, 1970–1990: An Annotated Bibliography.* New York: Greenwood Press, 1991.

Anell, Bengt. "The Origin of Death according to the Traditions in Oceania." *Studia Ethnographica Upsaliensia* 20 (1964): 1–32.

Bascom, William. "The Forms of Folklore: Prose Narratives." *Journal of American Folklore* 78 (1965): 3–20.

Boas, Franz. "The Origin of Death." *Journal of American Folklore* 30 (1917): 486–91.

Bødker, Laurits. *Folk Literature (Germanic).* Copenhagen: Rosenkilde and Bagger, 1965.

Dangel, R. "Mythen vom Ursprung des Todes bei den Indianern Nordamerikas." *Mitteilungen der Anthropologischen Gesellschaft in Wien* 58 (1928), 341–74.

De Laszlo, Violet S., ed. *Psyche and Symbol: A Selection from the Writings of C. G. Jung.* Garden City: Doubleday Anchor Books, 1958.

Dundes, Alan, ed. *The Blood Libel Legend: A Casebook in Anti-Semitic Folklore.* Madison: University of Wisconsin Press, 1991.

———. *Cinderella: A Casebook.* Madison: University of Wisconsin Press, 1988.

———. *Interpreting Folklore.* Bloomington: Indiana University Press, 1980.

———. *Little Red Riding Hood: A Casebook.* Madison: University of Wisconsin Press, 1989.

———. *Parsing through Customs: Essays by a Freudian Folklorist.* Madison: University of Wisconsin Press, 1987,

Edmunds, Lowell, and Alan Dundes, eds. *Oedipus: A Folklore Casebook.* New York: Garland, 1983.

Freud, Sigmund. "Psycho-Analytic Notes upon an Autobiographical Account of a Case of Paranoia (Dementia Paranoides)." In Sigmund Freud, *Collected Papers*, vol. 3. New York: Basic Books, 1959, 387–470.

Geddes, Virginia G. *"Various Children of Eve" (AT 758): Cultural Variants and Antifeminine Images.* Uppsala: Etnologiska Institutionen, 1986.

Jung, C. G., and C. Kerényi. *Essays on a Science of Mythology.* New York: Harper Torchbooks, 1963.

Lindzey, Gardner. *Projective Techniques and Cross-Cultural Research.* New York: Appleton-Century-Crofts, 1961.

Malinowski, Bronislaw. *Magic, Science and Religion.* Garden City: Doubleday Anchor Books, 1954.

Rank, Otto. *The Myth of the Birth of the Hero.* New York: Vintage Books, 1959.

Rycroft, Charles. *A Critical Dictionary of Psycho-Analysis.* New York: Basic Books, 1968.

Thompson, Stith. *Motif-Index of Folk-Literature.* 6 vols. 2d rev. ed. Bloomington: Indiana University Press, 1955–58.

PART III

A HISTORY WITHOUT STRUCTURE AND A STRUCTURE WITHOUT HISTORY: MYTH AND CULTURAL TRADITIONS

BRUCE LINCOLN

MYTHIC NARRATIVE AND CULTURAL DIVERSITY IN AMERICAN SOCIETY

AMONG THE MANY things I learned from Mircea Eliade is that the lives of cultures and individuals are shaped in significant measure by the stories they tell, particularly those of their origins. Although I have come to differ from my teacher and friend on any number of points—particularly on such questions as where these stories come from, what it is they reveal, and whose interests they serve—on this fundamental point we remain in full agreement. The following study picks up on the characteristic Eliadean concern with myths of beginnings and their ritual repetition, but pursues it in some non-Eliadean directions, focusing on a set of rituals and narratives more secular than sacred, and indicating the ways they are involved in the ongoing reconstruction, renegotiation, and sometimes even the violent alteration of the social groups who preserve and celebrate them. As an *exemplum* of these processes, I propose to treat a set of narratives within a narrative: the stories told on and about Thanksgiving by the Krichinsky family in Barry Levinson's wistfully autobiographical film *Avalon*.

As the film opens, the sky is illuminated by fireworks as a sonorous and richly accented voice begins to recount a familiar story: a story of beginnings and a creation myth of sorts. "I came to America in 1914, by way of Philadelphia. That's where I got off the boat."[1] As the voice continues, the camera pans slowly downward from the rockets' red glare past a neon-illuminated arch and finally comes to rest on the face of an eager young man, heavily mustached and smiling broadly, as he strides into the flag-lined arcade that will lead him to a new life in a new country. "And then I came to Baltimore. It was the most beautiful place you've ever seen in your life. There were lights everywhere. What lights they had. It was a celebration of lights. I thought it was for me. 'Sam was in America. Sam was in America.'"

The camera follows Sam as he wanders through the cobblestone streets of his promised city, pausing to gaze with appreciation and wonder at a host of American icons: a brass eagle, a miniature Statue of Liberty, a figure of Washington atop a high column, a plaque to Francis Scott Key, and a strolling incarnation of Uncle Sam, to whom this other, more recently and less fully Americanized Sam respectfully tips his hat, for all that his gesture goes unacknowledged. Everywhere he encounters the trappings of celebration: joyous crowds, star-spangled banners, red, white, and blue bunting, Roman candles, sparklers, and high-arching rockets. "I didn't know what holiday it was, but there were lights and I walked under them. There were fireworks and people cheered. What a welcome it was. What a welcome."

Lost and alone, Sam shows not a trace of timidity or apprehension, only eagerness for his quest and for the rich new world that opens to receive him. A guide appears, almost magically: a gnomish old man, who knows Sam's name and destination—a man who knows, moreover, on the strength of sustained professional experience, what it is like to walk in another man's shoes. "And I said, 'What a country is this! What a country! The wealthy don't even have to break in their own shoes.'" Finally, the hero of our narrative is led to the fabled castle of Avalon, where in other times the wounded Arthur came in quest of healing, and here his journey is crowned in success. From the turret above, his four lost brothers appear. They beckon warmly, and the family is reunited in love and celebration, just as heaven and earth are themselves connected by the mystic tower of Avalon. The camera cuts from a low angle shot of the brothers above to a reverse angle of Sam below, then pans back upward to the fireworks in the sky, and finally the image dissolves into a wisp of smoke that curls from the cigar of this very same man some thirty five years later, as Sam Krichinsky—the fictive embodiment of Levinson's beloved grandfather—tells the story with obvious relish in the moments before three generations of the Krichinsky clan will sit down to Thanksgiving dinner. "And that's when I came to America. It was the Fourth of July."

The camera shows the Krichinsky children enraptured by Sam's narration, but soon it is obvious that others find his story less captivating. Left to his own devices, Sam will go on to recount how the five Krichinsky brothers became wallpaper hangers; how they worked as musicians on weekends; how he met his wife, how beautiful she was, and how they fell in love; how the brothers organized a circle of mutual support, and brought relatives over from the old country; how his eldest brother, William, took sick and died. Given the slightest encouragement, he will add other chapters still, filled with details that strike everyone—save him—as trivial or banal, and he is also capable of segueing effortlessly into a host of densely interwoven but equally tangential narratives, such as the Horatio Algeresque tale of how the little man who broke in other people's shoes went on to become rich and famous. Not everyone is enthralled or infinitely patient, however. Among those given to impatience with Sam's rambling monologue is Eva, his long-suffering wife.

> Eva: Sam, how many times do we have to hear this story? They know this story. They heard it before. We all heard it before.
> Sam: If we don't tell the kids, they don't know . . .
> Eva: Sam, how many times do we have to hear this story? The children know the story.
> Sam: I'm telling them about when I came to America.
> Eva: Yeah, we know about it. We all heard it before.

In this moment of extraordinarily astute literary and social criticism, Eva offers us the finest definition of myth that I have yet to encounter. Myths, I would suggest, following her lead and that of Paul Veyne, are the stories that everyone knows and the stories that everyone has heard before. I would hasten to add that the nature of this "everyone" is a good deal more problematic than Eva indicates, since the people encompassed by this term participate within the social entity so designated only in imperfect and uneven fashion.[2] Granted, there are things they share that make them part of the group, but they also have their differences, which are capable of tearing it apart. Moreover, if we listen to Eva more closely, we find that this "everyone" is virtually interchangeable with "we," and both of these lexical markers index three groups that are logically separable but in this instance—and not coincidentally—happen to be coterminous. These are: (1) all the members of the Krichinsky family; (2) all those who will share the Thanksgiving dinner; and (3) all those who are "familiar" with the story, in the strict sense that their relation to it that is of a familial nature. And at this point, I want to suggest it is this story, this myth—or, more precisely, the memories embedded in the story and the sentiments it evokes in its hearers—that creates and recreates the Krichinsky family, just as the family creates and recreates the story with every successive telling.

In this example we can observe a moment of triadic co-definition: one of many moments in which a social group, a set of ritual performances, and a set of mythic narratives produce one another. This particular group of people comes to this particular Thanksgiving dinner and listens to this particular story because they are members of one family, a family that is not only defined but actively constructed through the stories they tell and the ceremonies they share. Moreover, these occasions are important, in large measure, precisely because they provide the opportunity to share the stories that actively remind their hearers of what holds them together and makes them who and what they are.

The temptation to stop telling a story, of course, is always present. Eva's remarks—"Sam, how many times do they have to hear this story?"—signals how annoying the repetitiousness of myths can be. Indeed, myths are the kind of stories that captivate everyone at first and bore them later, but remain capable of captivating them once again in new, different, and deeper ways. Being important, a myth gets repeated; being repeated, it gets tedious; being tedious, it gets ignored; and being ignored—but still important—it has to be repeated again. Through repetition it also becomes a collective narrative: a story in which all members of a group participate, albeit in varying ways that reflect (and define) the nature of their position within the group.

Those who tell such stories most often and those who are most fully captivated by them tend also to be those who stand at the head of the group, who believe most deeply in the group and in its myths (although sometimes it is a group's most manipulative and cynical members who become its narrators and leaders). On the other hand, classically, it is those who are just being socialized into a group as well as those who already belong to it most fully and unambiguously who constitute the most attentive and most appreciative audience for a mythic narration: children, for whom the story is most fresh, and elders, for whom it is most reassuring and comfortable. Others—adolescents, for example, or those who have married into the group (e.g., Eva)—are apt to be a good deal more detached and/or critical.

Those who recount such narratives generally understand their task as something both serious and playful, terribly easy at one level but also difficult in the extreme. Given that the stories are good—as they usually are, for as collective products they have been polished slowly and lovingly over the course of many tellings—it is a simple enough matter to attract and delight those who have not heard them before or for whom they are not yet familiar. Things are different, however, with those who know the stories well, for not only are they likely to find the contents tiresome from time to time, but they are equally likely to pounce on a narrator whose version compares unfavorably with others they have heard or one who introduces too many novelties into a story over which they share proprietary rights. For they rightly regard such a story as being "theirs" in a multiple sense: not only does it belong to them, it is also about them and it makes them who and what they are. Through their ability to correct and to criticize at any moment, they check the ability of a given narrator to embellish or to deviate, thereby protecting their story from the whims of any individual's forgetfulness, embroidery, or self-serving imagination. Moreover, it is just this kind of audience involvement that ensures the story is and remains a collective product: indeed, it is the product of that collective which is itself a product of the story.

Like many myths—I think, for instance, of the biblical Exodus account, Virgil's *Aeneid*, and the "wandering myths" told by the indigenous peoples of Australia—Sam's narrative describes a marvelous voyage and a discovery of fundamental importance. It speaks of a passage from one state of being to another, and it tells its hearers how it is they came to occupy the land they now inhabit, assuring them that this process, while arduous, was good, proper, and just. The story tells them not only *that* they belong but *where* and with *whom*. Other peoples' myths do the same things for them, but neither the stories nor their effects and consequences are readily transferable from one group to another, notwithstanding the claims of those scholars and others who speak all too glibly about the "universality" of myths.

To be sure, every group has its myths, although they do not always call them such, the word *myth* having acquired pejorative connotations ever since Plato felt the need to demolish the authority of narrative discourse in order to establish that of syllogistic argumentation. There are stories, however, that continue to command this kind of authority, notwithstanding the philosophers' best efforts, although these authoritative tales now tend to be called by some term other than myth: *history, tradition,* and *revelation* have long been popular choices in different circles, and *master narratives* has more recently become fashionable. But by whatever appellation they may assume, these are the stories through which groups accomplish the task of sociocultural reproduction by inscribing their values and sense of shared identity on those who are its members-in-the-making so that they will come to know and remember just who they are and just where they belong.

Insofar as one group differs from another, so will their myths, and insofar as the groups have certain similarities, in the same measure will their myths share common features. Thus, by stressing the extent to which their myths resemble one another, the members of different groups may draw closer together, just as they can maintain or increase their sense of estrangement by stressing the differences that exist in the stories they tell. I am attracted to the Krichinsky family myth, I realize, not for its intrinsic appeal or universal contents, but in large measure because its themes and structures closely resemble those of the stories that occasionally graced my own family's Thanksgiving celebrations. Yet in all of their significant details—the dates, the places, the focal incidents, and the names of the characters—my family's myths differ from those of the Krichinsky clan, and it is these specific differences that make us members of different families, for if I grew up hearing Sam's stories and not those my own grandparents told, I would be a Krichinsky and not a Lincoln. Insofar as our two stories do resemble each other, however, and insofar as we attend to their similarities, the Krichinskys and the Lincolns may come to understand themselves as part of a more nebulous and less cohesive group that exists at a higher level of integration than that of either family, for we—like others who tell similar tales—are Americans of Russian Jewish descent, whose ancestors came to the United States in the period before the First World War.

More distant to me than the Krichinsky myth is a set of stories to which I was introduced in school and in books, which celebrated the arrival of other groups to these shores: stories of Columbus, Vespucci, Cortés, Pizarro, Henry Hudson, Miles Standish, Capt. John Smith, Peter Stuyvesant, William Penn, Lord Baltimore, et al. In ways, of course, our stories are similar, for the stories of all American people—save those of the first—begin with the account of a voyage that transformed them from something else (Spaniards, Dutch, Africans, Irish, Italians, Armenians, Mexicans, Cubans, Vietnamese, Cambodians) into hyphenated ethnic-Americans of one sort or another and, in a few privileged cases, into Americans *tout court.*

Beyond the matter of names, dates, and points of departure—the importance of which is clear enough, and may be stressed for strategic advantage—there is another way in which some of these stories differ quite strongly from others, for in the course of their narration, all stories of passage must eventually describe the people that their protagonists encountered upon their arrival in the new land: people who preceded them in their voyage and who may therefore have been thought to possess older and better claims to that land. All manner of relations are possible with these predecessors, and I want to sketch out some of the possibilities that have been actualized at the interconnected levels of historic occurrence, narrative representation, and recurring attitudes and practice.

First, consider the original wave of European immigrants, those who made the passage to North America in the sixteenth, seventeenth, and eighteenth centuries and encountered the indigenous peoples of the Americas, whom they drove back militarily, justifying this expansion in and through heroic, imperialist, and racist stories in which the predecessors were systematically depicted as savages, heathens, and obstacles to be cleared. These stories differ significantly from the ones that treat the experiences of the next groups, who came in the nineteenth and early twentieth centuries from parts of Europe farther to the south and the east than did those in the first wave. In this set of stories, the voyagers of the first wave reappear, although they now figure as the predecessors—the "real Yankees"—whom the immigrants of the second wave encountered upon their arrival and whose language, dress, customs, and manners they struggled to assimilate. For the "greenhorn" protagonists of these tales understood and represented themselves as the social, cultural, and economic inferiors of their predecessors, and the tales told of them are more often comic than heroic, albeit a comedy tinged with great sadness.

The tales of passage that black Americans tell can focus on the forced voyage from Africa to southern plantations or on the later and only slightly less difficult passage from the postbellum South to northern metropolises. In such narratives, their white predecessors figure as people it was neither possible nor desirable to emulate or oppose openly but as oppressors and adversaries one could overcome by evading, defying, or outwitting them. Accordingly, the genres that predominate are tales of tricksters and outlaws, which celebrate ingenuity, resilience, and the skills and strategies of resistance.

Were I more knowledgeable, I would want to say something about the myths that Hispanic- and Asian-Americans have to tell, but it would be foolhardy for me to try. Accordingly, let me speak briefly about the stories that some Indians (e.g., the Navajo, Hopi, and Lakota) tell of how their ancestors took a journey that was vertical rather than horizontal and emerged from a subterranean realm onto the face of this land where they too encountered predecessors. These, however, were not humans, as in the other stories described above, but monsters, and more often animals, who are described as noble and powerful beings with whom the protagonists learned—to their mutual benefit—to co-exist in balanced, respectful, and mutually supportive relations. And if I have to characterize the genre of these stories, as I have for the others, I would not hesitate to call them romances. Indians also tell stories of conflict and hardship, of course, but the antagonists who figure in these stories are not any people whom they regard as their predecessors on this land but rather those who came later and regarded them as such.

It is possible to speak of all these materials as American myths and to see in them a general narrative pattern insofar as they all describe an originary voyage made by a set of primordial ancestors and the encounters those people had with others, whom they found already resident in this land. Yet the instant we move beyond this general and artificial plot summary and attempt to infuse some measure of narrative specificity into what is, in truth, a fairly bland and insipid outline, we begin to produce a story that can no longer be told by or about *all* Americans but only some. And the more specificity we introduce by adding names, dates, places, significant incidents, and the like, the smaller—but also the more coherent and cohesive—is the group whose historic experience, focal values, general outlook, and sense of social identity are encoded within and transmitted through that story. Different stories do not just characterize or belong to different groups, but help to create and sustain those groups. And rival versions of a story do the same for group factions, which remain bound together only as long as they care enough to dispute the details of the narratives they share.

With this, let us return to the Krichinskys. In particular, it is worth noting that when Sam speaks to the children, he tells them *his* story, but he does not presume to speak for his brothers, Gabriel, Nathan, or Hymie, all of whom have their own stories to tell. And when the full family is united at the festal table, the brothers do not speak of themselves; rather, they speak of their father. With this shift to a different generational level, they move away from their separate stories to those in which they all share interest and to which they all have an equally proprietary claim.

Others also enter the conversation at this time, including the women and the children of the Krichinsky family. All who participate speak from their own knowledge and from their own situation of interest. Occasionally they criticize, question, and heckle their relatives, who tell—and remember—things in a different way, while those so challenged show a praiseworthy capacity to rethink and revise their narratives in collaborative fashion. Generally, the exchanges are good-natured, but occasionally one glimpses the tensions and potential lines of rupture that run beneath the surface of Krichinsky conviviality.

Sam: Time to tell the kids about when my father came to America.

Anne (his daughter-in-law): Can't it wait till later?

Sam: The kids should hear this story. . . . We brought my father over in '25.

Gabriel (skeptically): '25?

Sam: William died in 1919. Hmmm. (He counts on his fingers). It was '25.

Gabriel: '25? It was later than '25.

Sam: He came the same year we brought Berle and Edith over.

Gabriel (emphatic): Berle and Edith came after!

Sam: After?

Gabriel: Yeah, after!!!

Sam (he pauses): It was '26.

Jules (Sam's son): Dad, Gabriel, what's the difference? He came to America, right?

Gabriel (insistent): It's a big difference between '25 and '26. One's '25 and the other's '26.

Jules: All's I'm saying is, *who cares* if it was '25 or '26?

Sam: Shhhh. Jules, Jules, if you stop remembering, you forget. (Pause. The camera comes in for a close-up). It was '26. I remember the excitement when we went to meet him.

Here we can see the incipient fault line dividing Sam's branch of the family from Gabriel's, and one between the generations. Although Sam hosts the celebration and presides at table, Gabriel, as the eldest, periodically feels the need to assert his authority. Usually, he does so by arriving late and forcing the others to wait for him before serving dinner, a practice they grudgingly accept. In the conversation quoted above, he challenges Sam more directly. Most immediately, Gabriel contests the date Sam gives for their father's arrival; beyond that, he disputes Sam's right to provide a definitive version of their common creation myth.

Sensing the danger in this moment, Jules moves to reconcile his father and uncle. At one level, the force of his intervention is to minimize the importance of their disagreement. But in doing this, he asserts that the story's details hold little interest for the younger Krichinskys, with an insouciance in which his elders perceive hints of irreverence, even disloyalty, for which he is gently rebuked. For the moment, however, all breaches are papered over as Sam stresses the importance of preserving the story whole and accurate, then graciously accedes to Gabriel's correction.[3] Other details of the narrative are then filled in, revisions raucously offered, pondered, and ratified. Finally, glasses are raised and healths drunk, as the unity of the family is not just celebrated, but actively recreated.

Avalon goes on to show two other Thanksgivings. The first of these comes after several eventful years have passed. In the interim, Jules has gone into business with his cousin Izzy (Hymie's son) and becomes extremely successful. The tokens of this are manifest: Jules dresses better, takes up golf, Americanizes his name from Krichinsky to Kaye, and he and his partner move their families to the suburbs. Sam and Eva go with them, but the other Krichinskys remain in town. The growing estrangement between the two branches is thus simultaneously socioeconomic, cultural, and emotional, but most obviously it is marked by the spatial distance between city and suburbs.[4] Tensions come to a head on the first Thanksgiving after the move, when Gabriel is even later than usual and the children start asking: "When can we eat?"

Sam: Gabriel should be here any minute.
Eva: That man would be late for his own funeral. (*General hoots and laughter.*)

Jules (*standing by the turkey and trying to get Sam's attention*):
    Dad . . . Dad . . . Dad, why don't we eat? (*Cheers.*)
Kids: I wanna eat. Yeah, I'm hungry.
Nathan: No, no, no, no. We should wait for Gabriel.
Sam: We should wait for Gabriel
Jules: Every year we have to go through the same thing. We can't
    cut the turkey because of Gabriel.
Sam (*close-up, and with a flourish*): Jules—Cut the turkey!!!

Over the course of this discussion, the camera pans from fid-
gety children to tense mothers whose desire to oblige their hungry offspring is held in check by the family's ethos and tradition.
It is this ethos and tradition that Jules now challenges, as leader
of the younger generation. Essentially, he urges that the needs of
the young be met and the privileges of the old curtailed. And
when Sam endorses this inversionary call, we experience it as
nothing less than a moment of liberation. Our happiness, however, is as short lived as that of the Krichinskys. A few minutes
later Gabriel and his wife enter, register shock, pain, and indigna-
tion, then storm out, with Sam in hot pursuit. At the curbside
they pause, and Gabriel makes his case.

Gabriel: You cut the turkey! It took us hours to get here. You live
    miles from nowhere. It's too far, for God's sake! Too far for
    relatives. You've got new relatives: relatives who live near you
    and who you wait for!
Sam (*soothingly*): Gabriel, for God's sake, let's not make an issue
    out of the turkey.
Gabriel: You know what it is? That's what happens when you get
    to be wealthy. You've got a wealthy son, so you don't even
    wait for your brother until you cut the turkey. The hell with
    you!
Sam: To hell with me?
Gabriel: Yes!
Sam: Jules making a good living has nothing to do with when we
    cut the turkey. Nothing.
Gabriel: When we lived in Avalon, nobody ate. You wait for every-
    one before you eat, much less cut the turkey without a
    brother! You move out here to the suburbs, and you think it
    doesn't matter any more?
Sam: The young ones are hungry. They carry on. They make a com-

motion. What do you want to do—stand on ceremony with
the family?

Gabriel: There's always young ones. There's always young ones and
they carry on and they want to eat. They got to wait until
every relative is there until the turkey is cut!!! I've said
enough. (*With this, he turns, gets into his car and drives
away. The camera follows him into the distance.*)

Like Sam, we are brought up short. It is not his privileges of
seniority that Gabriel defends but an ethic of egalitarianism and
absolute solidarity: no one eats until all are present. And to un-
derscore his case, he recites pieces from the family's mythology
of Avalon as primordial paradise. In prophetic tones, he curses
those who have erected a new system of privilege: one based on
wealth rather than age, one that lets the young, impulsive, and
amnesiac, overthrow tradition and make new rules to suit their
convenience, if only they are prosperous and headstrong enough.
His reproach is stinging, and a long silence follows his exit. Jules
may have succeeded in his rebellion through ritual, but if so his
victory is Pyrrhic. Neither the family, nor its rituals, nor its stories will ever be the same again. The following year, Jules, Ann,
and their children eat their turkey silently from individual trays,
and it is their TV set that supplies the evening's narration.

One can read *Avalon* as a nostalgic and cautionary film. Surely
it is enamored of old world traditions, mythic recitations, ritual
performances, family values and the value of family. Along these
lines, it is possible to understand it as a tragedy that starts from
the premise that fundamental values are encoded in every detail
of mythic texts and practice, then goes on to show how those
who fail to tell these stories and enact these rituals fully and perfectly bring disaster on themselves, their families, and the world
around them.

Such a reading is seductive, as may be the position itself, particularly for students trained in a field often awash with nostalgia.
Personally, I prefer a different reading and a different disciplinary
orientation. As I see it, while the film acknowledges the appeal of
nostalgia, *Avalon* neither denies nor resists historic change. And
while it appreciates the importance of myth and ritual, it does not
fetishize their capacity to escape, annihilate, or transcend history.
Rather, it treats them as supple, versatile, and potent instruments
that people produce, reproduce, and modify, and instruments they

use—with considerable but imperfect skill and strategic acumen—to produce, reproduce, and modify themselves and the groups in which they participate.

The processes through which social groups, ritual performance, and mythic narration coproduce one another are extraordinarily complex, and when change occurs in one corner of this triadic configuration, it has consequences for the others as well. Further, all details of myth and ritual are overdetermined signifiers of great density and import. As such, they are subject to multiple interpretations by different actors within the same social field, and can become sites of tension and struggle where those actors contest their rival interests, values, desires, and ambitions.

Sometimes these struggles are extremely dramatic, and as a work of fictionalized autobiography, *Avalon* makes the most of this potential for drama. By condensing, embellishing, and reworking such events as there were in the director's family, it creates a clear and forceful story line, and its clarity is what makes it a heuristically useful example. At the same time, artistic enhancement also makes the film misleading, both as a record of "what actually happened" and as a model for research. Although such potential is always present, rarely does the fate of a group turn on the moment a turkey is cut. More often, struggles play out at low levels over long periods of time without precise focus or definitive resolution. As groups of people change, the stories they tell and ceremonies they perform change also, and change in one sphere can be both cause and consequence of change in the others. Insofar as historians of religions understand history as their proper subject matter—and not as their enemy—they ought be attentive to these processes.

Notes

This lecture was presented at the Harvard University Center for the Study of World Religions, 12 October 1995. Earlier versions were presented at Metropolitan State University and St. Thomas University.

1. *Avalon,* written and directed by Barry Levinson.
2. Veyne can almost be heard offering a subtle, but significant, corrective to Eva's formulation: "The essence of myth is not that everyone knows it but that it is supposed to be known and is worthy of being known by all." See Veyne's *Did the Greeks Believe in Their Myths? An Essay on the Constitutive Imagination,* 45.
3. Regarding the capacity of ritual to paper over the sources of tension and conflict within a social system but not to resolve them, which results in the need for rituals to be ceaselessly repeated, see the classic discussion of

Max Gluckman "Les rites de passage," in Gluckman, ed., *Essay on the Ritual of Social Relations,* 1–52.

4. The film thus interweaves three narratives located at different generational levels, all associated with patriarchal figures and their voyages: (1) The story told by the Krichinsky brothers of how their father came to America; (2) Sam's story of his own arrival; (3) The story of Jules's move to the suburbs. The first two describe the loving welcomes given newly arrived members of the family, and thematize the value of solidarity. In contrast, the third describes the problems its mobile protagonists had with those whom they left behind, and thematizes the formation of a nuclear family as a result of schism.

Works Cited

Gluckman, Max, ed. *Essays on the Ritual of Social Relations.* Manchester: Manchester University Press, 1962.

Levinson, Barry, writer and director. *Avalon.* Produced by Baltimore Pictures, released by Tri-Star Pictures, © 1990 by Tri-Star Pictures, Inc.

Veyne, Paul. *Did the Greeks Believe in Their Myths? An Essay on the Constitutive Imagination.* Chicago: Univ. of Chicago Press, 1988.

FRANCISCA CHO BANTLY

ARCHETYPES OF SELVES: A STUDY OF THE CHINESE MYTHO-HISTORICAL CONSCIOUSNESS

> Active, successful natures act, not according to the dictum
> "know thyself," but as if there hovered before them the com-
> mandment: *will* a self and thou shalt *become* a self.
> —NIETZSCHE

IT IS THE proposed opposition between history and myth that serves as the impetus and framing device for this essay on China. The dualism of myth and history is perhaps most famously articulated by Mircea Eliade for most scholars of religion. What this configuration represents, however, is a paradigm of Western consciousness that has been repeatedly intoned and which voices an enduring concern with the opposition between the universal and the particular: Is it possible to exist within the transient, dynamic, and meandering particularities of history and still live within a static, enduring, and transcendent world of significance? In contrast to prior philosophies of history, Eliade articulates the shift in Western consciousness toward seeing the universal and the particular—myth and history—as being radically opposed. Other essays in this volume challenge such an opposition between myth and history and argue for various kinds of reconfigurations between the two, whether it be in the case of family histories of immigration to the United States (Lincoln), or in the case of Picasso's artistic interpretation of the historical destruction of Guernica (Apostolos-Cappadona). This essay will join these others in showing that traditionally Western opposition between myth and history to be an unproductive means of cultural analysis. More specifically, I will show how such Western consciousness is refracted in contexts in which the opposition between myth and history is not duly acknowledged. This is the case, as I have argued before, in the context of China.[1]

Any temptation to explain away this dualism of myth and history as peculiar to Eliade's experience and theology courts the danger of overlooking how representative Eliade is of Western intellectual self-conceptualizations. This polarity is ironically demonstrated, for example, in R. G. Collingwood's *The Idea of History*, where the author makes a case for the distinction between the natural and human sciences or, more properly, between natural and historical knowledge. In seeking to liberate history from the tyranny of the natural sciences, Collingwood asserts the distinctiveness and autonomy of history. Historical knowledge, he asserts, is an object that is created by and synonymous with the knowing subject (i.e., the historian). All historical knowledge, therefore, is a knowledge of mind, or a knowledge of thought, rather than the appropriation of external and empirical facts. Historical knowledge is lodged in the historian's mind rather than in an objective world outside his or her own thinking. What is notable about this view of history is its *historicism:* historical knowledge is possible because of our own rootedness in historical circumstances, which engenders our ability to imagine and relive the past. Historical knowledge is predicated, then, not on one's ability to abandon one's own standpoint, but on this standpoint itself. For Collingwood "the historical past is the world of ideas which the present evidence creates in the present. In historical inference we do not move from our present world to a past world; the movement in experience is always a movement within a present world of ideas."[2]

Collingwood's emphasis on the historical imagination leads him to point out the similarities between the historian and the fictional novelist. Because historical knowledge is enabled and conditioned by the culturally embedded observer, history by definition is opposed to static and universal constructs of meaning. Various attempts in the Western experience to create such a "science of human nature" constitute profoundly antihistorical episodes. This impulse can be traced back and laid at the doorstep of the ancient Greeks, for whom true knowledge was universal and best exemplified by mathematics. This "substantialism," as Collingwood labels it, "implies a theory of knowledge according to which only what is unchanging is knowable. But what is un-changing is not historical. What is historical is the transitory event."[3]

Collingwood's idea of history, with its reliance on perspectiv-ism and its opposition to the reality of the "event as such," is radically distinct from Eliade's own views of history. The opposi-tion between historical and scientific knowledge as Collingwood delineates them, however, is another way of enfleshing Eliade's two ontologies, or the basic opposition between the universal and the particular. The universal and static is embraced by the scien-tific, or "substantialist," mind that seeks truth only outside pro-fane time; and the processual and dynamic is embraced by the historical mind in its unyieldable mission to find value within the flux of history. Both Eliade and Collingwood agree in iden-tifying the ancient Greeks as the supreme defenders of archaic ontology. Hence, to Eliade "Plato could be regarded as the out-standing philosopher of 'primitive mentality,'" and Collingwood evokes the assertion of Aristotle that "poetry is more scientific than history, for history is a mere collection of empirical facts, whereas poetry extracts from such facts a universal judgment."[4]

In turning to the Chinese setting, the specific limits of this pa-per can be defined by beginning with a scholastic problem: What happened to myths in ancient China? Having addressed this ques-tion in a previous paper, I have already indicated that the impor-tance of this query stems from the importance of the category of myth itself in Western religious scholarship.[5] I expand that claim here to assert that myth is a weighty category in scholarly think-ing because it embodies the broader philosophical concern about the universal and the particular. Such a broad and ultimate ques-tion of meaning, however, is surely not the exclusive province of Western philosophical speculations. And yet many have been long and rightfully puzzled about the absence of myths in China. I have suggested that the dilemma this situation poses can be re-solved by recognizing that the significance of myth can be identi-fied with its ontologically creative function rather than with a certain narrative genre.[6] This essay will build on and further my contention that what makes a myth mythical is not its location in a specific kind of story but rather its articulation and perpetua-tion of archetypes—archetypes being defined as the templates that a culture creates in order to shape the world into a recognizable and meaningful reality. This position only draws out Eliade's own assertion that in mythical consciousness "an object or an act becomes real only insofar as it imitates or repeats an archetype."[7]

Eliade's reason for locating archetypes in narratives is that many cultures have exhibited the tendency to tell creation stories—cosmogonic myths—that take place in primordial (nonhistorical) time and that explain the origins of all that exists in the present. Through ritual means, these "archaic" cultures are capable of overcoming profane, historical time and returning to the primordial time of creation and thus participating in the activity of the gods—of regenerating time and creating the world anew. The concern with origins and beginnings is a critical ingredient of myth, for myth must allow us to relate our own time to that other sacred time. It is only through this capacity of myth that one can make good on the reneged promise of modernity: that one is free to make oneself, to play the role of creator.

Myth and History in China

In the Chinese case, the relationship between myth and temporality is radically reformulated. A significant thesis of this study is that in a Chinese context archetypes are constantly appropriated and repeated *within* historical time rather than outside of it. For the Chinese, history does not bring novelty as much as it provides an opportunity to demonstrate how much things remain the same. Despite the absence of extensive story cycles about gods who frolicked and ventured in primordial time and engendered the world, China is one of the most mythical of societies, and this mythical nature is readily apparent in its historical consciousness.

This thesis immediately violates, of course, the supposed contradiction between myth and history. It would be easy to dismiss the tension, perhaps, by reducing these two categories into narrative genres and therefore claiming that they are simply two different ways of doing the same thing. I concede, however, that style and function are not always readily disentangled from each other. Many have believed, for example, that the advent of historical or philosophical writing in a given society was a sign of the emergence of a new consciousness or mode of being—a development that can be explicitly contrasted to the prior mythic mode of that society.

Sarah Allan, one of the current field's foremost investigators of myth in China, suggests that the breach in mythical consciousness is brought about by the creation of historical records. Allan defines myth as a tale that violates natural reality, signifying that the story is concerned with the sacred rather than the profane. The separation from myth is created by recordkeeping. Historical records—which assert their own immovable evidence of an external reality—limit a society's ability to be unfettered by "what really happened." The shackles of history further hinder a person's ability to transcend the bounds of real possibility, constrained as he or she is by what the texts will allow. With the advent of history and recordkeeping, cultures learn to distance themselves from their prior immersion in mythic thought, thus allowing the development of analytical and critical thinking.[8]

It seems quite right that genre distinctions connote differences not only in literary style and convention but in humanistic aims, concerns, and perhaps even cognitive states. The notion of historical consciousness is often used to label a certain quality of thought and a certain orientation to reality that might be characterized as self-reflexive and critical. Reliance on witness and evidence, careful assessment of sources, and a vigilance toward the distinction between belief and fact constitute some of the qualities of the historical mode of thinking. And yet the reality of this form of consciousness is limited in that it is the product of specific brands of Western traditions of thought. Moreover, the rationalist faith in human critical faculties has already been superseded by our postmodern suspicion that objective, historical thinking comprises more an ideal than a reality.

The Chinese notion of history and historical thinking, in any case, is another breed altogether, although it participates in the general definition of history as the record and transmission of past events. China, which has long intoned the importance of history, has been credited with an exceptionally speedy appropriation of historical consciousness that has supposedly rendered Chinese culture rational and anti-superstitious from a very early age. The importance of history in China has led literary scholars of China to examine the significance of historical narrative in that culture, particularly in relation to other narrative forms.

Andrew Plaks's discussion of the history-fiction continuum in Chinese narratives points out that in both literary taxonomies and literary practice, it is often difficult to draw a neat line between the two.[9] Scholars of Chinese narratives, however, are united in informing us of the priority of history in the Chinese

literary tradition.[10] The Chinese prejudice for history indicates
one dominant mode in which that culture's observations on some
fundamental truths of human existence have been expressed.
These truths often entail observations on the sociopolitical realm
of being—as evinced by the didactic use and understanding of
history as a tool for better government and more virtuous rulers.
In addition, the positioning of biography and autobiography under
the rubric of history enabled the latter to co-opt the cultural
space in which the truths of self-identity and personal experiences were articulated.

It is important to note, however, that what qualifies as historical fact in the Chinese thought does not readily conform to the
logical-empirical speculations of Western philosophical traditions. Plaks identifies the function of all Chinese narratives
across the history-fiction continuum as "the transmission of
known facts," wherein such "facts" must withstand the scrutiny
of primarily moral rather than critical evaluation. In the words of
Plaks, "The necessary assumption of such transmission is that
every given narrative is in some sense a faithful representation of
what did, *or what typically does,* happen in human experience"
(emphasis mine).[11]

The confluence of "what happened" and "what typically happens" in Chinese historical thinking suggests a violation of genre
boundaries, particularly as indexed to Eliade's categories of myth
and history. "What typically happens" salutes the paradigmatic
and repetitive views of reality that are aligned with myth,
whereas "what happened" invokes the linear progression of facts
that are chronicled by history. In the Chinese setting, it quickly
becomes apparent that any attempt to emplace this culture on
one or the other side of the myth-history divide proves complicated at best.

Perhaps the most fruitful way of accessing a concrete instance
of the Chinese mythohistorical mind is to begin with another
example of genre confusion. Norman Girardot identifies one of
the more ambiguous—and hence interesting—mythic themes of
China as its "sage kings and model emperors."[12] Its ambiguity
derives from its position betwixt and between two literary categories, mythic narrative in the classical sense and historical legend.
My primary definition of myth as archetype, however, frees us
from concern with such categorical distinctions in favor of a more
functional consideration. Do sage kings and model emperors—
ideal types that I prefer to designate as culture heroes—offer an

archetype of cultural meaning that is repeatedly embodied and relived by historical individuals?

Confucius is perhaps best known for attempting to bridge the gap between the legendary and the possible by exhorting all men to become "the gentleman"—a model of identity explicitly lifted from China's culture heroes. Confucius's exhortation offers a significant addendum to the common thesis of reverse euhemerization through which sinologists have claimed that mythic gods were transformed into culture heroes—hence explaining the absence of myths in China.[13] The moral discourse of Confucius subsequently demanded that mere mortals assume the virtues of gods. The Confucian *junzi,* or its more prosaic incarnation as the scholar-official, has indeed animated the long course of Chinese history as a personal ideal and a sociopolitical category.

The persistence of this model of identity lends substance to yet another genus of mythical creation that will be the focus of the rest of this paper—archetypes of selves. Whereas my prior examination of myth as archetype focused on cosmological creation as enacted through the literary art of *The Book of Poetry,* my purpose here will be to illumine the creation of personal identities through the perpetuation and embodiment of enduring biographical myths. In particular, I will focus on female identities, culminating with a case study of Jiang Qing, the wife of Mao Zedong. I deliberately choose a contemporary figure in order to substantiate my thesis that myth is reenacted *in* historical time rather than in defiance of it.

Archetypes of Selves in China

A measure of the contemporary Western concern with the issue of self-identity is offered by the relatively recent proliferation of the study of autobiography. As some scholars suggest, the growth in critical literature on the autobiographical genre stems from postmodern ontological speculations on the substantiality of self and identity.[14] Janet Gunn refers to one prerequisite for autobiography stipulated by Georges Gusdorf—that the culture has emerged from the "mythic framework of traditional teachings" into the "perilous domain of history."[15] It seems that the modern Western search for self-identity is also framed by dualistic ontological self-conceptualizations. Gunn elaborates this condition by citing Eliade's notion of history: "Autobiography could emerge, then, only when men and women began to experience what Mircea Eliade has called the 'terror of history.' To be sure, history had been 'happening' long before its discovery in the nineteenth century; but it was by means of myth that human beings were able—in Eliade's word—to 'tolerate' it. Autobiography, I would add, continues to make tolerable the fullest inhabiting of that perilous domain."[16]

Here too the Western theory of autobiography postulates the split between the universal and the particular. The rise of autobiography, in this view, is the result of an intellectual age that throws us on our own devices when it comes to determining our identity and its meaning.

Within the Chinese pursuit of self-identity, the evolution and eventual split between mythical and historical consciousness never occurred. One significant result of this is the notable absence of an individualistic conception of selfhood. Rather than predicating the meaningfulness of a given life on its exceptional features, a self takes on identity and form only to the extent to which it animates one of a standard set of paradigms of selfhood. To wit, the absence of progression from mythical to historical consciousness collapses the distinction between mythical and autobiographical narratives. Chinese strategies for articulating the meaning of a life are to simply direct myths onto the concern for selfhood. The result is what I term *archetypes of selves*.

The Chinese concern with self-identity properly begins with the official biographies (*liezhuan*) that form the primary section of the dynastic histories (*zhengshi*). As part of the didactic historical tradition, these official biographies were designed to display public and sanctioned models of selves rather than supply an account of the inner life of individuals. Pei-yi Wu notes that the subservience of biography to the genre of history was a condition that characterized not only early China but premodern Europe as well. At that stage of development, personal life histories were inhibited by the absence of a literary vehicle. This lacuna was overcome only after the liberation of biography from the genre of history to the enabling media of belles lettres.[17] Thus, in opposition to the civically desirable figures pressed upon the readers of the official biographies, poetic versification and, much later, the Song dynasty accounts of Buddhist conversions supplied the means for more passionate (if sometimes veiled) forms of self-expression.

In women's biographies the tendency to typify in order to edify is also evident, and perhaps exaggerated because of the relative paucity of identities that a women could choose from. The earliest collection of women's biographies—the *Lienüzhuan* by Liu Xiang of the Han dyansty—enumerates seven categories of women:[18] (1) exemplary mothers (*muyi*), (2) capable and virtuous women (*xianming*), (3) benevolent and intelligent women (*renchi*), (4) chaste and undefiled women (*jenshun*), (5) chaste and righteous women (*jieyi*), (6) reasoning women (*biantong*), and (7) pernicious courtesans (*niebi*). Within this sanctioned list of female roles, the particular incarnation of the virtuous wife-widow perhaps stands out in terms of overall historical frequency. The category is particularly well attested to in the dynastic histories and provincial gazeteers. Of these biographies Pei-yi Wu observes: "Numbering in the tens of thousands, these good women for two millennia performed more or less the same deeds, each earning one of two lines of encomium in written history. They remain faceless and in most cases nameless, only identifiable by the surnames of their fathers or husbands. Their lives approach a proverb in that their roles are practically interchangeable and the outcome of their brief stories is completely predictable. What saves these biographical sketches . . . from total inanity is classical Chinese which, with its elegant set phrases and its own steadfastness . . . is well suited to handle the recurrent and the typical."[19]

The monotony and anonymity of these biographies should not be allowed to obscure the all-too-real lives of the women to which these accounts attest. This is particularly true of the Ming and Qing dynasties, when the state cult of honoring virtuous wives in the name of propagating Confucian morality encouraged and drove many a widow to suicide as the ultimate seal of her chastity.[20]

Scholars of China have begun to show more interest of late in the cult of chaste widows, such attention being merited by the exponential increase in biographical accounts devoted to this category of female identity in the late Imperial era. My own focus, however, shifts from this relatively well-documented instance of selfhood to a much rarer version—one that is less recorded and certainly less sanctioned: that of the woman in power, the would-be ruler, and in one or two cases, the female emperor.

The cases of women—usually the wives and mothers of emperors—who have wielded political power in China are expectedly few but more frequent than the official strictures on such practice would ideally allow for. Particularly notable are Empress Lü Zhi of the Former Han, Empress Wu Zetian of the Tang, and the

Empress-Dowager Ci Xi of the Qing. This list can be rounded out by the numerous regencies of empress dowagers, which, as Lien-sheng Yang points out, was an institution resorted to under particular but repeated circumstances.[21]

Although modern scholars have produced full-fledged biographies of some of these figures—particularly Wu Zetian and Ci Xi, very little speculation has been aimed at women in power as a cultural category. Despite the relatively few historical instances in which this category was instantiated, the Chinese awareness of and attitudes toward this possibility are discernible facts. The first historical document of China, the *Shujing*, or *Book of Documents*, asserts that "the hen does not announce the morning. The crowing of a hen in the morning indicates the subversion of the family."[22] This allegorical stricture on female power was invoked by periodic orders that prohibited the interference of the empress dowager in state affairs.

Priscilla Ching Chung's brief study of palace women in the Northern Song dynasty makes the point that male opposition to female power was not opposed to female rulers per se but was provoked by the fact that these women were allied to political forces hostile to those very ones who voiced objection. The alignment of political factions at court was often determined by familial and clan groupings, many of which were initially empowered by a female member who—in her capacity as wife or consort—held the favor of the emperor. Chung's article, however, focuses mainly on men who were able to gain political and social advantage through the key positioning of a female relative in the court. The actions of court women in this scenario demonstrate how, even within the seat of power, women were significant only to the extent to which they played out their familial roles.

Even with regent empress dowagers, the viability of their positions stemmed from the Confucian recognition of the prerogatives of a mother and wife. That is, an empress dowager was allowed to rule primarily because of her position as either wife or mother of an incapacitated emperor. It was impossible to attain power in any other way. The ideal empress dowager would gracefully step aside once the emperor proper attained self-sufficiency. Perhaps the negative historical judgment of Chinese males toward women in power is a reflection on those instances when the taste of power moved certain females to act in decidedly unmaternal and unfamilial ways. Empress Lü and Empress Wu are particularly remembered for their murderous proclivities, which were directed at everyone from their own husbands to offspring and relatives in their bids to hold on to the reins of power.

The archetype of female identity that most adequately encompasses the woman in power is the last and notably negative category of Liu Xiang's biographies—the pernicious courtesan. The fifteen biographies offered in this section of the *Lienüzhuan* tell the stories of women who bring utter ruin upon their states as a direct result of their lascivious natures. Again, the impact of these women is felt only through men. As wives and concubines, they bewitch their lords into doing their bidding—a vicarious means of going beyond their proper place. Indeed, women who meddle in affairs of state comprise an archetypal nightmare, prompting the lesson that "disorder comes not from heaven; . . . It is produced by a woman."[23]

The aspirations of these women, however, are notably modest. In their boldest instances, they connive to put their own son or lover into positions of power. In the vast majority of cases, however, these women manage to destroy nations almost nonchalantly, by embodying a prevalent view of femininity. The women profiled here are not individuals in any sense of our term but personifications of a particularly dangerous form of female sexuality. The voracious and irresistible nature of a woman's sexual appetite is rendered capable not only of captivating the man in question but of leading him to perversity. Female sexuality itself is portrayed as a form of deviance, expressing itself most frequently through adultery, incest, and abject cruelty. The most notable biographies target Moxi, consort of King Jie of the Xia dynasty, and Danji, wife of King Zhou of the Shang. Kings Jie and Zhou, of course, are infamous as the "last bad rulers" of their respective dynastic lineages. Their weakness as rulers, however, is not that they allow females to take over what is properly in their realm of control; instead, they allow themselves to be besotted by the frivolous and even baleful pursuits of women. Their women do not angle for power but merely distract their masters through the demands of their sensuality.

Perhaps the relative passivity of these women testifies to the very power of the hazards they pose. A lascivious act by a beautiful woman can cause empires to fall. This specter has been ever-present in the minds of Confucian moralists. Liu Xiang's biographies only cover the period up until the later Han, but the role of the pernicious courtesan was played to perfection in a much later era, according to popular Chinese judgment, by Yang Guifei, the consort of Emperor Taizong of the Tang. Stretching even further, various elements of Jiang Qing's biography—her beginnings as an actress, an entertainer, a bewitching outsider who beguiled the "emperor" (Mao Zedong) with her sexual charms and who then ultimately brought disaster upon the state—suggest how myths can model lives.

Ultimately, the model of the pernicious courtesan does not suffice in enfleshing a figure like Jiang Qing. Interestingly enough, the models that she herself suggested were Empresses Lü Zhi and Wu Zetian. The self-conceptualization is revealing, for indeed the pernicious courtesans of Liu Xiang's making were bit players within the rank of notable Chinese women. They did not even aspire to snatch away the reigns of empire. The likes of Wu Zetian, however, display a different category of female identity altogether—a woman (the only one in Chinese history) who actually succeeded in crowning herself emperor and founder of her own dynastic lineage. Jiang Qing's self-comparison spoke volumes about her own designs. It also immediately presented her with a dilemma: the judgment of Chinese history has not been kind to the women with whom Jiang Qing put herself in league. Nonetheless, Jiang had precious little choice of historical precedents or personal role models with which to legitimate her attempt to succeed Mao Zedong as chairman of the Communist Party.

The case of Jiang Qing is attractive by the very fact that the person she wished to become did not exist in the catalog of Chinese female selves. To be sure, her ambitions had been displayed before by an elite corps of women whose legacy was ultimately demeaned by history. The point is, a Wu Zetian hardly offered a paradigm of legitimacy—she was not a part of the cultural canon. What is instructive is that a Jiang Qing of the twentieth century—a woman of a revolutionary society that claimed to have broken from the limitations of its feudal past—chose to reactivate a traditional archetype of identity, no matter how problematic. This ostensibly modern woman was not willing or able to craft her life on the presumption that it was her qualities as an individual that merited her her place on the stage of history. Jiang Qing was compelled to instantiate herself in the mythical rather than historical mode.

What follows will be an analysis of how Jiang went about this process of mythical self-instantiation. The problem confronting her was manifest, as was its solution. The popular moral judgment on the ancient women with whom she paralleled herself with was harsh, creating a mandate to reconsider and revise that judgment. The vehicle for such deliberation came in the form of nothing other than historical criticism—an art that had garnered an added vitality and a new agenda by the Communist regime's embrace of Marxist historicism. Due to this paper's focus, what follows will concentrate on the mechanics of this historical criticism rather than on the intimate biographical details of Jiang or her predecessors.

Jiang Qing's Making of Myth-History

Jiang Qing's bid to become Mao's successor was not a plan that received the approval of the "emperor" himself. Jiang's ability to garner the support of her husband in her machinations waxed and waned according to her usefulness to him in his own struggle against rival claimants to the throne. After the uproar of the Cultural Revolution, the elite corps of the Communist Party settled down to face the new decade and the increasingly pressing question of who would succeed the aging ruler. Jiang Qing had ridden high during the Cultural Revolution, but a political reflex against its excesses, and the presence of other figures favored by the Son of Heaven, put Jiang in a precarious position as the decade of the seventies opened.

After the disgrace and exposure of Lin Biao, the defense minister who was expected to succeed Mao and who met his end in a suspicious plane crash in 1971, the remaining political lines shifted into place. They were drawn between the pragmatists like Premier Zhou Enlai and Vice Premier Deng Xiaoping, who favored a program of economic reform and openness to the West; and the leftists led by Jiang, head of the so-called Gang of Four, which represented the radical ideological politics rooted in the Shanghai region.

The outcome of the ensuing battles, of course, is now a matter of record.[24] Despite Jiang's efforts to tarnish the reputation of Zhou Enlai, the death of the premier in January 1976 presaged the events to come. The public outpouring of grief for the courtly and beloved premier took leaders by surprise. The spontaneous mass national day of mourning was also colored by explicitly vituperative references to Jiang and the Gang of Four. Despite this setback, Jiang's almost exclusive access to Mao—himself in ill health and fading to the point of senility—allowed her to thwart the promotion of Deng Xiaoping to premier. Deng was a long-standing political enemy who had excoriated Jiang's ideological and cultural activities. Having suffered a purge during the Cultural Revolution, Deng found himself exiled once more, while the callow minister for public security—Hua Guofeng—found himself catapulted to acting prime minister.

Events culminated upon the death of Mao Zedong on September 9 of the same year. Jiang sought to make good on her carefully executed maneuvers to become chairman of the Communist Party. Outright demands for her succession were answered by the Politburo a month later with orders for her arrest, swiftly followed by a roundup of the rest of the Gang of Four. The ensuing years of political shake-ups resulted in the waning powers of Hua Guofeng and the gradual ascendancy of Deng Xiaoping, sealing Jiang's fate with the opening of her trial in 1981.

This succession of events described in brief easily takes on a generic quality that can be readily distilled from the countless and repetitive power struggles that have been acted out in Chinese imperial courts. Scholars have commented on Mao's own consciousness of China's historical legacy: "Mao constantly referred to China's imperial past and to the role of the emperors."[25] The Soviet observer L. S. Perelomov notes that among the Chinese there is a particularly acute tendency to draw upon the past "for assurance not only about the legitimacy of [one's] origin but also [one's] rights in the present and future."[26] Perelomov documents this by pointing to a study that reveals that 47 percent of Mao's references in his collected works are to antiquity.[27]

Mao put his own words to this practice when he spoke about the "using the past for the present" (gu wei jin yun). He suggested the rationale for this policy in the following manner: "China's present new politics and new economy have developed out of her old politics and old economy, and her present culture, too, has developed out of her old culture; therefore, we must respect our own history and must not lop it off. However, respect for history means giving it its proper place as a science, respecting its dialectical development, and not eulogizing the past at the expense of the present or praising every drop of feudal poison."[28]

We might take this Maoist version of historical criticism as comprised of two principles: first, the "science" of history means interpreting events of the past through a Marxist lens; and second, the example of the past can be used both to illuminate and

legitimate the policies of the present. The two tasks were intimately related and ultimately, politically driven.

The Use of the Past

In 1971–72 a rather odd ideological and intellectual campaign was
launched that purported to "criticize Confucius" (*pipan kongzi*)
and rectify the interpretation of history. As one of the movement's spokesmen so accurately observed, "Records of history
have always served political struggle in real life."[29] The interpretation of history, he baldly admits, is not a matter of objectively
or critically determining "what happened." As an implement of
political struggle, history is subordinate to political ends. The reason why the interpretation of history must be strictly monitored
is that those interpretations can easily differ.

The fluidity of the meaning of history is an observation that
presses heavily upon the Western postmodern consciousness.
Our fascination with shifting boundaries of reality has sent us on
repeated rounds of the hermeneutical spin-cycle. When history is
an overt instrument of ideological struggle, however, the results
are not second-order reflections on the nature of knowledge. Instead, the primary concern involves determining which interpretation of history is "correct." More to the point, which interpretation serves the given expedient need?

Despite the academic cloak of the "criticize Confucius" campaign, its normative agenda was manifest in its division of party
members between those who "use the past to criticize the present" and those who "emphasize the present while slighting the
past." In political translation, the first camp referred to the politically retrograde who rejected the (Marxist) progression of history
in an attempt to cling to outmoded structures and forms of privilege. The latter, of course, designated the ideologically upright
who embraced the revolutions of the ever-evolving present. The
issue here was a question of how to use the past; that is, how to
appraise history critically in order to serve present political needs.

From a Marxist perspective, targeting Confucius made a great
deal of sense. More than anyone else, Confucius spoke for the
past, invoking the mythical belief that perfection lies in the past
and in its sacred models of being. Appropriating that divine model
is predicated on banishing history by enfleshing that timeless
ideal within oneself. One might also be tempted to see in the

Maoist mimicry of historical dialecticism a momentous breach in the Confucian-driven mythical orientation of China. Whatever the limitations and narrowness of Marxist philosophy of history, it nevertheless might be credited with catapulting Chinese historical thinking into the modern age. As the analysis to come will demonstrate, however, the Maoist principle of using the past to serve the present does not fundamentally deviate from the traditional Chinese use of history. In the present case, the past no longer represents the ideal of how things ought to be. Instead, it provides the measure of how far one has come in achieving a perfection that now lies in the immediate future. Despite the directional reversal in the location of the mythical golden age, the Chinese practice of history is still didactic; the events of the past hold meaning only because of what they tell us about how things ought to be. Given this agenda, the Maoist practice of history is less concerned with being objective than with being useful to present ends—it is the practice of myth-history.

The Myth-History of the Empresses

It is perhaps best to begin by looking at specific examples of Maoist historical criticism. As a self-styled student extraordinaire of Maoist thought, Jiang Qing actively applied his teachings to her historical-critical reinterpretations of the Empresses Lü Zhi and Wu Zetian. The major interpretive assertion made about these women was that they were profoundly anti-Confucian monarchs who followed the principles of the Legalists. Legalism is the Chinese school of realpolitik philosophy that was articulated in the pre-Han-dynasty era and definitively formulated in the third century B.C.E. by Han Feizi. The emperor Qinshi, who unified and ruled China (221–206 B.C.E.) in the aftermath of the Zhou dynasty, utilized Legalist principles to institute an absolute, repressive, and ultimately short-lived reign. Chinese judgment on the Qin dynasty has been unanimously disapproving. Qinshi's most frequently invoked legacy has been the infamous "burning of the books" incident of 213 B.C.E. in which all the classics were targeted; and the equally famous live burial of 460 Confucian scholars in a bid to quiet dissent. Jiang's revisionist move of praising Legalism was not of her own making but rather followed obediently in the footsteps of the "criticize Confucius" campaign.

The polemic against Confucius that was launched in the early 1970s purported to be a critical investigation of an important era of

Chinese history. The point was not simply to contrast the backward, Confucian-based feudal past with the Communist present. Rather, the aim was to demonstrate the principles of Marxist dialecticism operating in a slice of remote Chinese history. Led by scholars like Guo Moruo, president of the Academia Sinica, the focus of this movement fell upon China during the Warring States period of the Zhou dynasty (roughly seventh to third centuries B.C.E.). The thesis was asserted that these periods represented a significant class struggle and evolution in which slaveholding aristocrats—represented by Confucian ideology—gave way to a new landlord class tied to a centralized feudal state.[30]

The historical scaling of this supposed class revolution was fixed in such a way that the brunt of this momentous change fell squarely into the lap of Emperor Qinshi himself. In this scenario, the erstwhile tyrant was transformed into the vehicle and champion of dialectical materialism and historical progress. While his methods are acknowledged to be rather extreme (including the book-burning and scholar-burying incidents), they were "a necessary dictatorial means of the newly rising landlord class to deal with the restoration activities of the slave-owning aristocratic class."[31] The other side of the campaign to criticize Confucius, then, consisted of the mandate to elevate the Legalists. The class interests that Confucians and Legalists were supposed to represent is of secondary issue. Of greater import was the fact that Legalism represented the embrace of progress and of social radicalism. Confucianism, on the other hand, is seen as reactive; it is the retrogressive tendency of those who resist history because they themselves cannot move forward.

What is most important about this study of the struggle between the Confucians and Legalists is not that it offers a case study of the progression of Marxist dialectics. Much more significantly, it offers up an enduring *principle*—the struggle between progressive and conservative forces in history. This is the primary reason why so much ink was spilled by the Communist academic arm to reexamine Legalist scholarship and history.[32] The point was not to unearth the past as much as to draw an analogy for the present. The immediate purpose for drawing such an analogy began within a circumscribed context but soon took on perhaps unexpected proportions in the hands of Jiang Qing.

Both Western and Chinese observers are somewhat unclear about the immediate target of the "criticize Confucius" campaign. As Perelomov points out, however, the political dilemmas

that Mao Zedong faced in the early seventies make the utility of
the campaign palpable. Divisions within the Chinese Communist Party—particularly those critical of the Cultural Revolution
and other ultraleftist policies—had turned to examples from the
past to voice their discontent. Specifically, Mao's opponents drew
a parallel between the tactics of the Cultural Revolution and the
terrorist measures of Emperor Qinshi.[33] The likening of Mao to a
notorious feudal tyrant was not a substantive policy critique as
much as it was an expression of moral censure. The "criticize
Confucius" campaign that was launched in response, however,
took the ideological stance of proclaiming to defend Marxism
against revisionism. Its point was that Maoist policies represented the vehicle of Marxist progressivism in opposition to the
counterrevolutionary spirit of Mao's detractors.

Mao had been attacked both as a modern-day Qinshi and as a
Confucian. The criticism was not keyed into the differences between pre-Han-dynasty philosophical schools; its purpose was to
paint a metaphorical picture of Mao as a terrorizing autocrat. The
"criticize Confucius" movement quickly pointed to the distinction between Confucianism and Legalism in order to draw a historical and political lesson for the modern day. Conforming to the
suggestion that Mao was a latter-day Qinshi, the aegis of historical scholarship was used to argue that Legalism acted as the force
of historical progress and, more importantly, the principle of "emphasizing the present while slighting the past." This transformation of Qinshi into a forward-looking progressive supposedly had
precedents in scholarship before the Maoist campaign. At the
same time, the political expedience of the reevaluation is obvious.[34]

Whatever the scholarly merits of the reevaluation of Emperor
Qinshi and the Legalists, the easy utility of this kind of historical
criticism for those who desired to use the past to draw an expedient analogy for the present proved too tempting to resist. The
"criticize Confucius" campaign has been suspected by some to
have originated with Jiang Qing herself in an attempt to target
Zhou Enlai.[35] The premier successfully riposted by coupling the
name of Confucius with the now traitor Lin Biao. The failure of
this negative strategy was quickly supplanted in the spring of
1974 when articles about the Empresses Lü and Wu began to cir-
culate.

Appearing under various pseudonyms, numerous articles purported to show that these female rulers were Legalist champions

who advanced the movement of dialectical materialism. The claims made on their behalf are repetitive and incantatory: Empress Wu, for example, opposed Confucius and despised the classics. She restricted the large-scale land monopoly of great landlords. Herself a commoner, her reign marked the triumph of the commoner-landlord over the powerful gentry clans.[36] The real point of the articles need not be concealed by the pseudo-historical prose: women can be rulers; women can advance the cause of Marxist dialectics; a woman can succeed Mao and continue the revolution.

The politically driven zeal of this historical scholarship overlooked one critical point: Lü Zhi was the wife of Liu Bang, founder of the Han dynasty in the third century B.C.E. Wu Zetian was the wife of Gaozong, the second emperor of the Tang dynasty, and founder of her own dynasty in the late seventh century. The two figures were separated in history by 900 years; nevertheless they were proclaimed to be Legalists fighting the same landlords on behalf of the same commoners. The problematic nature of affixing the title *Legalist* to these figures notwithstanding, the result of these studies is that the progression of Marxist dialectics is robbed of its linear trajectory and imprisoned in a seemingly interminable circularity. Clearly, the term *Legalist* does not designate the primacy of Marxist historiography as much as a moniker of political approval. The Legalists are the good guys (and gals). The free range of this term is demonstrated in one article that points out the conflict between Confucianism and Legalism in yet another era: the rule of Wang Anshi in the eleventh century of the Song dynasty. In this scenario, the reformer Wang Anshi is a Legalist who is eventually overcome by his nemesis, Sima Guang the Confucian.[37]

After Jiang Qing was brought down as a "bourgeois careerist and conspirator," detractors rushed in to point out the fallacies in her historical reasoning. The criticisms are mainly twofold. First, the Confucian-Legalist conflict is contained within the ruling class; hence to paint the Legalists as champions of the peasants is a blasphemy that abolishes the reality of class conflict in Chinese history after the Qin dynasty. Second, to claim that the Legalists are akin to modern-day Marxists is absurd because Marxist theory itself mandates that the current era represents a complete breach with the past.[38] These criticisms explicitly point out a necessity of Marxist historical interpretation: the use of the past as an analogy for the present contradicts a theory of history that is relentlessly linear. As one observer critiques: "Marx spoke of 'striking similarities in history,' but similarities are different from sameness. Therefore, Marx firmly opposed superficial comparisons detached from historical conditions."[39] The Gang of Four's use of history, therefore, does not follow the "Marxist-Leninist-Mao Zedong" school of thought: "In their hands, history became a lump of damp flour they could shape into anything they wanted."[40]

Myth versus Ideology

A fair question to raise at this point concerns the sincerity of Jiang Qing's appropriation of Lü Zhi and Wu Zetian as models of self-identity. Given her tremendously self-serving display of historical criticism, did Jiang see these female models as genuine existential guides, or were they merely instrumental elements of an ideological campaign? This question, as such, supposes the possibility of separating Jiang's personal from her political identity—a distinction dubious at best. The important issue concerns why the claim and title of Legalism was made on behalf of these ancient empresses. Before the revisionist scholarship on Lü Zhi and Wu Zetian, the label of Legalism had already gained a certain cachet through the "criticize Confucius" campaign. Jiang clearly sought to transfer the sense of legitimacy conferred by this term to the women to whom not only Jiang, but her executioners as well, inevitably compared herself.

The point, of course, is the very inevitability of this comparison. In the absence of choices, Jiang's process of self-actualization was not ruled by a pursuit of sincerity or authenticity but rather by a public-relations campaign. Jiang sought to put her predecessors—who were indelible archetypes of female identity—in the best light possible. The most telling evidence is offered by her worst detractors: in attacking Jiang's claims about China's past empresses, never do they question the accuracy of the comparison—only the historical judgment on their moral stature. The spate of words that denounced Jiang Qing and the Gang of Four borrow the tone of academic argument over the interpretation of Legalism, Confucianism, and the Marxist "science" of history. In establishing their own conclusions, however, the analogy between Jiang Qing and the Empress Lü and Wu is reinforced. In examining the life of Empress Lü, one article proclaims, "It turned out the Empress Lü herself gave concentrated expression to the insidious, vicious, atrocious and tyrannical nature of the exploiting classes. Chiang Ch'ing and this woman were really cut from the same cloth."[41] Elsewhere, a scathing examination of Wu Zetian's policies lends an opportunity to assert "exact duplications" between Wu and the Gang of Four.[42]

The mythical impulse was expressed by both parties' assumption that the past served as an accurate model for the present. Despite the Marxist-Maoist rejection of the past and its attempt to impose a linear view of history, the actual practice of history demonstrated here (by both pro- and anti-Jiang forces) suggests the depth of the Chinese mythical reflex. This reflex is revealed specifically in the strategy of looking to past models, but it is perhaps more significantly embodied in the use of history itself.

The entire debate over the interpretation of history that commenced with the "criticize Confucius" episode might have provided a convenient matrix for Jiang Qing's political designs. The substance of this debate on history, however, is central to this study's concern with myth and history. To be sure, Jiang's myth-making in the service of her political kin is blatant and has been roundly condemned as such: "Whoever mocks history cannot but be punished by history."[43] But the question must be asked: Are the critics of Jiang's myth-history imposing a breakthrough in the understanding of history? Do they represent a new critical capacity that asserts the scientific practice of history over and against the ideological use of history in order to oppose the Party?

In the aftermath of Jiang's fall from grace, various ruminations appeared that offered to give the correct interpretation of Mao's directive to "make the past serve the present." Frequent reference is made to history as a scientific pursuit: "Historical research must be conducted in the scientific attitude of finding truth from facts and in no way should the pragmatic method of distortion, alteration, insinuation, and comparison by metaphor be adopted."[44] What quickly becomes evident, however, is that this "scientific attitude" has an explicit political purpose—"to serve the revolutionary cause of the proletariat." Mao's principle of making the past serve the present is candidly professed to have a "clear-cut class character." Another source asserts that "history is a branch of science having a very strong Party character." It goes on to conclude that one must clear up theoretical confusions "so that the study of history can really serve socialist revolution and construction."[45]

There is a consistent and optimistic confidence that the "scientific" study of history will reveal the theory of "Marxist-Leninist–Mao Zedong thought" operative in the practices of Chinese society. The distinction between historical theory and historical practice is implicitly recognized but quickly bridged by the imperative to "combine revolutionary quality and scientific quality."[46] The principle of "making the past serve the present" indeed evokes the long-standing Chinese assumption that the only point of studying history is to prove what one already knows. The divergence between fact and interpretation may be acknowledged (in passing) but it is not dwelled upon as the core of a hermeneutical dilemma. Rather, it is readily explained as a function of political error. The persistence of the didactic interpretation of history is nowhere more evident than in the assertion that "the fundamental interests of the proletariat are identical with the objective law of historical development."[47] The space between fact and interpretation is completely collapsed, not because Chinese historians are incapable of recognizing the distinction, but because the discipline of history is by definition the attempt to integrate fact and value.

Conclusion

The overall thesis of this study—that the mythical consciousness dominates Chinese historical thinking—can perhaps be too readily simplified into proof that some cultures never attained the breakthrough to critical thought. The point of this essay is neither to resuscitate Hegelian philosophies of history nor to dismiss them altogether. The Western tendency to divide its own history (along with the rest of the world) into a spectrum of consciousness between the poles of the mythical on the one hand, and the philosophical-historical-critical on the other, is a legacy that still dominates the conscience of comparative scholars. Within this context, whereas previous Western scholarship has generally conferred the description of "rational" and "nonmythical" to early Chinese thought, I have insisted on its consistently mythical—or archetypal—reflex.

It is necessary to qualify the extent of this claim. While it is a temptation to generalize and absolutize the *geist* of a culture, my primary focus here is on Chinese historical thinking. This focus is useful because it allows us to bring some questions to bear on our own assumptions about myth and history. Before making the results of this scrutiny explicit, a penultimate point must be made about this notion of critical analysis. If the practice of Chinese history is less than a stellar embodiment of historical methodology, the fault lies perhaps in the cultural constraints imposed on history rather than in a cognitive incapacity. It is a fact of all cultures that certain disciplines are married to the needs of orthodoxy and authority, while other practices are left to relative liberty. In recent times, science has guarded—indeed has come to represent—the principle of freedom of inquiry in the pursuit of truth. In every cultural context, however, one must ask the question of where to look. In the East Asian cultural sphere, the practice of a relatively unencumbered, critical reflection on reality has centered on the literary genres of poetry and fiction.

What perspectives, then, has this focus on the Chinese mythohistorical consciousness contributed to the study of myth in a postmodern age? The category of myth has long represented an experience of the world that the modern West has been conscious of being distant from. Eliade's "archaic" mind evokes a pristine age of innocence when societies lived in a universe of sacred meaning—a universe that is banished by our historical consciousness and its elevation of the event-in-itself. The advent of history suggests a world in which ultimate meaning is not possible; it heralds the mutual alienation of the universal and the particular.

It is this very polarization of event and meaning that Chinese historical thinking refuses to recognize. The convergence of "what happened" and "what typically happens," which is also equivalent to "what *should* happen," reveals perhaps a basic inability—or refusal—to recognize the distinction between the universal and the particular. This perhaps implicates China as one of the most profoundly mythical of cultures, in perfect conformity with Eliade's archaic ontology. This assessment seems to me to be wrongheaded, however, because the force of Eliade's archaic mind cannot be understood except in relation to its opposition—the modern historical mind. Eliade's category of traditional or archaic culture is a modern invention that is sustained by Western notions of the radical break between the past and present; between two different ontic modes of being. What is perhaps so notable about the Chinese historical mind is its very insistence on continuity despite its equal participation in, and observance of, the modern terrors of history.

The odd thing is that the more radical postmodern historicism becomes, the more positivist notions of history are discarded in favor of the Chinese strategy. R. G. Collingwood, for example, in asserting that "all history is the history of thought," is also led to question the distinction between event and meaning. Outward events, he claims, are simply the expression of inward thoughts—that is, the mental state, motivations, and beliefs of the historical agent. "For history, the object to be discovered is not the mere event, but the thought expressed in it. To discover that thought is already to understand it. After the historian has ascertained the facts, there is no further process of inquiring into their causes. When he knows what happened, he already knows why it happened."[48]

In Collingwood's view, historical understanding by definition consists of the apprehension of meaning. Despite both their tendencies to focus on the epistemological divide of the universal and the particular, Collingwood radically opposes Eliade with his claim that true meaning can only be found *within* history. We as historians can rethink the thoughts of those in the past by responding to their situation in the context of our own historical structure. Because our situation necessarily differs from that of the historical agent, our understanding of his or her actions is inherently critical and evaluative. Our rethinking of these past thoughts will simultaneously judge them from the perspective of our own realities. This deems, of course, that historical understanding and judgment will always alter as a function of the historian's own changing situation. In this sense, the historian herself is a part of the process she is studying; he "has his own place in that process, and can see it only from the point of view which at this present moment he occupies within it."[49]

Collingwood's view of history seems to concur with the Chinese tendency to emphasize normative reality. Here, however, historical meaning is derived from and sustained by the ever-transitory and transforming nature of reality. Collingwood is relentlessly hostile to fixed structures of meaning because they are inherently anti-historical. In this sense, the historical and the archetypal still collide. What is worth noting, however, is Collingwood's choice to embrace history. This is an affirmation that threatens Eliade's terror of history with exorcism: the assertion that meaning is not only possible within history but that it can only take place within it. Collingwood's historical understanding resonates with Chinese archetypal thinking in that the apprehension of meaning is always a creation of the present. My attempt to revalorize the notion of myth has focused on this creative function.

In my use of the broader idea of myth as cultural archetype, my point is to claim more than that myths provide patterns for living a life. Eliade saw the significance of myth in its common association with creation narratives. It is because myths narrate the creation of the world in a time before historical time that myths can be used to "banish history." The lack of distinction between a mythical and historical time in the Chinese case, however, obviates the need to relegate myths to some pristine and wistfully distant era. The point of an archetype is that it is constantly utilized as a model for creation in the present. The creation *narrative* can be traded in for a creation *function*. The patterns of selfhood suggested by Chinese archetypes of selves do not merely offer up "archaic" or "traditional" conceptions of model men and women. The enduring viability of these models sometimes requires an evolution in modes of expression: witness the transition between the legendary culture heroes as depicted in the Chinese classics and their alternate presentation in the ethical discourse of Confucius. The important point is that they provide a current cultural template by which actual lives and persons are formed. Thus the power of myth goes beyond a modeling function to manifest an ontological force.

Twentieth-century Existentialist ruminations on the terror of history have often found their way to an affirmation of the present moment, which is an affirmation of history itself. Karl Jaspers avers that it is through formulating the meaning of history as a whole—tempered as that universal view may be by our historical embeddedness—that allows one to transcend history: "The fundamental paradox of our existence, the fact that it is only within the world that we can live above and beyond the world, is repeated in the historical consciousness that rises above history. There is no way round the world, no way round history, but only a way through history."[50]

The question that remains is, What enables the historical being to negotiate her way through history? Clearly, no being—East or West—is capable of sustaining himself in a world defined by the event-in-itself. It is not possible to dispense with myths. But Eliade has already told us as much. There is one thing, however, that should be kept in mind. We have in our intellectual age banished

the fallacy of history; that is, the fallacy of an objective and brutish world of facts that robs us of our autonomy and self-
determination. Eliade's "terror of history" remains but with a
new definition: the terror derives not from our enslavement to
history but from our freedom to determine its meaning.[51]

We live in an age where myths must be created at will because
we lack archetypal models from the past. One must pause to consider the question of whether such willful myths really satisfy
the conditions of the term. Our investigation of the Chinese mythohistorical consciousness suggests that myths need not project
us back into a primordial, sacred time, but they nevertheless
must possess the power to remake the present in its own image.
The ontic force of myth has the power to repress as well as to
create. Jiang Qing herself might have preferred to live in a world
where she had the freedom to make herself of her own accord.
This freedom, nonetheless, does not suit the faint of heart nor the
weak of will. The dilemma is perhaps most succinctly posed by
reiterating a sentiment of Nietzsche: "Can you furnish yourself
with your own good and evil and hang up your own will above
yourself as a law? Can you be judge of yourself and avenger of
your law? It is terrible to be alone with the judge and avenger of
one's own law. It is like a star thrown forth into empty space and
into the icy breath of solitude."[52]

Notes

1. The argument appears in my article "Myth and Cosmology in *The Book of Poetry*," 283–85. Strictly speaking, the argument made by the article does not address the dualism of the universal and particular but rather the one of sacred and profane, also derived from Eliade. To the extent to which the sacred and profane are analogous to myth and history, however, the terms *universal* and *particular* also apply. I use these latter terms as a way of essentializing and converging some of the more significant categories of Eliade's thought.
2. Collingwood, *Idea of History*, 154.
3. Ibid., 42.
4. Eliade, *Cosmos and History*, 34, Collingwood, *Idea of History*, 24.
5. See note 1.
6. The ontologically creative function of myth is something that can be distinguished from the kind of ontological creativeness that has been observed of other forms of discourse, such as philosophy and metaphor. In "Myth and Cosmology," I derive the ontologically creative function of myth directly from Eliade's notion of myth as a ritual text that allows societies to banish historical time and return to the time of creation. I argued in that paper that this ontological creativity is not wedded to myth as a narrative but rather to myth as an articulation of archetypes.
7. Eliade, *Myth and Cosmos*, 34.

8. Allan, *The Shape of the Turtle*, 15.
9. As Plaks further points out, "In traditional China it is frequently the same group of literati who have indulged in both official historiography and more fictional (or at least less historical) forms of narrative" ("Towards a Critical Theory of Chinese Narrative," 312).
10. Anthony C. Yu for example, describes the development of prose fiction and its dependence on history, the derivative nature of the former being indicated by its common designation as "unofficial or fragmented history." Remarking on this nomenclature, Yu states that it "points already to the unmistakable supremacy of the original model [history] and the deviant nature of its imitator [fiction]" ("History, Fiction and the Reading of Chinese Narrative," 1).
11. Plaks, "Towards a Critical Theory," 313.
12. Girardot, "Chinese Religion: Mythic Themes."
13. The claim of reverse euhemerization was prevalent in early twentieth-century studies of China, most notably Granet's *Danses et Legendes de la Chine Ancienne.*
14. For introductions to the study of autobiography in the European-American context, see Weintraub's *Value of the Individual*, and Spacks's, *Imagining a Self.*
15. Gusdorf, "Conditions and Limits of Autobiography," 30.
16. Gunn, *Autobiography*, 4.
17. Wu, *Confucian's Progress*, 8.
18. My translation is taken from the full translation of the *Lienuzhuan* by Albert Richard O'Hara.
19. Ibid., 12–13.
20. For relatively recent accounts of this late Imperial-dynasty phenomenon of virtuous widows, see Mark Elvin, "Female Virtue and the State in China," *Past and Present* 104 (1984): 111–52; and T'ien Ju-k'ang, *Male Anxiety and Female Chastity: A Comparative Study of Chinese Ethical Values in Ming-Ch'ing Times.*
21. These circumstances were most frequently provided by the minority of the emperors, instances in which the emperor was ill or unable to attend to state affairs, and upon the sudden death of the emperor. See Yang, "Female Rulers in Imperial China," 51.
22. From "The Speech at Muh," Legge, *The Shoo King*, 302–3.
23. Liu Xiang is quoting *The Book of Poetry*. My translation is taken from the full translation of the *Lienüzhuan* by O'Hara (*The Position of Woman in Early China*, 194.)
24. For general accounts of the power struggle around the succession of Mao Zedong, see Hollingworth, *Mao and the Men against Him*; Terrill, *Mao*, and *The White-Boned Demon.*
25. Hsieh, "Rise and Fall of Comrade Chiang Ch'ing," 151.
26. Perelomov, "Mao, the Legalists, and the Confucianists," 64.
27. Ibid., 91 n. 4.
28. Mao Zedong, "On New Democracy," 381.
29. Hung, "Struggle," 128.
30. The Communist-controlled journal *Hongqi* (Red Flag) was the major vehicle for this new school of historical interpretation. Some articles include Lo Ssu-ting, "On the Class Struggle during the Period between the Qin and Han Dynasties," (8) 1974, 16–26; and "Forward on the Path of Socialism," (10) 1974, 5–7.

    Hung's article also clearly sketches out the basic thesis. See also Perelomov, "Mao, the Legalists, and the Confucianists" for an exposition of this movement.
31. Hung, "Struggle," 131.

32. For examples of this scholarship, see the translated articles in *Chinese Studies in History*, Fall/Winter (1974–75) issue.

33. Perelomov is referring to the document entitled "Outline of Project 571," which was allegedly written by Lin Biao's son in March 1971 and which detailed a plan for a political coup by Lin Biao and his followers against Mao. The document was eventually used to discredit and purge Lin Biao as a reactionary who tried to "turn back the wheel of history." See "Mao, the Legalists, and the Confucians," 69–70.

34. In the Introduction to the CHS volume on Ch'in Shih-huang (Emperor Qinshi) studies, Li Yu-ning gives one explanation for the revaluation of China's "first emperor": "Since the 'Outline of Project 571' showed that the 'counterrevolutionaries' had been anti–Ch'in Shi-huang, it seemed logical for revolutionaries to favorably interpret the First Emperor. And since the 'Outline' was to be so thoroughly discussed, the need for an authoritative interpretation of the First Emperor must have been realized" (lii).

35. Hollingworth, *Mao and the Men against Him*, 266.

36. See, e.g., Hu, Feng and Huang, "Female Emperor Wu Tse-t'ien"; and Li, "Wu Tse-t'ien: A Pro-Legalist, Anti-Confucian Stateswoman."

37. Lo, "Evolution of the Controversy between the Confucianists and the Legalists."

38. For examples, see Chou, "Distorting Ancient History to Serve Present Needs"; Survey of People's Republic of China Press, "The 'Gang of Four' Who Make a Mockery of History Have Been Punished by History"; Hsü, "Chiang Ch'ing and Empress Lü"; and Editorial Board of *Li-shih yen-chiu*, "Be Unrelenting in Beating Dogs."

39. Editorial Board, "Be Unrelenting in Beating Dogs," 30.

40. Ibid., 32.

41. History Writing Group, "Ghost of Empress Lü," 40.

42. Editorial Board, "Be Unrelenting in Beating Dogs," 35.

43. History Writing Group, "Ghost of Empress Lü," 43.

44. Li, "Correct Understanding," 46.

45. Hou, "Use Mao Tsetung Thought as a Guide in Critically Inheriting the Legacy of History," 64–65.

46. Li, "Correct Understanding," 46.

47. Ibid.

48. Collingwood, *Idea of History*, 214.

49. Ibid., 248.

50. Jaspers, *Origin and Goal of History*, 275.

51. Let us take a case in point from the pages of the mass media. In a recent column by Jonathan Yardley in the *Washington Post* entitled "Putting Our Own Spin on History" (Style Section, Monday, October 4, 1993), the author takes issue with two current events. The first has to do with the District of Columbia's movement toward implementing an Afrocentric curriculum in the public schools. Controversy raged throughout the summer of 1993 over this plan, fueled by questions about the intellectual integrity of the curriculum. The second event has to do with a book on Iwo Jima that raised questions about the famous flag-raising photograph, contending that it actually depicted the raising of a second and larger flag rather than a spontaneous moment in patriotic history. This deconstruction of a significant American image raised a storm of hostility and rejection.

The two events lead Yardley to reflect on the importance of history. The Afrocentric movement demonstrates the legitimate desire of all peoples to know their history and thus know who they are. The response to the revisionist history of Iwo Jima displays people's willingness to defend a mythical version of who they are. The incidents cause Yardley to lament the quixotic nature of history: "People believe what they want to believe. If

what most pleases or suits them happens to be true, fine; if it is not, then they would rather stick to comforting fiction rather than to disagreeable facts."
52. Nietzsche, *A Nietzsche Reader*, 241.

Works Cited

Abbreviations:
CSH: *Chinese Studies in History*
SPRCP: *Survey of People's Republic of China Press*

Allan, Sarah. *The Shape of the Turtle: Myth, Art, and Cosmos in Early China*. Albany: State University of New York Press, 1991.

Bantly, Francisca Cho. "Myth and Cosmology in the *Book of Poetry*." In *Myth and Fictions*. Edited by Shlomo Biderman and Ben-Ami Scharfstein. Leiden: E. J. Brill, 1993.

Chou Wen. "Distorting Ancient History to Serve Present Needs." CSH 11 (Winter 1977–78): 64–75.

Chung, Priscilla Ching. "Power and Prestige: Palace Women in the Northern Sung (960–1126)." In *Women in China: Current Directions in Historical Scholarship*. Edited by Richard W. Guisso and Stanley Johannesen. Youngstown: Philo Press, 1981.

Collingwood, R. G. *The Idea of History*. London: Oxford University Press, 1956.

Editorial Board of *Li-shih yen-chiu*. "Be Unrelenting in Beating Dogs Who Have Fallen in the Water—Liang Hsiao and Lo Ssu-ting." CSH 11 (Spring 1978): 28–48.

Eliade, Mircea. *Cosmos and History*. New York: Harper and Row, 1959.

———. *Myth and Reality*. New York: Harper and Row, 1963.

Elvin, Mark. "Female Virtue and the State in China." *Past and Present*, 1984.

Girardot, Norman. "Chinese Religion: Mythic Themes." *Encyclopedia of Religion*. New York: Macmillan Publishing Company.

Granet, Marcel. *Danses et Legendes de la Chine Ancienne*. Paris: Presses Universaires de France, 1959.

Gunn, Janet Varner. *Autobiography: Toward a Poetics of Experience*. Philadelphia: University of Pennsylvania Press, 1982.

Gusdorf, Georges. "Conditions and Limits of Autobiography." In *Autobiography: Essays Theoretical and Critical*. Edited by James Olney. Princeton: Princeton University Press, 1980.

History Writing Group of the Chinese Communist Party Kwangtung Provincial Committee. "The Ghost of Empress Lü and Chiang Ch'ing's Empress Dream." CSH 12 (Fall 1978): 37–54.

Hollingworth, Claire. *Mao and the Men against Him*. London: Jonathan Cape. 1985.

Hou Wai-lu. "Use Mao Tsetung Thought as a Guide in Critically Inheriting the Legacy of History." CSH 12 (Winter 1978–79): 60–65.

Hsieh Chen-ping. "The Rise and Fall of Comrade Chiang Ch'ing." *Asian Affairs* (New York) 5(Jan./Feb.1978): 148–64.

Hsü Hsün. "Chiang Ch'ing and Empress Lü." CSH 11 (Winter 1977–78): 56–63.

Hu Shen-shen, Feng Tan-feng and Huang Lung-chen. "Female Emperor Wu Tse-t'ien." CSH 8 (Summer 1975): 15–28.

Hung Shih-ti. "The Struggle between 'Emphasizing the Present While Slighting the Past' and 'Using the Past to Criticize the Present'." CSH, *The First Emperor of China: The Politics of Historiography* (Fall–Winter 1974–75): 91–115.

Jaspers, Karl. *The Origin and Goal of History*. New Haven: Yale University Press, 1953.

Ju-k'ang, T'ien. *Male Anxiety and Female Chastity: A Comparative Study of Chinese Ethical Values in Ming-Ch'ing Times*. Leiden: Brill, 1988.

Li Shih. "Wu Tse-t'ien: A Pro-Legalist, Anti-Confucian Stateswoman of the T'ang Dynasty." CSH 11 (Summer 1978): 26–33.

Li Shu. "A Correct Understanding of 'Making the Past Serve the Present.'" CSH 11 (Summer 1978): 42–47.

Li Yu-ning. Introduction. CSH, *The First Emperor of China: The Politics of Historiography*. (Fall/Winter 1974–75): xiii–lxxi.

Lo Ssu-ting. "Evolution of the Controversy between the Confucianists and the Legalists as Seen from Wang An-Shih's Reforms." CSH 9 (Fall/Winter 1975–76): 3–20.

———. "On the Class Struggle during the Period between the Qin and Han Dynasties." *Hongqi*, (8) 1974.

———. "Forward on the Path of Socialism." *Hongqi*, (10) 1974.

Nietzsche, Frederick. *A Nietzsche Reader*. Translated by R. J. Hollingdale. Harmondsworth: Penguin, 1977.

O'Hara, Albert Richard. *The Position of Woman in Early China*. Taipei: Mei Ya Publications, 1971.

Perelomov, L. S. "Mao, the Legalists, and the Confucianists." CSH 11 (Fall 1977): 64–93.

Plaks, Andrew. "Towards a Critical Theory of Chinese Narrative." In *Chinese Narrative: Critical and Theoretical Essays*. Edited by Andrew Plaks. Princeton: Princeton University Press, 1977.

Selected Works of Mao Tse-Tung. Volume 2. Oxford: Pergamon Press, 1961.

Shoo King (*Shujing*), in *Sacred Books of China: The Texts of Confucianism*, pt. 1, vol. 1. Translated by James Legge. Oxford at the Clarendon Press, 1879.

Spacks, Patricia Meyer. *Imagining a Self: Autobiography and Novel in Eighteenth-Century England.* Cambridge: Harvard University Press, 1976.

SPRCP. "The 'Gang of Four' Who Make a Mockery of History Have Been Punished by History." No. 6226 (Nov. 24, 1976), 118–28.

Sung, Marina. "The Chinese Lieh-nu Tradition." In *Women in China: Current Directions in Historical Scholarship.* Edited by Richard W. Guisso and Stanley Johannesen. Youngstown: Philo Press, 1981.

Terrill, Ross. *Mao.* New York: Harper and Row, 1980.

———. *The White-Boned Demon: A Biography of Madame Mao Zedong.* New York: William Morrow, 1984.

Weintraub, Karl Joachim. *The Value of the Individual: Self and Circumstance in Autobiography.* Chicago: University of Chicago Press, 1978.

Wu, Pei-yi. *The Confucian's Progress: Autobiographical Writings in Traditional China.* Princeton: Princeton University Press, 1990.

Yang, Lien-sheng. "Female Rulers in Imperial China." *Harvard Journal of Asiatic Studies* 23 (1960–61): 47–61.

Yardley, Jonathan. "Putting Our Own Spin on History." *Washington Post,* Style Section, Monday, October 4, 1993.

Yu, Anthony C. "History, Fiction, and the Reading of Chinese Narrative." *Chinese Literature: Essays, Articles, and Reviews* 10 (1988): 1–19.

Zedong, Mao. "On New Democracy." In *Selected Works of Mao Tse-Tung.* Vol. 2. Oxford: Pergamon Press, 1961.

LAURIE L. PATTON

MYTH AND MONEY: THE EXCHANGE OF WORDS AND WEALTH IN VEDIC COMMENTARY

A MYTH IN a Vedic commentary relates how Kakṣīvat, the son of a famous seer and poet Dīrghatamas, falls asleep in the forest. A king finds him sleeping and thinks that he would be an excellent son-in-law. They negotiate and come to an agreement. The story ends with a detailed discussion of the wealth bestowed upon him—chariots, brass, and strong-bodied steeds yoked in fours, among other gifts. The young poet sings a *mantra* from *Ṛg-Veda* (RV) 1.125 to thank him for the goods. A commentarial problem arises in the interpretation of the next verse of the Vedic hymn, which praises the good fortune of the person who has received such abundant wealth. The verse could easily be interpreted, true to Vedic dialogical style, as a reply from the king. But there is substantial disagreement in the commentary about who actually speaks this verse in praise of wealth. The consensus is that it is not the king but the young poet or the young poet's father.

The mythologist's question at this point is: Why all the fuss? Is this debate about the speaker of *Ṛg-Veda* 1.125.2 simply a matter of pedantic scholasticism, or is there something deeper at issue? I shall argue that there is indeed something larger at stake: These commentarial mythologies can be read not simply as "myths about money" or expressions of "Vedic materialism" but as meditations about the relative value of words and wealth as media of exchange in the early Vedic and late Vedic worlds. I will go on to show a historical shift in attitude toward these relative values. While the earlier Vedic texts show a fluidity of exchange between words and wealth as forms of currency, the later narratives found in Vedic commentaries will allow a king to give wealth but not to utter *mantras*. The relationship between the production of material wealth and the production of language as a form of social authority and prestige is no longer geared toward the performance of sacrifice but toward the fulfillment of *varṇa* (class) ideals. In examining this Vedic case in which money is an explicit concern, I make a larger argument about the way in which myths can be read as statements of relative value.

Making Money, Making History

Before moving to the historical work, it is important to address briefly the methodological problems raised by myths about money. The juxtaposition of mythology and money tends to create extreme reactions. The seemingly irreconcilable difference between the symbolic and the concrete, the figurative and the economic, frequently encourages mythologists to see one in terms of the other. In his introduction to *Taking Ancient Mythology Economically*, for example, Morris Silver views myth in terms of money.[1] He argues that, if one takes the idea of cultural diffusion in the ancient Mediterrenean seriously, many myths can be decoded to reveal their clear economic import: myths about the head are in fact myths about coinage; the throwing gesture symbolizes the advance of capital; opening a path represents the opening or keeping open of a trade route, and so on.[2]

Such an approach is surely welcome in the age of what might be called "post-mystification." Such reductionist moves (and I do not use the term pejoratively here) can and do have an extremely important function in the service of historicizing myths. Silver juxtaposes one discipline (the study of mythology) with another (economics) and thus opens up a whole new area of historical inquiry.[3] However, if used exclusively, such an approach to mythology ultimately perpetuates, even rigidifies, the dichotomy between practice and theory that Catherine Bell and others have argued can get in the way of clear thinking.[4] While Silver is careful enough not to claim that all mythology can be seen in this light, his interpretation proceeds in a single direction, from the narrative language—indeed, an analysis of particular words—to the economic practices behind them. Thus, all mythological words and the images that they portray are in the symbolic realm and the practices they represent are in the real realm, and never the twain shall meet.

The other approach to myths about money is to explain away their materialism by claiming that material survival was the paramount spiritual concern for those living under primitive conditions. While variations on this theme abound,[5] one of the most recent examples is a work on the Vedic period itself, Uma Gupta's *Materialism in the Vedas*.[6] She writes of the mythology of the ṛṣis (seers, or sages), "Religion . . . did not originate with a revelation of any divine or spiritual reality, but with man's consciousness of the powers supposed to be vitally affecting human life. To the Vedic Indian, life in this world was the dearest and most valuable thing. Religion . . . is a means of achieving this mundane value or goal. . . . The will to live positively aiming at material prosperity and negatively aiming at destruction of anything that stands in the way of enjoyment of life, is very prominent in the Vedic prayers and sacrifices."[7] Gupta's analysis of mythology follows upon these lines that the mundane and the supramundane are constitutively contrastive with each other. She writes of the mythology of the ṛṣis that, "in contrast with the spiritualistic religion," enemies are not the moral evils obstructive to the progress of spiritual life but the "concrete real objects" that threaten the very existence of this world.[8] In analyzing Vedic prayers for protection, Gupta continues in this vein, arguing that fear of losing life and anxiety for protection are "earth-bound" prayers, concerned with the "problems of mundane existence and have little to do with supramundane life."[9] While it would not be appropriate here to venture into a discussion of the history of the relationship between mind and matter, theory and practice, suffice it to say that views which see "materialist" religion as essentially different from "spiritual" or "symbolic" religion greatly affect the way in which one can read myths about exchange. Indeed, Gupta herself follows Vetter in characterizing Vedic prayers as "compelling, abusing and threatening the supernaturals should they fail to deliver the goods on demand."[10]

Several recent works are of great help in breaking down the material-symbolic dichotomy in the more general discussion of exchange. Marc Shell's recent works, *Money, Language and Thought* and *The Economy of Literature*, both address the ways in which money and language provide worth in Western Civilization and the relationships between linguistic and economic production in the medieval and modern eras. While his insights are helpful in the terms of Western literary practice, the language of symbolic anthropology also contributes important understandings of the dynamics of exchange within the contexts of myth and ritual. Building on the tradition of Marcel Mauss, Bronislaw Malinowski, Edmund Leach, Annette Weiner, and others,[11] Nancy Munn provides a helpful model of exchange in her study of the symbolism of value production among the Gawans, *The Fame of Gawa*. Breaking down the dichotomy between the symbolic and the nonsymbolic, she writes that a symbolic study need not be substantively retraced to the examination of myth or ritual or some special, predefined class of object. Rather, the practices by means of which actors construct their social world, and simultaneously their own selves and modes of being in the world, are thought to be symbolically constituted and themselves symbolic processes.[12]

Value, then, is measured in two ways according to Munn's symbolic anthropology. First, it can be seen in terms of its particular, essential capacities or key possible outcomes: for Gawans, giving food to overseas visitors has the capacity to yield not only return hospitality but also in the long run kula shells and renown. But the value of an act can also be expressed in a second way—that is, in terms of a differential proportion of some homogenous potency. Its value can then be expressed relatively in terms of a gauge (the kind of potency involved) along which value is, as it were, measured. Munn defines this more general value in Gawan terms as an act's capacity for spatiotemporal transformation—to expand a space-time of self-other relationships that are formed in and through acts or practices. It involves a deeper dimension of cultural meaning implicated in the substantive value of products and acts.[13]

Leaving aside for the moment the particular Gawan perspective on value, it is important for our purposes to note that value in this sense is not only particular and substantive but also general and relational. Such an idea has important implications for the study of myths about money. Just as kula shells are not simply the symbolic forms of the more materially grounded yams or canoes in the Gawan practice of exchange but exist along a continuum of relative value, so too myths about money are not simply the symbolic expression of a material reality. To be sure, such mythological narratives may express the particular potency of a certain kind of economic activity (e.g., the value of coins are best expressed through the symbolism of the head, as Silver argues).

However, that is not all they express. They can also act as kinds of meditation on the relative value of one form of symbolic construction as weighed against another.

Even more importantly for our purposes here, such a view of value encourages the historical analysis of how such values might change over time. While the problems of historical shifts in relative value are not addressed by Munn,[14] it would be fair to say that one could read particular myths in terms of their shifting presentations of value. The key word is, of course, *relative*. Munn's study focuses primarily on how value is relative to the contexts of the practices of exchange (e.g., the Gawan myth of the origins of the canoe depicts the relative value of male and female labor in the construction of canoes as media of exchange).[15] However, her study is suggestive to historians insofar as one might be able to trace such transformational productions of value relative to time itself. To put it in other words, if the symbolic process of value production is transformational, then it must be transformational not only in terms of the social roles and statuses of certain individuals and groups but also in terms of the mode of *value production itself*. The processes of exchange that constitute the production of value must undergo shifts, just as those engaging in them undergo shifts. Thus, the ways in which such value productions are represented in cultural narratives must also change over time. And it is this larger process of changing representation in which the historian of mythology is interested.

Mantra *and Wealth in the Vedic World*

Munn's symbolic analysis of value and its implications for historical work are particularly helpful in the context of Vedic mythology that deals with money, specifically myths that juxtapose material wealth with the more symbolic *mantra*, or sacred verse. In what follows I shall argue first that the stories about money and *mantra* are not simply the glorification of wealth;[16] I will argue instead that these myths are explicitly placed within Vedic commentary as a means of thinking about the relative worth of two important forms of exchange: speech and material wealth in the form of cows, chariots, gold, goats, and the like. I shall go on to argue that the mythological tradition not only parallels those changes in sacrificial practice but in fact can teach us more about the ways in which one can detect a change in attitude toward that relative worth as one reads myths from historical periods later than the *Rg-Vedic* texts upon which they are based. More specifically speaking, the ambiguous, fluid nature of the exchange between words and wealth, *mantra* and material goods discernible in the earlier Vedic texts becomes codified according to class in later Vedic commentaries. Despite the fact that the early texts indicate otherwise, in the later texts, only kings can give wealth, and only *rṣis*, as prototypical Brahmin priests, can utter *mantra*s. Moreover, the explicitly contestual, more violent forms of exchange implied in the sacrifical texts become tamed, sweetened into domestic reveries about the wanderings of a wayward poet whose wealth comes upon him unexpectedly.

Mantra *as Medium of Exchange:*
A Closer Look

It is a truism to say that words and wealth had a symbiotic relationship in the earliest Vedic period. Indeed, as discussed more generally above, the term *dāna*, ("giving," "gift") is a word of frequent occurrence in the *Rg-Veda*, uttered in praise of generous patrons.[17] One of the characteristics of the Brahmin priest is his right to receive gifts, which it is incumbent upon the other classes, or *varṇa*s, to present.[18] The relationship between words and wealth is even further codified in the term *dāna-stuti* ("praise of wealth") a term used in commentarial literature to refer to *mantra*s offered to the *dakṣinā*, or generous patron of the sacrifice.[19]

The exact nature of that relationship between *mantra* and money has been quite problematically characterized, however. Vedic language has been kept in the realms of two extremes: either it has been denigrated as a "cheap" form of exchange, and classified as "magic," or, more recently, it has been taken out of the realm of exchange altogether, and classified as "mystical." In either case, the possibility of mantric language simply being a player in the economy of symbols is denied.

To take the first extreme: the continuing use of the term *magic* as it is applied to Rg- and Atharva-Vedic utterances is commonplace.[20] Frequently, however, it is not clear exactly what is meant by the term. While it is not necessary at this point to delve into a history of the theories of magic in the history of religions, it is worth pointing out that in late nineteenth- and early twentieth-century Indology (a period when definitions of magic were both more simplistic and clearer than they are today), there is a definite economic undertone in the use of the term. *Magic* implies that something real is acquired cheaply—without cost, whether it be through the lack of physical effort ("sleight of hand," in the commonsense definition) or the lack of a commitment to community (in the Durkheimian sense), and so on.

In Vedic scholarship in particular, *mantra* has been classed as "magical"—a "cheap" way of attempting to affect reality, because language itself has not been taken as seriously as a valuable commodity in the system of Vedic exchange. When a goat, or even an oblation of warm milk, is given in exchange for Indra's favor, or for the possibility of rain, or for wealth, students of Vedic religion usually classify it as "sacrificial offering"—a legitimate, if mistaken, form of sacrificial exchange. This is true even when the more symbolic *mantra* accompanies the exchange (which is more often than not). However, when the offering is *mantra* and only *mantra*, unaccompanied by something more laborious, or costly in nature, the act is classed as a form of "magical spell."

A. B. Keith's treatment of the *hotṛ* priest is an excellent early example. The *hotṛ* is the priest of the sacrifice most responsible for the recitation of *mantra*. Because of this function, to Keith the *hotṛ*'s role is essentially that of a magician and should be contrasted with the *adhvaryu*, the ritualist:

> It is wholly impossible to doubt that, if the Adhvaryu really thought that the acts of the sacrifice and the actual offerings were what mattered, his view was not in the least shared by the *hotṛ*, who was of the opinion that his perfectly constructed hymns would give the god the greatest amount of pleasure. . . . The pride of the Vedic poets in their own powers is perfectly evidenced, when they claim that their hymns strengthen Indra for the slaying of Vṛtra or that through the prayers the steeds are yoked to the chariot of the god. Here as everywhere the tendency of the sacrifice to pass into magic is illustrated: the prayer which is really essentially free from magic is at last turned by the pride of its composers into nothing but a spell.[21]

The source of the pride here is, of course, that beautifully constructed words alone can effect the ends which the poet seeks.

The other attitude that takes language out of the realm of exchange is that of mysticism. To be sure, it is fair enough to call Vedic poets philosophers in some form, as do C. Kunhan Raja and

Antonio de Nicolas.[22] It is even arguable that they might be classed as devotees of the goddess of speech, as Willard Johnson has done. Wade Wheelock and Ellison Findly have gone some way in clarifying the issue by classifying *mantra* as performative.[23] Wheelock, in particular, sees *mantra* as one specific kind of speech act: following linguists J. L. Austin and John Searle, he classifies (and subclassifies) *mantra* as an illocutionary speech act *which serves to create and allow participation in a known and repeatable situation.* However, in all of these analyses, the language of exchange, so clearly present in the formulations of the poets themselves, is cut out of the picture. We are left solely with the expression of speculative thought, or of mystical experience—perhaps only a partial picture of the larger symbolic economy of which Vedic words are a part.

It is important to remember that *mantra* was exclusively neither a function of magic nor a function of personal meditation and inspiration. Its value was also placed within a context of exchange, as the Vedic poets themselves tell us. We must take the language of *mantra* at face value, and realize that the very self-reflexivity of the work—the references made to *mantra* and *sūkta* (hymn) in Ṛg-Vedic verses themselves—are more often than not explicitly linked to the expected return for the offering of the constructed word. It would be needless to multiply the staggering number of possible examples here.[24] Suffice it to say that one might read the simplest Ṛg-Vedic expression differently: "The man who honors you today, Agni and Soma, with this speech, bestow on him heroic strength, an increase of cows and noble steeds" (RV 1.93.2) can be seen as a statement of a transaction between two kinds of value, wherein one agent bestows the word and the other bestows the wealth.

Such an exchange-based view of language is also confirmed by the fact that language is spoken of as shaped and constructed—in a word, as a product in its own right. One need only turn to the well-known hymn RV 6.9, Agni and the young poet, to read images of language as constructed, or woven. The phrase "He is the one who knows how to stretch the thread and weave the cloth; he will speak the right words" (v.2) is not just a pretty way of talking about speech but a fundamental understanding of the way in which *mantra* participates in the larger economy of sacrifice. At times, speech is offered not only as an exchange for wealth, but its properties are also enumerated; RV 3.8.2 declares the speech of the poet to be "undecaying" (*ajaram*), presumably like the "great and good fortune" (*mahate saubhagāya*) that speech is said to bring.

Perhaps the most telling among numerous examples, RV 9.112 portrays the priest comparing his thoughts in the sacrifice to other forms of labor: "Our thoughts bring us to diverse callings, setting people apart: the carpenter seeks what is broken, the physician a fracture, and the Brahmin priest seeks one who presses Soma. O, Drop of Soma, flow for Indra," (v.1). And in v. 3, the economic connotations of the poetic act are made even more explicit "I am a poet, my Dad's a physician and Mum a miller with grinding stones. With diverse thoughts we all strive for wealth, going after it like cattle. O, Drop of Soma, flow for Indra." Poets, no less than those in other occupations, strive for wealth, using words as their primary form of earning potential. These are indeed well-studied Vedic expressions, whose meaning is clear. However, they are also utterances that can be fruitfully read with a different eye toward the role of language in symbolic exchange.

Fluidity of Identity: Mantra and
Exchange in the Sacrificial Texts

*Mantra*s are also integral parts of the process of exchange in the sacrificial texts in a number of intriguing and more complex ways than the simpler Rg-Vedic examples given above. Not only might *mantra*s be used as simple objects of exchange, as discussed above; they also act to effect the process of exchange. They do so in two particular ways.

First, *mantra*s complete ritual exchanges and give them a new reality. Without their being uttered, a number of sacrificial transactions would not be possible because they would not be "declared" as such. In this they are performative in a very particular way: they are not only requests for wealth that initiate exchange (as in the Rg-Vedic examples above), but they are declamatory of the fact that, because an exchange has taken place, a new ritual situation has come about, involving a change in the nature of the participants.[25] *Mantra*s function as agents of transformation that affect the identity of the individual in the process of exchanging.

Second, *mantra*s form a relationship between the person and the object of exchange. As both Munn and Weiner suggest in the New Guinea case,[26] the production of value involves a close identity between the person who has given a gift and the gift itself. At times, this identity manifests itself in the ways in which objects retain their original owner long after they have passed through several households in the process of exchange; this is part of the spatiotemporal transformation called fame in the Gawan context. In the Vedic context, this identity is achieved by the utterance of a *mantra*, declaring, as we shall see in an example below, the identity between *soma* (exchanged), and the consecrated sacrificer (the exchanger).

The basic Soma sacrifice, the *Agniṣṭoma*, described as the "fundamental and typical" Vedic sacrifice, should serve as a simple framework for illustration in an exceedingly complex corpus.[27] To sum up the sacrifice briefly: after several preliminary rites, involving the purchase of Soma, the construction of the altars, pressing pits, and a declaration of hospitality, the sacrifice proper consists of three pressings (morning, midday, and night) in which the Soma plant, also a deity, is crushed and offered to the gods. Each pressing has its own particular significance and its own modality of sacrificial exchange. Scholars have puzzled about the overall significance of the rite. Hillebrandt regards it as a rain charm in that Soma causes the waters of the sky to fall,[28] while others such as Oldenberg conjecture that it is a feeding of the gods with the lunar nectar that is Soma.[29] Hubert and Mauss describe the rites as the birth and death of the god Soma.[30] In his most recent book, *The Broken World of Sacrifice: An Essay in Ancient Indian Ritual*, Jan Heesterman places its meaning squarely in the middle of ritual contest for sacrificial wealth, a contest with potentially lethal consequences.[31]

The role of language—the *mantra*s and other formulas that are used in these processes—clearly reflects that agonistic element of exchange, particularly as the contestants struggle to achieve the identity of victorious sacrificer. These dynamics of *mantra* effecting a change of identity, mentioned above, are elucidated best by the figure of the *dīkṣita*, or consecrated sacrificer. Heesterman points out that the *dīkṣita* must undergo two periods of wandering before officially settling down for the Soma sacrifice proper, before and after his consecration (*dīkṣā*). While these periods of wandering are quite similar to those of the *brahmacārin*, or student,[32] and may have reflected an ancient initiation pattern, they were also intended as a way for the *dīkṣita* to collect the goods, or wealth, to be exchanged in the sacrifice, which was a campaign of conquest.

Let me attend first to the ways in which *mantra* completes—

indeed, transforms—the status of the sacrificer as the *dīkṣita*, the possessor of wealth, and all that such status entails. One such example is the purchase of Soma, the sacrificial substance itself. During the period of preparation before the Soma sacrifice proper, there is a ritual expedition to obtain the Soma materials. The ritual represents the buying of Soma in an elaborate bargaining scene, in which Soma is bartered for a cow. The contestual elements are clear: the verbal negotiation is not peaceful, and the Soma seller is beaten at the end.

More importantly for our purposes, the mantric language surrounding the transactions shows the transformation of identity in the process of exchange. The *mantras* uttered at the offering of the cow achieve the transformation of the contesting sacrificer into victorious sacrificer. Before the *mantra* is uttered, the cow has its seventh step sprinkled with *ghee* and the earth from that footprint cut out and divided over the fire hearths, with the sacrificer's wife equally receiving a part of it. The *mantra* accompanying the hoofprint is then uttered: "Here I cut the neck of the demon; the one who hates us and whom we hate, his neck I cut."[33] The *mantra* makes explicit the element of victory in contest over one's enemies, but perhaps even more importantly, articulates the price of a successful sacrificial exchange. The cow is the live representative of Iḍā, the goddess of the sacrificial meal, whose foot drips with *ghee* (*gṛhtapadī*), while the *ghee*-soaked print is the primordial altar.[34] Without the utterance of *mantra*, the exchange and distribution of the footprint would not be finished; its purpose would remain undeclared.

Other details within the sacrifice show the second way in which mantric language is involved with exchange: the establishing of an identity between the person exchanging and the object of exchange, as Munn and Weiner suggested above. The sacrificer identifies himself with the warrior god Indra and incorporates the Soma into himself. At various moments in the process of the sacrifice proper, the sacrificer is identified through *mantra* as the sacrificial conqueror. For instance, when the *dīkṣita* has obtained, or rather won, the Soma, he presses its stalks on his right thigh with the *mantra* "Enter into Indra's right thigh willing into the willing, soft into the soft."[35] *Mantra* effects his new status as Soma, the ultimate object of exchange. Moreover, the procession that follows is accompanied by a *mantra* that also refers to his new status as conqueror. The *mantra* declares that "they proceed, conquering, with Soma as their king; when a human king comes

into the house, it is in his power . . . King Soma has come to his
house; it is in his power."[36]

*Mantra*s also reveal an even more meaningful link between the
person exchanging and the thing exchanged. The conqueror is not
in an invulnerable position. Because the *dīksita* possesses the
goods of Soma, he is thus symbolically equal to the Soma, and
thus is himself vulnerable to being killed and crushed. Thus, he
himself *becomes* the mode of exchange, and this ambiguous status is reflected in the mantric exchange. In a more elaborate version of the *Agnistoma*, the *Rājasūya*, the king is announced at
his consecratory Soma feast with the *mantra* "This is your king,
Oh Bhāratas," and then, in a whisper, "Soma is our, the Brahmins', king."[37] This mantric identification of Soma with the king
is reflected in several Vedic texts that refer to Soma himself as
being killed, crushed as a sacrificial victim.[38] Even more complexly, the sacrificer can also be identified with another possessor
of Soma, the demon Vrtra, who held Agni and Soma within himself but ultimately had to face death as a consequence. As Heesterman puts it: "As his mythic prototype, the warrior god Indra,
must slay Vrtra, so the *dīksita* is called on to win by violent
means the goods of life, the Soma, and the fire, from his asuric
counterparts. And when successfully filling himself with the conquered goods he becomes, like Indra, what the slain Vrtra was
before."[39]

So far, then, the *Agnistoma* ritual involves the usage of *mantra*
that expresses the various forms of value that are part and parcel
of the dynamic exchange of the sacrifice. The first transforms the
status of the sacrificer to that of the conqueror, and the second—
that of Agni and Soma, fire and Soma stalks—puts the sacrificer
in the role of the victim. As mentioned above, value of the object
exchanged is also bound up with the persons involved in the act
of exchange. And, true to such analyses, mantric language involves the creation of an identity between the wealth acquired
and the person acquiring—in the Vedic case, the currency of exchange being the life and death of the person himself.

Specific *mantra*s aside, it is worth noting in concluding this
section that the more general description of the sacrificial roles
within the early texts is also clearly articulated in the language of
exchange. For instance, because the sacrificer fulfills both roles,
conqueror and conquered, simultaneously, he is thus in a quan-
dary from which the ritual texts tell us he must "buy himself
free" with an offering of a male goat. Like the Soma negotiation,

the sacrificial substitution—the he-goat offering—is articulated within the language of buying and selling. Indeed, the *Kauṣītaki Brāhmaṇa* goes on to say that, following this prototype, all ritual offerings are a "buying free" of oneself.[40]

Mantra *and the Fluidity of* Varṇa *Identity*

It is important at this juncture to add a further note about the identity of those performing and being transformed by such sacrificial exchanges—the producers of words as well as the producers of wealth. It is clear from the use of *mantra* in earlier sacrificial texts that the production of both *mantra*s and wealth was also fluid; the creation of value was not the sole prerogative of one class, or *varṇa*, or the other. Many of the sacrificial texts reveal a great deal of ambiguity—even interchangeability—between the roles of priest and patron in the process of exchange. Without delving into too much detail, it will be sufficient to note some examples: Indra is frequently identified both with the *brāhmaṇa* priest and the *hotṛ*, as well as the sacrificer; thus the roles of *brāhmaṇa* (overseer), *hotṛ* (chanter), and sacrificial patron are interchangeable and clustered in a single figure. Indra is at once symbolic of the *kṣatra* power, the garnerer and protector of wealth and yet is also depicted throughout the sacrificial literature as acquiring *brāhmaṇa* power, the garnerer and protector of speech.[41] Moreover, as Heesterman notes, sacrality is only fully recognizable in the *yajamāna* (patron of the sacrifice); it is he and not the officiant who has to submit to purification. And it is the Soma sacrificer (*dīkṣita*), mentioned above, who undergoes an entire rite of initiation. Nothing similar is required of the Brahmin officiant.[42]

The *mantra*s used in particular rites again tend to reinforce this ambiguity between *varṇa* roles. At the conclusion of that initiation rite, in fact, the *dīkṣita* is announced several times, "Consecrated is the *brāhmaṇa* so and so," irrespective of whether he is a Brahmin, a Kṣatriya, or a Vaiśya.[43] Thus the function of the *dīkṣā*, among other things, is to make the sacrificer closely resemble the *brāhmaṇa* power, which is here not just a priestly power but something much larger—what motivates the entire sacrificial performance.[44]

Relatedly, at the *Rājasūya*, or royal consecration, the royal sacrificer is surrounded by officiants and household officers. They exchange *mantra*s whereby the king addresses each of the priests, saying, "O Brahman," and the officiants respond in turn with the phrase, "You, O King, are brahman."[45] *Mantra* is produced by all participants in the *Rājasūya*, regardless of their *varṇa*.

The Fixing of Identity: Words and Wealth in Later Commentarial Mythology

The mutually supportive, interactive relationship between *mantra* and wealth seen in earlier poetic and sacrificial texts does not remain constant into the later Vedic period. The language of exchange still provides, as Munn might suggest, a framework within which to speak about the relative value of both as forms of prestige. There are some very specific differences, both in the way that the narratives are treated in the commentary after they are told and in the way in which the exchange itself, as well as the actors within the exchange, are portrayed. In later texts identities are fixed. Thus, *mantra*s do not effect a change of identity for all participants in the sacrificial process of exchange, but rather they become identified as forms of value for only one particular kind of person—that of the Vedic *ṛṣi*, who acts according to brahminical norms.

Three specific examples from the Vedic commentary of the *Bṛhaddevatā* (BD) will serve to illustrate these later attitudes. The *Bṛhaddevatā* is an index of Vedic deities with explanatory narratives interspersed throughout. According to the most recent philological research, the *Bṛhaddevatā's* indexical core is thought to have been constructed in the fourth century B.C.E. As for the content of the texts, the *Bṛhaddevatā* enumerates for each verse of the *Ṛg-Veda* the deity that properly belongs to it—and thus, by implication, the appropriate use of the *mantra*s in ritual.

Most of the narratives were added in the early Purāṇic period, between the first and fifth centuries C.E. Some later narratives and other philosophical interpolations are thought to have been added between the seventh and eleventh centuries C.E. The basic function of the *Bṛhaddevatā's* narratives is the explanation of *mantra* for ritual purposes. Such stories make *mantra*s meaningful and thus render the sacrifice more efficacious. In this aspect, the mythological narratives of the *Bṛhaddevatā* continue the particular projects of the *Nirukta* and *Mīmāṃsā* texts in asserting the everyday meaningfulness of the Veda.[46] In all of these texts, the various methods of making *mantra*s intelligible are caught up in the larger project of making the Veda transcendentally authoritative.[47]

More specifically, several of these narratives explicitly equate words with wealth as currency of exchange, in typical Vedic style. *Mantra*s are exchanged for goods, such as cattle, gold, and necklaces. In this way they continue the earlier Vedic portrait of the interchangeability, or exchangeability, of the two as forms of currency that are related to the overarching, value-producing activity of sacrifice.[48] As mentioned above, however, the modality of the exchange is portrayed and codified along very different lines. While the *Bṛhaddevatā*'s narratives are indeed concerned with the sacrifice, as are its earlier ritually oriented counterparts of the Brāhmaṇa texts, its narratives about words and wealth are only vaguely attached to their sacrificial context. Moreover, the mythological content focuses on the delineation of *varṇa* roles in the production of both *mantra* and money.

Wandering Currency

The following narrative introduces the theme of words and currency quite specifically. Not insignificantly, it is an addition of the author of the later recension of the text, who possesses a tendency to expand on Ṛg-Vedic hymns that celebrate the gifts of kings. As will be evident, the story shows some similarity to that of Śyāvāśva, to be narrated below.[49] In this, as in subsequent narratives, the words of the *Ṛg-Veda* are italicized, to show the ways in which *mantra* is integrated into the myth.

The *Bṛhaddevatā* begins as follows:

> After acquiring wisdom from his teacher Kakṣīvat was going to his own abode, [and] we are told, he became tired on the way, and fell asleep in the forest. The king by the name of Svanaya the son of Bhāvayavya, saw him as he traveled along in pursuit of amusement with his wife, his retinue, and his domestic priest. Then having seen [Kakṣīvat] endowed with beauty and resembling the son of a god, [the king] thought of giving him his daughter, there being no objection about class and family. Having awakened him, [the king] then asked him about his class, family, etc. The young man answered him, "I am of the race of Aṅgiras, O King. I am the son of the *ṛṣi* Dīrghatamas, son of Ucathya, O King." [The king] then gave him ten young women decorated with ornaments (based on RV 121.3), and the same number of chariots, strong-bodied steeds

yoked in fours, in order to carry the young women, money, and things made of brass, goats and sheep. Moreover, he gave a hundred golden necklaces and a hundred bulls. This is related with the next *sūkta* [beginning] *"A hundred"* (RV 1.126.2).[50] A hundred horses, a hundred necklaces, ten chariots with young women, those [horses] going in fours, and more than 1,060 cows. Kakṣīvat, who obtained all this from Svanaya Bhāvayavya, praised after receiving [it], and recited [that *sūkta* beginning] (RV 1.125) *"In the early morning having come, Svanaya bestows wealth; recognizing it and having accepted it, and by that increasing his offspring and life, he [presumably, the poet] comes with brave sons to abundant wealth,"* for his father (RV 1.125.1). Here his fruit [of praise] is for the most part set forth. His father saw the second [verse beginning], *"Rich in many cows, in gold and horses may he be; may Indra give great vital power to the one who stops you, returning in the early morning, by his treasure, like game caught by the net."* (RV 1.125.2) (BD 3.142-50)

The main point of this story is that the young Kakṣīvat was initiated as a *ṛṣi* through the appropriate exchange of words and gifts. Kakṣīvat has just returned from learning the Vedas, his period of studentship, and has not yet become a *ṛṣi*.[51] A *mantra*'s praise of a gift acts as a natural and expected return for the gifts of Svanaya to Kakṣīvat. It pays off the debt which Kakṣīvat now owes Svayana and thus restores a balance between men, just as, in other narratives of the *Bṛhaddevatā*, *mantras* restore balances between gods and men.[52]

In this the story reflects the typical Vedic perspective and has much in common with other mythological narratives of the same type. Indeed, the early texts reveal that the life of the *brahmacārin* training involves a pattern of setting out into the wilderness where one is initiated by a decisive revelatory experience; thereupon, one returns to affirm his newly acquired status. This may in fact be parallel to the action of the *dīkṣita*, who, though not performing service for a teacher, nonetheless undergoes a similar experience.[53] Moreover, the narrative mirrors the sacrificial situation: *mantras* confirm and bolster the production of wealth as they do in a multitude of Ṛg-Vedic hymns, and in various parts of the Soma sacrifice discussed above.

However, the story also contains some significant differences. First, there is very little reference to the sacrificial context at all.

Kakṣīvat appears out of nowhere. He is not a *dīkṣita*, garnering wealth in contestual fashion, but is simply described as "wandering in the forest." The king, moreover, is not concerned with his role as a potential or actual *yajamāna*; he is simply on holiday with his retinue. The only concern the king has, in fact, is that he make a match for his daughter that is appropriate to her *varṇa*. The meeting is serendipitous, almost fairy-tale-like in its quality, with no ritual basis whatsoever.

What is more, the story is not told by the commentators without some significant degree of puzzlement. After his narration of the story, the author of the *Bṛhaddevatā* feels compelled to continue a debate between earlier interpreters as to the ownership of the hymn. It might well be assumed that the last verse commented upon, RV 1.125.2, is part of a straightforward dialogue between the king and the *ṛṣi*, and the line is therefore the king's. However, for the commentators, a problem arises—perhaps because of the pronoun usage in RV 1.125.2: the words you and he are used to refer to Kakṣīvat and the generous king, respectively. According to the commentary, the person speaking, therefore, could not be the king himself but must be another person, either Kakṣīvat[54] speaking to his father, Dīrghatamas, about King Svanaya, or Dīrghatamas himself.[55] The text (3.152cd.–153) muses on this problem. "But [it might be asked,] how could this [verse] be indicated as one of Dīrghatmas? It is said, [to argue that point of view] that when [that (verse) beginning] 'At morning' was uttered [by Kakṣīvat], [Dīrghatamas] was rejoicing about the gift to his son; and then [Dīrghatamas] said a prayer for the king, which [begins] 'Having many cows . . . '" The potential solution that the *Bṛhaddevatā* provides is two: if Kakṣīvat recited it to his father, he could refer to King Svanaya in the third person, and thus he could mean the you to be his father, who was apparently accompanying him. The other reasonable assumption would be that the famous poet Dīrghatamas himself was the speaker, and he was addressing a series of joyful verses to his son.

The solution that is decidedly *not* provided, however, is the most straightforward one: that the king himself utters the verses, referring to himself in the third person (a linguistic device used in many other places in the RV and accepted by the BD). If one assumes that the verse 1.125.2 is King Svanaya's, it would introduce the thorny question of whether kings could produce *mantra*s and therefore become *ṛṣi*s—a problem that is neatly sidestepped in other parts of the *Bṛhaddevatā*. Kings produce gifts for *ṛṣi*s, to be sure—a fact which the author of the *Bṛhaddevatā* mentions in several places. The idea of kings producing *mantras*, however, is met with some ambivalence in many places in the text.[56] The omission of this possibility in the commentary is not without significance. Here we have the strong suggestion that *mantra* is the prerogative of the Brahmin (personified by the *ṛṣi*) and money that of the Kṣatriya (personified by the king Svanaya).

The Ṛṣi *Who Won a Wife with* Mantras

This next mythological narrative reinforces that perspective even more strongly. Its more fairy-tale-like overtones appealed to the European Indologists, who uncharacteristically take the time to comment on its merits as a narrative.[57] For the purposes of this analysis, however, the story is also quite rich because it intertwines the themes of *mantras* as agents of prestige, and *mantras* as a kind of currency of exchange, again echoing the typical Vedic themes. As we shall see, however, there is more to the story than what meets the earlier Vedic eye. The narrative runs as follows:

> There was a royal *ṛṣi* known by the name of Rathavīti Dārbhya. The king [Rathavīti Dārbhya], intending to sacrifice, went to Atri and propitiated him. Making himself and his intended purpose known, standing with folded hands, he chose the seer Arcanānas, son of Atri, as his sacrificial officiant. He, with his son, went to the king in order to give the sacrifice. Now the son of Atri's son, Arcanānas, was Śyāvāśva, who was gladly taught by his father the Vedas, with their *aṅga*s [limbs] and sub-*aṅga*s. Arcanānas, having gone with his son, performed the sacrifice for the king. As the sacrifice was going on, he saw the splendid daughter of the king; the thought occurred to him, "The daughter of the king might be my daughter-in-law." The heart of Śyāvāśva also became attached to her, and so he said to the *yajamāna*, "Join up with me, O king!" The king, wanting to give his daughter to Śyāvāśva, said to his own queen, "What is your thought [if] I give my daughter to Śyāvāśva? For a son of Atri would not be an ineffectual son-in-law for us." She said to the king, "I have been born into a family of royal *ṛṣi*s. One who is not a seer [is] not our son-in-law. This one has not seen *mantra*s. Let the girl be given to a *ṛṣi*; thus she would be a mother of the Veda. [One] regards one who sees *mantra*s as a father of the Veda."[58] The king, after having thought it over with his wife, rejected him, saying, "No one who is not a *ṛṣi* is worthy to be our

son-in-law." The ṛṣi, thus rejected, returned when the sacrifice had finished. But the mind of Śyāvāśva did not return from the girl. Thus the two [Arcanānas and Śyāvāśva] returned. They both ran into Queen Śaśīyasī, King Taranta and King Purumīḷha. The two kings Taranta and Purumīḷha were ṛṣis, sons of Vidadaśva. These two kings themselves paid honor to the two ṛṣis. And the king presented the ṛṣi's son to his queen. With the agreement of Taranta, she gave wealth several-fold. Queen Śaśīyasī [gave] goats and sheep, cows and horses to Śyāvāśva; honored by the yajamānas, father and son went to their own aśram to Atri. They reverently addressed Atri, the great ṛṣi of shining brilliance. A thought occurred to Śyā-vāśva: "Because of the non-seeing of mantras, I have not obtained the girl, beautiful in all her parts. If I were also a seer of mantras, my happiness would be great." As he thought out of doors, a host of the Maruts appeared. He saw standing at his own side, quite similar in form, and equal in age, the Maruts, with gold on their breasts. Having seen the gods, similar in age, and with the figures of men, Śyāvāśva asked, in wonder, "Who are you, most excellent leaders, who come one by one from a place very far away?" (RV 5.61.1) He then became aware that they were the gods the Maruts, the sons of Rudra. Having observed this, he praised them [with the verse]: "They who are born by swift horses, drinking the intoxicating liquid, they receive great exaltation here" (RV 5.61.11). For the ṛṣi [the father] thought it a transgression of his own, that having seen thus, [his son] did not praise, but asked, "Who are you?" Being praised, and pleased with their praise, the sons of Pṛśni [the Maruts], as they went off, having taken off the gold from their breasts, then gave [it] to him [Śyāvāśva]. When the Maruts had gone forward, the splendid Śyāvāśva went with his mind to the daughter of Rathavīti. He, only just [now] a ṛṣi, wanting to proclaim himself to Rathavīti, thus engaged [the goddess] Night on an errand with the verse, "Turning away, O night, bring to Dārbhya this song of praise of mine; convey my praises, O goddess, as a charioteer. And say to Rathavīti for me, when the Soma juice is poured out, that my desire does not go away" (RV 5.61.17,18). To Night, who did not see Rathavīti, [he said],[59] seeing with the eye of a ṛṣi, "Here this wealthy Rathavīti lives upon the Gomatī, and has his home on the Himavat" (RV 5.61.18–19). Inspired by the goddess Night, having learned of the errand of the ṛṣi, the son of Darbha, taking the girl, approached Arcanānas, grasped his feet, and stood, bent forward, with his hands folded. "I am Rathavīti, son of Darbha," he announced his name. "I refused you before when you desired an alliance with me. Now forgive me, I give homage to you, and do not be angry with me, honorable one. You are the son of a *ṛṣi,* yourself a *ṛṣi,* and the father of a *ṛṣi,* O honorable one. Here, take this [girl] as a daughter-in-law," he said. Then the king himself honored him with a mixture of honey and milk, the water of reception, and water for his feet. Having given him a hundred white horses he let him go back to his home. And the *ṛṣi,* too, having praised Queen Śaśīyasī, Taranta and King Purumīḷha with the six [verses beginning,] *"She has given cattle of horses, cows, and hundreds of sheep, the one who threw her arms around the hero [Taranta] whom Śyāvāśva praised"* (RV 61.5–10), went to his home. (BD 5.50–5.81)

As with the story of Kakṣīvat, there is much to recommend this story as reflecting the typical Vedic situation. There is a great deal of ambiguity in the notion of the family of royal *ṛṣi*'s whence Rathavīti Dārbhya's family hails. He is both a *ṛṣi* and a sacrificial sponsor and chooses another *ṛṣi,* Arcanānas, to perform his sacrifice. Moreover, his wife, the queen, calls herself a "mother of the Veda," from a lineage of royal *ṛṣis.* He is both *yajamāna* and seer at once, and so is his wife.

And yet here is where the narrative progression begins to part company with the Vedic situation. As in the previous story, the young man meets the kingly retinue fortuitously on the path, apart from the realm of the sacrifice. Moreover, his goods have very little to do with the mechanics of sacrificial exchange that we encounter in the earlier figure of the *dīkṣita,* who intentionally goes out to wander in search of booty. And nonetheless, even more serendipitously than in the previous story, great wealth—goats and sheep, cows and horses—is bestowed upon Śyāvāśva. In the beginning of the story, Śyāvāśva is not prestigious enough to win the daughter of the king; he is only an apprentice accompanying his father on his sacrificial duties. Now, thanks to the fortuitous generosity of the kings and queen, he also has wealth. Yet there is still one more problem. The fact that Śyāvāśva has not "seen" his Vedic verses yet, and therefore has not yet become a *ṛṣi* is even more of a major stumbling block to the queen in the match of her daughter to his family. The words of the queen reinforce this quite strongly: he is not a *ṛṣi,* and thus cannot be the father or marry a mother of the Veda.

Therefore, Śyāvāśya must be initiated into being a *ṛṣi,* and only the gods can do this for him. Obligingly, the Maruts appear and in a comical moment's blunder, he asks them who they are. Responding to his father's horror, he remembers that *mantras* must indeed be produced and does so accordingly. The *mantras* satisfy the Maruts, who give him their breastplates, and he, "only just a *ṛṣi*," sends the goddess Night off on an errand to recite *mantras* as proof of his newfound status. Thus the father, Rathavīti Dārbhya, is convinced. The king apologizes profusely, allows Śyāvāśva to take his daughter, and gives him gifts besides.

In this story, *mantras* appear as powerful agents of exchange on three different levels: they make it possible for Śyāvāśya to earn the status of a *ṛṣi*, to win the bride, and to obtain gifts. All three benefits are produced from the *mantras* arising from a single vision of the Maruts—a powerful fruit of praise indeed! Moreover, even after the exchange has been successfully completed and the bride has been won, even further wealth is garnered in the form of one hundred white horses, as an apology from the erroneous king himself.

There is a crucial difference, however. Unlike the earlier sacrificial material, where wealth is identified with both the consecrated sacrificer and the *brāhmaṇa* priests, here the production of value is quite clearly delineated between the two. The roles are clarified in very particular ways. No matter how much wealth the kings may give Śyāvāśva, kingly wealth cannot create *ṛṣi*hood. After gaining wealth, Śyāvāśva has become as powerful as a king, as the *yajamānas*, and could return to the sacrifice, as the *dīkṣita* does after his period in the wilderness, filled with booty to present. In the words of the mythological narrative itself, however, such wealth is immaterial. Even after he gains the booty of the kings Taranta and Purumīḷha, and Queen Śaśīyasī, Śyāvāśva knows that wealth alone will not be the right form of exchange to win the daughter of Rathavīti Dārbhya. The straightforward sacrificial model for gaining booty is not enough; he must become initiated through words as well as wealth.

The division of *varṇa* lines is reinforced even further when, after the story has made it clear that royal wealth is insufficient, the great king Rathavīti Dhārbya also apologizes to the young *ṛṣi* who has proved himself by reciting *mantras*. In status, the pure *ṛṣi*, Śyāvāśva, becomes greater and more powerful than the more ambiguously defined kingly *ṛṣi* who has put him to the test. He has the power not only to propitiate the gods through sacrifice, as Rathavīti himself clearly does, but also to control the gods, as his indenture of the goddess Night as errand-runner clearly attests.

In subtle but significant ways, then, the story presents us with a very different picture from that of the earlier material. *Mantras* are the sole prerogatives of *ṛṣis*, and gift-giving is the sole prerogative of kings. Moreover, at the end of the narrative, the power imbalance between the king and the Brahmin has been reversed, and the younger, newly initiated Brahmin seer is clearly the powerful figure. While the process of exchange between words and wealth remains, its rules are different, and it proceeds within a much more socially codified world.

Mantras *Begetting Wealth Begetting*
Mantras *Begetting Wealth*

In addition to the emerging codification of *varṇa* roles in the process of exchange, the myths of Kakṣīvat and Śyāvāśva also illustrate an increasing distance from the realm of violent exchange within the sacrificial contest. The exchanges have become domesticated in this sense—not only placed outside the realm of sacrifice but in fact never really returning to it as the buyer of *soma* or wandering *dīkṣita* would. Moreover, the story of Śyāvāśya and his victory also shows the increasing intimacy between the *ṛṣi* and deity; he receives the golden breastplates of the Maruts and embarks immediately upon a working relationship with the goddess Night to boot. Like other stories in the *Bṛhaddevatā* which I have treated elsewhere, [60] this next story continues this process of domestication, and further develops the devotional aspects of the relationship between *ṛṣi* and god. This creates a kind of nonsacrificial, *bhakti*-like (devotional) relationship that is far more common to the classical religious texts, the Purāṇas than it is to the Vedic worldview.[61]

Although simple in narrative progression, this next myth, like the two previous myths, is somewhat Vedic in that it illustrates the ever-increasing expansiveness with which the cycle of exchange between gifts and *mantras* can revolve.[62] That cyclical exchange, however, takes place entirely without reference to sacrifice. In fact, the narrative moves the entire process of exchange to the context of the devotional relationship with the god.

There is praise of the royal seer [Sobhari] for Trasadasyu[63] in [the verse beginning] *"He has given me . . ."* [RV 8.18.36–7]. [He gave] fifty young women and three [herds] of seventy cows. He also [gave] horses, camels, and garments of various kinds, jewels, a brown bull, the leader who led those [herds]. Having made this marriage, the *ṛṣi*, going along, recited this to Indra, and with the *sūkta* [beginning], "*We invoke you, O Indra who is ever new,*" (RV 8.21) [praised] Śakra. The Lord of Śaci, pleased by this, [said,] "O Ṛṣi, choose a boon." Bowing, the *ṛṣi* answered him, "O Lord, [may] I enjoy the fifty Kākutstha[64] women all at once, and the assumption of many forms at will—youth, and eternal enjoyment, the conch treasure and the lotus treasure always to remain in my houses. May that Viśvakarman make palaces of gold by your grace, and a flower garden with celestial trees for each one of them. Let there be no rivalry of co-wives among them." And [Indra] said, "Let all of this be." (BD 6.51–57)

Here, the *ṛṣi* Sobhari praises the liberality of King Trasadasyu, with whom, we can infer from the text, he has arranged a marriage. Sobhari, in true Vedic style, enumerates his gifts accordingly. Sobhari also tells Indra about the manifold generosity of Trasadasyu while at the same time praising Indra. Interestingly enough, unlike the previous story, where the Maruts are praised only after they appear in front of him, here it is as if Sobhari is praising Indra for no reason other than to confide in him, like a child telling a parent about a recently received present. Yet despite the fact—that Indra has not appeared before him—these *mantras* of Sobhari's in praise of Indra result in further wealth, for Indra is pleased and asks him to choose a boon.

Thus, as Derrida writes in "White Mythologies," words, like more solid forms of currency, have the power to increase exponentially. In this myth Sobhari's words result in an ever-growing income, like a series of returns on a wise initial investment. The first words of praise are in exchange for material gifts of Trasadasyu; they result in further words of praise for Indra. These further words of praise for Indra result in even more fantastic forms of material rewards. The nature of the rewards is also unusual; the *ṛṣi* chooses as his boon states of mind and states of pleasure as well as the concrete wealth of the conch treasure and the lotus treasure. Such a request paints an engaging portrait of what the ideal life of a *ṛṣi* actually might look like!

Even more importantly for our purposes, the myth has moved the entire process of exchange to the celestial level, in the context of the intimate relationship between devotee and boon-granting deity. Sobhari asks for miraculous powers, such as the ability to assume many different forms at will. Indeed, his requests have a

Purāṇa-like air of fantasy about them, such as the golden palaces created by Indra himself. In addition, he requests the conch treasure spoken of in the popular *Pañcatantra* 11.10, and the lotus treasure (said to be 100,000,000 pieces of money). What began as a human interaction between king and *ṛṣi* has gone through yet another cycle and become a process of exchange in the midst of loving devotion with a happily-ever-after ending. Such a scene is indeed a long way from the Heestermanic cycle of violent exchange with which we began.

Conclusion

The scene is not, however, at all inconsistent with the Heestermanic hypothesis about the singular fate of the sacrificial contest and the arrival of the classical paradigm. As he argues on the basis of the ritual texts, the various opposing roles of the contestual sacrifice, the *dīkṣita* (consecrated sacrificer-to-be) became fused with the munificent sacrificer (already established). The *dīkṣita*, being at the same time the sacrificer who sets the *brahman* (power) of the sacrifice in motion, must logically be a *brāhmaṇa* from the outset. Explaining his analysis of the *prāṇāgnihotra* (the ritual for the Brahman taking his meal), Heesterman writes: "Whereas the *brahman* power originally had to be won or vindicated in the sacrificial arena, it was not straightforwardly ascribed. In short, the classical *brāhmaṇa* had arisen. Permanently fixed in his role he ideally upholds in, by, and for himself alone the ultramundane order of the ritiualistic *śruti*. As the *brāhmaṇa* is fixed in his role, so is the warrior—once a warrior always a warrior."[65] The Vedic *brāhmaṇa* thus comes to act alone as the Brahmin householder in the classical period, a single ritualist engaging in a ritual without contenders.[66] And, by logical extension, wealth becomes a separate issue, a problem for the Brahmin to resolve, as Manu and other dharmaśāstric literature give ample testimony. Indeed, the fourteenth-century Vijayanagaran commentator Sāyaṇa uses the occasion of RV 125 (the hymn referring to the story of Kakṣīvat, discussed above), to discuss at length whether it is a fault that the Brahmin *ṛṣi* accepted a gift from a king, as the *Manu Smṛti* prohibits it!

Our mythological analysis shows the ways in which this change was achieved, providing a kind of intermediate stage in the progress of the Vedic sacrifice toward the classical period. The opponents of the contestual sacrifice are now friendly, mutual

supporters—be it King Svanaya and Kakṣīvat, or Rathavīti Dhārbya and Śyāvāśva—who make their exchanges in codified ways.
Moreover, the visionary poet gives words for wealth not in order
to return to the sacrifice but simply to win a wife or, in the case
of the narrative of the ṛṣi Sobhari, to develop a *bhakti*-like relationship with the god Indra. While *mantra* and money remain
powerful vehicles for exchange, the standards of domestic and devotional life are emerging as paramount.

To return, then, to the problems of myth and money: the language of symbolic anthropology has helped to portray in a more
refined way the use of canonical language as a form of exchange
in the Vedic world. Once *mantra* is shown to be one value-laden
entity among others—indeed, a value that can have transformative power—there can be a resulting shift in analytical focus. The
modality of exchange between words and wealth comes more
clearly into view, putting concerns with magical or materialist
practices in the background. Such a focus can be productively
used for historical purposes, revealing intriguing shifts from sacri-
ficially coded exchange to socially coded negotiations between
households as well as between devotee and gods.

When they encounter myths about money, then, mythologists
need not take refuge in either the materialist or the mystical extremes. They can fruitfully rest in the tension between the concrete and the symbolic, the economic and the figurative, resisting
the temptation to reduce one to the other. They can view mythological narrative as one of the ways in which certain exchanges
are portrayed, and also one of the ways in which changing attitudes toward the rules for such exchange are contemplated and
expressed.

Notes

1. My critique of Silver's *Taking Ancient Mythology Economically* should not
   detract from the excellent philological and historical insights that the
   book possesses.
       Many have recently argued against the mystification of myths by struc-
   turalists and morphologists alike, reiterating the now well known claim
   that myths are authored (in the Ancient Near East, even finished with an
   authorial colophon) and historical: they do not arise "spontaneously" from
   the "people" as an "expression of faith."
2. Silver, *Taking Ancient Mythology Economically*, 73 passim.
3. Strenski, in his *Religion in Relation*, discusses reductionism in just this
   manner. He argues that, if reduction is seen as the juxtaposition of one field
   to another, we need not see it as an inherently problematic pursuit but a
   creative one in which new fields of inquiry may arise.

4. Bell, *Ritual Theory, Ritual Practice.*
5. Some of the more straightforward theses of this kind include Edwards's *Philosophy of Religion* and Huxley's *Religion without Revelation.*
6. Other works preceding Uma Gupta's make intriguing judgments as to where materialism should be placed—mostly alongside other, "baser" human instincts. See, for instance, Shastri's *Short History of Indian Materialism, Sensationalism, and Hedonism;* or Lefever's *Vedic Idea of Sin.*
7. Gupta, *Materialism,* 41.
8. Ibid, 40.
9. Ibid.
10. Ibid, 29. Also see Vetter, *Magic and Religion.*
11. Mauss, "Essai sur le don." See in particular Malinowski, *Argonauts of the Western Pacific;* Leach and Leach, *Kula: New Perspectives on Massim Exchange;* Weiner, "A World of Made Is Not a World of Born: Doing Kula on Kiriwana," in Leach and Leach, *Kula;* Weiner, "Inalienable Wealth."
12. Munn, *Fame of Gawa,* 7.
13. Ibid, 8–9.
14. So, too with Silver (*Taking Ancient Mythology Economically,* 42.): one might argue that despite the larger argument that the mythical gorgon's head has monetary value, one can be more specific and state that a gorgon's head might have value as trading currency in the sixth century, and yet later it functioned as a guardian of treasury or depository where merchants displayed their wares.
15. Munn, *Fame of Gawa,* 139–41.
16. Nor, in the cases of the more bizarre narratives, the products of "scribal error" as some scholars have claimed. See the discussion of the myth of "selling Indra in the marketplace," n. 47, below.
17. See, for starters, *Ṛg-Veda* 1.128.5; 5.53.5; 5.30.7; 5.33.6; 7.18.22; 8.46.4; 8.50.6; 10.141.5,6.
18. See, for instance, *Śatapatha Brāhmaṇa* 11.5.7.1.
19. See *Bṛhaddevatā* 6.45, 92. Also see *Sarvānukramaṇī* on *Ṛg-Veda* 8.2; 8.4; 8.5; 8.74.
20. For two random recent examples of the use of the term *magic* to describe the Vedic worldview, see Hopkins, *Hindu Religious Tradition,* 27–28; Zysk's groundbreaking work *Asceticism and Healing in Ancient India,* chap.1.
21. Keith, *Religion and Philosophy of the Vedas and the Upaniṣads,* 310.
22. Raja, *Poet-Philosophers of the Ṛg-Veda.* See my "Poets and Fishes" for a full discussion of Kunhan Raja. Also see de Nicolas, *Meditations through Ṛg-Veda.*
23. This debate engages not only the question of *mantra* but the entire question of the possibility of meaning. For an approach which posits a certain continuity of *mantra* usage in the midst of cultural change, see Renou, "Les Pouvoirs de la Parole" in *Etudes Védiques,* 1–27; Gonda, *The Vision of the Vedic Poets;* Gonda, "Indian Mantra," 244–97. For a more mystical, *bhakti*-oriented view of *mantra,* see Johnson, *Poetry and Speculation in the Ṛg Veda.* For a strictly syntactical analysis of *mantra* usage, see Staal, "Concept of Metalanguage and Its Indian Background"; "*Ṛg Veda* 10:71 on the Origin of Language"; "Ritual Syntax"; "Meaninglessness of Ritual"; "Sound of Religion"; "Vedic *Mantras,*" in *Mantra,* ed. Alper, 48–95. For a more performative perspective, see Wheelock, "Ritual Language of a Vedic Sacrifice"; "Taxonomy of *Mantras* in the New and Full Moon Sacrifice"; "Problem of Ritual Language"; "*Mantra* in Vedic and Tantric Ritual," in *Mantra,* ed. Alper, 96–122; and Findly, "*Mantra kaviśasta* Speech as Performative and Patton, "Vāc Myth or Philosophy?"
24. *Ṛg-Veda* 1.23.19–21; 1.43.4; 1.89.4; 1.157.4; 2.33.2; 2.33.13; 6.74.3; 7.46.2–3; 8.20.23; 9.5,15; among countless others.

25. Wheelock argues that the ritual language of *mantra* is not only beneficially classified as a "speech act" but can be further subdivided into four categories: the presentation of characteristics; the presentation of attitudes and wishes; the presentation of intentions; and the presentation of requests ("Mantra in Vedic and Tantric Ritual," 99). Thus, *mantra* as it participates in the process of exchange could be classified as both the presentation of requests and also the presentation of characteristics—i.e., the new characteristics of the person who has just finished exchanging.

26. See in particular Munn, "Fame," in *Fame of Gawa,* 105–18. See also Weiner, "Inalienable Wealth," 217.

27. To summarize briefly: Soma is the sacrificial plant which is pressed to make a drink as well as the deity to whom many hymns of praise are sung. The sacrifice to Soma is performed annually in the spring, and consists of several preliminary operations: the purchase of the Soma and a declaration of a hospitable reception to King Soma once he arrives, including the *tanunapatra,* or "pact of hospitality"; the measuring out and building of the altars; the preparation and installation of the two chariots for the Soma, as well as huts, hearths, and planks for pressing; the creation of four cavities which amplify the sound of the Soma stalk when it is pressed. Preliminary rites conclude with the procession of deified Agni Soma, the oblation of a goat, and the carrying procession of the night-passing waters.
   At the sacrifice proper, after the preparatory rites, three pressings take place: the morning pressing, the midday pressing, and the evening pressing. The morning pressing is a series of oblations of Soma, but also of pressing cakes—including barley cakes, flour in sour milk, parched rice, etc. During these pressings musical passages and recitations also take place, and another sacrifice of a goat, dedicated to Agni. At the midday pressing, while similar in structure to the morning pressing, the honoraria are given out: the sacrificer is to give cows of a specific number, and in some texts, "all his wealth," including his daughter, whom he may marry to one of the officiants. The evening pressing involves two chants and two recitations, of which the last, "Praise of Agni," is the one that gives its name to the whole ceremony. The closing rites, called "the tail of the sacrifice," consist of libation, expiatory rites, a salute to the sun, a dissolution of the alliance and the sacrifice of a sterile cow, or eleven other animals. While all of the gods occupy a special place, Indra has a particularly special role, and the midday Soma pressing falls to him. See Caland and Henry, *L'Agniṣṭoma,* for a full exegetical treatment.

28. Hillebrandt, *Vedic Mythology.*

29. Oldenberg, *Religion of the Veda,* 204–5.

30. Hubert and Mauss, *Sacrifice.*

31. Heesterman, *Broken World of Sacrifice.*

32. See Heesterman's discussion of the parallels between the *brahmacārin* collecting goods for his patron and teacher and the *sanīhāras* collecting goods for the *dīkṣita* in the process of sacrifice. See *Broken World of Sacrifice,* 166 passim, and particularly his analysis of the story of Satyakāma Jābāla in *Chandogya Upaniṣad* 4.4.5.

33. *Taittirīya Saṃhitā* 1.2.5 d-e: See also Manu's riddle challenge, 1.8; Caland and Henry, *L'Agniṣṭoma,* no. 31; Heesterman, "Somakuh und Danaergabe."

34. See *Taittirīya Saṃhitā* 1.2.5c: I pour you on the head of the earth, on the place of the sacrifice, on the ghee-dripping footprint of Iḍā (*iḍāyāḥ pade ghṛtavati*). Also discussion in Heesterman, n. 263.

35. *Taittirīya Saṃhitā* 1.2.79; see also *Āpastamba Śrauta Sūtra* 10.27.3. The ritual also involves the explicit dissociation of the sacrificer from the Soma during the *vaisarjana,* or "setting free" of the Soma, when the Soma stalks

are brought from the śālā (hall) to the mahavedi (great altar); in uttering one particular mantra, the sacrificer explicitly sends it to the gods through Savitṛ. Taittirīya Saṃhitā 6.3.2.4–5; Kāṭhaka Saṃhitā 26.2:124.1; Maitrāyaṇī Saṃhitā 3.9.1:113.14; Śatapatha Brāhmaṇa 3.6.3.1; Āpastamba Śrauta Sūtra 11.18.3.

36. Maitrāyaṇī Saṃhitā 3.9.1:112.4–8; Kāṭhaka Saṃhitā 26.2:123.17.
37. See Heesterman, Ancient Indian Royal Consecration, 71; 75–78.
38. Āpastamba Śrauta Sūtra 4.8.1; Taittirīya Saṃhitā 2.7.1.2, 4; Kāṭhaka Saṃhitā 37.9.89.3.; 37.5..87.8.
39. Heesterman, Broken World of Sacrifice, 174.
40. This also incidentally, explains why it is forbidden to eat the dīkṣita's food in the Agniṣṭoma ritual. Partaking of the dīkṣita's food can thus readily be seen as partaking in the sin of Indra's Vṛtra-slaying violence and ultimately as man-eating in the sense of inguritating what he has violently integrated in his person. See Heesterman, ibid., 175.
41. In fact, Indra's role in the sacrifice, and his identification with the sacrificer, may give us some clue to another curious myth, whereby the god himself is the currency of exchange. The story goes as follows:

> [When] her embryo said, "I will not be born straightforwardly" (Ṛg-Veda 4.18.2). [Aditi] scolded her son, Indra, she wishing only for her own welfare (Ṛg-Veda 4.18.1). Indra, as soon as he was born, challenged the ṛṣi in a fight. Vāmadeva, fighting him, after having made strength for himself for ten days and nights, was victorious over him with his might. Gautama, selling him [Indra] in the convocation of ṛṣis, in "Who buys this, my Indra, with ten milk cows; when he has killed enemies, then let [that buyer] give him again to me" (Ṛg-Veda 4.24.10), himself praised [Indra] with that [sūkta beginning], "No one, O Indra, is superior to you; no one more excellent; killer of Vṛtra, there is no one the likes of you" (Ṛg-Veda 4.30.1). And in "What, then, O Vṛtra-slayer, are you not fiercest in your anger, O Maghavan? Thus you have slain the son of Danu [Vṛtra]" (Ṛg-Veda 4.30.7), he dispelled his anger by half. Then in this way the ṛṣi proclaimed his form and heroisms, his actions of fortitude and his various deeds to Aditi. In the triplet [beginning] "I am Manu and Sūrya; I am the wise ṛṣi" (Ṛg-Veda 26.1), [there] is self-praise; its praise seems to be his [Indra's]. That is, the seer praises himself as if he were Indra (Bṛhaddevatā 4.130cd–35).

In the second part of the story told above, the battle between Vāmadeva and Indra results in Indra's defeat and his subsequent sale in the marketplace. Here, in this odd mixture of Vedic motifs, not only does the ṛṣi exchange words for gifts, praise for praise, but he also exchanges god himself in the marketplace once he has defeated him.

The hymn has been the object of debate by various Indologists. (See Nītimañjarī on Ṛg-Veda 4.18 quotes BD 4.130 and 131. Also see Sieg, Sagenstoffe, 179–86, and Pischel and Geldner, Vedische Studien 11: 42–44.) Sieg thinks that the thrust of the Ṛg-Vedic verse 4.24.10 about selling the god Indra is an ironic question. It does not ask, "Who will buy this Indra?" but "Who would be so stupid as to buy a god when he can slay his enemies?" In Sieg's opinion this line was misunderstood by Vedic interpreters early on and was carried into commentatorial tradition by Sāyaṇa on Ṛg-Veda and others. The fact that the Bṛhaddevatā takes advantage of this misunderstanding is in character with its tendency to exonerate the ṛṣi as much as possible. According to its interpretation, this Ṛg-Vedic verse is quite power-

ful; as Sāyaṇa also comments on this verse, Vāmadeva, having subjugated
Indra by much praise, says he will adhere to his bargaining price.

Yet, thanks to Heesterman and, before him, Caland and Henry, we might
have another clue as to why Indra is sold in the marketplace. It is, in a
sense, a logical outcome of the series of identifications made in the Soma
sacrifice: the victorious Soma-bringer is also identified with Soma itself,
and in turn identified with Indra. The god is the sacrificial victim, and also
that which is bought and sold as the sacrificial offering.

42. Heesterman, *Broken World of Sacrifice*, 160.
43. *Taittirīya Saṃhitā* 6.1.4.3; *Śatapatha Brāhmaṇa* 3.2.1.40. *Kāṭhaka Saṃhitā*
    23.5.:80.4; *Maitrāyaṇī Saṃhitā* 3.6.9:72.1 do not specify *brāhmaṇa* at all.
44. Heesterman, *Broken World of Sacrifice*, 163.
45. See Heesterman, *Ancient Indian Royal Consecration*, 93, 226, n.79.
46. *Nirukta* 1.15 ff., where Yāska argues with Kautsa, an opponent who ques-
    tions the authority of the Vedas and asserts that Vedic *mantras* are mean-
    ingless. And see *Pūrva Mīmāṃsā Sūtras* 1.5 denoting the eternal
    relationship between words and their meaning, 1.26 for an assertion of the
    everyday quality of Vedic language, and 2.1–23 for a discussion of signifi-
    cance of *arthavada*—explanatory passages which are subordinate to *co-
    dana*, or ritual injunctions, but nonetheless meaningful as passages which
    provide incentives to and augments of sacrificial action. The substance of
    Kautsa's criticisms of Yāska and Yāska's rejoinder is discussed and amplified
    in the first chapter of Jaimini's *Pūrva Mīmāṃsā Sūtras*. See also Francis X.
    Clooney, *Thinking Ritually*. Even more specifically, the declaration of past
    deeds was called *bhutarthavada*—a thing which happened in the past and
    cannot be proved or disproved by direct perception. See Mohan Lal Sandal's
    introduction to *Mīmāṃsā Sūtras*.
47. More specifically, these narratives are used to explain a certain group of
    Ṛg-Vedic hymns, called *saṃvāda*, or "dialogue hymns," which involve a
    conversation among several characters. *Itihāsas* and *ākhyāna*s elucidate the
    circumstances in which the verses of these Ṛg-Vedic hymns were uttered—
    designating the speakers of each verse and the situation of the characters
    involved. Scholars have deemed these *itihāsas* necessary to the "coherence"
    of the Ṛg-Veda; such narratives complete and explain the spotty references
    and histories contained within the Ṛg-Vedic text. As such, they have been
    called the "saga-like" counterpart to the more "poetic" Ṛg-Veda. (In fact,
    in many Vedic commentaries such as the *Bṛhaddevatā* and the *Nirukta*,
    authorities disagree as to whether a Vedic hymn should be called a dialogue;
    it could also be called *a narrative* in and of itself. Whatever the appellation
    of the hymns, commentators such as Yāska, Śaunaka, and later Sāyaṇa do
    not give a ritual application [*viniyoga*] for these hymns, but prefer to tell a
    story in order to explain them.)
48. In modern parlance, *mantras* are the inverse of Derrida's concept of *usure*,
    expounded in "White Mythologies." There, Derrida traces how language is
    represented by the language of coinage; for him, the image of currency can
    be used to describe how metaphors lose their initial ontological persua-
    siveness and "value," and become directly equated with the concept for
    which they initially stood in a creative indirect relationship. For Derrida,
    the history of language in the West is a record of how language usage over
    time functions as a kind of "usury," whereby a metaphor's "value" de-
    creases, like a coin. At the same time, however, *usure* also implies the re-
    verse—the hope that in the process of exchange words would not become
    exhausted, but would "increase [their] return in the form of revenue, addi-
    tional interest, linguistic surplus value." The *Bṛhaddevatā* shows us that,
    despite Derrida's revolutionary intentions, this idea is far from new. Its nar-
    ratives clearly show that language's value increases with usage. The basic

Vedic concept of the performance of sacrifice begetting wealth is here particularized to a specific part of the sacrifice—the *mantra*.

49. See Tokunaga, "Text and Legends," p. 117, n. 62. Although not directly relevant to the discussion, it is worth commenting on the intriguing ownership of the *sūkta* which both belongs to a particular ritual and has a particular *itihāsa*. The *Bṛhaddevatā* (3.141) "A *sūkta* of Kakṣīvat, [beginning] '*When indeed will Indra, the protector of men and bestower of wealth, listen to the praises of the Aṅgirasas, who are devoted to the gods!*' (*Ṛg-Veda* 1.121), usually regarded as belonging to Indra, is indicated as indirectly belonging to the all-gods in the Svarasāmans." In the *Kauṣītaki Brāhmaṇa* (24.9), Svarasāmans are the rites by which the Atris rescued the sun from darkness, when it had been pierced by Svarbhanu. Those who perform those rites expel evil from both worlds. The hymn is used as replacement for the Nābhānediṣṭha hymn (*Ṛg-Veda* 10.61), and is described as a "Crypto-Vaiśvadeva" hymn—one in which the gods are not mentioned. Here and in the following verses, the *Bṛhaddevatā* juxtaposes without comment or judgment the *yājñika* and the *aithāsika* perspectives; both the deity of the *sūkta* and its ritual use are mentioned. The addition of ritual commentary is also a habit of the later recension.

50. The wording of the story then emulates the two stanzas of *Ṛg-Veda* 126.23, just cited.

51. These lines are in all probability a later interpolation of *Bṛhaddevatā*. Additionally, the order of Ṛg-Vedic hymns is violated in this *itihāsa*, where 1.126 comes before 1.121 and 1.125. The plot thus assumes more importance than the actual order of the *sūkta*s and verses themselves—a modification of canon quite typical of the second recension.

52. See my discussion of the "balancing" function of these narratives in *Myth as Argument*, chap. 7.

53. *Atharva Veda Saṃhitā* 11.5.3.; *Śatapatha Brāhmaṇa* 11.5.4.12; also see discussion in Horsch, *Vedische "Gāthā" und "Śloka" Literatur*, 136 ff.; and Heesterman, *Broken World of Sacrifice*, 165–70.

54. "The Venerable Śaunaka says the whole is Kakṣīvat's (*Bṛhaddevatā* 3.152ab)."

55. Also, Macdonell (1904) sees *Bṛhaddevatā* 3.151–153 as a possible interpolation, as *Sarvānukramaṇī* does not mention the passage and its style is suspicious.

56. In the next verse, the *Bṛhaddevatā* attempts to classify the exchange according to "praise of men," which is intimately related to "praise of gifts" as a form of appropriate exchange for gifts. "154. The verses in which the actions of kings and their gifts, great, small, and middle sized, are told, are to be understood as *narāśaṃsī*—praise of men; the praise of kings in the ten [*maṇḍalas*] is through [these verses]." Sāyaṇa mentions this praise of men in his comment on *Ṛg-Veda* 1.125, which also includes the Kakṣīvat story. In fact, he uses the occasion of *Ṛg-Veda* 1.125.2 to discuss at length whether it is a fault that the brahmin *ṛṣi* accepted a gift from a king, as the *Manu Smṛti* prohibits it.

57. This story is quoted by Ṣaḍguruśiṣya on *Ṛg-Veda* 5.61 with the omission of occasional *śloka*s. Sāyaṇa, in introduction to 5.61, tells the story in another metrical form. Sieg (*Sagenstoffe*, 50–64) treats the story in its various manifestations. He also states the relation of its various forms (51). For the present purposes, there are no significant differences between the versions.

58. I have rendered "one" as the subject of the sentence here, taking it as a general normative statement on the part of the queen. Macdonell, following the same emendation he makes in Ṣaḍguruśiṣya (177), would read "a certain seer." In either case, the normative tone is apparent.

59. The phrase "who did not see Rathivīti" is taken from the next verse.

60. See in particular "Beyond the Myths of Origin."
61. To be sure, such devotional relationships can be found in the earliest of Vedic poetry. However, they usually occur specifically within the realm of sacrifice, and these stories occur outside that realm altogether. (See also my "The Transparent Text.")
62. Not surprisingly, this *itihāsa* is added by the second recension of the *Bṛhaddevatā*, with its penchant for the gifts of kings to *ṛsis*.
63. Macdonell (1904) has here "the royal seer Trasadasyu" but Trasadasyu is named elsewhere as a king, not a seer; thus I translate "praise of the royal seer for Trasadasyu." Elsewhere in the *sūkta* (verse 32), the *ṛsi* is named as Sobhari "We the Sobharis, have come to the universal sovereign the ally of Trasadasyu, for his protection." Sāyaṇa, moreover, names the *ṛsi* as Sobhari.
64. This word is probably used in the text owing to the close association of Indra with Kakutstha. (See Macdonell, *Bṛhaddevatā* 2 224.)
65. Heesterman, *Broken World of Sacrifice*, 213.
66. The development of the ascetic path in Vedic India has its own implications for the relationship between words and wealth. With the development of the concept of *ātman*, the sacrificer identifies himself completely with the sacrifice and becomes *ātmayājin*, the one who performs the sacrifice for himself and by himself. He is thus sovereignly independent, and to be contrasted to the *devayājin*, who is still dependent on and subservient to the gods.

   If indeed the act of exchange is replaced by an act of internal self-transcendence, then such a hypothesis has real implications for the exchange between words and wealth. *Mantra* is no longer one kind of currency given in exchange for another, wealth. Instead, language is part of the *ātmayājin*'s transcendent power, whose maintenance requires no external fire but the speaking and acting of truth (*satya*). As Heesterman puts it, the *ātmayājin* "construes with Ṛg-, Yajur-, and Sāmaveda . . . a transcendent, heavenly body" (Ibid. 216). Such transcendence means that the sacrificer comes to possess the power of language in its own right; he is equivalent to Veda, and thus to *mantra*.

Works Cited

SANSKRIT SOURCES

Āpastamba Śrauta Sūtra. Edited by Richard Garbe. Delhi: Munshiram Manoharlal, 1983.

Atharva Veda Saṃhitā. Edited by V. Bandhu. 4 vols. Hoshiarpur: Vishveshavaranand Vedic Research Institute, 1960–62.

———. Translated by W. D. Whitney. 2 vols. Harvard Oriental Series, vols. 7 and 8. Cambridge: Harvard University Press, 1905.

Bṛhaddevatā. Edited and translated by Arthur Anthony Macdonell. 2 vols. Harvard Oriental Series. Cambridge: Harvard University Press, 1904.

Bṛhaddevatā, or an Index to the Gods of the Rig Veda by Śaunaka, to which have been added Ārṣānukramaṇī, Chandonukramaṇī "and Anuvākānukramaṇī" in the Form of Appendices. Bibliotheca Indica Sanskrit Series, nos. 722, 760, 794, and 819 (new series). Calcutta: Baptist Mission Press, 1893.

Jaiminīya Brāhmaṇa. Edited by R. Vira and L. Chandra. Nagpur: Sarasvati Vihara Series, 1954.

———. Incomplete translation by H. W. Bodewitz. *Jaiminīya Brāhmaṇa* 1:1–65. Leiden: E. J. Brill, 1973.

Katyāyana Śrauta Sūtra. Translated by H. G. Ranade. Poona: Dr. H. G. Ranade and R. H. Ranade, n.d.

———. Edited by Albrecht Weber. Chowkhamba Sanskrit Series, no. 104. Reprint: Varanasi: Chowkhamba Sanskrit Series Office, 1972.

Kāṭhaka Saṃhitā. Edited by Śrīpāda Dāmodara Sātavalekara. Pāraḍi, Ji. Balasāḍa: Svādhyāya-Maṇḍala, 1983.

Kauṣītaki Brāhmaṇa. Edited by H. Bhattacharya. Calcutta Sanskrit College Research Series, no. 73. Calcutta: Sanskrit College, 1970.

Maitrāyaṇī Saṃhitā. Edited by Leopold Von Schroeder. Leipzig: F. A. Brockhaus, 1885.

Manu Smṛti. Edited by J. H. Dave. 5 vols. Bhāraitīya Vidyā Series. Bombay: Bhāratīya Vidyā Bhavan, 1972–82.

Manu Smṛti. Translated by George Bühler. *Sacred Books of the East*. Oxford: Clarendon Press, 1886; reprint ed., New York: Dover Publications, 1969.

———. Translated by Wendy Doniger with Brian Smith. New York: Penguin, 1992.

The Nighaṇṭu and the Nirukta, The Oldest Indian Treatise on Etymology, Philology, and Semantics, Critically Edited from Original Manuscripts and Translated by Lakshman Sarup. London and New York: Oxford University Press, 1920–27.

Pañcatantra Pūrnabhadra. Edited by Johannes Hertel. Harvard Oriental Series 11. Cambridge: Harvard University Press, 1908.

Pañcaviṃśa Brāhmaṇa. Edited by P. A. Cinnaswami Sastri and P. Parrabhirama Sastri. 2 vols. Kashi Sanskrit Series, no. 105. Benares: Sanskrit Series Office, 1935.

Pūrva Mīmāṃsā Sūtras of Jaimini. Edited and translated by Mohan Lal Sandal. 2 vols. In *Mīmāṃsā Sūtras of Jaimini*. Delhi: Motilal Banarsidass, 1980.

Ṛg Veda Samhitā, together with the Commentary of Sāyaṇa Āchārya. Edited by F. Max Müller. 4 vols. Varanasi: Chowkhamba Sanskrit Series, 1966.

Ṛg Veda Vyākhyā Madhavakrta. Edited by C. Kunhan Raja. Adyar: Adyar Library, 1939.

Śabara Bhāṣya. Translated by Ganganatha Jha. 3 vols. Baroda: Oriental Institute, 1933–36.

Sarvānukramaṇī, with Commentary of Ṣaḍguruśiṣya. Edited by Arthur Anthony Macdonell. Oxford: Clarendon Press, 1886.

Śatapatha Brāhmaṇa. 5 vols. Bombay: Laxmi Venkateswar Steam Press, 1940.

———. Translated by Julius Eggeling. *Sacred Books of the East.* Oxford: Clarendon Press, 1882–1900.

Taittirīya Brāhmaṇa. 3 vols. Ānandāśrama-saṃskṛta-granthāvaliḥ, granthānkha no. 42. Poona: Ānandāśrama, 1979.

———. Partial translation by P. E. Dumont. *Proceedings of the American Philosophical Society,* 92, 95, 98, 101, 107–9, 113.

Taittirīya Saṃhitā of the Black Yajur Veda With the Commentary of Bhaṭṭa Bhāskara Miśra. Edited by A. Mahadeva Sastri and K. Rangacharya. Delhi: Motilal Banarsidass, 1986.

SECONDARY SOURCES

Alper, Harvey, ed. *Mantra.* Albany: State University of New York Press, 1989.

Bali, Suryakant, ed. *Historical and Critical Studies* in the Atharva Veda. Delhi: Nag Publishers, 1981.

Bell, Catherine. *Ritual Theory, Ritual Practice.* Cambridge: Cambridge University Press, 1991.

Biderman, S., and B.-A. Scharfstein, ed. *Myths and Fictions: Their Place in Philosophy and Religion.* Leiden: E. J. Brill, 1983.

Bloomfield, Maurice. *A Vedic Concordance.* Harvard Oriental Series, no. 10. Cambridge: Harvard University Press, 1906; reprint ed., Delhi: Motilal Banarsidass, 1964.

Böhtlingk, Otto, and Rudolph von Roth. *Sanskrit-Wörterbuch.* 10 vols. St. Petersburg: Buchdruckerei der Kaiserlichen Akademie der Wissenschaften, 1875.

Caland, W., and V. Henry. *L'Agniṣṭoma.* Paris: Ernst Leroux, 1906.

Chakrabarti, S. K. "On the Transition of the Vedic Sacrificial Lore." *Indo-Iranian Journal* 21 (1979): 181–88.

Clooney, Francis X. *Thinking Ritually.* Vienna: DeNobili Press, 1990.

Dandekar, R. N. *Vedic Bibliography.* 4 vols. Bombay: Karnatak Publishing House, 1946.

de Nicolas, Antonio. *Meditations through the Ṛg-Veda: Four Dimensional Man.* Boulder: Shambala, 1978.

Derrida, Jacques. "White Mythologies." In *Margins of Philosophy.* Chicago: University of Chicago Press, 1982, 207–72.

Edwards, D. M. *The Philosophy of Religion.* London: Hodder and Stoughton, 1924.

Findly, Ellison Banks. "*Mantra kaviśasta:* Speech as Performative in the Ṛg Veda." In *Mantra,* ed. Harvey Alper, 15–48.

Gonda, Jan. *Change and Continuity in Indian Religion.* The Hague: Mouton, 1965.

―――. *A History of Indian Literature.* Vol. 1, fac. 2: *The Ritual Sūtras.* Wiesbaden: Otto Harrassowitz, 1977.

―――. *A History of Indian Literature.* Vol. 1, fac. 1: *Vedic Literature (Saṃhitās and Brāhmaṇas).* Wiesbaden: Otto Harrassowitz, 1975.

―――. "The Indian Mantra." *Oriens* 16 (1963): 242–97.

―――. *The Vision of the Vedic Poets.* The Hague: Mouton, 1963.

―――. Mantra *Interpretation in the* Śatapatha-Brāhmaṇa. New York: E. J. Brill, 1988.

―――. *Prayer and Blessing: Ancient Indian Ritual Terminology.* New York: E. J. Brill, 1989.

Grassmann, Hermann. *Wörterbuch zum "Rig Veda" 4., unveränderert.* 4th ed. Wiesbaden: Otto Harrassowitz, 1964.

Gupta, Uma. *Materialism in the Vedas.* New Delhi: Classical Publishing, 1987.

Hacker, Paul. *Grundlagen indischer Dichtung und indischen Dekens.* Vienna: Institut für Indologie der Universität Wien, 1985.

Heesterman, J. C. *Ancient Indian Royal Consecration.* The Hague: Mouton, 1957.

―――. *The Inner Conflict of Tradition: Essays in Indian Ritual, Kingship and Society.* Chicago: University of Chicago Press, 1985.

―――. "Somakuh und Danaergabe." *XXIII Deutscher Orientalistentag: Wurzburg 1985.* Stuttgart (1989): 349–57.

―――. *The Broken World of Sacrifice: An Essay in Ancient Indian Ritual.* Chicago: University of Chicago Press, 1993.

Hillebrandt, Alfred. *Vedic Mythology.* Translated by Sreeramula Rajeswara Sarma. Vol. 1. Delhi: Motilal Banarsidass, 1980.

Hopkins, Thomas J. *The Hindu Religious Tradition.* Belmont, Calif.: Wadsworth Publishing, 1971.

Horsch, Paul. *Die Vedische Gāthā und Śloka Literatur.* Bern: Francke Verlag, 1966.

Hubert, H., and M. Mauss. *Sacrifice: Its Nature and Function:* Translated by W. D. Walls. Chicago: University of Chicago Press, 1964.

Huxley, J. *Religion without Revelation.* London: Max Parrish, 1957.

Inden, Ronald. *Imagining India.* London: Basil Blackwell, 1990.

―――. "Orientalist Constructions of India." *Modern Asian Studies* 20 (1986): 401–55.

Johnson, Willard. *Poetry and Speculation in the Ṛg Veda.* Berkeley: University of California Press, 1980.

Kane, Pandurang Vaman. *History of Dharmaśāstra*. 2d ed. 5 vols. Poona: Bhandarkar Oriental Research Intitute, 1968–75.

Keith, Arthur Berriedale. *Rigveda Brāhmaṇas: The Aitareya and Kauṣītaki Brāhmaṇas of the Rigveda*. Delhi: Motilal Banarsidass, 1981.

———. *The Religion and Philosophy of the Vedas and the Upaniṣads*. Delhi: Motilal Banarsidass, 1989.

Keith, Arthur Berriedale, and A. A. Macdonell. *Vedic Index of Names and Subjects*. 2 vols. Delhi: Motilal Banarsidass, 1967.

Leach, J., and E. Leach. *The Kula: New Perspectives on Massim Exchange*. Cambridge: Cambridge University Press, 1983.

Lefever, H. *The Vedic Idea of Sin*. Travancore: London Mission Press, 1935.

Macdonell, Arthur Anthony. *A History of Sanskrit Literature*. Oxford, 1899; reprint ed., Delhi: Motilal Banarsidass, 1971.

———. *Vedic Mythology*. [1892]. Issued as Bd. 3, Hft. 1A of *Grundriss der indo-arischen Philologie und Altertumskunde*, edited by G. Bühler; reprint ed., Varanasi: Indological Bookhouse, 1963.

———. *The Religion of the Veda*. Translated by Shridhar B. Shrotri. Delhi: Motilal Banarsidass, 1988.

Malinowski, Bronislaw. *Argonauts of the Western Pacific*. London: Routledge and Kegan Paul, 1922.

Mauss, Marcel. "Essai sur le don. Forme et raison de l'échange dans les sociétés archaïques." In *Année Sociologique, Nouvelle Série 1*, 1923–34.

Munn, Nancy. *The Fame of Gawa*. Cambridge: Cambridge University Press, 1986.

Oldenberg, Hermann. *The Religion of the Veda*. [1917]. Translated by Shridhar B. Shrotri. Delhi: Motilal Banarsidass, 1988.

Patton, Laurie L. "Beyond the Myths of Origin: Narrative Philosophizing in Vedic Commentary." In *Myths and Fictions: Their Place in Philosophy and Religion*. Edited by Biderman and Scharfstein. Leiden: E. J. Brill, 1993, 225–54.

———. "The Transparent Text: Purāṇic Trends in the *Bṛhaddevatā*." In *Purāṇa Perennis*, ed. Wendy Doniger. Albany: State University of New York Press, 1993, 3–29.

———. *Myth as Argument*.

———. *The Bṛhaddevatā as Canonical Commentary*. Religions Geschichtliche Versuche und Vorarbeiten. Berlin: De Gruyter Mouton, 1996.

———. "Poets and Fishes: Modern Indian Interpretations of the Vedic Rishi." In *Authority, Anxiety, and Canon: Essays in Vedic Interpre-*

tation, ed. Laurie L. Patton. Albany: State University of New York Press, 1994, 281–308.

———. "Dis-solving a Debate: Toward a Practical Theory of Myth with a Case Study from Vedic Commentary." In *Religion and Practical Reason*, ed. Frank Reynolds and David Tracy. Albany: State University of New York Press, 1994, 213–62.

———. "Vāc: Myth or Philosophy?" In *Myth and Philosophy*, ed. Frank Reynolds and David Tracy. Albany: State University of New York Press, 1990, 183–214.

Pischel, Richard, and Karl F. Geldner. *Vedische Studien*. Band I, 1889; Band II, 1897; Band III, 1901. Stuttgart: W. Kohlhammer.

Raja, C. Kunhan. *Poet-Philosophers of the Ṛg-Veda*. India: Ganesh and Co., 1963.

Renou, Louis. *Les Ecoles Védiques et la Formation de Veda*. Cahiers de la Société Asiatique, vol. 9. Paris: Imprimerie Nationale, 1947.

———. *Vocabulaire du Rituel Védique*. Paris: C. Klincksieck, 1954.

———. *Etudes Védiques et Paninéènnes*. 17 vols. Paris: Publications de l'Institut de Civilisation Indienne, 1955–69.

Shastri, D. R. *A Short History of Indian Materialism, Sensationalism, and Hedonism*. Bookland: Calcutta, 1957.

Shell, Marc. *Money, Language and Thought*. Berkeley: University of California Press, 1993

———. *The Economy of Literature*. Baltimore: Johns Hopkins University Press, 1993.

Sieg, Emil. *Die Sagenstoffe des Ṛg-Veda und die indische Itihāsa-Tradition*. Stuttgart: W. Kohlhammer, 1902.

Silver, Morris K. *Taking Ancient Mythology Economically*. Leiden: E. J. Brill, 1992.

Smith, Brian K. *Reflections on Resemblance, Ritual and Religion*. New York: Oxford University Press, 1989.

Staal, J. Frits. "The Concept of Metalanguage and Its Indian Background." *Journal of Indian Philosophy* 3 (1975): 315–54.

———. "*Mantra*s and Bird Songs." *Journal of the American Oriental Society* 105 (1985): 549–58.

———. "The Meaninglessness of Ritual." *Numen* 26 (1979): 2–22.

———. "*Ṛg Veda* 10:71 on the Origin of Language." In *Revelation in Indian Thought: A Festschrift in Honour of Professor T. R. V. Murti*, ed. Harold Coward and Krishna Sivaram. Emeryville, Calif.: Dharma Publishing, 1977, 3–14.

———. "Ritual Syntax." In *Sanskrit and Indian Studies: Essays in Honour of Daniel H. H. Ingalls*, ed. M. Nagatomi et al. Dordrecht, Holland; Boston: D. Reidel, 1980, 119–43.

————. "The Sound of Religion." *Numen* 33 (1986): 33–64.

Strenski, Ivan. *Religion in Relation.* Columbia: University of South Carolina Press, 1993.

Tambiah, Stanley. "The Magical Power of Words." *Man,* n.s. 3 (1968): 175–208.

Tokunaga. "The Text and Legends of the *Bṛhaddevatā.*" Ph.D. diss., Harvard University, 1979.

Vetter, G. B. *Magic and Religion.* New York: The Philosophical Library, 1958.

Weiner, Anette B. "Inalienable Wealth." *American Ethnologist* 12 (1985): 210–27.

Wheelock, Wade. "The Ritual Language of a Vedic Sacrifice." Ph.D. diss., University of Chicago, 1978.

————. "A Taxonomy of *Mantra*s in the New and Full Moon Sacrifice." *History of Religions* 19 (1980): 349–69.

————. "The Problem of Ritual Language." *Journal of the American Academy of Religion* 50, no. 1 (1982): 49–69.

Zysk, Kenneth. *Asceticism and Healing in Ancient India.* Oxford: Oxford University Press, 1991.

PART IV

CONTINUITIES AND INTERRUPTIONS: MYTH, ART, AND LITERATURE

ERIC J. ZIOLKOWSKI

SANCHO PANZA AND NEMI'S PRIEST: REFLECTIONS ON THE RELATIONSHIP OF LITERATURE AND MYTH

WHEN CLAUDE LÉVI-STRAUSS lamented in 1955 that the study of myth had remained for fifty years "a picture of chaos," his complaint was not simply against predecessors and colleagues in his own field.[1] As he put it, "Precisely because professional anthropologists' interest has withdrawn from primitive religion, all kinds of amateurs who claim to belong to other disciplines have seized this opportunity to move in, thereby turning into their private playground what we had left as a wasteland."[2] Among the "amateurs" he had in mind were undoubtedly the same literary critics whom the folklorist Stith Thompson faulted that year for "recent perversions of the word 'myth.'"[3] Such sentiments are still echoed in essays in this volume, both by anthropologist Mary Douglas and folklorist Alan Dundes. Such contempt for literary-critical treatments of myth was shared by the anthropologist David Bidney, who, also in 1955, warned that "contemporary philosophers and theologians, as well as students of literature in general, who speak of the 'indispensable myth' in the name of philosophy and religion, . . . are undermining faith in their own disciplines and are contributing unwittingly to the very degradation of man and his culture."[4]

These attitudes were expressed during the heyday of critical consideration of the relationship of myth and literature. Northrop Frye, cited by Bidney as one of those literary scholars who

abetted human degradation by attributing a positive value to
myth, once recalled how in writing his famous study of Blake's
prophetic poems, *Fearful Symmetry* (1947), "I had to learn something about myth, and so I discovered, after the book was published, that I was a member of a school of 'myth criticism' of
which I had not previously heard."[5] As the Germanist E. W. Herd
observed in 1969, no such *school* in the strict sense ever existed.
Yet "the more extravagant devotees of this approach to literature,
and their more fiery opponents, both tend to give the impression
that myth criticism is a well-defined movement."[6] By then, even
as sober-minded an exponent as John B. Vickery could accurately
call myth criticism "one of the most distinctive trends in contemporary literary study."[7]

That trend waned over the next decade, despite the appearance
of several notable surveys of myth criticism and despite an official
reaffirmation by the Modern Language Association of America
that the area of "literature and myth" is worthy of scrutiny on a
level equal with "literature and linguistics," "literature and philosophy," "literature and religion," and nine other areas of interdisciplinary literary study.[8] In a 1980 essay in one of the last
major volumes devoted to the subject, Vickery had both bad news
and good to report on the current status of myth criticism in the
Anglo-American scene. Myth critics had "both come a long way
and . . . scarcely moved an inch," becoming "more aware and sophisticated" in their questions and approaches while remaining
"fitful at best and confused or uncertain at worst" in their understanding. Because this "paradoxical situation" seemed to mark
"the dropping away of spurious issues, the increased self-
awareness of methodologies, and the concomitant recognition of
the [inherent theoretical] complexities," he considered myth
criticism "better today than a decade ago": it had "gained in direct proportion to its decline in amount or quantity and its movement away from the position it once occupied of critical fad."[9]
Vickery's careful optimism was not shared by Klaus Weissenberger with regard to "mythopoesis" in German literary criticism.
In reassessing the "total concept of poetry" developed in the late
1950s and the 1960s by Wladimir Weidlé and Wolfgang Schade-
waldt—a concept that establishes the autonomous value (*seins-
heteronome Eigenwürde*) of poetry and furnishes criteria for defining the main genres on the basis of their different mythopoetic
manifestations—Weissenberger in 1980 deemed it "regrettable

that theories with such far-reaching consequences hardly find any echo nowadays in Germany."[10]

By the mid-1980s, at the height of the much younger vogue for poststructuralism and deconstruction, the scholarly status of myth-critical approaches to literature had declined even further in America and abroad. "Mythological literary criticism" was no longer "widely influential," claimed one authority: "When it was, it seems to have been tied to the suggestion that the presence of a mythological motif necessarily means that earlier instances of that theme represent the best resource for understanding the later work. It remains, however, a lively component of a complex and robust criticism that is aware of possible prefigurative aspects in a literary work."[11] While it is unclear what "complex and robust criticism" this scholar was thinking of, today one would be hard-pressed to find a mythological approach serving as a "lively component" of any criticism still widely practiced. Of two lexicons of literary criticism and theory that appeared in 1992, one lacks any entry on myth criticism while the other's substantial entry on the topic refers to only three sources published after 1980, the latest of which appeared in 1984.[12] Likewise, of two new major reference guides to literary criticism and theory that came out in 1993 and 1994, only one contains an entry on myth criticism, and the most recent source to which that entry refers was published in 1983.[13] The absence of more recent sources seems consistent with the frank obituary pronounced in Oxford's *Dictionary of Literary Terms* (1990): "Myth criticism has been widely dismissed as a form of reductionism that neglects cultural and historical differences as well as the specific properties of literary works."[14]

This statement encapsulates the most devastating of four main charges against myth criticism, the others being that the method arbitrarily imposes a mythic pattern upon literary texts; that it overemphasizes and misuses analogy in interpretation; and that it ignores, distorts, and violates historical data and evidence pertinent to substantiating mythic elements in literary texts.[15] The severity of these charges is not all that has boded ill for myth criticism in recent decades. While it has been suggested that the future viability of myth criticism as a critical approach will depend in part "upon the success of literary theorists in appropriating the empirical and conceptual investigations of myth by other disciplines," the meaningfulness of myth criticism's two most basic categories, myth and literature, has been questioned by philosophers, literary theorists, and theorists of myth and religion.[16] By dissipating the dichotomy of ordinary and nonordinary language and leveling the hierarchy that privileges such "serious" modes of discourse as philosophy, history, and journalism over literature (the paradigm of "nonserious" discourse), deconstruction in the 1970s and 1980s attempted to obliterate the distinction between literature and those other modes, to regard them all as literature, and thus, by making literature all-encompassing, to deny that literature can be defined or have an essence.[17] Fostering this development was the idea that all modes of discourse are at their roots metaphorical and hence mythic in nature—even Western metaphysics, *la mythologie blanche* (a phrase adapted by Derrida from Anatole France), which purportedly "erased" the *mythos* out of which it sprang.[18] The idea that myth underlies discourse strangely inverts Max Müller's long-rejected philological theory of myth as a "disease of language," in effect making all human discourse a disease of *myth*.[19] The same idea also anticipates Ivan Strenski's thesis that myth, in seeming to be everything, is nothing.[20]

Notwithstanding the unfavorable winds of theory, my own conviction is that the investigation of myth and literature in their relationship not only remains theoretically tenable but is essential for a full understanding both of literary structure and meaning and of the processes of mythic transmission and transformation. It is no accident, for example, that elsewhere in this volume, the work of literary theorist Marc Shell becomes useful for Laurie Patton to make her argument about the mythic representations of words and money in Vedic India. In considering first the history and diversity of the ways this relationship has been construed, I shall in effect be replying to the charge that to explore the relationship is reductionist; if the implicit thrust of this charge is to discourage myth criticism, the very diversity of approaches such criticism has involved exposes the accusation itself as reductionist. I shall then consider a lineage of texts that reflect the increased bearing of theories of myth upon the incorporation of myths per se in modern literature. And I shall conclude by demonstrating through a comparison of a classic novel and a classic comparative study of myth and ritual how such a study can be theoretically bound to the same particular *mythos* as a literary text.

This essay aims at suggesting that the study of myth in literature, if it is to advance, will have to take into greater account certain theoretical factors that hitherto have been generally ignored.

The Greek word *mythos*, meaning speech or narrative, is first employed as a technical term in literary theory by Aristotle, who uses it in his *Poetics* to denote plot, or the arrangement of incidents in an action. But the controversy over the truth or value of mythic events had already begun by Plato's time a generation earlier. This debate, with its obvious ramifications for the interpretation of literary texts that incorporate myths, would continue through the centuries, with the pendulum of opinion on the matter oscillating dramatically from age to age up through the Enlightenment. Anticipated by Vico's exposition of myth as "poetic metaphysics" in his *Scienza nuova* (1725), there developed a notion of myth that opened an entirely new outlook on the relationship of myth and literature. This notion began with Friedrich Schlegel and F. W. J. Schelling, and continued with other German Romantics and such English and American counterparts as Coleridge and Emerson. For them all, myth, like poetry, embodied a kind of truth, a means supplementary to reason, logic, or science, by which to grasp experience, representing "a comprehensive vision (as opposed to metaphysical explanation) of the world clothed in narrative."[21]

This Romantic understanding of myth has informed many if not most of the views expressed in our own century about the relationship of myth and literature. If the restored interest in myth among literary artists and critics is largely attributable to the impact of James G. Frazer, whom we shall later discuss, and to the pervasive currency of Freudian and Jungian theories as well, a most important aspect of the modern concern with myth that finds its roots in the Romantic view is the stress laid upon myth as literary content, in addition to myth as literary form.[22] Quite distinct from Aristotle's concentration on myth as plot, this emphasis was given philosophical ballast by the mythico-symbolic writings of Ernst Cassirer and his follower Susanne K. Langer and achieved consummate expression in Hermann Broch.[23] In effect, Broch inverts the Aristotelian understanding of *mythos* in its relation to *logos*: whereas for Aristotle, *mythos* as plot finds its "antonym and counterpoint" in *logos*, Broch identifies *mythos* with meaning and content (*Inhalt*), and *logos* with structure and form (*Form*), construing the two together as the dual foundations of all human expression.[24]

In practice, literary artists and critics over the past half-century have tended to find myth related to literature in six distinct ways that span a wide spectrum between emphases on myth as form and on myth as content.[25] The most obvious way is displayed by fictional or poetic works that expressly retell a particular mythic or legendary tale in its original setting.[26] Critical treatment of such works requires analyzing the myth in its original and other traditional forms and assessing the manner in which those forms have been adapted or transformed in the more recent text. This involves "consideration of the author's attitude towards the original myth, of the way in which this attitude is communicated through the new form, of style and of structure."[27]

Second, mythological elements derived from earlier cultures often manifest themselves in individual literary texts through specific allusions, themes, images, names, motifs, symbolic characters, inherited plots and scenes.[28] Analysis on this level evolved from Frazer's encyclopedic investigations into the origins of primitive and ancient myth and ritual and the subsequent research of anthropologists Gilbert Murray at Oxford and F. M. Cornford and Jane Harrison at Cambridge. Observing "the widespread dispersion of similar myths," they concluded, much as Vico had done two centuries earlier, that "if these commonalities cannot be explained by transmission from one culture to another, the alternative appears to be that the human mind (or human experience as processed by the mind) is so constructed that certain modes of thought and correlative narratives are produced by all peoples." Picking up on this conclusion and often considering it confirmed by Freud's theories of the unconscious, myth critics "assumed that myths express fundamental human responses to life which are finally inexpressible in any other way."[29] Their studies therefore concentrate on tracing ways prefigurative mythic materials are received and adapted in the work of later authors, whether directly or by transformation, and whether consciously or unconsciously on the authors' part.[30]

The key theoretical question on this level of analysis is: How are primary myths transformed into literature? Frye and Slochower offered two complementary explanations. Frye, whose views are more closely associated with the fourth level discussed below, termed the transformation of myth in literature *displacement*, construing myth as one extreme of literary design and naturalism as the other. In between lies the whole area of romance, or "the tendency to displace myth in a human direction," where, for example, the sun god or tree god from a myth may be replaced by the portrayal of a person who is significantly associated with the sun or trees.[31] Slochower terms derivative mythic versions in literature *mythopoesis* to distinguish them from primary myth. Mythopoesis in his sense occurs in texts likes Camus's *Le Mythe de Sisyphe* (1955), which sever the myths upon which they are based from their ritual origins, adapting the stories exclusively as aesthetic structures. Mythopoeic texts appear when the literal account of the myths or legends they adapt can no longer be accepted. In modern literature, the link between the mythic and the literary may seem external and tangential, with mythology appearing as, in Marcelino Peñuelas's words, "un elemento accesorio de la literatura, un tema más." Even in the earliest manifestations of literary art, especially epic poetry and the theater, the link is not essential: "La mitología aquí aparece como un elemento previo, anterior a su expresión literaria. Así puede decirse que la mitología es literatura en potencia."[32]

Summing up the enterprise of analyzing mythopoesis and mythic transformations in literature, Vickery relates the "strategies of incorporation and displacement" to six categories: poetics, structure, theme, character, narrative, and point of view.[33] Of these categories, that of structure (*mythos* in an Aristotelian sense) elicits what amounts to a third, separate level of analysis. In certain literary texts, the plot structure, as distinct from the narrative materials employed in it, may be found to be adopted implicitly or explicitly from a particular myth or legend (in the sense of a mythic account of a historical person or event). Like mythic materials, mythic structure may be employed consciously or unconsciously by the author; and, when done consciously, the employment may be avowed or tacit. But such concerns, Herd maintains, "should not worry those whose sympathies lie with the New Critics, as the critic's concern here is not with the author's intentions but with the integral structure of the work."[34]

Another understanding of myth in literature focuses upon the recurrence of universal archetypes that are usually alleged to find their source in the collective unconscious. Derived originally, like the view informing the second level of analysis discussed above, from the work of Frazer and the Cambridge anthropologists (including Murray), and popularized by Jungian psychology, this view crystallizes most notably in Maud Bodkin's *Archetypal Patterns in Poetry* (1934) and Northrop Frye's *Anatomy of Criticism* (1957). Critics such as these are concerned "not with the specific mythological motifs or figures that interest Slochower and the thematologists, but rather with . . . general archetypal patterns" such as rebirth or apocalypse, the quest of the hero, the eternal return, and the lost paradise.[35] The assumption that universal themes and motifs must all approximate some basic, central Ur-narrative flourishes in Joseph Campbell's idea of the "mono-myth" of the hero and in Frye's vast critical system of *mythoi*, "phases," and "modes," which depicts all literary genres as derivations from the quest myth.[36] As exemplified by Bodkin, Campbell, and Frye, critics interpreting on this level tend to be indifferent as to whether such structural patterns in a text may have emerged there with or without conscious development by the author; instead, the critical challenge is to demonstrate that the pattern constitutes "a coherent and meaningful whole within the overall structure of the work."[37]

Most objections to this fourth approach center around the concept of archetype upon which it depends. What makes the approach unacceptable in the eyes of its detractors is its usual linkage with Jung's theory of the collective unconscious, which one critic compares to "the creature from the black lagoon. It's lying in wait to emerge from that oily water and devour us all."[38] In associating archetypal patterns in literature with this theory appropriated from another discipline (psychology), Bodkin and critics like her were seen to be imposing upon literary criticism a category incompatible with it.[39]

Still, the association with the theory of a collective unconscious is not all that has led some to reject the search for archetypes in literature. Frye considered such a theory "unnecessary" in literary criticism.[40] Yet he was repeatedly taken to task for basing his critical system upon a concept of archetype, despite his explicit resistance to the confusion of his own use of the term archetype with Jung's.[41] Frank Kermode found Frye's system invalidated by what he deemed its failure to acknowledge that literature is fundamentally different from myth and ritual: if literature does the work that myth and ritual once did, "they can obviously no longer do it."[42] (This last point is debatable, as it seems belied by modern literary texts that incorporate mythic or ritual materials, albeit in displaced forms, that are by no means defunct in the minds of many readers.)[43] Literature, Kermode contends, is distinguished by "a different reality principle, appropriate, in an expression of Eliade's which Frye himself quotes, to *this* time as myth was appropriate to *that* time. The difference between *illud tempus* and *hoc tempus* is simply willed away in Frye's critical system, but it is essential to the very forms of modern literature, and to our experience of it." So "when you hear talk of archetypes, reach for your reality principle."[44]

Derived ultimately from Herder via Schelling's *Philosophie der Mythologie* (1842), and extending naturally from the Romantic assumption that all great literature must possess an underlying mythology, the fifth and most controversial way literature and myth are considered related has to do with texts that are proclaimed by their authors, or perceived by their critics and readers, to embody newly created myths.[45] The term myth is invoked to characterize modern literary works whose vision seems to epitomize certain basic human desires or experiences. Such figures as Hamlet, Faust, Don Juan, Don Quixote, and Robinson Crusoe, and the narratives of such authors as Hawthorne, Melville, Dostoevsky, Kafka, and Hesse have been viewed as "new myths" or "literary myths" in this sense, "though none is based explicitly on motifs originally associated with a ritual or on universal archetypal patterns."[46] In accord with such eminent novelists and short-story writers as Mann, Broch, and Eliade, who pursued avowedly "mythic" ends in their literary art, students of literature have been wont to speak of the "mythmaking" of poets like Blake, Shelley, Wordsworth, Rilke, Yeats, Eliot, Hart Crane, and Dylan Thomas.[47] One critic has even lauded "the poetic revitalization of myth" in our time.[48]

Against the notion of literary mythmaking it is commonly asserted that a myth cannot be created, believed in by choice, or brought into being by will, since the book has "succeeded" myth.[49] Attributing mythic status to literary works becomes problematic when perceived as a means by which critics try to confer upon fiction the prestige of traditional myths, even when a work may not possess any definitive traits of those myths.[50] As Philip Rahv points out, by "confusing" the power of myth and the power of poetry, "the inflaters of myth are able to credit it with properties that really belong to art."[51] Moreover, warns Herd, critics who try to trace "new myths" in literary works risk leading themselves into a trap. If the "new myth" departs completely from the patterns of established myths, the literary critic's point can only be proved through recourse to other disciplines. If the critic uncovers a new structural pattern, there seems no compelling reason to characterize it as a myth.[52]

Taken to an extreme, the understanding of certain literary texts or heroes as myths can lead to a notion that such texts or heroes spring into existence of their own accord, with their authors serving merely as mouthpieces for their expression. Unamuno and Jung went so far as to claim that it was not Cervantes and Goethe that created Don Quixote and Faust, but Don Quixote and Faust that created Cervantes and Goethe.[53] This way of construing a literary hero or text, again, leads the discussion of myth and literature beyond the boundaries of literary criticism and into realms of psychology, philosophy, and other disciplines. The same is the case with yet another, sixth way that mythic and literary phenomena are said to be connected, and this is by linking myth and the process of literary creation. One might contend, as Peñuelas does, drawing upon theories of Jung and Mark Schorer and testimonies of modern literary artists, that the creative process establishes an "auténtica fusión" where myth and literature "aparecen como un mismo tronco que toma savia de las mismas raíces." But Peñuelas's admission that the creative process is a theme "tanto de sicología como de literatura" exposes why this theory, which commits the long-condemned "genetic fallacy," offers little to the literary critic interested in strictly textual analysis.[54]

Here, an important literary-historical point needs to be made if one is to speak of the "displacement" (Frye) or the "degeneration" and "camouflaging" (Eliade) of primordial and ancient myths in modern literature. From the Enlightenment on, not only particular myths themselves but also developments in the *theoretical reflection upon* the general phenomenon of myth, especially among exponents of the newly developing disciplines of anthropology, comparative religion, and, later, depth psychology, conditioned how mythic content and mythic structures were assimilated or "made" in literary works. Obviously, if a concern over authors' intentions may haunt some efforts to analyze mythic incorporations or "mythmaking" in literary works, so too may a concern with the responses of readers to those works.[55] Less obvious, but perhaps equally decisive in the case of each text, is how its author conceived of the phenomenon of myth in general (as opposed to particular myths); how that concept influenced the author's adaptation of whatever particular traditional myth, mythic materials, or mythic structure might have informed the text; and in turn, how we as readers conceive of myth in general and how our own concept influences our interpretation of the text's mythic dimensions.

As Strenski reminds us, the leading theories of myth reflect "the larger theoretical, professional and cultural projects assumed" by their postulators.[56] Given the propensity of literary art to be equally if not more reflective of the time and place in which it is produced, it should come as no surprise that a considerable portion of modern Western literature, by virtue of being created within the same culture and period as that growing modern "industry" of myth to which Strenski refers, has been demonstrably susceptible to the sway of certain dominant modern theories of myth.

Theories of myth are most clearly reflected in those rare works of literature that broach the concept or phenomenon of myth as an explicit subject for discussion. A first step toward the development of this phenomenon is taken in Thomas Carlyle's fictional treatise Sartor Resartus (1833–34). The book's hero, the eccentric German professor Diogenes Teufelsdröckh, finds "the Mythus of the Christian Religion look[ing] not in the eighteenth century as it did in the eighth" and announces as the foremost need of the age "to embody the divine Spirit of that Religion in a new Mythus."[57] This statement, in M. H. Abrams's view, sums up a central enterprise of the preceding generation of Romantics in England and Germany, whose tendency was "to naturalize the supernatural and to humanize the divine."[58]

In echoing Friedrich Schlegel's call for a "new mythology" to be formed "out of the uttermost depth of the spirit," Teufelsdröckh stops short of theorizing upon the nature of myth.[59] To be sure, in adapting Goethe's ideal of Bildung as an invitation to embrace the totality of what is known of human experience, including the diversity of religious faiths, Carlyle may be credited as "the pioneer of Comparative Religion in England."[60] But the locus classicus for literature reflecting the tendency within that discipline to theorize about myth is Middlemarch (1871–72), which is set in the period immediately prior to Sartor's publication. In George Eliot's novel, the aged pedant Mr. Casaubon, who does not know German, aspires to reveal "The Key to All the Mythologies," not knowing—as Eliot and Casaubon's cousin Will Ladislaw knew—that Karl Otfried Müller had published Prolegomena zu einer wissenschaftlichen Mythologie (1825), which exposed the fallacy of the whole "mythography" enterprise.[61] What makes Casaubon different from a fictional character modeled after some figure of a traditional myth (for example, Dr. Frankenstein, whom Mary Shelley presented as "the modern Prometheus," or Prince Myshkin, whom Dostoevsky modeled

partially after Christ), is that he is a fictional character who is
aware of, and who *theorizes about,* myth as a phenomenon.

Such self-conscious appropriation of the theory of myth in literature does not stop with *Middlemarch.* Another stage of appropriation is reached in C. S. Lewis's fantasy novel *Perelandra*
(1944), whose protagonist, the philologist Ransom, finds himself
transported mysteriously from his home on Earth to a floating
island on the planet Venus. There, he is cast into a scenario un-
mistakably reminiscent of Adam's in the pre-Fall Garden of Eden,
complete with a pristine gardenlike setting, the presence of a solitary, beautiful, innocent, naked virgin woman, and the awareness
that her destiny rests on her ability to obey a special injunction
(not to dwell on "the Fixed Land") issued by an unseen divine
being (Maleldil). As Ransom himself is quick to recognize these
parallels, he begins wondering whether "all the things which appeared as mythology on earth [were] scattered through other
worlds as realities," and he senses that he is "enacting a myth."[62]
Two subsequent developments complicate the analogy with the
pre-Fall Eden scenario. First, there is the arrival of another earth-
ling, the mad scientist Weston. As the "Un-man" completely
taken over by the force of evil, he promptly assumes the role of
Eden's serpent by tempting the woman to defy the divine injunction. Second, there are the disclosures that this woman is to be
joined by a male companion whom she has yet to meet; that she
and this mate-to-be are both parentless and the only natives of
the planet; and that they, like Adam and Eve, are to become
queen/mother and king/father of an entire race.

The extraordinary innovation of *Perelandra* is its portrayal of a
character who not only consciously reflects upon myth as a phenomenon but finds himself a participant in a particular myth
with which he is already familiar and which seems to be re-
peating itself before his eyes. His sense of déjà vu leads him to
suspect that "the old myths [were] truer than the modern myths,"
such as "evolution," and he concludes that "the triple distinction
of truth from myth and of both from fact was purely terrestrial—
was part and parcel of that unhappy division between soul and
body which resulted from the Fall."[63] True to the Miltonic implication of his name, Ransom is eventually awed at realizing that
his true "mission" on Venus is to act as Maleldil's agent, serving
a quasi-messianic role aimed at saving the Venusian Eve from
succumbing to her Tempter.[64] Acting upon that realization, Ran-

som slays the "Un-man" and thereby averts the impending Fall. By the end of the novel, he is as aware as are the readers that he has taken part not simply in a reenactment of one biblical myth but in a blending and reformulation of two: the Fall and the Atonement, which, as now combined, become the story of an *averted* fall. When the embodiments of the classical deities Mars and Venus appear before him near the novel's close, he affirms from his experience the realness of myth: "The Muse is a real thing. A faint breath, as Virgil says, reaches even the late generations. Our mythology is based on a solider reality than we dream: but it is also at an almost infinite distance from that base. . . . Ransom at last understood why mythology was what it was— gleams of celestial strength and beauty falling on a jungle of filth and imbecility."[65]

Ransom's revelation harmonizes with a pair of categorical assumptions that governed the thinking of two of our century's most influential students of religion. First, the "almost infinite distance" he posits between "mythology" ("gleams of celestial strength and beauty") and the "jungle of filth and imbecility" accords with the "absolute heterogeneity" by which Emile Durkheim distinguished *le sacré* from *le profane* in his seminal exposition (1912) of those terms.[66] Second, Ransom's emphasis on myth's "reality" anticipates the classic definition of myth offered more than ten years after the appearance of *Perelandra* by Eliade, a chief adopter of Durkheim's distinction.[67] In fact, the phenomenon of fictional characters reflecting upon the theory of myth crystallizes supremely in Eliade's own epic novel, *La Forêt interdite* (1955). Set in Rumania and several other European sites during the tumultuous period 1936–48, this voluminous narrative transposes its author's own notion of myth as an escape from the "terror of history" into an obsession of the main protagonist and other characters.[68]

From Carlyle through Eliade, the appearance of characters in literature who reflect upon myth epitomizes a crucial, though largely unappreciated, truism concerning the mythic aspects of modern literary texts. In any text where mythic incorporation, mythic displacement, mythic structuring, or mythmaking occurs, whatever theory of myth it is that informs or is reflected in those dimensions of the text may bear decisively upon the text's meaning. In this respect Lillian Feder's analysis of the creative adaptation of ancient Greek and Roman myth in Yeats, Pound,

Eliot, and Auden is distinguished by the special attention she pays to the direct impact the theories of myth in Vico, Frazer, Freud, and Jung had upon those poets' thinking and writing.[69]

What I am suggesting is that, at least since Vico, with his notion of myth as a poetic metaphysic, and especially from the time of the early Romantics, with their new idea of myth as the basis of literature, the *theory* of myth has played a more and more decisive role in the incorporation, displacement, structuring, and making of myths or mythic elements in literary texts. This development corresponds to the increasingly hermeneutic stance of the modern mind toward myth. For modern people, as Paul Ricoeur observes, belief in myths has yielded its place to the interpretation of myths: "[Modern man] alone can recognize the myth as myth, because he alone has reached the point where history and myth become separate."[70] As a result, concepts of what myth is and of how it functions, especially those concepts that became the most dominant, have figured increasingly—in some cases as crucially as the informing myths themselves—in those texts that possess mythic dimensions.[71]

Frazer, even more so than Freud or Jung, is the scholar credited for "the bulk of modern literary interest in myth and ritual."[72] In what remains of this essay I shall depart from the well-trod path of demonstrating Frazer's nonpareil impact upon subsequent literature and proceed in an opposite direction, considering *The Golden Bough* in association with a classic work of fiction completed exactly three hundred years before Frazer's culminating third edition (12 vols., 1911–15), and roughly two centuries before myth and literature began to be consciously equated by the Romantics: Miguel de Cervantes's novel *Don Quijote de la Mancha* (pt. 1, 1605; pt. 2, 1615), known in English as *Don Quixote*.[73]

Why compare these two works? For Hermann Broch "the whole history of European literature is strung between Homer and Tolstoy," having emerged from myth with the former and returned to myth with the latter. Notwithstanding Broch's view of *mythos* as the original ancestor (*der Ur-Ahn*) of all forms of narrative expression, however, the modern literary "return" to myth was not really a return at all, precisely because it involved a theoretical awareness of myth as something to return to.[74] A genuine myth cannot be conscious of itself as a myth, or even of the phenomenon of myth; once myth, or the people conceiving it, attains that consciousness, it ipso facto becomes something else: what Tillich called a "broken myth."[75] This may explain why a contributor to Yves Bonnefoy's *Dictionnaire* of mythologies could discern in modern poetry, from Hölderlin on, a "progressive movement by which the gesture of confidence in the use of a mythic model loses if not its validity at least its force of credibility."[76]

Most of Frazer's scholarly methods, ideas, and hypotheses have long been rejected.[77] Given that much myth criticism was based upon his writings, the diminishment of his reputation over time clearly encouraged detractors of that criticism. Nonetheless, *The Golden Bough* is deemed a primary stimulus behind our century's obsession with myth. My aim hereon shall be to reveal the modern theoretical detachment from myth, as epitomized by Frazer, to have been prefigured by the *Quixote*, which, as "the first and unsurpassed model of the modern realist novel," figured in the development of practically every important novelist since Cervantes and engendered the genre's most distinctive theme: the conflict of fantasy and reality.[78] While not succumbing to a temptation to deny the generic distinction between the *Quixote* and *The Golden Bough*, the following comparison will reveal how Frazer's epochal "study in comparative religion" and "magic and religion," in its treatment of primitive myths and rituals from around the world, is impelled by an obsession with the same basic Western *mythos* that is found displaced in Cervantes's novel.[79]

One can only wonder whether Frazer, who had read the *Quixote* as a boy and went on a three-week walking-tour of Spain as a young man, was aware of certain striking commonalities between Cervantes's masterpiece and *The Golden Bough*.[80] Each work apparently originated out of a single initial idea (to parody books of chivalry through the depiction of a crazed, bibliophilic hidalgo and to explain the bizarre succession of priesthood of Diana at Nemi or Aricia), and neither author began writing his work with any intimation of its eventual magnitude.[81] An identical period of ten years elapsed between the publications of the *Quixote*'s two parts, and between the appearances of *The Golden Bough*'s first two editions, and in both cases the intervening decade saw the first part or edition achieve extraordinary popular success that crucially affected the formation and substance of the second.[82]

Together with the ironic style that characterizes both authors' prose, there is also an unmistakable kinship between the particular "stage" of mental evolution with which Frazer is most interested, and the mental affliction that defines the character of Cervantes's hero.[83] The seemingly endless chain of illusions through which the mad hidalgo proceeds once he sallies forth into the world as a "knight," mistaking prostitutes for damsels, flocks for armies, windmills for giants, and so forth, could for all intents and purposes be established upon the first of the "two different misapplications of the association of ideas" that Frazer attributes to the "savage" mind: the "association of ideas by similarity."[84] Frazer's caution to his readers against making "the perpetually repeated mistake of judging the savage by the standard of European civilization," and against assuming "that all races of men think and act much in the same way as educated Englishmen," recalls the *Quixote*'s central psychological conceit: the dichotomy, repeatedly emphasized by the narrator, between the knight's "madness" (*locura*) and the "sanity" (*cordura*) of all the characters he meets, with the possible exception of Cardenio (1:24).[85] For Michel Foucault this dichotomy has far-reaching consequences, since "the madman, understood not as one who is sick but as an established and maintained deviant, as an indispensable cultural function, has become, in Western experience, the man of *primitive* resemblances."[86] I emphasize *primitive*, a term used more or less synonymously with *savage* in *The Golden Bough*, to suggest how analogous the psychological alienation of the *Quixote*'s madman—"the man who is *alienated* in *analogy*"—is to the sense of psychological estrangement that Frazer seeks to implant in his readers as they contemplate the "savage" mentality.[87] Cervantes's narrator and Frazer highlight the supposed psychological distance between the "madman" and "sane" society, and between the "savage" and the "educated Englishmen," ultimately in order to play the same trick of exposing the supposition of that distance as problematic, if not illusory.[88]

This is not the only trick played by the author of *The Golden Bough* on his readers. Only at his completion of the third edition did he reveal the now notorious truth about his usage of the figure of Nemi's priest, "the nominal hero of the long tragedy of human folly and suffering which has unrolled itself before the readers of these volumes. . . . He, too, for all the quaint garb he wears . . . , is merely a puppet, and it is time to unmask him before laying him up in the box."[89] Much has been written about this last-minute "unmasking," which for Jonathan Z. Smith exposes Frazer's whole enterprise as a "bad joke."[90] This jocular theme beckons our attention to what we shall see to be a remarkable correspondence between the vast entirety of *The Golden Bough* and the longest sustained episode of the *Quixote*.

In his discussion of magical ceremonies that originated with the intent of ensuring the revival of nature in spring, Frazer speculates over what happens to such primitive rites once "man" realizes their futility:

> With the advance of knowledge these ceremonies either cease to be performed altogether or are kept up from force of habit long after the intention with which they were instituted has been forgotten. Thus fallen from their high estate, no longer regarded as solemn rites on the punctual performance of which the welfare and even the life of the community depend, they sink gradually to the level of simple pageants, mummeries, and pastimes, till in the final stage of degeneration they are wholly abandoned by older people, and, from having once been the most serious occupation of the sage, become at last the idle sport of children. It is in this final stage of decay that most of the old magical rites of our European forefathers linger on at the present day.[91]

Considered in the light of the *Quixote*, Frazer's explanation of "decayed" rituals (an explanation for which he acknowledges his debt to Wilhelm Mannhardt) gives pause for thought. It seems only natural that the *Quixote* should incorporate certain themes, motifs, structural patterns, and other elements discernibly derived from mythic and ritual sources. For José Ortega y Gasset, the transition from epic to novel represented by the *Quixote* is a movement from the objective world of myth and romance into "the inner world in all its vast extension, the *me ipsum*, the consciousness, the subjective"; myths now become internalized in the mind of the protagonist.[92] In helping spawn the modern novel, the *Quixote* embodied a kind of "half-way house" between that genre and the earlier genre it satirized and replaced: the books of chivalry or romances.[93] As chivalric literature constitutes a virtual repository of displaced mythic patterns and mythic materials (derived largely from the mythically-saturated literature of ancient Greece and Rome), the *Quixote* could hardly have satirized it without incorporating and further displacing some of its more prominent mythic features.[94]

The place in the *Quixote* that displays a Frazerian myth-ritual pattern "degenerated" or "decayed" to the point of appearing farcical, like "the idle sport of children," is the extended episode of Sancho Panza's governorship of Barataria (2:44–45, 47, 49, 51, 53), the most elaborate of the long series of "jests" (*burlas*) whose unwitting dupes the mad knight and his peasant squire become while sojourning as guests of the actual duke and duchess (2:30–57). Anyone who has read *The Golden Bough* will remember the prominent roles the ritual of the mock-king-for-a-day and the mythic pattern of dying and resurrecting take on in Frazer's quest (itself a jest!) to explain the Arician priesthood. As we shall see, these two motifs, together with a number of other mythic and ritual motifs that Frazer draws into association with the unfortunate figure of the priest of Nemi, recur in the Barataria episode.

Over the centuries interpreters have typically set Sancho Panza in a reductive opposition to Don Quixote as sanity to insanity, body to soul, realism to idealism, rationalism to faith, prose to poetry, and so forth.[95] During the past half century, when not still being viewed this way, he has been seen as an embodiment of the whole human and the eternal peasant type, in his blending of individual and universal qualities; a spokesman for Spanish philosophy, in his quoting of proverbs; an emblem of the Spanish people, in his virtues and vices; and a representative of the modern human, in his alienation.[96] Critics trying to locate Sancho's origin in learned or popular traditions have associated him with the figure of *el rústico* in the tradition of the theater prior to Lope de Vega; the rustic in the broader dramatic tradition; the countryman of the oral tradition of the Age of Gold; the Western folkloric type of the "clever fool" (*tonto-listo*); or the *rey del Carnaval* of the popular tradition of carnival.[97]

This last interpretation, offered by Augustin Redondo, is of special interest. In associating the portrayal of Sancho in the Barataria episode with the carnivalesque tradition, Redondo makes no mention of Frazer. However, he draws considerably upon Mikhail Bakhtin's analysis of Rabelais, and it was Bakhtin who, in a single, passing parenthetical allusion, credited Frazer for performing "a considerable task in the study of the origin and character of various themes and symbols pertaining to the culture of folk humor."[98]

Redondo's linkage of the Barataria episode with carnival accords with Bakhtin's own perception of the *Quixote* as one of the "greatest" and "most carnivalesque novels of world literature," and will later provide us a key for understanding how the affinities between the Barataria episode and a certain ritual and mythic pattern studied in *The Golden Bough* might be explained by historical and cultural connections rather than by some theory of archetype and a collective unconscious.[99] For the tradition of folk-carnival humor displays, albeit in "degenerated" or "decayed" forms, that same pattern of motifs that can be found displaced even further in the *Quixote*'s Barataria episode.

The germinal conceit behind the episode of Barataria is Sancho's quest to become governor of an island. His primary incentive for entering Don Quixote's service as a squire stems from the knight's promise of such a governorship to him during their initial dialogue (1:7), and the squire's aspirations are fueled by later reiterations of that promise (e.g., 1:30, 35, and 2:3). The first analogy between Sancho and the Arician priest, who assumed his position by slaying his predecessor in single combat, is that just as each priest reigned under the title of Rex Nemorensis, or King of the Wood (until he was likewise slain by his successor), so Sancho immediately inflates his own desire to be a governor into a wish to be a king (*rey*).[100] Another analogy is suggested by the requirement that the King of the Wood be a runaway slave "in memory of the flight of Orestes, the traditional founder of the [Arician] worship."[101] Sancho is never a slave; but as an impoverished peasant he subsists at the bottom of the social scale and, as Don Quixote's "servant," must regard him as "master" (*amo*). Nor is Sancho a runaway when he first appears; but he does leave behind his wife and children to follow Don Quixote, and, after helping his master free a band of the king's galley slaves (1:22), he and Don Quixote become fugitives from the Inquisition.

The encounter of the knight and squire with the duke and duchess (2:30) initiates a chain of events and motifs that seem Frazerian *avant la lettre*. One particular association evoked by the portrayal of the duchess in this scene proves uncannily suggestive. When first spotted "coming out of the wood," she appears as the "fair huntress" in the company of her hawking party, a being of such elegance and beauty that she seems more than human: "Splendor itself seemed personified in her" (2:591). Just as the sacred charge of the King of the Wood was to serve Diana Nemorensis (Diana of the Wood), goddess of the hunt (who is mentioned by name in other connections elsewhere in the novel), so Sancho presents himself on his knees before this "fair huntress" of the wood, enlists his master and himself in her service, and soon thereafter, with his master, finds himself situated in her country estate as her "favorite" (2:31, 594).

The whole subsequent sojourn of Don Quixote and Sancho at the ducal palace constitutes an elaborate joke concocted by their hosts, who are believed to have been modeled by Cervantes after

the actual duke and duchess of Luna and Villahermosa, the own-
ers of a country estate at Pedrola, near Zaragoza.[102] As the duke
and duchess in the novel "had read the First Part of this history,
and from it were aware of Don Quixote's strange ideas, they . . .
[meant] to humor him and agree with everything he said, and, so
long as he stayed with them, to treat him as a knight-errant, with
all the ceremonies usual in the books of chivalry they had read"
(2:30, 592). Out of this scheme, the ducal couple mastermind and,
with the assistance of numerous lackeys, dueñas, and vassals,
carry out a series of "jests" with the knight as their unwitting
butt: his nocturnal encounter with "Merlin," who instructs Don
Quixote on how the "disenchantment" of his beloved Dulcinea
might be brought about (2:35; for her original "enchantment" see
2:10); his "flight" with Sancho on the wooden horse Clavileño
(2:41); the (feigned) amorous advances made upon him by the
duchess's "lovesick" damsel, Altisidora (2:44 and thereafter); and
his "battles" with a cat (2:46), with a band of pinching "phan-
toms" (2:48), and with the lackey Tosilos (2:56).

Despite their cruelty, which epitomizes a pervasive feature of
the whole novel, these ostensibly playful jokes furnish striking
support to Huizinga's concept of *homo ludens*.[103] More precisely,
the spectacle of the deluded madman being set up and treated
temporarily as a knight (with the significant result that "this was
the first time that he thoroughly felt and believed himself to be a
real knight-errant and not an imaginary one" [2:31, 595]), only to
be reduced to an object of constant ridicule, seems a displaced
illustration of what Huizinga observes of the "archaic" human
habit of "playing at nature": "Through this ritual play, savage society acquires its rude forms of government. The king is the sun,
his kingship the image of the sun's course. All his life the king
plays 'sun' and in the end he suffers the fate of the sun: he must
be killed in ritual forms by his own people."[104] Don Quixote (cf.
the archaic "king") is allowed to "play" the knight (cf. the "sun")
while suffering humiliation (cf. the sun's fate) through "jests" (cf.
the "ritual forms") perpetrated by his hosts (cf. the king's "own
people").

But Don Quixote is not the only butt of the ducal humor. Sancho too becomes their butt, and the central joke at his expense—
his imagined governorship of Barataria—displaces even further
the ritual of killing the king. This point brings us back to Frazer,
whose fascination with regicide stemmed from his preoccupation
with the mystery of the Arician priesthood. According to Frazer,

the regicidal act that was habitually committed by certain "savage" peoples at the end of a fixed term, or upon the failure of the king's strength or health, or in the aftermath of some great calamity such as a drought or famine, eventually became "modified" and "softened down." In some societies, the act of regicide evolved into the practice of annually replacing the king with a surrogate "temporary king," who "at the close of his short reign . . . is no longer killed, though sometimes a mock execution still survives as a memorial of the time when he was actually put to death."[105]

From the point in the *Quixote* where the duke pretends to confer upon Sancho the government of an "island" (2:32, 602), this new joke of allowing Sancho to realize his ambition of becoming a governor (which complements the joke of allowing Don Quixote to believe he himself really is a knight) closely resembles the practice of mock-kingship in societies around the world. Sancho, as we have seen, thinks of governorship in terms of kingship. And at least ten motifs associated by Frazer with divine kingship and with what he views as its derivative, mock-kingship, find analogies in Sancho's governorship.

The Mock-King's Peasant Origin

This feature of a number of the traditions of mock-kingship considered by Frazer has an obvious bearing upon the joke of Sancho's governorship, as Cervantes's text calls our attention explicitly to the motif of the peasant-king.[106] While listening to Don Quixote's paternalistic counsels before assuming the governorship, Sancho reminds him: "Not all governors come from royal stock." To which Don Quixote responds: "Glory in your humble birth, Sancho, and be not ashamed of saying you are peasant-born. . . . Countless are they who, born of low parentage, have risen to the highest dignities, pontifical and imperial" (2:42, 655).

Association with Fertility, Vegetation, and Spring

Frazer appeals to this next association of divine kingship in general, and of the Rex Nemorensis in particular, to illustrate his theory that primitive peoples put their kings to death out of a conviction that a king's life was sympathetically bound up with his country's prosperity: should the king's strength fail, so would the power of nature to support the land and its people.[107] *The*

Golden Bough also surveys rituals that involve slaying the tree spirit (whose incarnation the priest of Nemi was believed to be), and such springtime and early summer festivals of European peasants as the May tree and Maypole which he regards as modern "relics" of tree worship. The same associations with spring and fertility recur in the *Quixote*. The duke tells Sancho, as he is about to assume his governorship, that "his islanders were already looking out for him as for showers of May [*el agua de mayo*]" (although the whole episode takes place in August), and that the "real, genuine island" which he is to rule is "uncommonly fertile and fruitful" (2:42, 653). Through these associations Sancho is cast mockingly in the role of sustainer of the natural order on which the citizens of his rustic "island" depend. From a Frazerian perspective, this role would seem ultimately derived from the divine kings of archaic peoples; through its "decay" in the carnival rituals of Spanish popular culture, the role of sustainer would have availed itself to Cervantes's imagination.

Triumphal Procession

Like the mock-king of Cambodia (the so-called Sdach Méac or King February), who, according to Frazer, ruled in the place of the real king for three days in the month of Méac (February), Sancho is dispatched by the ruler he "replaces" (the duke) and is led on a triumphal, crowded, spectacular procession to the place of his governorship. The descriptions of the two processions in the *Quixote* and *The Golden Bough* are remarkably similar, and seem all the more so when it is remembered that both processions are essentially parodic.[108]

Royal Taboo

Among the taboos imposed upon supernaturally endowed kings by "savage" societies, one of the more common ones Frazer discusses is the restriction of the royal diet.[109] As governor, the gluttonous Sancho is hilariously victimized by the same taboo. As soon as he assumes office he is forbidden by his official physician to eat to his heart's content, and in his resulting hunger and frustration he threatens to murder the offending doctor (2:47). This parallel was noted by Freud, an avid reader of Frazer. Citing *The Golden Bough* several times to support his own theory of the ceremonial taboo of kings as an expression of their subjects' unconscious hostility and revenge against them, Freud notes: "The experiences of Sancho Panza (as described by Cervantes) when he was Governor of his island convinced him that this view of court ceremonial was the only one that met the case."[110]

Settler of Disputes

Frazer cites a case from Siam of a mock-king to whom "all disputes about fields, rice, and so forth" were referred during his temporary "reign."[111] As governor, Sancho is similarly called upon by the inhabitants of his "island" to judge in various legal disputes and other matters (2:45; 2:49; 2:51). His judgments prove so sound that all witnesses "were filled with amazement and looked upon their governor as another Solomon" (2:45, 672), and the majordomo whom the duke and duchess had commissioned to report back to them for their amusement "could not make up his mind whether he was to . . . set him down as a fool or as a man of sense" (673).[112] Appealed to here is a Christian theme as old as the Pauline epistles: the wise fool. Sancho himself points out that "God sometimes guides those who govern in their judgments, even though they may be fools" (673)—a thought that is later reiterated by Don Quixote (see 2:51, 709).

Battle of Succession

"In the sacred grove there grew a certain tree round which at any time of the day, and probably far into the night, a grim figure might be seen to prowl. *In his hand he carried a drawn sword, and he kept peering warily about him as if at every instant he expected to be set upon by an enemy.*"[113] This unforgettable image from the opening page of *The Golden Bough* occurs as part of a 466-word portrait of Nemi's priest, of which more than half is "Romantic nature prose-poetry derived entirely from Frazer's fancy."[114] Yet, turning from this grim portrait to the *Quixote's* comical vignette of Sancho making his vigilant nocturnal round of Barataria as governor, with staff in hand (2:49), the reader is bound to feel a sense of déjà vu. Chronologically, would it be putting the cart before the horse, or the antitype before the type, to imagine the Cervantine scene as a distant parodic displacement of the grim classical image conjured by Frazer? That both images present a king/governor circling about a sacred grove/island in his charge, with sword/staff in hand, may be purely coincidental. But the possibility of a direct link between them is suggested by the fact that Frazer's sole reference for the line italicized above, Strabo, had figured importantly in sixteenth-century critical discussions of chivalric literature and the classical aesthetic.[115]

Another analogy may not be purely coincidental. The nocturnal paranoia betrayed by the wary priest in the passage above presumably stems from his awareness as *"a priest and a murderer"* that—as Frazer goes on to infer, still basing on Strabo the words I have italicized—*"the man for whom he looked* was sooner or later to murder him and hold the priesthood in his stead."[116] Likewise, Sancho is awakened on the seventh night of his governorship by bell ringing and shouts, and told: *"To arms, to arms,* señor governor, *to arms!* The *enemy* is on the island in countless numbers, and we are lost unless your skill and valor come to support us. . . . *Arm at once,* your lordship, *if you would not have yourself destroyed* and the whole island lost" (2:53, 719, emphasis mine). To prepare Sancho for the battle which is staged as yet another joke by the duke's cronies, the jokers bind and immobilize him between two long shields, with a lance placed in his hand— thereby rendering (whether Cervantes was aware of it or not) an apt parody of the paranoid, sword-wielding priest described by Strabo (and Frazer).

What also seems to connect this image of Sancho to the Strabo-Frazer portrait of Nemi's priest is the theme of mock-battle. As the priest's inferred paranoia would stem from his anxiety over an impending attack by his own murderer-successor, and as Frazer's intent is to link this murderous ritual of succession with widespread archaic rituals of regicide, so the mock-battle that hastens Sancho's governorship to its end is virtually identical with what Frazer finds to be a common feature of such rituals. Among some "barbarous races," he points out, succession to the royal throne was achieved by "vanquishing the king in battle."[117] And in the alleged "Great Sacrifice" festival sponsored every twelfth year by the king of Calicut, the king staked his life and crown on the ability of his soldiers to defend him against a staged but gruesomely spectacular and real attack.[118]

Regicide

The "attack" on Barataria climaxes when Sancho, still bound between the two shields, falls to the ground and is trampled by the jokers play-acting the battle (2:53). While I am not aware that a satisfactory source for this scene has been identified, it would be hard to overlook the scene's affinity with one of the harvest customs of modern European peasantry that Frazer deems analogous to ancient Greek and Near Eastern conceptions of the annual death and resurrection of a god: "The person who cuts or binds or threshes the last sheaf . . . is bound up in the last sheaf, and, thus encased, is carried or carted about, beaten, drenched with water, thrown on a dunghill," and so forth.[119] Regardless of whether the scene of Sancho and the shields (cf. the sheaf) was inspired by any such custom (and it is plausible that it was, given the breadth of Cervantes's first-hand knowledge of the Spanish peasantry), the same regicide motif that Frazer found still present in the European folk culture of his own day is discernibly present in the denouement of the Barataria episode.[120] This is true even of the Sacaea festival of ancient Babylon, in which a prisoner condemned to death was dressed up as a king, seated on the king's throne, fed whatever he requested (unlike Sancho), and allowed for five days to issue whatever commands he pleased and even to sleep with the king's concubines, only to be brutally killed at the festival's close. Like Sancho's governorship, this custom was, Frazer allows, perhaps "merely a grim *jest* perpetrated in a season of *jollity* at the expense of an unhappy criminal."[121]

There are, of course, important differences between Sancho and a victim of actual regicide. Unlike such a victim, who is killed so as to be replaced by a new successor, Sancho is not killed; he survives, albeit bruised, traumatized, and depressed, and his village "defeats" its attackers. And whereas Frazer believed that the killing and replacing of kings in the prime of their life expressed a primitive desire "to bring the relentless revolution of the great wheel to a stand, to keep youth's fleeting roses for ever fresh and fair," Sancho's governorship is brought to an end because the jokers who contrived it begin to fear the joke may go stale.[122] Thus Sancho again resembles a mock-king, whose temporary reign, being essentially a joke, interrupts for a short period, in some cases only a day, the reign of a real king.

Yet, true to Frazer's theory of mock-kingship, the episode of Sancho's governorship might also seem to display residual traits of actual regicide, grim traits that become humorous only in the Cervantine context. While governor, Sancho repeatedly claims to be "dying of hunger" as the result of the dietary restrictions imposed on him by his physician (2:47, 679), whom he considers a "public executioner" (680) who is actively "killing me with

hunger" (2:51, 711; cf. 2:49, 691). This anxiety leads him to expect—like a victim-to-be of regicide—"to take leave of [this
government] and my life together" (2:51, 712). Ultimately the
majordomo himself, the chief perpetrator of the joke, sees to it
that Sancho is fed, as "he felt it against his conscience *to kill* so
wise a governor by hunger" (2:50, 708, emphasis mine).

Regifugium

Following the mock-attack, which in effect, if not by Cervantes's
conscious intent, parodies a thwarted regicide, there occurs in his
narrative another closely related motif that finds a counterpart in
Frazer's discussion of the succession to kingdom in ancient Lat-
ium. In the manner of the Roman *regifugium* (flight of the king),
though not for the same conjectural reasons offered by Frazer for
that rite, Sancho flees his island, convinced that "ploughing and
digging, dressing and pruning grapevines are more in my line than
defending provinces or kingdoms" (2:53, 721).[123]

This flight episode is immediately preceded by allusions to, and
later ends with a symbolic enactment of, what becomes the culminating theme of *The Golden Bough.*

Death and Resurrection

Once the "attack" on Barataria had been rebuffed, and before his
flight, the trampled and traumatized Sancho demanded to be released from office so that he could "go look for my past life, and
resurrect from this present death [*para que me resucite de esta
muerte presente*]" (2:53, 721). This turn of phrase, together with
the doctor's ensuing offer to revive Sancho with "a potion for falls
and bruises that will make you as sound and strong as ever" (721),
calls to mind Frazer's account of a ritual of Saxony and Thüringen
in which the representative of the tree spirit, after being slain, is
brought to life again by a doctor: "This is exactly what legend
affirmed to have happened to the first King of the Wood at Nemi,
Hippolytus or Virbius, who after he had been killed by his horses
was restored to life by the physician Aesculapius. Such a legend
tallies well with the theory that the slaying of the King of the
Wood was only a step to his revival or resurrection in his successor."[124]

If "The Ritual of Death and Resurrection" is the culminating
theme of *The Golden Bough,* it is self-evident how crucially Fra-

zer's conjectural linkage of that theme with regicide and mock-kingship bears upon his own quest for an explanation of Nemi's priesthood.[125] Of interest to us is not the question of the legitimacy of Frazer's linkage but the prefiguration of that linkage in the denouement of the Barataria episode.

As the coda of that episode, Sancho's flight ends with his undergoing a comically symbolic death, resurrection, and atonement. After falling with his donkey into a deep, dark pit (sima) or cave (gruta), where they lie entrapped, he becomes convinced that they will die there, "buried alive [sepultado en vida]" (2:55, 732; cf. 729). Don Quixote, upon finding him there, blames the misfortune on Sancho's "sins," and a witness to Sancho's release describes him jokingly as a "sinner . . . out of the depths of the abyss [abismo], dead with hunger [muerto de hambre]" (732). Sancho himself attributes eschatological significance to his figurative resurrection from the cave: "If heaven had not sent me my master Don Quixote, I'd have stayed there till the end of the world" (733).

Sancho's cave incident, itself a parodic echo of his master's earlier adventure in the cave of Montesinos (2:22-23), is not the last episode in the novel to involve the theme of death and resurrection. This theme comes to the fore in the feigned death and resurrection of Altisidora, the final joke played by the duke and duchess on Don Quixote and Sancho (2:69). To be sure, this joke is played long after Sancho's departure from Barataria, and only after he and Don Quixote have left the ducal castle, proceeded to Barcelona, and started back toward their village following Don Quixote's defeat by the Knight of the White Moon (Sansón Carrasco) on the Barcelona beach (2:64). Yet the episode of Altisidora's resurrección highlights another motif that finds an analogue in The Golden Bough, and this motif illuminates further the implications of those residual traits from the ritual of temporary kingship in the Barataria episode.

Scapegoat

The final joke played by the duke and duchess begins when Don Quixote and Sancho are kidnapped one evening on the road by a band of armed horsemen who carry them back to the ducal castle. There, they are brought before a "bier" on which lies the "dead body" of the beautiful Altisidora, whom they are led to believe died out of her unrequited love for Don Quixote. This episode has been read as an allegorical satire of an auto-da-fé, presenting the

arrested culprits (Don Quixote and Sancho), the entry of the prisoners with escorts into the court (the ducal castle), the fatuity of
the judges (the dukes' lackeys), and so forth.[126] Sancho is forced
to wear the painted tunic and pointed cap (coroza), the sanbenito
of Inquisitional convicts. To achieve the "dead" woman's "resurrection" and "salvation" (la salud), he is ordered by the "judge"
to submit to a specified number of pinches and pinpricks by the
ducal dueñas, which he unwillingly receives. Afterwards, with
Altisidora "risen" before him, he complains of being "the scapegoat"—la vaca de la boda, literally, the wedding cow—"in order
to cure other people's ailments" (2:69, 807). This statement
squares with his earlier claim as governor that, under the diet
imposed by his doctor, "I find that I have come to do penance as
if I were a hermit" (2:51, 711). As soon as he and Don Quixote
depart from the ducal castle the next night, he is pressured by his
master into playing a penitential-scapegoat role again. To fulfill
the penance prescribed much earlier by "Merlin" (one of the first
ducal jokes) as the antidote to Dulcinea's "enchantment," he is
required to inflict 3,300 lashes upon his own naked back, which
he pretends to do by slapping the whip against trees in the dark
within earshot of his pleased but deceived master (2:71).

If Sancho's lot as scapegoat seems hilarious poetic justice for a
man who has repeatedly boasted about being an "old Christian"
(cristiano vieje)—a label claimed in Spain to avoid being suspected of blood kinship to those true scapegoats, the Jews—his
responsibility for "resurrecting" and "disenchanting" others
would have had patent, far-reaching implications for Frazer.[127] In
primitive societies around the world, as well as among such
groups as the gypsies of southern Europe in Frazer's own time,
the public scapegoat as a material vehicle for the expulsion of
evils could be anything from an inanimate object, such as a
wooden bandbox, to a living creature, such as a bird, wild animal,
or human being. Through conjectures and analogies, Frazer could
perceive a human scapegoat like the Tibetan Jalno as "a successor
of those temporary kings, those mortal gods, who purchase a
short lease of power and glory at the price of their lives."[128] The
parallel with the Roman Catholic papal institution seemed obvious. With regard to the Jalno of Lhassa, Lhassa being "the Rome
of Asia," and the Jalno being the "temporary vicar" of the Grand
Lama ("the pope of Lhassa"), Frazer observes: "The analogy of
many customs in many lands points to the conclusion that, if this
human divinity stoops to resign his ghostly power for a time into

the hands of a substitute, it is, or rather was once, for no other reason than that the substitute might die in his stead.[129] Thus through the mist of ages unillumined by the lamp of history, the tragic figure of the pope of Buddhism—God's vicar on earth for Asia—looms dim and sad as the man-god who bore his people's sorrows, the Good Shepherd who laid down his life for the sheep."[130]

Sancho's awareness of his own function as scapegoat for Altisidora's resurrection seems consistent with the analogy between his role in the earlier Barataria episode and the role of a mock king or "degraded" divine king, a figure Frazer regards as a prototype of the scapegoat. The same awareness also suggests a humorous analogy between the Barataria episode and the *mythos* of Christ, the Good Shepherd whom Frazer regards as a scapegoat.

We shall return to this point momentarily.

Conclusion

As we have seen, the episode of Sancho's governorship involves ten motifs that find analogies in Frazer's discussion of rituals of divine and mock-kingship. How are these analogies to be explained? And what do they signify? My intent here is neither to support nor to dismiss but to ignore psychological theories of archetype or of a collective unconscious. In suggesting instead a strictly literary and cultural-historical explanation for the analogies in question, I shall assume a definition of *mythos* as a ritually rooted story that bears a distinctive plot structure and theme, involving superhuman beings and deeds, which embodies a paradigm for religious beliefs and ritual actions and is considered revelatory of fundamental truths about humanity and the world by the persons or communities who relate it.

That ten mythic and ritual motifs associated by *The Golden Bough* with divine and mock-kingship crop up in the *Quixote*'s Barataria episode should come as no surprise, despite there being no reason to suspect that the *Quixote*, written in Counter-Reformation Spain by an ostensibly faithful Roman Catholic (possibly of Jewish descent), exerted any influence upon the writing of *The Golden Bough* by an outspoken rationalist atheist in late Victorian England. The first motif, the mock-king's peasant origin, finds countless variations in legends, stories, and other lore that have saturated Western culture for centuries.[131] Indeed, the idea of the peasant-turned-king (or peasant-turned-governor) is the thematic equivalent of the breaking down of the classical separation of "high" and "low" styles (*Stiltrennung*) that Erich Auerbach considered a defining legacy of Christian literature stemming from the New Testament, and Cervantes was an important representative of that legacy.[132]

Fortuitously, Frazer provides a helpful clue as to Cervantes's most plausible source for virtually all ten of the motifs we have found incorporated in the Barataria episode. Noting a similarity between the Saturnalia of ancient Italy and the carnival of modern Italy, Frazer observes that "in Italy, Spain, and France, that is, in the countries where the influence of Rome has been deepest and most lasting"—in two of which (Spain and Italy) Cervantes spent most of his life—"a conspicuous feature of the Carnival is a burlesque figure personifying the festive season, which after a short career of glory and dissipation is publicly shot, burnt, or otherwise destroyed, to the feigned grief or genuine delight of the populace. . . . This grotesque personage is no other than a direct successor of the old King of the Saturnalia, the master of revels, the real man who personated Saturn and, when the revels were over, suffered a real death in his assumed character."[133]

As Redondo has shown, the characterization of Sancho draws upon the carnivalesque tradition, casting him in the role of carnival (*Carnaval*, synonymous with joy, recreation, abundance, and freedom) in its opposition to his master's embodiment of Lent (*Cuaresma*, synonymous with sadness, abstinence, and submission to the ascetic spirit dictated by the rules of the church). Redondo's uncovering of the "carnival structure" of the Barataria episode allows us to see the consistency of all ten of that episode's Frazerian motifs with the festivities of carnival leading up to Shrovetide (*Carnestolendas*) and Lent. As Sancho, the simple, chubby, and bearded peasant, approximates the typical madman (*loco*) or fool (*tonto*) who personifies carnival, so Sancho's association with fertility, vegetation, and spring ("the showers of May") corresponds with the calendrical setting of carnival; his procession from the ducal castle to Barataria, with that of the carnival king from the city gate to the church; his unsolicited dietary restrictions, with the ascetic repression of the approaching Lent; his role as settler of disputes, with the "play-court of justice" (*juego del tribunal*) during Shrovetide; the mock battle, in which he is trampled between two shields, with the symbolic combat between carnival and Lent, which may involve a ritual trampling of a puppet personification of the festival king between two bucklers; his subsequent flight from Barataria (a parodic *regifugium*), with the ouster of carnival by Lent; his thwarted mock-regicide, with the mock-execution of the carnival king; his symbolic death and resurrection, with that king's play-acted *nacimiento-muerte-resurrección*; and his role as penitential scapegoat, with that king's association with biblical humiliation.[134]

These structural, thematic, and character links between the Barataria episode and carnival would seem to furnish for that episode points of entry into Frazer's "grammar of the human imagination" (Frye's description for *The Golden Bough*).[135] What might be signified by the episode's fit in this "grammar"?

Mirroring the increased sanctification of Don Quixote in the responses of "soft," Romantic readers of Cervantes over the past several centuries, the *Quixote* has been perceived as parodying, or even incorporating and transforming, the *mythos* of Christ's life and sufferings.[136] At the same time, from Freud to Frye, sympathetic readers of *The Golden Bough* have been captivated by its association of the execution of temporary kings, and of the "survivals" of that practice in rituals of mock kingship like Carnival, with rituals and myths of Christianity—most notably the Eucharist (deity-eating) and the story of Christ's Passion.[137]

My conviction is that the affinities between the *Quixote* and *The Golden Bough* reflect the powerful structural and thematic sway exerted upon the authors of both texts by the Christ *mythos*, particularly as expressed through the Roman Catholic and carnival traditions.

Cervantes was probably neither the orthodox, reactionary spokesman for Tridentine didacticism as some have viewed him nor the iconoclastic freethinker as others have viewed him but rather a man of a "profoundly undoctrinaire" religious consciousness, "alive with a complex ferment of spiritual and secular tendencies."[138] It is thought plausible that he studied grammar with the Jesuits at Seville and attended lectures by Father Pedro Pablo de Acevedo in the Colegio de Santa Catelina; if he did so, he would have been sensitive to the tradition of thought and piety emanating from the legacy of the Jesuits' founder, Ignatius of Loyola, whose *Spiritual Exercises* (composed 1521–41) devotes the third of its four constitutive "weeks" to contemplation of the events of Christ's Passion. In the *Quixote*, the Passion *mythos* with its dominant image of the Man of Sorrows seems to emerge, displaced, in the portrayal of the Knight of the Sad Countenance as either an object of parody or a source of serious inspiration, depending on whether the reader laughs at or pities the hero in his misfortunes. Given that Sancho's illusory governorship is itself a parody of Don Quixote's illusory knighthood, it only follows that Sancho as governor should invoke Christ as his own model for governing, and that one of his later statements should seem to associate his own "foolishness" (tontería) with Paul's praise for the "foolishness of the Cross."[139]

In contrast to Cervantes, Frazer was an outspoken opponent of religion, particularly Christianity, and inhabited a non-Roman-Catholic country.[140] But these facts do not necessarily imply that in writing The Golden Bough he was in no way compelled by the mythos of Christ. As his texts and other evidence reveal, among his authorial motivations was an ever-intensifying aim to demonstrate the similarities of that mythos, and of various doctrines and rituals stemming from it (especially those of the Catholic tradition), to beliefs and practices from primitive societies, and thus to expose the "savage" heritage of that mythos and the presumed fallacies of privileging it over other analogous myths and of attributing a divine status to its hero.

This aim was cautiously concealed in the first edition, where Frazer left those similarities to speak for themselves, with no explicit reference to Christianity.[141] Of course his readers did notice and take an interest in those similarities. As his biographer points out, in the second edition, which introduces Frazer's theory of the progression of magic, religion, and science as a theoretical framework, Frazer "drops his caution and brings his rationalist and antireligious intentions into the open" through an elaborate conjectural analysis of three ancient pagan festivals: the Persian Sacaea, the Roman Saturnalia, the Babylonian Zakmuk.[142] Combining features from each to formulate the scenario of a priest-king who is bloodily sacrificed to ensure the fertility and health of his domain, Frazer links those festivals and that scenario to the Jewish celebration of Purim and reinterprets the Christian Passion narrative accordingly: as the main protagonist in a Purim-like Passover ritual, Christ "played" Haman, the mock-king who was killed, while Barabbas, as the true king Mordecai, was spared; hence Christ falls directly in line with such other dying and reviving gods as Adonis, Attis, and Osiris.[143] Although Frazer, in the first version of his study (1906) named after those three gods, retreats from the "aggressive irreligion" of the second edition of The Golden Bough, his relativization of the Christ mythos and of the mysteries and rituals that grew out of it persists in the third edition.[144] The image connecting St. Peter's Cathedral with Nemi's grove at the close of each of the three editions and the abridgment seems a final indication of Frazer's true intentions.

Our comparison of *The Golden Bough* and the *Quixote* has shown that the scholarly study of myth and ritual, and their incorporation and displacement in a literary text, can be compelled in remarkably similar directions and are therefore, as activities, not so unrelated as might be thought. The same tradition of carnivalesque myth and ritual that provided Cervantes with the structure and theme for the episode of Barataria furnished Frazer with data to support his own theories in comparative religion. And just as the carnival underpinnings of the Barataria episode, being themselves displacements of the Christ *mythos* and the pagan Saturnalia, foster the image of Sancho as a Saturnalian scapegoat and a distant, humorous displacement of the Christ-figure, so Frazer, as cited earlier, compares the "slain" carnival king to the "slain" Saturnalian king in order to link both figures to the slain Rex Nemorensis, whom we are to see as an analogue to Christ.[145]

This comparison implies that fruitful study of myth and literature must entail an awareness of the literary ramifications of theories of myth. Anyone inclined to dismiss this conclusion as an overgeneralization based on a single comparison should be reminded that examples of it abound among other classic theorists of myth from this century. Thus Freud, who connected myth with the same processes of the unconscious as dreaming and poetic creation, predicted in his preface to the third edition (1911) of *Die Traumdeutung* (1900, *The Interpretation of Dreams*) that future elaborations of his work would have to afford closer contact with imaginative writing and myths.[146] The theory Eliade shared with Frye of a continuity between myth and literature, and of the capacity of both to facilitate an escape from time, finds fulfillment in much of Eliade's own fiction.[147] Bonnefoy, drawing upon Eliade, deems it essential "that myth appear not only as an act of speech about the divine, but *as a text* in which the divine is infinitely embedded in signifiers."[148] And, in the Bororo myths in Lévi-Strauss's *Mythologiques* (1964–71), Vickery discerns "more than a touch of absurdist humor playing around the scenes and details, which is not to say that the Bororo do. . . . Our traditional modes of treatment . . . seem unable to capture the perceived and felt realities of [these] narratives, and by this failure they stand forth as almost parodies in themselves. Can it be—and there are already more than a few signs on the horizon—that criticism, like literature and myth, will increasingly become deliberately parodic as it endeavors to attest meaningfully to the age's dominant forms and perceptions of myth and literature?"[149]

This question was posed almost a decade and a half ago, and

the answer is still forthcoming. But two things have been evident from as far back as Plato. Few theorists are as self-aware as Socrates, who, when he slips from an appeal to theory to an incorporation of myth at the juncture of books 6 and 7 of *The Republic*, does so self-consciously. And while cities might always banish poets for conjuring myths, myths could never be banned from poems.

Notes

1. Lévi-Strauss, "The Structural Study of Myth," in Sebeok, ed., *Symposium*, 82.
2. Ibid., 81.
3. Thompson, "Myths and Folktales," ibid., 170.
4. Bidney, "Myth, Symbolism, and Truth," ibid., 23.
5. Frye, "The Road to Excess," in Slote, ed., *Myth and Symbol*, 3.
6. Herd, "Myth Criticism," 69.
7. Introduction to Vickery, ed., *Myth and Literature*, ix.
8. E.g., Ostendorf, *Der Mythos*; Righter, *Myth and Literature*. See Barricelli and Gibaldi, eds., *Interrelations*, whose thirteen essays by different scholars include Vickery's "Literature and Myth" (67–89). *Interrelations* reconsiders and adds to the list of "literature and" topics from an earlier volume, Thorpe, ed., *Relations*, whose seven essays include Northrop Frye's "Literature and Myth" (27–55).
9. Vickery, "Literary Criticism and Myth," in Strelka, ed., *Criticism and Myth*, 211.
10. Weissenberger, "Mythopoesis in German Literary Criticism," in Strelka, ed., *Criticism and Myth*, 270.
11. Doty, *Mythography*, 181.
12. Hawthorn, *Glossary*. Hawthorn's inclusion of entries on such younger theoretical movements as deconstruction, postmodernism, poststructuralism, and New Historicism makes the absence of an entry on myth criticism all the more noteworthy. Although he does include an entry on myth itself (158–60), that entry focuses on the general theories of Claude Lévi-Strauss, Roland Barthes, and Clemens Lugowski, while failing to mention Maud Bodkin, Northrop Frye, Philip Wheelright, Herbert Weisinger, or any of the other critics most often associated with myth criticism.
    Cf. Cuddon's *Dictionary*, 3d ed., which appeared a year before Hawthorn's *Glossary*, and which likewise contains an entry on myth (562–63) but lacks one on myth criticism. Harris, *Dictionary*, s.v. "Myth Criticism," 244–53: The original publication dates of the twenty studies cited from the last five decades in this entry give a telling quantitative account of the rise and decline of myth criticism over that period: two of these studies appeared in the 1930s; two in the 1940s; eleven—by far the highest number—in the 1950s; then, three in the 1960s; and two in the 1970s.
13. Charles Eric Reeves, "Myth Theory and Criticism," in the 1994 *Johns Hopkins Guide*, ed. Groden and Kreiswirth, 520–23, cites twenty-one sources whose original dates of publication range from 1913 to 1983. Makaryk, gen. ed. and comp., *Encyclopedia*, which appeared a year before the *Hopkins Guide*, lacks any entry on myth criticism but contains one on myth, by Alvin A. Lee (596–97). The latter cites five primary sources by Frye, Lévi-

Strauss, Barthes, Tzvetan Todorov, and William Ray, whose dates of publication range from 1957 to 1984.

14. Baldick, *Dictionary*, s.v. "Myth Criticism," 144.

15. See Vickery, who seeks to refute each of these charges ("Criticism and Myth," 225–35). Vickery provides references to critics who expressed each charge. See also Doty, *Mythography*, 175–76. A variation on the charge that the method neglects the uniqueness of specific texts is Kermode's remark: "It is a common enough complaint that the search in novels for mythical order reduces their existential complexity" (*Continuities*, 40). Cf. the specific criticisms of Frye in Kermode, *Continuities*, 119–20; and in his *Puzzles*, 64.

16. Reeves, "Myth Theory and Criticism," in *Johns Hopkins Guide*, 523.

17. See Culler, *Deconstruction*, 182.

18. Derrida, "White Mythology" ("La Mythologie blanche" [1971]), 213.

19. See, e.g., Müller's *Science of Language*, 1:21 (cf. 2:432); *Science of Religion*, 44; and *Contributions*, 1:68–70.

20. Strenski, *Four Theories*, 1. Cf. the poet Basil Bunting's assertion that haggling over the meaning of the term myth is futile, because it does not seem to have any specific meaning.

21. Harris, *Dictionary*, 245. Cf. Kermode, *Continuities*, 40; and Wellek and Warren, *Theory*, 190–91.

22. On the literary impact of the Freudian and Jungian theories and the distinctions between them, see Kermode, *Continuities*, 39; and Feder, *Ancient Myth*, 34–59.

23. See Doty, *Mythography*, 174–75.

24. Wellek and Warren, *Theory*, 190; "Mythische Erbschaft der Dichtung," in Broch, *Dichten*, 239.

25. My following survey of these six ways draws upon, synthesizes, and elaborates upon a number of similar discussions by other scholars: Peñuelas, who finds literature related to myth on several different *niveles* (*Mito*, 107–27); Herd, who outlines five "basic literary situations" in which myth criticism can be used to consider "the function of myth as part of the total structure of a given work" ("Myth Criticism," 70–73; quote on 70); Theodore Ziolkowski, who distinguishes three "senses" in which the term *myth* is commonly employed in modern criticism ("Hesse, Myth, and Reason," in Wetzels, ed., *Myth and Reason*, 131–34); Lilian Feder, who summarizes three "major ways" that myths are used in literature ("Myth, Poetry, and Critical Theory," in Strelka, ed., *Criticism and Myth*, 53); John J. White, who sums up three "distinct, yet complexly related senses" involved in most critical discussions of myth in fiction ("Mythological Fiction and the Reading Process," in Strelka, ed., *Criticism and Myth*, 72); Doty, who finds four "relationships" between myth and literature (*Mythography*, 181–82); and Harris, who summarizes six "meanings" associated with myth in current literary criticism (*Dictionary*, 244–53). Of the six ways in which myth and literature will be related in my discussion, *way 1* corresponds to Herd's first "situation," and Doty's fourth "relationship"; *way 2*, to Peñuelas's first and second "niveles," Herd's second "situation," Ziolkowski's first "sense," Feder's first and second "ways," White's second "sense," Doty's second "relationship," and Harris's fifth "meaning"; *way 3*, to Herd's third "situation," Feder's second "way," White's first "sense," and Doty's third "relationship"; *way 4*, to Peñuelas's third (and to some extent his fourth) "nivel," Herd's fourth "situation," Ziolkowski's second "sense," and Harris's fourth "meaning"; *way 5*, to Herd's fifth "situation," Ziolkowski's third "sense," Feder's third "way," White's third "sense," and Harris's third "meaning" (and, by extension, Harris's second "meaning"); *way 6*, to Peñuelas's fourth "nivel."

26. Examples that come immediately to mind are Thomas Mann's treatment of the Joseph stories; Mary Renault in her treatments of Theseus and Alexander; and Zora Neale Hurston and Anthony Burgess in their separate treatments of Moses.

27. Herd, "Myth Criticism," 70.

28. Doty, it should be noted, consigns to a separate category of "relationship" between myth and literature cases where there may appear, in literary works, particular characters who bear highly suggestive names of mythic characters (i.e., names "that trail long wakes of associations") but who are not further related to the prototypes whose names they carry, as in the case of John Barth's *Chimera* (*Mythography*, 181–82).

29. Harris, *Dictionary*, 247, 248. Gilbert Murray's lecture "Hamlet and Orestes" (1914), in his *Classical Tradition*, 205–40, is (as Harris notes) cited by Stanley E. Hyman, "The Ritual View of Myth and the Mythic," in Sebeok, ed., *Symposium*, 141, as the earliest application of the ritual view of myth "outside Greek studies."

30. This sort of analysis is typified by Diéz del Corral, *Función del mito*; Slochower, *Mythopoesis*; Frenzel, *Stoffe*; Stanford, *Ulysses Theme*. See also T. Ziolkowski, "A Practical Guide to Literary Thematics," in his *Varieties*, 201–27.

31. Frye, *Anatomy*, 137: "The central principle of displacement is that what can be metaphorically identified in a myth can only be linked in romance by some form of simile: analogy, significant association, incidental accompanying imagery, and the like." On the complementariness of this theory and Eliade's "morphology of the sacred," see my "Between Religion and Literature," 518–19.

32. Peñuelas, *Mito*, 107–8.

33. Vickery, *Myths and Texts*.

34. Herd, "Myth Criticism," 71. Of the plethora of twentieth-century Western novels exhibiting this usage of myth, the most obvious paradigm is Joyce's *Ulysses* (1922).

35. T. Ziolkowski, "Hesse, Myth, and Reason," 132.

36. See Campbell, *Hero*; and Frye, *Anatomy*, whose system is extended in his *Great Code* and *Words with Power*.

37. Herd, "Myth Criticism," 71.

38. A. L. Willson, in "Round-Table Discussion" transcribed in Wetzels, ed., *Myth and Reason*, 174.

39. E.g., Herd, "Myth Criticism," 72.

40. Frye, *Anatomy*, 112.

41. See Frye, *Spiritus Mundi*, 117, where he does acknowledge the resemblance of his own view of literature to Jung's mandala vision.

42. Kermode, "Frye Reconsidered" (1965), in *Continuities*, 120.

43. Not all religious rituals and myths whose work literature may now "do" are defunct. For example, does the fact that the Roman Catholic Eucharist, together with its attendant concept of transubstantiation, informs the climactic scene of Graham Greene's novel *Monsignor Quixote* (1982) mean that the ritual of Mass, and the myth of (the episode of the Last Supper in) Christ's life which it recalls, "can obviously no longer do" their work in the minds of Roman Catholic practitioners?

44. Kermode, "Frye Reconsidered," 121. Cf. Kermode's distinction between "fictions," which are assumed to be nonfactual even when they help us make sense of the world, and myths, which are fictions taken as fact (*Sense of an Ending*, 39).

45. See Block, "Myth of the Artist," in Strelka, ed., *Criticism and Myth*, 3–21, esp. 6–7. Cf. Harris, *Dictionary*, 246, 247.

46. T. Ziolkowski, "Hesse, Myth, and Reason," 133. For the comparison of Don

Quixote, Don Juan, and Faust as myths, see also, e.g., Sánchez-Castañer y Mena, *Penumbra;* Watt, *Rise of the Novel,* 85–86; Laffont-Bompiani, *Dictionnaire,* 2:211. See also the entry "Romantic Myths of the Rebel and the Victim" in Bonnefoy, *Mythologies,* 2:767–71, where the modern "literary" myths of Faust, Ahasuerus, and Don Juan are juxtaposed with the ancient myths of Satan, Prometheus, Cain, Job, and Empedocles.

47. Under the constant encouragement of Karol Kerényi, Mann consciously cultivated in his fiction what he called his "affinity for the mythical" ("Mythology and Humanism," 195). Cf. the other numerous allusions to myth intermittently throughout the Mann-Kerényi correspondence. Broch yearned for a literary genre that would express "der Mythos der neuen Kultur" ("Mythische Erbschaft," 248; cf. Herd, 73). Mircea Eliade envisioned a "new literature of the fantastic" that, in retrieving under "camouflage" the treasured mythic, symbolic, and ritual elements of the past, would constitute "a *new mythology*" (*Journal,* 279).

48. Wheelwright, "Myth," in Preminger, ed. *Princeton Encyclopedia,* 416.

49. See Guastalla, *Mythe et le livre;* Wellek and Warren, *Theory,* 192.

50. Kermode, *Puzzles,* 35. To exemplify the view Kermode opposed, White, "Mythological Fiction," also cites Barbara Hardy's claim that "all art worth discussing achieves myth" ("Golding's First Phase," 22).

51. Rahv, *Myth and the Powerhouse,* 9–10.

52. Herd, "Myth Criticism," 73.

53. Unamuno, *Our Lord,* 445–63; Jung, *Modern Man,* 197. Cf. Peñuelas, *Mito,* 119.

54. Peñuelas, *Mito,* 109.

55. The intentionalist concern, though denied by Herd in a passage quoted earlier in our discussion of the third way myth and literature have been considered related, is included as the sixth in Stanford's list of eight basic causes of variation in the successive portraits of any well-known mythical hero or theme: (1) the different ways by which the authors adapting the hero acquired their information about the tradition around him; (2) the amount of information to which those authors had access; (3) the language(s) in which they presented their portraits of the hero; (4) the authorial habit of assimilating old material to contemporary fashions and customs; (5) problems of morality, such as the question of how to treat the hero's traditional morals; (6) the authors' technical intentions (e.g., regarding whether to adapt the hero to a heroic, tragic, satiric, or other context); (7) the authors' personal reactions to the hero's traditional personality; and (8) above all, the presentation of the hero in his earliest definitive portrait (*Ulysses Theme,* 2–7). The affectivist concern is given precise formulation by White (who draws upon the reader-response theories of Stanley Fish and Robert Scholes) in his "Mythological Fiction," 74–75: "One basic and largely underestimated feature of [mythological fiction], whose plot is in some way anticipated by the myth(s) to which it alludes, is that we must read it in a different way from works for which no such classical analogy has been offered."

56. Strenski, *Four Theories,* 2.

57. Carlyle, *Sartor,* 194.

58. Abrams, *Natural Supernaturalism,* 68. The expression "Natural Supernaturalism"—borrowed by Abrams in his title, and paraphrased in the quote just given—is from Carlyle, who introduced it in a letter of 1830 to Goethe (quoted by C. F. Harrold, Introduction to Carlyle, *Sartor,* xxiv), and later repeated it through Teufelsdröckh (*Sartor,* 254).

59. Schlegel, *Gespräch über die Poesie* (1800), in *Kunstanschauung,* 185, as cited by Abrams, *Natural Supernaturalism,* 67.

60. ApRoberts, *Ancient Dialect,* 3.

61. Ibid., 2. Interestingly, apRoberts views Ladislaw as an embodiment of Car-

lyle, insofar as he "embodies the new German learning that Carlyle was to import and domesticate in England."

62. Lewis, *Perelandra*, 45, 47.
63. Ibid., 102, 144.
64. For Milton, as Scott Elledge points out, Christ's death represents a payment of "ransom" to liberate mankind "from the bondage of Satan, sin, and death into which Adam sold himself and all his progeny by his disobedience" ("Notes on Certain Important Concepts and Topics in *Paradise Lost*," in Milton, *Paradise Lost*, 399).
65. Lewis, *Perelandra*, 201.
66. Durkheim, *Elementary Forms*, 53–54.
67. Eliade, *Sacred*, 95: "The myth, then, is the history of what took place *in illo tempore*, the recital of what gods or the semidivine beings did ... *ab origine*. Once told, that is, revealed, the myth become apodictic truth; it establishes a truth that is absolute. ... It is for this reason that myth is bound up with ontology; it speaks only of *realities*, of what *really* happened, of what was fully manifested. Obviously these realities are sacred realities, for it is the *sacred* that is pre-eminently *real*" (italics in text; originally translated from the French and published in Germany by Rowohlt Taschenbuch as *Das Heilige und das Profane* [1957]).
68. E.g., the hero Stefan asks: "Do you really believe that only through death can we be freed from Time and History? Then human existence would have no meaning! Then our being here in life, in History, is a mistake!" (*Forbidden Forest*, 128).
69. Feder, *Ancient Myth*.
70. Ricoeur, *Symbolism of Evil*, 161, cf. 5.
71. My point here corresponds, I think, to the following remark by Vickery on the effect which consideration of "the problematic of point of view and self" in literary texts has on the critic: "Instead of the reader or critic taking myth to be the interpreter of literature—as is the case when the focus is upon the metonymic organization of a work's structure—he here finds literature itself to be a process of metaphoric substitution. It is this which reverses the relationship, *making literature the interpreter of myth insofar as it, explicitly or implicitly, establishes an attitude, a point of view toward specific myths*" (*Myths and Texts*, 186, emphasis mine).
72. Vickery, *Literary Impact*, 4.
73. In the early 1920s T. S. Eliot had predicted that Frazer and other anthropologists would "not fail to have a profound effect upon the literature of the future" ("Prediction," 29). Cf. Eliot, "Euripedes and Gilbert Murray," 38, cited by Haskell M. Block, "Cultural Anthropology and Contemporary Literary Criticism," in Strelka, ed., *Myth and Literature*, 131. Eliot's prediction was echoed by Trilling in 1965: "Perhaps no book has had so decisive an effect on modern literature" (*Teaching*, 14). Cf. Vickery, *Literary Impact*, 120. The most thorough studies of Frazer's literary legacy remain the latter book by Vickery, and Fraser, *Sir James Frazer*. See also Doty, *Mythography*, 169–71.

    The following abbreviations will be used to refer to the different editions of *The Golden Bough: GB* 1st ed. (1890); *GB* 2d ed. (1900); *GB* 3d ed. (1911–15); *GB* ab. (abridged edition, 1922). Wherever a specific quote from one edition of *GB* is repeated verbatim in later editions, references to later instances of the quote are given in parentheses following the reference to the earliest instance. All quotes in English from Cervantes, *Don Quixote* (cited hereafter as *DQ*) are from the Ormsby translation, ed. Jones and Douglas. All quotes in Spanish are from the Riquer edition.
74. Broch, "Mythische Erbschaft," 239. The quote is from "The Style of the Mythical Age," in Broch's *Dichtung*, 249, which reiterates (in Broch's English) many of the points made in "Mythische Erbschaft".

75. Tillich, *Dynamics of Faith*, 50.
76. Bonnefoy, *Mythologies*, s.v. "Modernity's Challenge to Myth, in the Poetry of Hölderlin, Heine, Baudelaire, Mallarmé, T. S. Eliot, and Rilke," by John E. Jackson, 2:778–81.
77. Consider Leach's well-known attack on Frazer's methodology, "Golden Bough . . . ?"; and the exposé of Frazer's substantive errors and inconsistencies in J. Z. Smith's "Bough Breaks," in *Map Is Not Territory*, which concludes: "Frazer becomes the more interesting and valuable precisely because he deliberately fails" (239). Cf. Fraser, *Making*, 210. According to Fraser, twentieth-century social anthropology has been dominated by Malinowski's recantation of Frazer ("The Face beneath the Text: Sir James Frazer in his Time," in Fraser, ed., *Sir James Frazer*, 4). Cf. Ackerman, *Frazer*, 1, 256. Frazer has had defenders from other disciplines. E.g., Eliade revered *GB* despite "all its shortcomings" as a seminal classic in religious studies (*Quest*, 14), and appreciated it as a "cultural fashion" in itself ("Cultural Fashions"). And Frye esteemed Frazer's masterpiece as a "grammar of the human imagination" (*On Culture*, 89), viewing it "primarily" as a study in literary criticism (*Fables*, 17). See also Frye, *Anatomy*, 109; and his "Literature and Myth," 30. But Eliade and Frye themselves were attacked for some of the same reasons as Frazer, most notably for their perceived tendency toward ahistoricism and generalization. With Ackerman's observation that "what has been rejected is [Frazer's] way of collating items culled from literally everywhere and every age to produce sweeping synthetic results" (*Frazer*, 105), cf. the criticisms of Eliade and Frye cited by E. Ziolkowski, "Between Religion and Literature," 503, including notes 23–27.
78. Menéndez y Pelayo described *DQ* as such during the tercentenary (1905) in his lecture "Cultura literaria de Miguel de Cervantes y elaboración del 'Quijote,'" in his *Estudios*, 135, and this view has been reiterated by innumerable critics and literary artists since then. See Levin, *Grounds*, 224–43.
79. For readings of *GB* as a literary text see Vickery, "The Golden Bough: Impact and Archetype," in Slote, ed., *Myth and Symbol*, 174–96; Hyman, *Tangled Bank*, 189–291; Smith, "Glory," 9. Smith himself compares *GB* to Laurence Sterne's *Tristram Shandy* (1759–67)("Glory," 13–15). Cf. Ackerman, *Frazer*, 103–5, 108, 248. The stylistic and thematic debts of Sterne's novel to the *Quixote* are well known; e.g., Welsh, *Reflections*, intermittently throughout. Those debts, together with the easy susceptibility of both *DQ* and *Tristram Shandy* to "deconstructive readings" (e.g. Flores, *Rhetoric*, 88–144), might seem to make seductive the idea of analyzing the two texts "intertextually." "A Study in Comparative Religion" is the subtitle of *GB* 1st ed. "A Study of Magic and Religion" is adopted as the subtitle of *GB* 2d ed., and retained for *GB* 3d ed. and *GB* ab.
80. See Ackerman, *Frazer*, 8, 9, 30–31. Frazer's "Diary" from the tour he took to Spain with his friend James Ward, dated March 13–April 8, 1883, contains only one reference to Cervantes's hero: "After leaving Alcazar we soon passed through the village (Argamasilla de Alba), of which Don Quixote is represented as having been a native" (19; entry of March 26). I am grateful to the Master and Fellows of Trinity College, Cambridge, whose library provided me with a photocopy of the complete diary.
81. We know this for sure of Frazer (from *GB* ab., v) and can be all but certain of it in Cervantes's case (see, e.g., Northrup, *Introduction*, 257).
82. In *DQ* pt. 2 the knight encounters characters who have read pt. 1 and recognize him, the "real" man, as the book's hero. The text, as a result, "turns back upon itself, thrusts itself back into its own density, and becomes the object of its own narrative. The first part of the hero's adventures plays in the second part the role originally assumed by the chivalric romances. Don Quixote must remain faithful to the book that he has now become in reality; he must protect it from errors, from counterfeits, from apocryphal se-

quels; he must fill in the details that have been left out; he must preserve its truth" (Foucault, *Order,* 48). In *GB* 2d ed., likewise, Frazer meant to preserve the "truth" of *GB* 1st ed., whose "scope and purpose . . . [had] been seriously misconceived by some courteous critics" (pref., *GB* 2d ed., 1:xvii, reprinted in *GB* 3d ed., 1:xxi). As an expanded investigation of the problem of the succession of the Arician priesthood, *GB* 2d ed. extends its own comparative scope centrifugally around that problem to encompass a wider mass of data and conjecture than *GB* 1st ed. had examined, including certain newly available materials on Aboriginal Australian cultures and religions. In contrast *DQ* pt. 2, as a sequel, presses its narrative linearly forward from the point where pt. 1 left off, but does so while repeatedly reflecting upon pt. 1.

83. It must be granted that irony is a notoriously slippery term and that Frazer's irony seems derived from a tradition different from Cervantes's. For Fraser, Frazer's "habit of irony based on a conviction of the profound folly of the generality of mankind" seems an inheritance from Hume (who was himself an admirer of *DQ*), and both Frazer and Hume share this quality with Edward Gibbon (*Making,* 21). Although the origins of what the German Romantics exalted as Cervantes's "Godlike irony" remain a mystery, it is tempting to accept it upon conjecture as a cultural holdover from his possibly converso descent; e.g., as suggested by Byron, *Cervantes,* 24–32. But both authors' irony allows them—as they address their audiences alike as "gentle reader" (*desocupado lector,* translated as "idle reader" in the Norton ed. of *DQ* 1:prol., 9) and "indulgent readers" (*GB* 3d ed., 10:v–vi)—to convey a similarly bemused, if at times sardonic in Frazer's case, detachment from their subjects. *DQ*'s narrator satirizes books of chivalry by portraying a madman who retains belief in their veracity in an age when the medieval worldview that spawned them is defunct. Frazer, in analyzing "magical" and "religious" worldviews that (as he contends, beginning in *GB* 2d ed.) evolved successively and in opposition to each other during prehistorical and later times, treats those worldviews from the modern "scientific" perspective that exposes the "erroneous" logic underlying them and, to his satisfaction, renders them obsolete.

84. *GB* 3d ed., 1:53 (ab., 13). Cf. 2d ed., 1:62. (The second misapplication is "by contiguity.") Indeed, for Foucault, who makes no appeal to Frazer, Don Quixote is "the hero of the Same," whose "whole journey is a quest for similitudes" (*Order,* 46, 47). Just as homeopathic or imitative magic, founded on the law of similarity, "commits the mistake of assuming that things which resemble each other are the same" (*GB* 3d ed., 1:53 [ab., 13]), so Don Quixote's madness, revolving around the law of analogy or similitude, leads to his "attempt to transform reality into a sign" (Foucault, *Order,* 47). It follows that *DQ* and *GB* share the theme of sorcery and enchantment. The crucial difference is that, while any two similar "things" that might be mistakenly identified with each other by Frazer's preliterate "savages" must exist in the objective world (a man, say, and an image of him that might be destroyed with the intent of causing him to perish), the "signs" into which Cervantes's overly literate madman transforms objects from "reality" are drawn not from reality, but from his obsessive reading of chivalry books. In contrast to the magicians whom Frazer portrays as virtuosi upholders of the law of similarity, the cruel *encantadores* by whom Don Quixote imagines himself to be constantly persecuted and who ironically are themselves imaginary figments derived from his reading serve not as sustainers, but as would-be destroyers of the similitudes conjured by his imagination. Thus the (imagined) transformations wrought by these (imagined) enchanters furnish the "model" for "nonsimilitude"—a model, say, for the reality that the windmills are *not* giants, a reality that Don Quixote,

upon confronting it after being knocked from his horse by the one he attacked, in turn takes to be an illusion conjured by the enchanters (see Foucault, *Order,* 47).

85. *GB* 3d ed., 4:197–98 (ab., 342).

86. Foucault, *Order,* 49, emphasis mine. For Foucault's interpretation of the history behind this transformation, see his *Madness.*

87. Foucault, *Order,* 49, emphasis in the text; long before Foucault and countless other theorists from our own time would create a vogue for categories of "otherness" and "difference," Frazer's "civilized" Victorian readers sought the thrills of exotica in *GB*—a fact that helps explain the book's extraordinary success. In doing so, those "educated Englishmen" proved themselves real-life, armchair counterparts of Sansón Carrasco, that character in *DQ* who, above all others, emerges as both the most highly educated and the one most intensely preoccupied with that quality of Don Quixote that makes him *different:* his madness. A young bachelor of theology from Salamanca University, Carrasco can only purge himself of his obsession with the madman by actively pursuing him on his journey from La Mancha to Barcelona, and by tracking him down there, bringing him to his senses by defeating him in battle and requiring him to return home. Likewise, Frazer's readers, to satisfy their obsessive curiosity about racial and cultural "otherness," must follow Frazer as a knight in quest of the Grail on his "voyage of discovery . . . [through] many strange foreign lands, with strange foreign peoples, and still stranger customs" (*GB* 3d ed., 1:43 [ab., 10]), a "voyage" which ends only in the final paragraph of *GB* ab. with the return of the narrative to its initial scene, the woodland lake of Nemi. Thus for David Richards, "*The Golden Bough* is that 'Other' of the Victorian imagination as it struggles to free itself from too much history by reconstructing its remote past in speculative reformulations of human evolution" ("A Tower of Babel: Frazer and Theories of Language," in Fraser, ed., *Sir James Frazer,* 81). And for Vickery, Frazer's work is a "gigantic quest romance couched in the form of objective research" ("*The Golden Bough:* Impact and Archetype," in Slote, ed., *Myth and Symbol,* 184). Cf. Ackerman, *Frazer,* 174, 178. The "voyage" motif recurs in *GB* 3d ed., 11:308 (ab. 827): "Our long voyage of discovery is over and our bark has drooped her weary sails in port at last." Cf. Frazer, *Aftermath,* vi; and *GB* 2d ed., 3:462, where we are invited to "revisit once more in imagination the scene from which we set out on our long pilgrimage."

88. While Cervantes's contemporaries read his novel exclusively as a funny burlesque about a mad buffoon, by the mid-eighteenth century in England a reader like Fielding could view Don Quixote sympathetically as a symbol for the "madness" of all the world, particularly the English. See E. Ziolkowski, *Sanctification,* esp. 47–50. Consistent with suggestions in *DQ* pt. 2 that those who play jokes on the knight must be as crazy as he, if not more so, it has long been observed that he has a tendency to "quixotize" those whom he encounters, by which is meant either that he incites them to accept illusions of their own or causes them to behave as foolishly as he himself. The ultimate effect of such *quijotización* is to blur the distinction between madness and sanity beyond practical meaningfulness. In *DQ* see, e.g., the conversation between Sansón and Tomé Cecial (2:15, 502–3) and the narrator's comments on the duke and duchess (2:70, 810). For seminal discussions of "quixotization" in *DQ* see Unamuno, *Our Lord,* intermittently throughout; Madariaga, *Introductory Essay,* esp. 137–45; and Romero Flores, *Biografía,* 135–52. (This process of *quijotización* is found to be accompanied by a reciprocal process of *sanchificación* ["sanchification"] or disillusioning of the knight by his squire. See Madariaga, *Introductory Essay,* 146–56; Romero Flores, *Biografía,* 153–66.) Frazer achieves a similar

effect by subverting his and his readers' own evolutionary distinction between "savage" and "civilized" societies. Sensing, as Freud will do also, "the permanent existence of such a solid layer of savagery beneath the surface of society" (GB 2d ed., 1:74 [3d ed., 1:236; ab., 64]), Frazer acknowledges "our debt to the savage": "For when all is said and done our resemblances to the savage are still far more numerous than our differences from him" (GB 1st ed., 1:211 [2d ed., 1:449; 3d ed., 3:422; ab., 307]).

89. GB 3d ed., 10:vi.
90. J. Z. Smith, "Glory," 109. Cf. the Afterword to his "Bough Breaks," 239.
91. GB 3d ed., 4:269 (ab., 375). The use of the terms *degeneration* and *decay* here prefigures their use by Eliade to describe the fate of primordial myths in modern literature.
92. Ortega y Gasset, *Meditations*, 138.
93. See Williamson, *Half-way House.*
94. Consider the following four examples: (1) *DQ*'s narrative revolves around the theme of the hero's quest, whose connection to the "monomyth" outlined in Campbell's *Hero* speaks for itself. (2) The knight's twin adventures in the cave of Montesinos (2:22–23) and on the "flying" horse Clavileño (2:41), adventures that are explicitly linked with each other in one of the knight's statements (see 2:41, 653), appeal to the pervasive theme of the otherworldly journey in medieval romance (see, e.g., Patch, *Other World,* esp. 230–319), and beg humorously to be associated with the myths, symbols, and rituals of ascension and descent pervading the religions of the world as surveyed by Eliade, and the whole of Western literature as surveyed by Frye. For references to Eliade's discussions of ascent symbolism, mystical flight, levitation, and their opposite, *descensus ad inferos,* see E. Ziolkowski, "Between Religion and Literature," 519 n. 126. See also Frye's discussion of the "four primary narrative movements" of which he finds all stories in literature to be "complications" or "metaphorical derivations": descent from a higher world; descent to a lower world; ascent from a lower world; ascent to a higher world (*Secular Scripture,* 97). (3) Don Quixote's ongoing desire to restore the Age of Gold appeals directly to a widespread myth of ancient origins; see Levin, *Myth of the Golden Age,* esp. 162–63. (4) The concepts of Fortune, Fortune's wheel, and the winds of Fortune which are alluded to recurrently throughout *DQ* and, as I have argued elsewhere, crystallize metaphorically in the windmill the mad knight tilts against, are traceable back through Renaissance, medieval, and classical literature to myths expressing Greco-Roman cosmology. See E. Ziolkowski, "Don Quijote's Windmill." To acknowledge these four and any number of other mythic resonances in *DQ* does not require a Jungian reading of the sort promoted by Bleznick, "Archetypal Approach."
95. See E. Ziolkowski, *Sanctification,* 7, 16–17, 129, 131, 200–201, 210–12, 240, 241. See also appendix 11, "Don Quixote and Sancho as Opposites," in Flores, *Sancho,* 189–90.
96. For these four views see, respectively, Sánchez y Escribano, "Sancho Panza"; Romero Flores, *Biografía;* Pabón Núñez, "Exaltación"; Willis, "Prototype."
97. For these five views see, respectively, Hendrix, *Comic Types;* Márquez Villanueva, "La génesis literaria de Sancho Panza," part 1 of his *Fuentes,* 20–94; Chevalier, "Literatura oral"; Molho, "Raíz folklórica de Sancho Panza," part 3 of his *Raíces folklóricas,* 217–336; and Redondo, "Tradición carnavalesca" (who cites the other four articles in this note).
98. Bakhtin, *Rabelais,* 54. I am unaware of any other mentioning of Frazer in Bakhtin's writings.
99. Bakhtin, *Problems,* 128. Cf. Bakhtin's intermittent references to Cervantes in *Rabelais.*

100. Thus Sancho tells Don Quixote in their first conversation: "If I should become a king by one of those miracles your worship speaks of, even Juana Gutiérrez, my old lady would come to be queen and my children princes" (*DQ*, 1:7, 58; cf. 1:50, 389).

101. *GB* 3d ed., 4:213 (ab., 350). See also 1st ed., 1:3; 2d ed., 1:4; 3d ed., 1:10–11; ab., 3.

102. Noted by the editors in *DQ*, 592 n. 1.

103. See Collingwood, *Principles*, 87; and Nabokov, *Lectures*, 52. Cf. the remarks of Sansón Carrasco in *DQ*, 2:3, 439.

104. Huizinga, *Homo Ludens*, 15, drawing upon Frobensius, *Kulturgeschichte Afrikas*.

105. *GB* 1st ed., 1:228 (2d ed., 2:26; 3d ed., 4:148; ab., 330). See also Frazer, "Killing."

106. E.g., *GB* 1st ed., 1:232–33 (2d ed., 2:31; 3d ed., 4:154–55; ab., 334–35).

107. E.g., *GB* 3d ed., 4:v, 9, 14–46; ab., 309–18.

108. Compare the following two passages:

> On a favourable day fixed by the astrologers the temporary king was conducted by the mandarins in triumphal procession. He rode one of the royal elephants, seated in the royal palanquin, and escorted by soldiers who, dressed in appropriate costumes, represented the neighbouring peoples of Siam, Annam, Laos, and so on. In place of the golden crown he wore a peaked white cap, and his regalia . . . were of rough wood. After paying homage to the real king, . . . together with all the revenues accruing during that time . . . , he moved in procession round the palace and through the streets of the capital. (*GB* 1st ed., 1:228–29 [2d ed., 2:27; 3d ed., 4:148–49; ab., 330])

> Sancho at last set out attended by a great number of people. He was dressed like a lawyer, with a very full, brown plush camel's hair overcoat and a cap of the same material, and mounted Moorish-style on a mule. Behind him, in accordance with the duke's orders, followed Dapple with brand new ass-trappings and ornaments of silk, and from time to time Sancho turned round to look at his donkey, so well pleased to have him with him that he would not have changed places with the emperor of Germany. On taking leave, he kissed the hands of the duke and duchess and got his master's blessing. (*DQ*, 2:44, 663)

109. See esp. *GB* 1st ed., 1:116–18; 2d ed., 1:309–13; 3d ed., 3:8–11, 116–19, 291–93; ab., 199–200, 230–31, 277.

110. Freud, *Totem*, 51.

111. *GB* 1st ed., 1:230 (2d ed., 2:28; 3d ed., 4:150; ab., 331).

112. Cf. *DQ*, 2:51, 706.

113. *GB* 3d ed., 1:8–9, emphasis mine. The same passage occurs with slight variations in punctuation and wording in 1st ed., 1:2; 2d ed., 1:2; ab., 1. I have followed J. Z. Smith in italicizing that portion of the passage Frazer based on the following account of Nemi's priest given in Strabo's *Geographica* 5.3.12: "He is appointed priest who, being a runaway slave, has managed to murder the man who was priest before him; he is always armed with a sword, keeping watch against attacks and ready to ward them off" (as cited by Smith, "Bough Breaks," 214).

114. J. Z. Smith, "Bough Breaks," 214. Smith's complete analysis of that portrait encompasses 212–26.

115. See Forcione, *Cervantes, Aristotle*, 56, 57, 58, 60, 63, 78, 80, 153, 269. From Forcione's discussion it would seem almost impossible for Cervantes not to have known Strabo's work at least secondhand. Whether he read

him directly and knew the passage on Nemi's priest must, as far as I know, be left to speculation.

116. *GB* 1st ed., 1:2 (2d ed., 1:2; 3d ed., 1:9; ab., 1), emphasis mine.
117. *GB* 3d ed., 4:196 (ab. 341). Cf. for example 3d ed., 4:51 (ab. 323).
118. *GB* 3d ed., 4:49–51 (ab., 321–23).
119. *GB* 1st ed., 1:367 (2d ed., 2:225–26; 3d ed., 7:218; ab., 494).
120. Another instance in which a joke played on Don Quixote's squire seems to be based upon an actual peasant practice is the "blanketing" of Sancho (1:17), which finds a striking, albeit more serious analogy in Frazer's account of how Naya, the uncle of Kublai Khan, was put to death by his nephew "by being wrapt in a carpet and tossed to and fro till he died" (*GB* 3d ed., 3:242 [ab., 266]).
121. *GB* 1st ed., 1:226 (2d ed., 2:24–25; 3d ed., 4:114; ab., 328), emphasis mine. Frazer proceeds in each succeeding edition to reject this explanation.
122. *GB* 3d ed., 4:vi. Cf. v, 9–10. Not long after Sancho assumes office, even the majordomo must acknowledge—as he says to Sancho—"that I am filled with wonder when I see a man like your worship, entirely without learning (for I believe you have none) say such things, and so full of maxims and sage remarks, very different from what was expected of your worship's intelligence by those who sent us or by us who came here. Every day we see something new in this world; jokes become realities, and the jokers find the tables turned on them" (*DQ*, 2:49, 692). It is no mere coincidence that soon afterwards, the jokers begin plotting how to bring the joke of Sancho's government to an end (see 2:50, 708; 2:51, 712).
123. See *GB* 2d ed., 2:67; 3d ed., 2:308–10; 4:213; ab., 182, 350.
124. *GB* 2d ed., 2:67 (3d ed., 4:213–14; ab., 350).
125. See *GB* 1st ed., 2:342–58; 2d ed., 3:422–46; 3d ed., 11:225–78; ab., 802–12.
126. See Puigblanch, *Inquisition,* 1:339–350n, whose interpretation is rejected by Castro, *Pensamiento,* 291, 325 n.171.
127. E.g., *DQ,* 1:21, 150; 1:47, 372; 2:3, 441.
128. *GB* 2d ed., 3:116 (3d ed., 9:221; ab., 664).
129. *GB* 2d ed., 3:116, 117 (3d ed., 9:221, 222; ab., 664, 665).
130. *GB* 2d ed., 3:117 (3d ed., 9:222–23; ab., 665).
131. Consider, e.g., the Slavonic legend of Piast, the peasant boy who became the first Polish king, or the story, "The Clever Man and the Simple Man," told by Rabbi Nachman of Bratzlav, about a simple cobbler who becomes a successful prime minister (Buber, *Tales,* 71–94, esp. 86–94). The dream of the unlanded peasant to possess and to govern land as king has recurrently found expression in Western literature and thought—from Jesus' claim that the meek shall inherit the earth; through the desire of Shakespeare's drunken butler, Stephano, to "inherit" Prospero's island (*Tempest* 2, 2, 171.); to the wish of the Cowardly Lion to become "King of the Forest" (in the film version of *The Wizard of Oz*).
132. See Auerbach, *Mimesis,* intermittently throughout. Cf. Watt, *Rise of the Novel,* 79. Auerbach examines *DQ* in his chapter "The Enchanted Dulcinea" (*Mimesis,* 334–58).
133. *GB* 2d ed., 3:143 (3d ed., 9:312; ab., 679).
134. See Redondo, "Tradición carnavalesca," esp. 41, 50–70, which links the Barataria episode with carnival while making no mention of Frazer.
135. Frye, *On Culture,* 89.
136. See E. Ziolkowski, *Sanctification,* esp. 37–61, 91–262.
137. E.g., Freud, *Totem,* 51, 154; Frye, *On Culture,* 87, 90.
138. Forcione, *Cervantes,* 354. On Cervantes's apparent views on religion, particularly Ignatian piety, and the clergy, see E. Ziolkowski, *Sanctification,* 24–30.
139. Cf. E. Ziolkowski, "Don Quijote's Windmill," 896–97, where Don Qui-

xote's career as a knight and Sancho's career as a governor are both shown to follow the same circular pattern of the *regno-regnavi* theme derived from the medieval and Renaissance concept of *fortuna*. Thus Sancho observes to the duke: "I don't know much about letters, for I don't even know the A B C; but it's enough for me to have the Christus in my memory [*bástame tener el* Christus *en la memoria*] to be a good governor" (*DQ*, 2:42, 654]. And as noted earlier Sancho affirms that "it might be seen that God sometimes guides those who govern in their judgments, even though they may be fools [*tontos*]" (2:45, 673). Redondo, who cites both these statements, observes of the first: "Claro está que Sancho utiliza *Christus* en el doble sentido de la palabra: el de la cruz que precede al abecedario en la cartilla de los niños y el de Jesús, refiriéndose de tal modo a la doctrina evangélica" ("Tradición canavalesca," 57 n.81). On the association of Sancho's observation with the Pauline notion of "foolishness," see ibid., 47–49.

140. As Frazer wrote in a letter of September 22, 1900, to his friend Solomon Schechter, with regard to *GB* 2d ed.: "There are things in it which are likely to give offence both to Jews and Christians, but especially, I think, to Christians. You see I am neither the one nor the other, and don't mind knocking them impartially" (quoted by Ackerman, *Frazer*, 169–70).

141. See Frazer's first letter concerning *GB* to his publisher George Macmillan (November 8, 1889), quoted by Ackerman, *Frazer*, 95; and the comments of Macmillan's literary advisor, John Morley, soon thereafter in his assessment of the manuscript, as quoted by Ackerman, 96. Cf. Fraser, *Making*, 112–13.

142. Ackerman, *Frazer*, 167.

143. See *GB* 2d ed., 3:186–98; and Ackerman, *Frazer*, 167–69.

144. Ackerman, *Frazer*, 239. See *GB* 3d ed., 5:253–57, 304–10; 6:119; 9:222–23; 10:140–46, which correspond to ab. 400–402, 416–19, 445, 665, 712–15. (A revision of Frazer's *Adonis, Attis, Osiris* [1906] is incorporated as vol. 6 of *GB* 3d ed.) No attempt is made in *GB* ab. to incorporate the seemingly far-fetched hypothesis posited in the extended note in 3d ed., 412–23 (drawn from the text of 2d ed., 3:186–98), by which Frazer tried to link Christ's Passion and Crucifixion with certain aspects of the Sacaean, Saturnalian, and Purim traditions.

145. Cf. Redondo, "Tradición carnavalesca," 57, who also associates Sancho as governor with the Saturnalian tradition.

146. Freud, *Interpretation*, xxviii.

147. See E. Ziolkowski, "Between Religion and Literature," 516–19.

148. Bonnefoy, Preface to *Mythologies*, 1:xxvi, emphasis mine. See also Eliade, "Toward a Definition of Myth," ibid., 3–5.

149. Vickery, "Literature and Myth" in Barricélli and Gibaldi, eds., *Interrelations*, 86–87.

Works Cited

Abrams, M. H. *Natural Supernaturalism: Tradition and Revolution in Romantic Literature*. New York: Norton, 1973.

Ackerman, Robert. *J. G. Frazer: His Life and Work*. Cambridge: Cambridge University Press, 1987.

apRoberts, Ruth. *The Ancient Dialect: Thomas Carlyle and Comparative Religion*. Berkeley: University of California Press, 1988.

Auerbach, Erich. *Mimesis: The Representation of Reality in Western Literature.* Translated by Willard R. Trask. Princeton: Princeton University Press, 1953.

Bakhtin, Mikhail. *Problems of Dostoevsky's Poetics.* Translated by Caryl Emerson. Minneapolis: University of Minnesota Press, 1984.

———. *Rabelais and His World.* Translated by Hélène Iswolsky. Bloomington: Indiana University Press, 1984.

Baldick, Chris. *The Concise Dictionary of Concepts in Literary Terms.* Oxford: Oxford University Press, 1990.

Barricelli, Jean-Pierre, and Joseph Gibaldi, eds. *Interrelations of Literature.* New York: Modern Language Association of America, 1982.

Benardete, M. J., and Angel Flores, eds. *The Anatomy of Don Quixote: A Symposium.* Ithaca, N. Y.: Dragon Press, 1932.

Bleznick, Donald W. "An Archetypal Approach to *Don Quixote.*" In *Approaches to Teaching Cervantes' "Don Quixote,"* edited by Richard Bjornson. New York: Modern Language Association, 1984, 96–103.

Bodkin, Maud. *Archetypal Patterns in Poetry: Psychological Studies of Imagination.* London: Oxford University Press, 1934.

Bonnefoy, Yves. *Mythologies, compiled by Yves Bonnefoy: A Restructured Translation of "Dictionnaire des mythologies et des religions des sociétés traditionnelles et du monde antique."* Prepared under the direction of Wendy Doniger. 2 vols. Chicago: University of Chicago Press, 1991.

Broch, Hermann. *Dichten und Erkennen.* Vol. 6 of *Gesammelte Werke.* 10 vols. Edited by Erich Kahler et. al. Zurich: Rhein, 1953–61.

Buber, Martin. *The Tales of Rabbi Nachman.* Translated by Maurice Friedman. 1956. New edition, with Introduction by Paul Mendes-Flohr and Ze'ev Gries. Atlantic Highlands: Humanities Press International, 1988.

Byron, William. *Cervantes: A Biography.* Garden City, N.Y.: Doubleday, 1978.

Campbell, Joseph. *The Hero with a Thousand Faces.* New York: Bollingen, 1949.

Carlyle, Thomas. *Sartor Resartus: The Life and Opinions of Herr Teufelsdröckh.* Edited by Charles Frederick Harrold. Indianapolis: Odyssey, 1937.

Castro, Américo. *El pensamiento de Cervantes.* New ed. Barcelona: Noguer, 1972.

Cervantes, Miguel de. *Don Quixote de la Mancha.* 2 vols. Edition and notes by Martín de Riquer. Barcelona: Juventud, 1955. New edition, 1979.

———. *Don Quixote.* Translated by John Ormsby. Revised and edited by Joseph R. Jones and Kenneth Douglas. New York: Norton, 1981.

Chevalier, Maxime. "Literatura oral y ficción cervantina." *Prohemio* 5, nos. 2–3 (September-December 1974): 193–95.

Collingwood, R. G. *The Principles of Art.* Oxford: Clarendon, 1938.

Cuddon, J. A. *A Dictionary of Literary Terms and Literary Theory.* 3d ed. Oxford: Blackwell, 1991.

Culler, Jonathan. *On Deconstruction: Theory and Criticism after Structuralism.* Ithaca, N.Y.: Cornell University Press, 1982.

Derrida, Jacques. "White Mythology: Metaphor in the Text of Philosophy." In *Margins of Philosophy.* Translated by Alan Bass. Chicago: University of Chicago Press, 1982.

Diéz del Corral, Luis. *La función del mito clásico en la literatura contemporánea.* Madrid: Gredos, 1957.

Doty, William G. *Mythography: The Study of Myths and Rituals.* Tuscaloosa: University of Alabama Press, 1986.

Drake, Dana B. *"Don Quijote" (1894–1970): A Selective Annotated Bibliography,* vol. 1. Chapel Hill: University of North Carolina Department of Romance Languages, 1974.

———. *"Don Quijote" (1894–1970): A Selective and Annotated Bibliography,* vol. 2. Miami: Ediciones Universal, 1978.

Durkheim, Emile. *The Elementary Forms of the Religious Life.* Translated by Joseph Ward Swain. New York: Macmillan, 1915.

Eliade, Mircea. *The Sacred and the Profane: The Nature of Religion.* Translated by Willard R. Trask. New York: Harcourt Brace Jovanovich, 1959.

———. "Cultural Fashions and the History of Religions." In *The History of Religions: Essays on the Problem of Understanding,* edited by Joseph M. Kitagawa. Chicago: University of Chicago Press, 1967.

———. *The Quest: History and Meaning in Religion.* Chicago: University of Chicago Press, 1969.

———. *Journal II: 1957–1969.* Translated by Fred H. Johnson, Jr. New York: Harper and Row, 1977; reprint, Chicago: University of Chicago Press, 1989.

———. *The Forbidden Forest.* Translated by Mac Linscott Ricketts and Mary Park Stevenson. Notre Dame: University of Notre Dame Press, 1978.

Eliot, T. S. "Euripedes and Gilbert Murray." *Arts and Letters* 3 (1920).

———. "A Prediction in Regard to Three English Authors: Writers Who, though Masters of Thought, are Likewise Masters of Art." *Vanity Fair,* February 1924, 29, 98.

Feder, Lillian. *Ancient Myth in Modern Poetry.* Princeton: Princeton University Press, 1971.

Flores, Ralph. *The Rhetoric of Doubtful Authority: Deconstructive*

Readings of Self-Questioning Narratives, St. Augustine to Faulkner. Ithaca, N.Y.: Cornell University Press, 1984.

Flores, R. M. *Sancho Panza through Three Hundred Seventy-Five Years of Continuations, Imitations, and Criticism 1606–1980.* Newark, Del.: Juan de la Cuesta, 1982.

Forcione, Alban K. *Cervantes, Aristotle, and the "Persiles."* Princeton: Princeton University Press, 1970.

———. *Cervantes and the Humanist Vision: A Study of Four "Exemplary Novels."* Princeton: Princeton University Press, 1982.

Foucault, Michel. *Madness and Civilization: A History of Madness in the Age of Reason.* Translated by Richard Howard. New York: Pantheon, 1965.

———. *The Order of Things: An Archaeology of the Human Sciences.* New York: Random House, Vintage, 1973.

Fraser, Robert. *The Making of "The Golden Bough": The Origins and Growth of an Argument.* New York: St. Martin's, 1990.

Fraser, Robert, ed. *Sir James Frazer and the Literary Imagination: Essays in Affinity and Influence.* Houndmills, Basingstoke, Hampshire: Macmillan, 1990.

Frazer, James G. Diary of tour in Spain, 1883 (March 13–April 8). Unpublished handwritten diary kept at Trinity College, Cambridge.

———. *The Golden Bough: A Study in Comparative Religion.* 2 vols. London: Macmillan, 1890. 2d ed., rev. and enl., retitled *The Golden Bough: A Study in Magic and Religion.* 3 vols. London: Macmillan, 1900. 3d ed., rev. and enl., London: Macmillan, 1911–15. 1-vol. abr. ed., London: Macmillan, 1922.

———. *Adonis, Attis, Osiris: Studies in the History of Oriental Religion.* London: Macmillan, 1906; 2d ed., rev. and enl., 1907.

———. "The Killing of the Khazar Kings." *Folklore* 28 (1917): 382–407.

———. *Aftermath: A Supplement to the Golden Bough.* London: Macmillan, 1937.

Frenzel, Elisabeth. *Stoffe der Weltliteratur: Ein Lexikon dichtungsgeschichtlicher Längsschnitte.* 1962. 4th ed. Stuttgart: Kröner, 1976.

Freud, Sigmund. *Totem and Taboo: Some Points of Agreement between the Mental Lives of Savages and Neurotics.* Translated by James Strachey. New York: Norton, 1950.

———. *The Interpretation of Dreams.* Translated by James Strachey. New York: Avon, 1965.

Frobenius, Leo. *Kulturgeschichte Afrikas, Prolegomena zu einer historische Gestaltehre; Schicksalskunde im Sinne des Kulturswerdens.* Zurich: Phaidon, 1933.

Frye, Northrop. *Fearful Symmetry: A Study of William Blake.* Princeton: Princeton University Press. 1947. 1st pap. ed., 1969.

———. *Anatomy of Criticism: Four Essays.* Princeton: Princeton University Press, 1957.

———. *Fables of Identity: Studies in Poetic Mythology.* San Diego: Harcourt Brace Jovanovich, 1963.

———. *Myth and Symbol: Critical Approaches and Applications.* Edited by Bernice Slote. Lincoln: University of Nebraska Press, 1963.

———. "Literature and Myth." In *Relations of Literary Study: Essays on Interdisciplinary Contributions,* edited by James Thorpe. New York: Modern Language Association, 1967.

———. *The Secular Scripture: A Study of the Structure of Romance.* Cambridge: Harvard University Press, 1976.

———. *Spiritus Mundi: Essays on Literature, Myth, and Society.* Bloomington: Indiana University Press, 1976.

———. *On Culture and Literature: A Collection of Review Essays.* Edited by Robert D. Denham. Chicago: University of Chicago Press, 1978.

———. *The Great Code: The Bible and Literature.* New York: Harcourt Brace Jovanovich, 1983.

———. *Words with Power: Being a Second Study of "The Bible and Literature."* Harcourt Brace Jovanovich, 1990.

Groden, Michael, and Martin Kreiswirth, eds. *The Johns Hopkins Guide to Literary Theory and Criticism.* Baltimore: Johns Hopkins University Press. 1994.

Guastella, R. M. *Le Mythe et le livre: Essai sur l'origine de la littérature.* Paris: Gallimard, 1940.

Hardy, Barbara. "Golding's First Phase." In *Daily Telegraph.* April 20, 1967.

Harris, Wendell V. *Dictionary of Concepts in Literary Criticism and Theory.* New York: Greenwood Press, 1992.

Hawthorn, Jeremy. *A Glossary of Contemporary Literary Theory.* London: Edward Arnold, 1992.

Hendrix, W. S. "Sancho Panza and the Comic Types of the Sixteenth Century." In *Homenaje ofrecido a Menéndez Pidal.* Madrid: Librería y Casa Editorial Hernando, 1925, 485–94.

Herd, E. W. "Myth Criticism: Limitations and Possibilities." *Mosaic* 2, no. 3 (1969): 69–77.

Huizinga, Johan. *Homo Ludens: A Study of the Play-Element in Culture.* Boston: Beacon, 1966.

Hyman, S. E. *The Tangled Bank: Darwin, Marx, Frazer and Freud as Imaginative Writers.* New York: Atheneum, 1962.

Jung, C. G. *Modern Man in Search of a Soul.* Trans. W. S. Dell and Cary F. Baynes. New York: Harcourt, Brace, and World, 1934.

Kermode, Frank. *Puzzles and Epiphanies: Essays and Reviews 1958–1961.* New York: Chilmark, 1962.

———. *The Sense of an Ending.* Oxford: Oxford University Press, 1967.

———. *Continuities.* New York: Random House, 1968.

Kitagawa, Joseph M., ed. *The History of Religions: Essays on the Problem of Understanding.* Chicago: University of Chicago Press, 1967.

Laffont-Bompiani. *Dictionnaire des personnages littéraires et dramatiques de tous les temps et de tous les pays.* Edited by Jacques Brosse. 2 vols. Paris: Société d'Edition de dictionnaires et encyclopédies, 1960.

Leach, Edmund. "Golden Bough or Gilded Twig?" *Daedalus* 90 (1961): 371–99.

Levin, Harry. *Myth of the Golden Age in the Renaissance.* Bloomington: Indiana University Press, 1969.

———. *Grounds for Comparison.* Cambridge: Harvard University Press, 1972.

Lewis, C. S. *Perelandra: A Novel.* 1944. New York: Macmillan, 1965.

Madariaga, Salvador de. *Don Quixote: An Introductory Essay in Psychology.* London: Oxford University Press, 1935. Rev. 1961.

Makaryk, Irena R., gen. ed. and compiler. *Encyclopedia of Contemporary Literary Theory: Approaches, Scholars, Terms.* Toronto: University of Toronto Press, 1993.

Mann, Thomas, and Karol Kerényi. *Mythology and Humanism: The Correspondence of Thomas Mann and Karol Kerényi.* Translated by Alexander Gelley. Ithaca, N.Y.: Cornell University Press, 1975.

Márquez Villanueva, Francisco. *Fuentes literarias cervantinas.* Madrid: Gredos, 1973.

Menéndez y Pelayo, M. *Estudios cervantinos.* Buenos Aires: Plata, 1947.

Milton, John. *Paradise Lost: An Authoritative Text, Backgrounds and Sources, Criticism.* Edited by Scott Elledge. New York: Norton, 1975.

Molho, Mauricio. *Cervantes: raíces folklóricas.* Biblioteca Románica Hispánica. Madrid: Gredos, 1976.

Müller, F. Max. *Lectures on the Science of Language.* Delivered at the Royal Institution, 1861 and 1863. New York: Charles Scribner, 1865.

———. *Introduction to the Science of Religion.* Lectures at the Royal Institution, 1871. London: Longmans, Green, 1873.

———. *Contributions to a Science of Mythology.* 2 vols. London: Longmans, Green, 1897.

Müller, Karl Otfried. *Prolegomena zu einer wissenschaftlichen Mythologie.* Göttingen: Vandenhoeck und Ruprecht, 1825. Reprint with foreword by Karl Kerényi. Darmstadt: Wissenschaftliche Buchgesellschaft, 1970.

Murray, Gilbert. *The Classical Tradition in Poetry.* Oxford: Oxford University Press, 1927.

Nabokov, Vladimir. *Lectures on Don Quixote.* Edited by Fredson Bowers. New York: Harcourt, Brace, and World, 1983.

Northrup, George Tyler. *An Introduction to Spanish Literature.* Rev. and enl. by Nicholson B. Adams. 3d ed. Chicago: University of Chicago Press, 1960.

Ortega y Gasset, José. *Meditations on Quixote.* Translated by Evelyn Rugg and Diego Marín. New York: Norton, 1963

Ostendorf, Bernard. *Der Mythos in der Neuen Welt: Eine Untersuchung zum amerikanischen Myth Criticism.* Frankfurt: Thesen, 1971.

Pabón Núñez, Lucio. "Sancho, o la exaltación del pueblo español." *Cuadernos Hispanoamericanos* 63 (1964): 541–80.

Patch, Howard R. *The Other World according to Descriptions in Medieval Literature.* Cambridge: Harvard University Press, 1950.

Paz, Octavio. *The Bow and the Lyre: The Poem, the Poetic Revelation, Poetry and History.* Translated by Ruth L. C. Sims. Austin: University of Texas Press, 1973.

Peñuelas, Marcelino C. *Mito, literatura y realidad.* Madrid: Gredos, 1965.

Preminger, Alex ed. *The Princeton Encyclopedia of Poetry and Poetics.* Enl. ed. Princeton: Princeton University Press, 1974.

Puigblanch, D. Antonio. *The Inquisition Unmasked.* Translated by William Walton. 2 vols. London, 1816.

Rahv, Philip. *The Myth and the Powerhouse.* New York: Farrar, Straus and Giroux, 1965.

Redondo, Augustin. "Tradición carnavalesca y creación literaria del personaje de Sancho Panza al episodio de la ínsula Barataria en el 'Quijote.'" *Bulletin Hispanique* 80 (1978): 39–70.

Ricoeur, Paul. *The Symbolism of Evil.* Translated by Emerson Buchanan. Boston: Beacon, 1969.

Righter, William. *Myth and Literature.* London: Routledge and Paul, 1975.

Romero Flores, Hipólito R. *Biografía de Sancho Panza filósofo de la sensatez.* Barcelona: Aedos, 1952

Sánchez-Castañer y Mena, Francisco. *Penumbra y primeros albores en la génesis y evolución del mito quijotesco: Lección inaugural del curso 1948–1949.* Valencia: Vives Mora, 1948.

Sánchez y Escribano, Frederico. "Sancho Panza y su cultura popular: un aspecto de sociología cervantina." *Asomante* (San Juan, Puerto Rico) 4, no. 3 (1948): 33–40.

Schlegel, Friedrich. *Kunstanschauung der Frühromantik.* Edited by Andreas Müller. Leipzig: Reclam, 1931.

Sebeok, Thomas A. *Myth: A Symposium.* Bibliographical and Special Series of American Folklore Society vol. 5. Indiana: American Folklore Society, 1955; reprint, Bloomington: Indiana University Press, Midland Books, 1965.

Slochower, Harry. *Mythopoesis: Mythic Patterns in the Literary Classics.* Detroit: Wayne State University Press, 1970.

Slote, B., ed. *Myth and Symbol: Critical Approaches and Applications.* Lincoln: University of Nebraska Press, 1963.

Smith, Jonathan Z. "The Glory, Jest and Riddle: James George Frazer and *The Golden Bough.*" Ph.D. diss., Yale University, 1967.

―――. "When the Bough Breaks." In *Map Is Not Territory.* Leiden: E. J. Brill, 1978.

Stanford, W. B. *The Ulysses Theme: A Study in the Adaptability of a Traditional Hero.* 2d ed. Ann Arbor: University of Michigan Press, 1968.

Strelka, Joseph P., ed. *Literary Criticism and Myth.* University Park: Pennsylvania State University Press, 1980.

Strenski, Ivan. *Four Theories of Myth in Twentieth-Century History: Cassirer, Eliade, Lévi-Strauss and Malinowski.* Iowa City: University of Iowa Press, 1987.

Thorpe, James, ed. *Relations of Literary Study: Essays on Interdisciplinary Contributions.* New York: Modern Language Association of America, 1967.

Tillich, Paul. *Dynamics of Faith.* New York: Harper and Row, 1957.

Trilling, Lionel. "On the Teaching of Modern Literature." In *Beyond Culture: Essays on Literature and Learning.* New York: Viking, 1965.

Unamuno, Miguel de. *Our Lord Don Quixote: The Life of Don Quixote and Sancho with Related Essays.* Translated by Anthony Kerrigan. Princeton: Princeton University Press, 1967.

Vickery, John. *The Literary Impact of "The Golden Bough".* Princeton: Princeton University Press, 1973.

―――. *Myths and Texts: Strategies of Incorporation and Displacement.* Baton Rouge: Louisiana State University Press, 1983.

Vickery, John B., ed. *Myth and Literature: Contemporary Theory and Practice.* Lincoln: University of Nebraska Press, 1966.

Vico, Giambattista. *The New Science of Giambattista Vico.* Unabridged translation of the 3d ed. (1744). Translated by Thomas Goddard Bergin and Max Harold Fisch. Ithaca, N.Y.: Cornell University Press, 1948. Rev. ed., 1968.

Watt, Ian. *The Rise of the Novel: Studies in Defoe, Richardson and Fielding*. Berkeley: University of California Press, 1957.

Wellek, René, and Austin Warren. *Theory of Literature*. 3d. rev. ed. New York: Harcourt Brace Jovanovich, 1975.

Welsh, Alexander. *Reflections on the Hero as Quixote*. Princeton: Princeton University Press, 1981.

Wetzels, Walter D., ed. *Myth and Reason: A Symposium*. Austin: University of Texas Press, 1973.

Williamson, Edwin. *The Half-way House of Fiction: Don Quixote and Arthurian Romance*. Oxford: Clarendon Press, 1984.

Willis, Raymond S. "Sancho Panza: Prototype for the Modern Novel." *Hispanic Review* 37 (1969): 207–27.

Ziolkowski, Eric J. "Don Quijote's Windmill and Fortune's Wheel." *Modern Language Review* 86 (1991): 885–97.

———. *The Sanctification of Don Quixote: From Hidalgo to Priest*. University Park: Pennsylvania State University Press, 1991.

———. "Between Religion and Literature: Mircea Eliade and Northrop Frye." *Journal of Religion* 71 (1991): 498–522.

Ziolkowski, Theodore. *Varieties of Literary Thematics*. Princeton: Princeton University Press, 1983.

BENJAMIN CALEB RAY

THE GILGAMESH EPIC: MYTH AND MEANING

THE GILGAMESH EPIC has attracted scholarly interest since 1872 when parts of the Flood account in the eleventh tablet were first translated by the enterprising George Smith.[1] Subsequent scholarship, the discovery of more tablets, and advances in understanding the Akkadian language have resulted in a series of improved translations. For English readers an important milestone was reached with the publication in 1955 of E. A. Speiser's authoritative version in *Ancient Near Eastern Texts.* More recent textual progress and further discoveries together with the epic's increasing popularity have resulted in several new, more complete versions. Five English translations have appeared within the last ten years, including the splendid free-verse rendering by David Ferry.[2] A refreshing diversification of scholarly interpretation has also occurred at the hands of younger Assyriologists and scholars in classics and comparative literature. Equally important within the Assyriological camp is Jeffrey Tigay's outstanding 1983 study *The Evolution of the Gilgamesh Epic,* which reviews the text's literary history, examines the progress made in resolving some of its textual and linguistic problems, and evaluates important interpretive issues.

After a century of nearly exclusive treatment by Assyriological scholars and their philological and historical methods, the epic now appears to have gained sufficient textual integrity, despite several sizable gaps, so that it is available to scholars in other disciplines and to other critical approaches. In light of this, we might ask in the manner of the literary critic Stanley Fish, "Is there a text in this discussion?"[3] The answer appears to be an enthusiastic "No!" That is, with the introduction of new critical perspectives, there is now no recognized normative interpretation of the text or method for discovering it, such as the source-critical

method of the older Assyriologists. There are now several different literary critical perspectives, all dependent upon somewhat
different interpretive communities and personal convictions. To
be sure, most scholars still profess to know the author's intention
and try to find the text's universal meaning, critical claims that I
myself cannot endorse. Nevertheless, thanks to the work of generations of Assyriologists, both the original text and its recent
translations, as well as its wider literary context, have achieved a
sufficient degree of scholarly confidence that there is opportunity
for new interpretive frames of reference—each bringing its own
interests and purposes to bear.

To regard this as a positive development is, of course, to agree
with the postmodern claim that interpreters create meanings in
the texts they interpret. For most of us, perhaps, and certainly the
authors in this volume, this once-radical viewpoint has now
come to be recognized as the more commonplace notion that different interests issue in different readings of texts.[4] This essay
joins those of Doniger, Lincoln, and Grottanelli in arguing that
to endorse, even to celebrate, such interpretive diversity is in no
way to deny that we can still judge some readings to be better
than others—to offer more insight, take a fuller account of the
text and its historical environment, discriminate more sharply
between qualities of certain characters and situations, and so on.
The point is that while we shall always read the text in the context of *some* interests and purposes, knowing that we cannot privilege any single reading as universally valid, we must nevertheless
justify the interpretive choices we make by a careful treatment
of the text as a historical document and as a coherent, though
sometimes heterogeneous, whole.

Recognizing that a single text may support several different but
equally good interpretations, Richard Rorty prefers what he calls
"inspired" readings.[5] These are the sort that make a difference in
our lives, changing our conceptions of ourselves and our priorities
in life, readings that are moved by love and hate, in contrast to
merely methodical readings that treat texts as examples of types.[6]
Literary criticism, Rorty argues, is a moral matter, a question of
treating texts not simply as means but as ends in themselves.
This position, Rorty admits, comes very close to taking the side
of traditional humanistic criticism against the professional theorists whose methodical readings are, by contrast, boring and predictable.

I find myself in agreement with Rorty, because he comes into the hermeneutical circle straight on. He recognizes the holistic character of our understanding and, hence, that our judgments, moral assumptions, theoretical choices, personal preferences, and emotional responses are fully involved: interpretation is ineluctably contextual and personal. In this portrait of the literary critic, we recognize Wendy Doniger's image of the historian of religions as a "hunter/sage," the sympathetic scholar whose study of myth is moved by the heart and disciplined by the mind.[7] Like Doniger, I would argue that, in addition to the conventional apparatus of objective scholarship, based on detailed linguistic, historical, and cultural study, the interpretation of myth should be self-involving and self-aware. In studying other peoples' myths we should be learning about other peoples' local truths and learning truths about ourselves, exercising both scholarly objectivity and personal subjectivity. This, as Doniger says, enables us "to realize things about ourselves that we did not or would not notice about the image that we saw in the mirror of our own culture . . . in other peoples' mirrors we may see ourselves face to face." In *Other Peoples' Myths* Doniger explains why certain myths and stories appealed to her and how at various times they served as guides for her life. For her, the story of the Rabbi of Cracow, who sought a hidden treasure in a distant place only to discover that it lay within his own house, is a serious methodological guide: "There *is* treasure for us to find in other peoples' myths."[8]

Thus it is surprising that, until recently, Assyriologists and comparative religionists have found the Gilgamesh epic less than appealing and discovered little "treasure" in it. Most of these scholars focus upon Gilgamesh's failure to achieve immortality and find the story pessimistic. Writing just before the turn of the century, Morris Jastrow pronounced the epic to be "unsatisfactory" because "Gilgamesh revolts against the universal law of decay and is punished . . . [he] cannot escape the doom of death."[9] The Sumerologist Samuel Noah Kramer called the epic a "forceful and fateful episodic drama of the restless, adventurous hero and his inevitable disillusionment."[10] Alexander Heidel concluded that the epic ends on a "sad and somber note," while Thorkild Jacobsen held Gilgamesh's failure to be a "jeering, unhappy, unsatisfying" conclusion.[11] Mircea Eliade, perhaps influenced by these views, interpreted the epic as a "dramatized illustration of the human condition, defined by the inevitability of death," and suggested that the story was "a dramatized account of a failed initiation."[12] In keeping with these views, Jonathan Z. Smith has commented upon the epic's "relentless" account of Gilgamesh's failure to escape death. Smith also denies that the epic concerns the mortal condition of Everyman, as is usually assumed.[13]

By contrast with these interpretations, classicists, comparative literature scholars, and contemporary Assyriologists claim to have discovered new and more positive meanings in the story. Reading it against the background of Homeric epics, these scholars, not surprisingly, make Gilgamesh appear to be a heroic and humanistic figure of exemplary significance. According to Hope Nash Wolf, Gilgamesh's knowledge consists of "the experience of going to the limit," leading to an "acceptance of himself."[14] Gerald K. Gresseth sees the epic as "the first embodiment . . . of the idea of humanism," which became more fully expressed in the Homeric epics.[15] Going a step further, George F. Held finds parallels with Plato's *Symposium* such that the epic "seems specifically designed to teach, that man can develop himself, fulfill his nature, and obtain true happiness . . . only through the pursuit of virtue and knowledge and not mere pleasure."[16] Writing in the *Encyclopedia of Religion*, William L. Moran states that "acceptance of human limitations, insistence on human values—this is the teaching of the life of Gilgamesh."[17] In a more psychological fashion, Thomas van Nortwick proposes that the epic is a tale of Jungian individuation and achievement of self-mastery.[18] David M. Halperin believes Gilgamesh to be a hero who finally finds "pride and contentment in the achievements of civilized life" and thus reads the epic as "an argument for the adequacy of mortal life—and, especially, of civilized life—as the only sort of life livable for man."[19] Assyriologist Benjamin Foster, employing a Platonic perspective, goes even further and argues that the story reaches beyond the conventional values of its own royal ideology and that Gilgamesh achieves genuinely self-transcending knowledge.[20]

A close reading of the text, I believe, will show, that it supports each of these interpretations of Gilgamesh's failure, the negative as well as the positive, and that it does not uphold any interpretation definitively. Each is a partial reading: Gilgamesh returns to Uruk in "bitterness," "disillusionment," and "quiet resignation"; Gilgamesh returns "grown up" with heroic "pride and contentment"; Gilgamesh returns and achieves a higher wisdom. Moreover, although Gilgamesh is the chief protagonist, his views about life and death are not the only ones of importance in the story.

The views of each of the other characters, together with Gilgamesh's changing attitudes, can be seen as manifestations of important dramatic forces within the epic that play off each other to the very end of the story. A careful job of laying this out will delineate the logic of the text more adequately than has been done previously.

For me, the point of such an exercise is not to undermine any and all interpretations but to explore and articulate the story's aesthetic richness. The genius of the Gilgamesh epic, it seems to me, is its deliberate openness towards the several readings it allows, an openness that enhances its thought-provoking power. I shall argue that the epic reaches no point of closure either in regard to Gilgamesh's own views about life and death or in regard to the other views offered within the text by other characters. That a single scholar, the distinguished Assyriologist Thorkild Jacobsen, has changed his mind and proposed three different readings over the course of forty years of work on the epic clearly supports the notion that the epic admits of multiple interpretations, even for the same scholar.[21] For me, the most stimulating way to read it is to see it as a literary kaleidoscope of dramatically expressed attitudes toward life and death. The epic itself recommends none absolutely, and in praising the wisdom of the story, the opening section implicitly praises the process of encountering them all.

In this respect, I find the literary critic Walter Benjamin's observations on the art of storytelling highly suggestive. Benjamin points out that storytellers, in dealing with what he calls the "epic side of truth," convey their wisdom by weaving it through the real-life fabric of a story's narrative, while keeping the narrative largely free from explanation. In this way "the psychological connection of events is not forced upon the reader. It is left up to him to interpret things the way he understands them, and thus the narrative achieves an amplitude that information lacks."[22] Similarly, the author of the Gilgamesh epic does not offer any explanation at the end of the story but has his hero make only a conventional verbal gesture, praising the great walls of his city to his traveling companion. That Gilgamesh's concluding words repeat part of the opening section creates the strong impression that the story is a never-ending one that thrusts the burden of its interpretation back upon its readers to ponder again and again.

First, I shall outline the important aspects of story's textual history.[23] In 1872 George Smith, a brilliant, self-taught Assyriologist at the British Museum, caused a scholarly sensation when he translated a fragment of the Flood story in Tablet XI of the Gilgamesh epic and presented it to the Society of Biblical Archaeology.[24] The possibility that a long-lost pagan text anticipated the Bible's story of the Flood and Noah's Ark aroused considerable public excitement. The fragment Smith translated was found in the ruins of the palace library of Ashurbanipal, the Assyrian king (668–627 B.C.E.) who assembled the greatest library of the ancient Near East in his capital at Nineveh. A newspaper publisher quickly raised funds and sent Smith on three expeditions to Nineveh to bring back more cuneiform tablets in hopes of further revelations. Smith found more tablets, including additional parts of the Gilgamesh text, but unfortunately fell ill during his third trip and died.

All twelve tablets of what is now called the standard version of the Gilgamesh epic, written in Akkadian, were found in the ruined libraries at Nineveh, and hence this text is known as the Nineveh version. The text is unusual in having an author's name, Sin-leqi-unnini, attached to it, although nothing is known about him, except for his title which identifies him as an incantation priest. Parts of the Gilgamesh story also exist on fragments of five tablets dating from the Old Babylonian period (c. 1900–1600 B.C.E.) that were found later at different sites in ancient Babylonia. The differences between that text and the Nineveh text show that the author of the latter text greatly expanded and carefully reworked the story. The Old Babylonian version, which exists only in fragments of tablets that do not overlap, incorporates five much older Sumerian tales about Gilgamesh, which probably date from the third dynasty of Ur (c. 2100–200 B.C.E.). The Old Babylonian version also lacks the didactic prologue of the Nineveh text. Archeologists have found several more texts of a slightly later date that range across a wide geographical area, written in Akkadian, Hittite, and Hurrian languages.

Scholars now recognize that the Gilgamesh story never became standardized and was constantly altered through contact with a continuing oral tradition. Each period and locality seems to have had its own version of the story, and some of its themes may also have found their way into Homer's epics and into Arabic literature. The general purpose for which the Gilgamesh epic and its folk-tale elements existed in both oral and written form appears to have been entertainment in the contexts of royal courts, private houses, encampments along the desert caravan routes, or aboard ships sailing the rivers of the Indus Valley.[25]

An important feature of the Nineveh text is the unusual character of its twelfth (and last) tablet. Tablet XII begins rather abruptly with Gilgamesh speaking to Enkidu, who is still alive, despite his dramatic death in Tablet VII, and tells of Enkidu's visit to the underworld and entrapment there. Scholars agree that this tablet is stylistically at odds with the rest of the work, whose introduction and epilogue provide a unified literary framework for Tablets I–XI, and that it shows no attempt at thematic adaptation. Tablet XII is virtually a straight translation into Akkadian of the much older Sumerian tale "Gilgamesh, Enkidu, and the Netherworld," retaining the Sumerian portrayal of Enkidu as Gilgamesh's servant, rather than his intimate friend, and lacking any logical transition from the scene of Gilgamesh's return to Uruk.

Not knowing what to make of the contradictions and discontinuities of Tablet XII, some scholars dismiss it as an "inorganic appendage," the work of an incompetent scribe. Others recognize that its purpose, though crudely handled, is to explain to Gilgamesh (and the reader) the various fates of the dead in the Afterlife. Through Enkidu's voice the tablet describes the different conditions of the dead: men who accomplish something in their lives by way of siring sons or by dying gloriously on the battlefield fare better in the Afterlife than those who die without these accomplishments and have no one to mourn them. Men who produce seven sons become "close to the gods," and fare best of all. Tablet XII appears to be simply a further step in the literary evolution of the text. It is quite possible to read Tablet XII as an awkward attempt to bring closure to the epic, to show how the already wise and knowledgeable Gilgamesh receives further knowledge about the secrets of the Afterlife, a realm that he later governs as one of the judges of the dead. Tablet XII can therefore be seen as but another turn of the "hermeneutic wheel" (to use Rorty's expression) in the hands of a perceptive scribe.[26]

Let us begin with the epic's introduction, which praises Gilgamesh's wisdom and exhorts us to read the story:

> He who has seen everything, I will make known to the lands.
> I will teach about him who experienced all things,
> Anu granted him the totality of knowledge of all.
> He was the Secret, discovered the Hidden,
> he brought information of (the time) before the Flood.
> He went on a distant journey, pushing himself to exhaustion,
> but then was brought to peace.[27]
> He carved on a stone stela all of his toils,

and built the wall of Uruk-Haven,
the wall of the sacred Eanna Temple, the holy sanctuary.
Look at its wall which gleams like copper,
inspect its inner wall, the like of which no one can equal!
Take hold of the threshold stone—it dates from ancient times!
Go close to the Eanna Temple, the residence of Ishtar,
such as no later king or man ever equaled!
Go up on the wall of Uruk and walk around,
examine its foundation, inspect its brickwork thoroughly.
Is not the brick structure made of kiln-fired brick,
and did not the Seven Sages themselves lay out its plans?
One league city, one league palm gardens, one league lowlands,
    the open area of the Ishtar Temple,
three leagues and the open area of Uruk it (the wall) encloses.
Find the copper tablet box,
open the . . . of its lock of bronze,
undo the fastening of its secret opening.
Take and read out from the lapis lazuli tablet
how Gilgamesh went through every hardship.[28]

The introduction begins by praising Gilgamesh for the breadth of his experience and the totality of his knowledge.[29] As Tigay points out, the introduction is unique in ancient Near Eastern literature in emphasizing the understanding that the hero gained from his deeds rather than the deeds themselves.[30] Gilgamesh's deeds are mentioned later on but given secondary place.

Yet although the introduction praises Gilgamesh for his unsurpassed wisdom, it never says exactly in what this wisdom consists or why he returned "at peace" or what this means. Tigay and Foster correctly suggest that the story's wisdom is the story itself and that the understanding Gilgamesh gained lies within it.[31] However, like other scholars, they proceed to reduce the variety of views about life and death the story presents to the question of Gilgamesh's view at the end, ignoring the story's genuine ambiguity on this point. For this reason, as well as literary-critical reasons, we must therefore question the assumption that the story has a single point and that it is to be found in Gilgamesh's rather obscure frame of mind at the story's conclusion.

In addressing the reader, the introduction in fact points both to Gilgamesh's wisdom and to the question of the reader's perception of it. The introduction tells us that to appreciate Gilgamesh's greatness and wisdom it is necessary to take the measure of his magnificent works: the massive wall of Uruk, the incomparable Temple of Ishtar, the well-proportioned area of the city which the wall encloses. We are to climb upon the wall, observe how well it is built, and see how it encompasses the city, revealing its order and majesty. Then we are to open the container buried in the wall's foundations, take out the inscribed tablets, and read aloud the story of Gilgamesh's adventures. As our viewing of the wall will reveal something of Gilgamesh's greatness as a king, so our reading the story of his search for immortality will reveal the greatness of the wisdom it contains. Thus, Gilgamesh provides us with a model of the activity of seeing, searching, and understanding as an end in itself; it is the intensity of the activity and the breadth of the search, not Gilgamesh's final state of mind at the end, that seem to count.

I shall focus upon four episodes that convey distinctive viewpoints about the meaning of life and death, beginning with the fear of death that both Gilgamesh and his friend Enkidu experience as they prepare to fight the forest-dwelling monster Humbaba.

The story opens with the young and physically powerful Gilgamesh oppressing the people of Uruk, "like a wild bull." He physically abuses the young men and unmarried women of the city in ways that are still not understood, perhaps by dominating the men in contests of strength and by taking sexual advantage of the women. In response to the people's complaints, the gods create Enkidu to be Gilgamesh's physical match in order to divert his violent and libidinous attentions so that Uruk can have peace. Gilgamesh dreams twice of the coming of Enkidu. His mother, Ninsun, interprets these dreams and tells him that he will love and cherish Enkidu as a wife and that Enkidu will be his friend, protector, adviser, and brother. Gilgamesh's enthusiastic response indicates that he has longed for a companion, someone equal to him in strength and valor with whom he can share a life of heroic adventure.

The friendship that develops between Gilgamesh and Enkidu occurs not only because they are well matched in strength and courage but because each becomes a mirror of the other's soul. In dramatic moments of self-doubt and triumph, Gilgamesh and Enkidu reveal their deepest feelings to one another. Gilgamesh learns that only through his friendship with Enkidu is he able to accomplish heroic deeds and achieve a sense of fulfillment.

In their adventures together, death figures only as the fear of defeat which the heroes must overcome if they are to accomplish their goal. Gilgamesh counsels the frightened Enkidu to "pay no heed to death," for together they will prevail and "establish fame." Death is here denied for the sake of fame which can outlive it. Although this part of the Nineveh text is fragmented, its ideas parallel closely those in the Old Babylonian version in which Gilgamesh says to Enkidu: "Who, my Friend, can ascend to the heavens? / Only the gods can dwell forever with Shamash. / As for human beings, their days are numbered, / and whatever they keep trying to achieve is but wind! / Now you are afraid of death— / What has become of your bold strength? / I will go in front of you. . . . / Should I fall, I will have established my fame. / (They will say:) "It was Gilgamesh who locked in battle with Humbaba the Terrible."[32]

Here, Gilgamesh utters the conventional view that risking death in battle is justified because such heroism gains the warrior a lasting name, a kind of social immortality. The hero either succumbs in battle and wins immortal fame or escapes death and lives to fight again. In either case, death is denied.

After Gilgamesh and Enkidu slay Humbaba, the goddess Ishtar attempts to seduce Gilgamesh into becoming her husband. Gilgamesh's rejection of her advances turns out to be another triumph, this time over a powerful and treacherous goddess whose marriage proposal conceals an intent to conquer, even to kill.[33] Moreover, Gilgamesh not only insults Ishtar but implicitly boasts of his superiority over her previous lovers who succumbed to her deadly purposes. The two heroes reach the peak of their fame by slaying the death-dealing Bull of Heaven sent by the vengeful Ishtar. They save the inhabitants of Uruk from destruction and receive the gratitude and honors of the city. Enkidu, unfortunately, gets caught up in Gilgamesh's bravado and clumsily tries to insult Ishtar by throwing into her face the thigh of the freshly killed Bull of Heaven. This brings down Ishtar's fury onto the unsuspecting Enkidu whom the gods decide must die.

At first, Enkidu is fearful at the prospect of dying. He becomes angry and curses the hunter who captured him and the prostitute Shamhat who introduced him to human civilization. It was Shamhat who took him from his state of nature and made him a civilized man by means of fine food and drink, elegant clothing, and sexual pleasure. Shamash, the god of justice, intervenes at this moment and tells Enkidu that he is being unfair in cursing

Shamhat. Shamash reminds Enkidu of the luxurious lifestyle he enjoyed at Gilgamesh's court, of his deep friendship with Gilgamesh, and of the widespread mourning that will follow his death and the tomb Gilgamesh will build for him.

Foster suggests that Shamash's speech is ironic and satirical in tone, a god stooping to calm an upstart creature who has taken a socially privileged life for granted.[34] Shamash's words, however, are effective. Upon hearing him speak, Enkidu's "heart grew calm, his anger abated." By reminding Enkidu of the luxurious life he led and of his cherished friendship with Gilgamesh, Shamash helps him to realize that although his life was short, it was fulfilled.

After removing his curse and blessing the harlot, Enkidu grows silent and resigns himself to death. But recurrent dreams of the miserable existence in the Afterlife make him despair, and he calls out to Gilgamesh to remember their courageous deeds. Enkidu's changing attitudes toward death—fear, anger, and acceptance, tempered by moments of delirium and despair—make a powerful impression upon Gilgamesh.

Gilgamesh becomes fully drawn into Enkidu's "stages of death and dying," to use Kübler-Ross's well-known expression for this process.[35] He does his best to reassure and comfort his friend, staying with him day and night. He tells him that the whole kingdom, men and animals alike, will be plunged into mourning and honor him with lavish displays of grief; and he promises to make a fine statue and tomb and offer prayers to the gods in his name.

Enkidu's death scene is dramatic and rhetorically powerful. It is the climactic phase of the deepening friendship and fraternal love between the two young heroes. Such deathbed scenes must have been familiar to members of the literate upper-class at times when beloved family members and friends died tragically and senselessly in the prime of life. The descriptions of the violent and tender practices of mourning must also have been familiar, as well as the great tombs built to honor the memory of the dead, for it was believed that the well-honored dead who received offerings and prayers at their tombs continued to live well in the otherwise desolate underworld. Shamash's reminders about the value of friendship, the pleasures of luxurious living, as well as the honors accorded in death to the rich and famous, must also have been familiar as ways of giving meaning to death. Up to this point, Gilgamesh's behavior shows complete acceptance of the conven-

tional attitudes toward life and death voiced by Shamash. A life
filled with friendship, achievements, social privilege, and public
recognition is a life for which to be thankful, despite a premature end.

Several scholars see Gilgamesh as now having reached an important stage in his moral and psychological development.[36] They
believe that his friendship with Enkidu has taught him an important lesson about the value of social relationships in giving
meaning to life, turning him away from his previously ego-
centered behavior. This interpretation, however, depends partly
upon one's reading of the story's ending, a question which I shall
consider later. After Enkidu dies, Gilgamesh becomes obsessed
with the fear of death. Instead of continuing upon a trajectory of
psychological maturity and social fulfillment, Gilgamesh reverts
to a wholly self-preoccupied quest for immortality. The pain and
loss that Gilgamesh feels is, of course, the result of the happiness
and sense of social fulfillment that he had achieved with Enkidu.
But his friendship made him vulnerable in a way that he never
realized before. He now wants to achieve the status of an immortal god, untouchable by death—a condition that is also detached
from any serious involvement in human affairs. Gilgamesh's apparent acceptance of Enkidu's death quickly becomes translated
into a preoccupation with his own death and desire to separate
himself entirely from the human condition.

Wearing the rustic garb of a mourner, he turns his mourning
for Enkidu, which would normally have been a seven-day ritual
period, into a personal quest for immortality.[37] Gilgamesh thus
rejects the accepted cultural patterns by which the social and personal impact of death is both expressed and contained. He also
appears to be thinking of death that comes in the prime of life,
cutting off the possibility of future deeds and acts of greatness, as
it did to Enkidu. Each time Gilgamesh explains his quest to those
he encounters on his journey, he tells of Enkidu's youthful prow-
ess, the "wild ass who chased the wild donkey, the panther of the
wilderness." He concludes: "Enkidu, my friend whom I love, has
turned to clay! / Am I not like him? Will I lie down never to get
up again?"[38]

Obsessed by fear of death, he sets out to find Utnapishtim, the
survivor of the flood who together with his wife is the only immortal human being. Confident of his prodigious strength, Gilgamesh imagines that he can not only travel to the ends of the

earth where no one has been before but also, upon meeting Utnapishtim, confront him and obtain the secret of eternal life. Gilgamesh has accomplished all his deeds by means of physical
strength, and he conceives of achieving immortality in the same
terms.

Gilgamesh embarks upon his journey to find Utnapishtim, getting past the terrifying Scorpion men and traveling onward until
he meets Siduri, the divine tavernkeeper of the gods. In the Nineveh version, she listens to his plight and gives him directions
to Utnapishtim. In the Old Babylonian version, Siduri speaks directly to his desire to obtain immortality, telling him that "When
the gods created mankind / they fixed Death for mankind, / and
held back Life in their own hands." Then she proceeds to give
some advice about the meaning of life in words that are often
treated as a Babylonian version of carpe diem: "Now you, Gilgamesh, let your belly be full! / Be happy day and night, / of each
day make a party, / dance in circles day and night! / Let your
clothes be sparkling clean, / let your head be clean, wash yourself
with water! / Attend to the little one who holds onto your hand, /
let a wife delight in your embrace."[39]

Scholars have pointed out that Siduri's words are not as they
seem, an exhortation to a life of hedonism. In the context of
Gilgamesh's mourning apparel and ritual dishevelment, Siduri's
speech calls upon him to end his fruitless search and his excessive
mourning behavior. She tells him to eat in a festive manner, re-
joice in life, cleanse himself and his garments, and resume sexual
relations—in short "to assume behaviors of joy that mark the termination of the mourning cycle."[40] Her words also resonate with
a topos in ancient Near Eastern wisdom literature to the effect
that humans should take joy in life through eating, drinking,
dancing, bathing the body, wearing clean garments, and engaging
in marital relations.[41] Hence, her words convey an effort to direct
Gilgamesh's attention away from his futile quest for immortality
toward the world of the living and the joys of this life. Thinking
of the Homeric heroes of the Iliad and Odyssey and the humanistic values of civilization and domestic life, Gerald Gresseth believes that Siduri's speech eloquently states "what the epic is all
about," that "Gilgamesh and a fortiori all other men are only—
and should only strive to be—human beings." This, says Gresseth, was "the first statement at least in germinal form, of the
idea of humanism, a belief we ordinarily associate with the rise
of Greek culture."[42] Halperin, like Foster, sees Siduri's speech as

part of the process of educating Gilgamesh so that he will appreciate the value of a fully developed social life with male friends, a wife and children.

But if Siduri's words convey one of the central messages of the epic, Gilgamesh's reply shows that he gives it no serious thought: "What are you saying, alewife? / My heart is grieving for my friend. . . . Show me a track . . . / If it is possible [let me cross] the sea."[43] Haunted by the thought of his own death, Gilgamesh makes Siduri give him directions to Utnapishtim and continues on his way. Any teleological reading of Gilgamesh's character development and "ethical progress," as Held calls it, is undercut at this point by Gilgamesh's persistent egocentrism.

When Gilgamesh meets Utnapishtim, he is surprised to find not a superhuman being but a human like himself. Utnapishtim immediately confronts him with a series of questions all implying that he should end his mourning for Enkidu and stop his exhausting and fruitless search.

> Through toil you wear yourself out,
> you fill your body with grief,
> your long lifetime you are bringing (to a premature end)!
> Mankind, whose offshoot is snapped off like a reed in a canebreak,
> the fine youth and lovely girl
> . . . death,
> No one can see death,
> no one can hear the voice of death,
> yet there is savage death that snaps off mankind.
> For how long do we build a household?
> For how long do we seal a document?
> For how long do brothers share the inheritance?
> For how long is there to be jealously in the land (?)
> For how long has the river risen and brought the overflowing waters,
> so that dragon flies drift down the river?
> The face that could gaze upon the face of the Sun
> has never existed ever.
> How alike are the sleeping and the dead.
> The image of Death cannot be depicted.[44]

In addressing the subject of Gilgamesh's obsession, the untimely death of the young, Utnapishtim uses an image from nature. He likens the death of "the fine youth and lovely girl" to offshoots in a reed-bed that are "snapped off" in the prime of life, suggesting that premature death is part of the natural order of things. Utnapishtim then shifts to the context of the domestic life cycle: we build a house, the father dies, and the brothers divide up the estate. Nothing human lasts forever. Utnapishtim returns to the subject of premature death and uses another metaphor from nature. It is the image of dragonflies settling on the waters during the annual flood of the rivers. They get caught in an eddy and disappear from view. That they die in the prime of life, Utnapishtim seems to suggest, is part of the nature of things, the great cycle of life and death. Finally, Utnapishtim juxtaposes the image of sleep with that of death, conveying the idea that death is fundamental to life; it is as natural as sleep and as unavoidable as sleep, a truth Utnapishtim will later demonstrate to Gilgamesh.

I read Utnapishtim's speech (unfortunately, broken in key places) as an attempt to place the apparent unnaturalness of premature death, such as Enkidu's, into the same category as the more natural death that occurs in old age.[45] Both belong to the given order of things, which is fundamentally impermanent. What Utnapishtim questions is Gilgamesh's exhausting struggle for immortality, which may result in his dying prematurely. There is the strong implication, too, that Gilgamesh is avoiding his royal responsibilities to worship the gods and to make something of himself as a king.

Only after these words does Gilgamesh realize that the figure who has been speaking to him is Utnapishtim. He also recognizes that Utnapishtim cannot be forced into granting him immortality, which can only be obtained from the gods. Without reflecting upon what Utnapishtim has said, Gilgamesh asks Utnapishtim how he managed to appear before the Assembly of the Gods and receive immortality. Utnapishtim tells him one of the "secret of the gods," that is, the story of the Flood and how he and his wife were spared and made immortal. The Flood story reveals another secret, namely, that the gods not only instituted death by old age but also premature death from predators (lions, wolves), famine, and disease.

Without giving Gilgamesh a chance to respond, Utnapishtim decides to teach him about mortality by means of a simple physical test: he tells Gilgamesh not to fall asleep for six days and seven nights. Exhausted from his travails, Gilgamesh immediately falls asleep, and Utnapishtim awakens him only after six days and seven nights. Realizing he has failed the test of immortality, Gilgamesh voices his despair: "O woe! What shall I do, Utnapishtim, where shall I go? / The Snatcher has taken hold of my flesh, / in my bedroom Death dwells, / and wherever I set foot there too is Death!"[46]

At this point, Gilgamesh appears to be stymied; and for the first time he is reduced to inaction. Utnapishtim, who has maintained control over Gilgamesh from the beginning of their encounter, gently compels the distraught hero to prepare to return home and end his fruitless quest. He makes Gilgamesh take off his mourning garb, bathe and anoint himself, and put on a noble robe. The washing and dressing in new clothes effectively ends Gilgamesh's protracted state of mourning, and the symbolic reinvestiture with a royal robe prepares him to return to Uruk and resume his kingship. In Utnapishtim, Gilgamesh has met his match. He knows it and silently accepts the ritual termination of his quest and reinvestiture as king. Thus Utnapishtim brings closure to Gilgamesh's desperate quest. A crucial turning point has occurred: Utnapishtim has used the conventional ritual symbolism of the ending of mourning to make Gilgamesh accept his own death.[47] Gilgamesh can no longer deny his mortality or try to find a way out of it; he must return to his kingdom and reckon with it.

Taking pity on Gilgamesh, Utnapishtim's wife proposes that he be given something for his valiant efforts, so that he will not have to return empty-handed to Uruk. Utnapishtim tells him of a magical plant, another "secret of the gods," called "The Old Man Becomes a Young Man," which will restore youth. Gilgamesh dives to the bottom of the sea and retrieves the plant. He resolves to bring it back to Uruk, test it on an old man, and then try it himself to "return to the condition of my youth." On his way home, Gilgamesh stops to bathe in a pool of water. He sets the flower aside, and a serpent, emerging from the pool, steals it and carries it off. Immediately, the snake sloughs its skin, rejuvenated, and slips away.

The loss of the flower of youth appears to affect Gilgamesh as deeply as his failure to achieve immortality. Gilgamesh gives way to utter despair. Weeping, tears streaming down his face, he laments to his companion: "*Counsel me*, O Ferryman Urshanabi! / For whom have my arms labored, Urshanabi? / For whom has my heart's blood roiled? / I have not secured any good deed for myself, / but done a good deed for the 'lion of the ground'!"[48] This is the low point of the story. Gilgamesh, the would-be god, has failed again. He must now deal not only with mortality but with human frailty and old age.

The story ends a brief ten lines later. After traveling thirty leagues, Gilgamesh and his guide Urshanabi stop for the night. The next day they arrive at Uruk, and Gilgamesh says to Urshanabi: "Go up, Urshanabi, onto the wall of Uruk and walk around. / Examine its foundation, inspect its brickwork thoroughly— / is not the brick structure of kiln-fired brick, / and did not the Seven Sages themselves lay out its plan? / One league city, one league palm gardens, one league lowlands, / the open area of the Ishtar Temple, / three leagues and the open area of Uruk it (the wall) encloses."[49]

Most contemporary scholars want to find in these lines what Jacobsen, writing in 1976, called a "late and dearly won resignation," an "acceptance of reality."[50] For Jacobsen, the wall of Uruk "stands for all time as Gilgamesh's lasting achievement." Hence, he finds a fresh optimism in Gilgamesh's final words commending the walls of the city: "Man may have to die, but what he does lives after him. There is a measure of immortality in achievement, the only immortality man can seek."[51] Moran argues similarly that Gilgamesh's words praising the walls of Uruk bring "us back to where we began and to a sense of achievement."[52]

There is nothing, however, to prevent a very different reading. Writing in 1990, Jacobsen revised his heroic interpretation and offered a more sober view, tied to his own conviction that "man can never at heart really accept the fact of death."[53] In this essay Jacobsen no longer finds any optimism in Gilgamesh's final words but views them as merely a "common sense" ending, showing that Gilgamesh simply grew up and became "normal and sensible," a perspective in keeping with Jacobsen's stated refusal to accept death. In praising the walls of Uruk to his companion, Gilgamesh is in fact doing nothing more than uttering conventional phrases, like all city-praise poems.[54] That Gilgamesh addresses these words to such a minor character as the boatman also undercuts their impact.[55] We might even imagine that in these words Gilgamesh is taking refuge in utterly conventional phrases to cover up his true feelings of defeat and despair.

Unlike Odysseus, Gilgamesh was not in fact presented with an actual choice between mortality and immortality. Utnapishtim's sleep test was merely a means of demonstrating to Gilgamesh his mortal nature. Having failed the test and finally grasped his own mortality, Gilgamesh is faced with reconciling himself to it. His return to Uruk and praising its walls can be viewed as but the beginning of this process. Despite the views of most scholars, Gilgamesh's praising of the walls does not express any opinion about life and death, neither Held's heroic realism, Foster's superior wisdom, nor Jacobsen's sober common sense.

To see Gilgamesh's words as deliberately inconclusive on this point—not explicitly proposing a lesson about the meaning of life but simply concluding the search for it—is in keeping with two of the most interesting texts in the Babylonian wisdom literature. Much of this literature is entirely conventional, consisting of pious precepts and moral admonitions. But two texts, the so-called *Dialogue of Pessimism* and the *Theodicy*, present seriously ambivalent views of the meaning of life.

The *Dialogue* is a conversation between a master and a slave. The master calls upon his servant and tells him he wishes to undertake a certain activity. The slave responds enthusiastically and offers good reasons for the master's decision. Then the master changes his mind and decides he will not undertake the proposed activity; whereupon, the slave endorses that with equal enthusiasm and justification. For example:

> Slave, listen to me! —Here, I am, master, here I am!
> —Quickly! Fetch me the chariot and hitch it up:
> I want to drive to the palace!
> Drive, master, drive! It will be to your advantage
> When he will see you, the king will give you honors!
> —O well, slave I will not drive to the palace!
> —Do not drive, master, do not drive!
> When he may see you, the king may send you
> God knows where,
> he may make you take a route you do not know,
> he will make you suffer agony day and night![56]

The dialogue presents ten such proposals and reversals of action, each justified with sound reasons. The impression conveyed to the reader is that there are compelling conventional reasons both for and against any particular action or decision. At the end the master asks facetiously whether the best way to commit suicide is by having one's neck broken or by being drowned in a river. The slave answers cleverly with the question, "Who is so tall as to ascend to heaven? / Who is so broad as to encompass the entire world?" which is to say that humankind can never know the answer to such a question, only the gods can know. Whereupon, the master proposes, again factiously, to kill the slave, so he can go to the Afterlife and find out the answer. The slave responds that if the master did so, he himself would soon die because he could not live long without his slave!

Jean Bottéro has argued, rightly I believe, against those who take this poem to be either a serious expression of pessimism, "the negation of all values," or a satire, a lampoon on the folly of human life. Bottéro suggests that the *Dialogue* is both satirical and serious; it mocks conventional wisdom expressed in the slave's ready-made responses in order to emphasize the limited nature of human knowledge. Thus he proposes that the *Dialogue*'s conclusion is that "no one in this world can answer the question of the meaning of human life."[57]

Bottero arrives at this interpretation by reading the *Dialogue* against the background of an earlier text called the *Poem of the Righteous Sufferer*, which also deals with questions about the meaning of life. The *Righteous Sufferer* asks in Job-like fashion why pious people suffer apparently arbitrary reversals of fortune, and concludes by praising the god Marduk who eventually restores the sufferer to health and posterity. "Indeed, I thought (my piety) to be pleasing to the gods! / But, perhaps what is proper to oneself is an offense to them? / And what one thinks to be blasphemy may be proper to them? / Who can know the will of the gods in heaven? / Who understands the plans of the underworld gods? / How could the mortals understand the plans of the gods? / He who prospered yesterday is dead today. / (He who) was dejected for a minute, suddenly is exuberant. / One moment people are singing in exultation; / the other they groan like professional mourners!"[58]

In the end, this thoughtful and meditative text concludes that humankind is incapable of explaining the misfortunes and contradictions of life, only the gods know the answers to such questions and only continued trust in them can bring deliverance. While it is plausible to interpret the *Dialogue* in the same fashion, I read it in less pious terms. The *Dialogue* mocks conventional opinion, even the worship of the gods, by placing its words of advice in the mouth of a clever slave, who outwits his master by using commonsense reasoning against itself. The implication is that we, too, should reject the simple answers, whether pious or impious, and that we should think carefully for ourselves in a world of conflicting values and opinions. If this interpretation appears to be too modern, too expressive of an individualistic perspective on life, I would argue that what makes these texts appealing is their resistance to the pious platitudes of their day. They invite the reader to explore the limits of culturally received ideas and religious conventions, as Gilgamesh himself did.

It is possible, of course, to take a historicist approach, such as Jacobsen's early essay on Mesopotamian literature, and treat the epic as a conventional expression of its day, typifying what Jacobsen calls "a civilization grown old" whose prominent mood was "scepticism toward all values, utter negation of the possibility of a 'good life.'"[59] But Jacobsen's historicist approach merely attempts to justify his reading of the text by attributing it to a certain historical "age" or "period." My answer to both "old" and "new" historicism is that it not only deprives literature (or myth) of the possibility of any genuine countercultural point of view, it refuses to take seriously the value of different readings, preferring a single conformist point of view, the "representation" of the putative ideology of the age in question.[60] While we must give considerable weight to the local character of all knowledge, the point to emphasize, as Fish, Doniger, and others remind us, is that such knowledge is never monolithic nor do we find it unmediated from our personal selves.

The *Theodicy* is another wisdom text that questions the conventionally unquestionable. It is an acrostic poem whose acrostic words read: "I, Saggil-kinam-ubbib, the incantation priest, am adorant of the god and the king." Although the poem bears this pious message, its argument, which takes the form of a dialogue between a "sufferer" and a "friend," presents disturbingly contradictory assertions. On the one hand, the two speakers assert that the gods are just; on the other hand, they agree that the gods make human beings prone to injustice. The "sufferer" and the "friend" agree that the gods punish the wicked, but they also affirm that the wicked prosper unpunished. This is a deeply ambiguous text, because, as W. G. Lambert points out, it does not reconcile the conventional view that the gods are just with the testimony of experience that confirms the opposite.[61] The poem ends with the "sufferer" weakly asserting his trust in the justice and mercy of the gods. For the reader, this unsettling poem can only invite critical reflection upon the conventional pieties of religious faith.

The Gilgamesh epic, as I read it, has a similar purpose in calling upon its readers to question conventional wisdom and think for themselves. It presents a variety of contemporary views about the meaning of life and death, which Gilgamesh dramatically undercuts, until he is left with only one certainty: his own death. We

see him return to his kingdom ready to begin life again, powerfully conditioned by this knowledge. Since the introduction tells
us that Gilgamesh wrote down the epic for posterity, we can
imagine that he is conditioned not only by the awareness of his
own mortality but also by all that he learned and experienced
before and after his quest; hence his desire to write down the full
story for the benefit of others. In recommending the story to us,
the heavily didactic introduction seems to suggest that we, like
Gilgamesh, should think seriously about death as something personal, that we should suffer and agonize over it as deeply as Gilgamesh, that we should do so while still in the prime of life, that
we should do so in the context of both religious belief and conventional wisdom, and that we should live the rest of our lives
conditioned by this experience.

The basis of the story's powerful impact upon the reader is, of
course, its presentation of Gilgamesh as a fully human though
larger-than-life figure who suffers the mental anguish of real
people while challenging human norms. As Samuel Kramer aptly
notes: "In this poem it is man who holds the center stage—the
man Gilgamesh, who loves and hates, weeps and rejoices, strives
and wearies, hopes and despairs."[62] Such deeply expressed human
emotions pull us into the story so we can identify with him. Gilgamesh is not, of course, Everyman, for he is a partly divine figure, but his feelings and values are wholly human; and it is these
with which we identify. To persuade the reader to adopt any one
of the epic's many views about life and death does not seem to be
the point. The story's "wisdom" is to present them all in a single
dramatic and gripping tale so that we might be moved to reflect
upon them, to experience vicariously the full range of Kübler-
Ross's attitudes toward death while still in the prime of life and
in this way arrive at "inspired" readings that move us in important ways.

The epic may be especially suited to young adults, not just because the hero is young, but because the young are still to some
extent outsiders to a society's cultural norms. The story's teaching will have effect only if its message about facing up to death
can make a difference in the readers' lives as they adapt to civilization's values. The story's deliberate failure to show us the difference Gilgamesh's experiences make in his life when he returns to
Uruk is part of its purpose. Its purpose is to have an effect on us,
to make us identify with Gilgamesh's attitudes of denial, grief,
anger, struggle, despair, and acceptance and reflect both upon

what Gilgamesh has learned and what we have learned in thinking about his story.

After reading this story and identifying with the hero's plight,
we can no longer suppose that death cannot happen to us—a typical adolescent and young-adult attitude—for the story places it
too firmly in our minds, as it did for Gilgamesh. But if we are not
told what Gilgamesh thinks about it, we are told that the whole
experience, especially the toil and suffering it involved, made him
the wisest king of all time: a king who achieved a deep awareness
of death and, perhaps, transcended his fear of it.

The awkward addition of Tablet XII makes sense in this context, for, as other scholars have noted, it tells how men fare in the
Afterlife, giving pride of place to the warrior who dies in battle
and to the man who begets many sons. The fact that Gilgamesh
asks Enkidu's spirit to tell him about the fate of the dead implies,
perhaps, that Gilgamesh was reconciled to death: "Tell me, my
friend, tell me, my friend, / Tell me the Earth's [Underworld's]
conditions you've found." By informing the reader about the Afterlife, Tablet XII also encourages reflection upon the meaning of
life. This is consistent with the story's aim which, I think, is to
instill in its readers a deep awarness of death and awaken a mood
of meditation upon it, so that, like Gilgamesh, we will be inspired
by it as we turn to the business of everyday life and work out
what it will mean.

Notes

I am grateful to my colleagues Gary Anderson and Jenny Geddes for their critical
comments on earlier drafts.

1. G. Smith, *Assyrian Discoveries,* 9–14; McCall, *Mesopotamian Myths,*
   13–14.
2. Gardner and Maier, *Gilgamesh* (1985); Kovacs, *Epic of Gilgamesh* (1989);
   Dalley, *Myths from Mesopotamia* (1989); Temple, *He Who Saw Everything*
   (1991); Ferry, *Gilgamesh* (1993). For a long time, the prose version by Sandars, *Epic of Gilgamesh* (1960), was the most readily available text, despite
   its many shortcomings. Unless otherwise indicated, I have used Kovacs's
   version because of its literalness of translation, despite its omission of Tablet XII.
3. Fish, "Is There a Text in this Class?"
4. Stout, "What Is the Meaning."
5. Rorty, "Pragmatist's Progress."
6. For example, Rainer Maria Rilke's enthusiastic appreciation of the epic: "In
   the fragments . . . is a colossal happening and presence and fearing. . . . Here
   is the epic of the fear of death, arisen from that which is immemorial
   among human beings for whom the separation between death and life had

become definitive and ominous" (Moran, "Rilke and the Gilgamesh Epic," 209).

7. O'Flaherty, *Other Peoples' Myths*.
8. Ibid., 140, 139.
9. *Religion of Babylonia and Assyria*, 514.
10. Kramer, "Epic of Gilgamesh," 19.
11. Heidel, *Gilgamesh Epic*, 10; Jacobsen, "Mesopotamia," 227. The opinion of European Assyriologists is much the same. According to Hugo Gressman, "The mood of the epic is gloomy and heavy. With the most profound pessimism, the poet contemplates the lot of mankind whose greatest yearning cannot be fulfilled" (*Gilgamesh-Epos*, 170). F. M. Th. Bohl finds the ending so unattractive that he believes that "the Akkadian epic as we have it is a torso, and therefore the ending is unsatisfactory" ("Ewige Leben," 261). Benno Landsberger writes that "The answer [to the question of the value of life] is entirely pessimistic: all is to no purpose. Only friendship . . . and the belief in fate against which humanity struggles stand as the positive points in the melancholy atmosphere of the epic" ("Einleitung," 174). Even Von Guiseppe Furlani, who praises the epic as a "hymn to friendship," characterizes the epic as an "immense tragedy" ("Gilgamesh Epos").
12. Eliade, *History of Religious Ideas* I, 77–80.
13. J. Z. Smith, *Drudgery Divine*, 105, 122. For a similar view, see Bendt Alster, "Paradigmatic Character."
14. Wolf, *Study of the Narrative Structure*, 20–21.
15. Gresseth, "Gilgamesh Epic and Homer," 16.
16. Held, "*Gilgamesh* and Plato's *Symposium*," 133.
17. Moran, "Gilgamesh," 559.
18. Van Nortwick, *Somewhere*, 36–38.
19. Halperin, *One Hundred Years*, 79–80.
20. Foster, "Gilgamesh."
21. Jacobsen, "Mesopotamia" (1949); *Treasures of Darkness* (1976); "Gilgamesh Epic" (1990).
22. Benjamin, *Illuminations*, 89. I want to thank Laurie Patton for drawing my attention to Benjamin's writings.
23. See, Tigay, *Evolution of the Gilgamesh Epic*.
24. McCall notes that when Smith discovered the fragment of the Flood account, "He was so overcome with excitement that he rushed around the room and began tearing off his clothes" (*Mesopotamian Myths*, 14).
25. Lambert, "Ancestors, Authors, and Canonicity"; Dalley, *Myths from Mesopotamia*; "Gilgamesh and the Arabian Nights"; Moran, "Ovid's *Blanda Voluptas*."
26. Cf. Tigay, *Evolution*, 107, n. 27.
27. This line concludes with an important term that translators have rendered either as *shup-shu-uq*, "in pain," or *shup-shu-uh*, "at peace." Consensus now identifies the term as *shup-shu-uh*, which means "calm" or "peaceful." The use of this word suggests the ultimate calming of Gilgamesh's "stormy heart" and acceptance of his mortality, hence Dalley's translation of the word as "resigned" (Tigay, *Evolution*, 262; Moran, "Gilgamesh," 559; Jacobsen, "Gilgamesh Epic," 247; Dalley, *Myths from Mesopotamia*, 50). I am indebted to my colleague Gary Anderson for assistance on this point.
28. Kovacs, *Epic of Gilgamesh*, 3–4.
29. The term translated as "knowledge, experience, wisdom" is *nemequ*. According to the *Chicago Assyrian Dictionary*, *nemequ* is a broad and inclusive word that refers "to a body of experiences, knowledge, skills, and traditions which are the basis of a craft or occupation, or form the basis of civilization as a whole" (160 n. 2).

30. Tigay, *Evolution*, 143–44.
31. Ibid., 125; Foster, "Gilgamesh," 42; cf. Vanstiphout, "Craftsmanship," 67.
32. Kovacs, *Gilgamesh*, 19–20.
33. On this point, see Tzvi Abusch's excellent article "Ishtar's Proposal."
34. Foster, *Gilgamesh*, 39.
35. Kübler-Ross, *On Death and Dying*. This study has stimulated a widespread response, much of it critical of the implied universality of Kübler-Ross's "stages." See Schultz and Aderman, "Clinical Research" and Retsinas, "Theoretical Reassessment."
36. Jacobsen, *Treasures of Darkness*; Halperin, *One Hundred Years*; Foster, "Gilgamesh."
37. This is clearer in the Old Babylonian verson. See Anderson, *Time to Mourn*, 78; Moran, "Gilgamesh," 559.
38. Kovacs, *Gilgamesh*, 91.
39. Ibid., 85.
40. Anderson, *Time to Mourn*, 80–81; cf. Abusch, "Gilgamesh's Request," 12–17.
41. Tigay, *Evolution*, 168–69.
42. Gresseth, "Gilgamesh," 13.
43. Gilgamesh (Old Babylonian version), Dalley, *Myths from Mesopotamia*, 150.
44. Kovacs, *Gilgamesh*, 93.
45. For a different reading, see Lambert, "Theology of Death."
46. Kovacs, *Gilgamesh*, 105.
47. I owe this fundamental insight to Moran, "Gilgamesh," 559.
48. Kovacs, *Gilgamesh*, 107.
49. Ibid., 107–08.
50. Jacobsen, *Treasures*, 208.
51. Ibid., 108. Another scholar attributes more specific thoughts to Gilgamesh: "He returns to his city of Uruk, realizing that for him the true meaning of life resides in the optimal fulfillment of his civic (and for him, royal) tasks" (Vanstiphout, "Craftsmanship," 65).
52. Moran, "Gilgamesh," 559.
53. Jacobsen, "Gilgamesh Epic," 249.
54. Tigay, *Evolution*, 149–49.
55. Foster, "Gilgamesh," 42.
56. Bottéro, *Mesopotamia*, 253.
57. Ibid., 263.
58. Lambert, *Babylonian Wisdom Literature*.
59. Jacobsen, "Mesopotamia," 231.
60. For excellent evaluations of the problems of New Historicism, see Myers, "New Historicism"; Fish, "Commentary"; and Cantor, "Greenblatt's New Historicist Vision."
61. Lambert, *Babylonian Wisdom Literature*, 64.
62. Kramer, "Epic of Gilgamesh," 7.

Works Cited

Abusch, Tzvi. "Ishtar's Proposal and Gilgamesh's Refusal: An Interpretation of the Gilgamesh Epic, Tablet 6, Lines 1–79." *History of Religions* 26 (1986): 143–87.

———. "Gilgamesh's Request and Siduri's Denial. Part II: An Analysis and Interpretation of an Old Babylonian Fragment about Mourning and Celebration." *Journal of Ancient Near Eastern Society* 22 (1993): 12–17.

Alster, Bendt. "The Paradigmatic Character of Mesopotamian Heroes." *Revue d'Assyriologie* 68 (1974): 49–60.

Anderson, Gary A. *A Time to Mourn, a Time To Dance: The Expression of Grief and Joy in Israelite Religion.* University Park: Pennsylvania State University Press, 1991.

Assyrian Dictionary of the Oriental Institute of the University of Chicago. Edited by Erica Reiner et al. Chicago: Oriental Institute, 1980.

Benjamin, Walter. *Illuminations.* New York: Schocken Books, 1968.

Bohl, F. M. Th. "Das Ewige Leben im Zyklus und Epos des Gilgamesch" (1953). In *Das Gilgamesh-Epos*, edited by Karl Oberhuber, 237–75. Darmstadt: Wissenschaftliche Buchgesellschaft, 1977.

Bottéro, Jean. *Mesopotamia: Writing, Reasoning, and the Gods.* Translated by Zainab Bahrani and Marc Van De Mieroop. Chicago: University of Chicago Press, 1992.

Cantor, Paul. "Stephen Greenblatt's New Historicist Vision." *Academic Questions* (Fall, 1993): 21–36.

Dalley, Stephanie, trans. and ed. *Myths from Mesopotamia.* Oxford: Oxford University Press, 1989.

———. "Gilgamesh and the Arabian Nights." *Journal of the Royal Asiatic Society*, ser. 3, 1, no. 1 (1991): 1–17.

Eliade, Mircea. *A History of Religious Ideas.* Vol. I. Translated by Willard R. Trask. Chicago: University of Chicago Press, 1978.

Ferry, David. *Gilgamesh: A New Rendering in English Verse.* New York: Noonday Press, 1993.

Fish, Stanley. *Is There a Text in This Class?* Cambridge: Harvard University Press, 1980.

———. "Commentary: The Young and the Restless." In *The New Historicism*, ed. H. Aram Veeser, New York: Routledge, 1989.

Foster, Benjamin. "Gilgamesh: Sex, Love, and the Ascent of Knowledge." In *Love & Death in the Ancient Near East*, ed. John H. Marks and Robert M. Good, 21–42. Guilford, Conn.: Four Quarters Publishing, 1987.

Furlani, Von Guiseppe. "Das Gilgamesh Epos als Hymnus auf die Freundschaft" (1946). In *Das Gilgamesh-Epos*, edited by Karl Oberhuber, 219–36. Darmstadt: Wissenschaftliche Buchgesellschaft, 1977.

Gardner, John, and John R. Maier, trans. *Gilgamesh.* New York: Vintage Books, 1985.

Gresseth, Gerald K. "The Gilgamesh Epic and Homer." *Classical Journal* 70, no. 4 (1975): 1–18.

Gressman, Hugo, and Arthur Ungnad. *Das Gilgamesh-Epos: Forschungen zur Religion und Literatur des Alten und Neuen Testamenta* 14. Göttingen: Van den Hoeck and Ruprecht, 1911.

Halperin, David M. *One Hundred Years of Homosexuality: And other Essays on Greek Love.* New York: Routledge, 1990.

Heidel, Alexander. *The Gilgamesh Epic and Old Testament Parallels.* Chicago: University of Chicago Press, 1949.

Held, George F. "Parallels between *The Gilgamesh Epic* and Plato's *Symposium.*" *Journal of Near Eastern Studies* 42 (1983): 133–41.

Jacobson, Thorkild. "Mesopotamia." In *Before Philosophy,* edited by H. and H. A. Frankfort. Harmondsworth: Penguin Books, 1949.

——. *Treasures of Darkness.* New Haven: Yale University Press, 1976.

——. "The Gilgamesh Epic: Tragic and Romantic Vision." In *Lingering over Words: Studies in Ancient Near Eastern Literature in Honor of William L. Moran.* Harvard Semitic Studies, edited by Tzvi Abusch, John Huehnergard, and Piotr Steinkeller. Atlanta: Scholars Press, 1990, 231–40.

Jastrow, Morris, Jr. *The Religion of Babylonia and Assyria.* Boston: Ginn, 1898.

Kovacs, Maureen Gallery, trans. *The Epic of Gilgamesh.* Stanford: Stanford University Press, 1989.

Kramer, S. N. "The Epic of Gilgamesh and Its Sumerian Sources." *Journal of the American Oriental Society* 64, no. 1 (1944): 7–23.

Kübler-Ross, Elizabeth. *On Death and Dying.* New York: Macmillan, 1969.

Lambert, W. G. "Ancestors, Authors and Canonicity." *Journal of Cuneiform Studies* 11 (1957): 45–49.

——. "The Theology of Death." In *Death in Mesopotamia,* edited by Bendt Alster, 53–66. Copenhagen: Akademisk Forlag, 1980.

——. *Babylonian Wisdom Literature.* Oxford: Clarendon Press, 1982.

Landsberger, Benno. "Einleitung in das Gilgamesh-Epos" (1960). In *Das Gilgamesch-Epos,* edited by Karl Oberhuber. Darmstadt: Wissenschaftliche Buchgesellschaft, 1977, 171–77.

McCall, Henrietta. *Mesopotamian Myths.* Legendary Past Series. Austin: Universtiy of Texas Press, 1990.

Moran, William L. "Rilke and the Gilgamesh Epic." *Journal of Cuneiform Studies* 32, no. 4 (1980): 208–10.

——. "Gilgamesh." In *The Encyclopedia of Religion,* edited by Mircea Eliade. New York: Macmillan, 1987.

——. "Ovid's *Blanda Voluptas* and the Humanization of Enkidu." *Journal of Near Eastern Studies* 50, no. 2 (1991): 121–27.

Myers, D. G. "The New Historicism in Literary Studies." *Academic Questions* (Winter, 1988–89): 27–36.

O'Flaherty, Wendy Doniger. *Other Peoples' Myths.* New York: Macmillan, 1988.

Pritchard, James B., ed. *Ancient Near Eastern Texts: Relating to the Old Testament.* 2d. ed. Princeton: Princeton University Press, 1955.

———. *The Ancient Near East: Supplement to Ancient Near Eastern Texts.* Princeton: Princeton University Press, 1968.

Rorty, Richard. "The Pragmatist's Progress." In *Interpretation and Overinterpretation: Umberto Eco,* edited by Stefan Collini. Cambridge: Cambridge University Press, 1992, 89–108.

Retsinas, Joan. "A Theoretical Reassessment of the Applicability of Kübler-Ross's Stages of Dying." *Death Studies* 12 (1988): 207–16.

Sandars, Nancy K., trans. *The Epic of Gilgamesh.* 2d. rev. ed. Harmondsworth: Penguin Books, 1972.

Schultz, Richard, and David Aderman. "Clinical Research and the Stages of Dying." *Omega* 5, no. 2 (1974): 137–43

Smith, George. *Assyrian Discoveries.* 3d. ed. New York: Scribner, Armstrong, 1876.

Smith, Jonathan Z. *Drudgery Divine: On the Comparison of Early Christianities and the Religion of Late Antiquity.* Chicago: University of Chicago Press, 1990.

Stout, Jeffrey. "What Is the Meaning of a Text." *New Literary History* 15 (1982): 89–108.

Temple, Robert. *He Who Saw Everything: A Verse Translation of the Epic Gilgamesh.* London: Rider Books, 1991.

Tigay, Jeffrey H. *The Evolution of the Gilgamesh Epic.* Philadelphia: University of Pennsylvania Press, 1982.

Van Nortwick, Thomas. *Somewhere I Have Never Travelled: The Second Self and the Hero's Journey in Ancient Epic.* New York: Routledge, 1990.

Vanstiphout, H. L. J. "The Craftsmanship of Sin-leqi-unninni." *Orientalia Lovaniensia Periodica* 21 (1990): 45–79.

Wolf, Hope Nash. *A Study of the Narrative Structure of Three Epic Poems: Gilgamesh, The Odyssey, Beowulf.* New York: Garland Publishing, 1987.

DIANE APOSTOLOS-CAPPADONA

PICASSO'S *GUERNICA* AS MYTHIC ICONOCLASM: AN ELIADEAN INTERPRETATION OF THE MYTH OF MODERN ART

ALTHOUGH I WAS never privileged to be a formal student of the historian-of-religions Mircea Eliade, I have found that his theories and texts provided me with both an enduring influence and the seedbed for the study of religion and the arts. Eliade's encyclopedic view of religion and of the religious allows for the necessary inclusion of the arts into religious studies. Nonetheless, this was neither an inclusion he chose to study in depth nor one in which our mutual conclusions would have agreed. For example, my proposed methodology of "mythic iconoclasm" is never directly employed by Eliade in any of his written texts. It seems clear to me, however, from an attentive study of all his texts on the arts, published and unpublished, that he laid the groundwork for a clearly defined creative hermeneutical method for the analysis of the existential situation of the artist and of the role of art in society that I have chosen to build upon and to employ in my analyses of the mutuality of the aesthetic and the religious, especially in the Secular Century.

Pablo Picasso's *Guernica* (1937, Centro de Arte Reina Sofia, Madrid) (fig. 1) was painted allegedly in response to the artist's horror at the saturation bombing of the Basque village from which the painting gets its name. Much has been written about

Fig. 1. Pablo Picasso, *Guernica* (1937, Centro de Arte Reina Sofía, Madrid). Courtesy, Giraudon / Art Resource, New York. The works of Pablo Picasso ©1996 S.P.A.D.E.M., Paris/A.R.S., New York.

Guernica—it has been analyzed and interpreted from a variety of scholarly perspectives including art history and criticism, iconology and iconography, cultural history, anthropology, sociology, and classical mythology.[1] Acclaimed as Picasso's masterpiece, *Guernica* has been described as a religious painting—Herbert Read called it "a modern calvary," Paul Tillich characterized it as the "best present-day Protestant religious picture," and Joseph Campbell analyzed it as "a reorganization of mythological motifs."[2] One must wonder, first, whether there is anything more to say about this painting, and second, why it is that this of all of Picasso's paintings has so captivated and fascinated scholars, critics, and the public.

I would like to suggest that there is more to say about *Guernica*—at least one more attempt at interpretation and analysis that may bring us closer to an understanding of why this painting has continued to attract both popular and scholarly attention. In this examination of *Guernica*, I will build upon Eliade's study of artistic creativity and genius as dependent upon an intuitive (also read imaginative) mode-of-being-in-the-world. Although he never fully developed a method of analysis for the creative arts, there are implications in Eliade's regular references to symbolism and the arts for the extrapolation of such a hermeneutical method.

While Eliade was criticized, perhaps appropriately, for his emphasis on the "intuitive" and the "ahistorical" in his own hermeneutical analyses of religious phenomena including myth, I would agree with David Cave that such critiques of Eliade may be appropriate only from the traditionally defined methodology of history.[3] I differ, however, from Cave in my rationale for finding such criticism inadequate as Eliade was clearly interpreting a philosophy of history, not reporting history. For me, Eliade represented what Ivan Strenski terms a "creative hermeneutics."[4] In distinction from Strenski, I find that Eliade's methodology of a creative hermeneutics—perhaps better said as a hermeneutics of creativity—for the study of religion and by implication the study of religion and the arts is a major contribution to twentieth-, if not also to twenty-first-century scholarship. Eliade's creative hermeneutics suggests that *homo religiosus* is *homo aestheticus*. Thus his emphasis on the intuitive in his analyses of religious phenomena accesses the human imagination as a vehicle for interpretive discovery, especially in terms of the deciphering of symbolic values that may be latent or camouflaged in the secularity of the twentieth (and twenty-first) century.

Eliade carefully defined the creative process as having a religious (if not mythological) nature and understood the centrality of intuition and atemporality to the creative personality.[5] Creative personalities are capable of suspending "fate" through the momentary absence of recognizable time and space categories in the act of "making," and thereby of momentarily experiencing transcendence—that is, living in the *mundus imaginalis*. As a novelist and playwright, Eliade himself was personally cognizant of this artistic reality. At the same time, I would argue that his scholarly writings not only benefited in thematic exposition but also in the experiential tonality of his written prose. It is these "words of manifestation," to use David Tracy's description, that permit Eliade's scholarly texts to be open to and on the aesthetic dimensions, thereby affirming my conviction that *homo religiosus* is *homo aestheticus*.[6]

Such an empathy, however, did not provide Eliade with the necessary critical skills for more than a superficial appraisal of the religious character(s) of works of art. For example, consider his own abridged analysis of *Guernica*:

> Such a case was Picasso's "Guernica," because nothing in it—except possibly the bull, the only clear religious symbol—was there to tell us that this was a very important religious painting. . . . The symbols put there, unconsciously or not, the colors, the organization of the painting, all present a world of meanings which is fundamentally religious, telling us about the despair of a man who is destroyed by man, without having a God to ask for help. The religious meaning of it is discerned by a critical hermeneutical analysis. It is a creation of the human mind in the sense that Picasso, depressed by the historical situation, rediscovered a series of symbols and images of religious significance. But this world of meaning is not his creation; "Guernica" is his creation. Its religious meaning is the set of patterns which he put there without being aware of their significance, which gives to us a religious meaning. This is the dividing line of creation and discovery: Picasso has created "Guernica," and in so doing, he has discovered a world of religious meaning previously closed to him.[7]

Despite Eliade's inadequacies as an iconographer or his partially developed methodology for a hermeneutics of the arts, a careful iconographic study of *Guernica* and its place in Picasso's oeuvre through an Eliadean lens permits a (re-)viewing of this painting that may prove closer to the painter's original intentions. In his essays on modern art, Eliade, continually referred to the "breakdown of traditional symbols and images" and the need for the "destruction of traditional aesthetic universes."[8] Expanding the primal meaning of iconoclasm—that is, simply as image breaking—to that of image breaking *without* the destruction of *all* images, he stated, "Moreover, all the modern artistic movements seek, consciously or unconsciously, the destruction of the traditional aesthetic universes, the reduction of 'forms' to elementary, germinal, larval states in the hope of re-creating 'fresh worlds'; in other words, these movements seek to abolish the history of art and to reintegrate the auroral moment when man saw the world 'for the first time.'"[9] In conjunction with his theories of ritual, especially that of the New Year, and of the camouflage of the sacred in the modern world, Eliade implied that iconoclasm must occur regularly to allow for the re-emergence of meaningful and adequate images. "Such works represent closed worlds, hermetic universes that cannot be entered into except by overcoming immense difficulties, like the initiatory ordeals of the archaic and traditional societies. On the one hand, one has the experience of an 'initiation,' an experience that has almost vanished from the modern World; on the other hand, one proclaims to the 'others' (i.e., the 'mass') that one belongs to a select minority . . . to a gnosis that has the advantage of being at once spiritual and secular in that it opposes both official values and the traditional churches."[10]

Iconoclasm is thereby, a creative activity.[11] Moreover, Eliade's reading of modern art's "destruction of traditional forms and fascination for the formless" was specifically a mythic iconoclasm, that is, the breaking down of recognizable traditional images into the essential visualization of a culture's fundamental myths.[12] What I have thus termed *mythic iconoclasm*—implied throughout Eliade's texts—I will further propose as an appropriate methodology for interpreting modern art and the existential situation of the modern artist in the so-called Secular Century, in particular, Picasso and what he referred to as "the *Guernica*."[13]

As a twentieth-century artist who lived in political exile from his native Spain, and in spiritual exile from his natal Roman Catholicism, Picasso can be characterized appropriately as embodying what Eliade describes as modern humanity's "nostalgia for paradise."[14] For Eliade, however, these twentieth-century artists lived within a specialized category of the "nostalgia for para-

dise"—not simply the Adamic paradise lost to all human beings—but also the "paradise" of one's childhood or youthful
homeland from which the adult was in political exile.[15] This lost
childhood or youthful paradise—to which one could never return
either physically or politically—became a source of both constant
melancholy and personalized iconography.[16] Picasso's nostalgia
for the lost paradise of the idyllic and free Spain of his childhood
was both an inspiration for and symbolic subject matter in his
art. Eliade's category of the twentieth-century artistic nostalgia
for paradise clarifies Picasso's immediately personalized and haptic response to the bombing of this now infamous Basque city.

Guernica is not the only image that Picasso made to reflect
both his horror at the Spanish Civil War or his disdain at the ascendancy to power of Generalissimo Francisco Franco. Picasso
also completed a series of etchings entitled Sueno y Mentira de
Franco (Dreams and Lies of Franco) (1937, Museum of Fine Arts,
Boston)(fig. 2). Other artists reflected the shock and disbelief at
the total destruction of Guernica in their own oeuvres, perhaps
no one more persuasively and persistently than the late Robert
Motherwell in his lifelong series of black-and-white paintings
entitled Elegy to the Spanish Republic, identified by serial number. Picasso did not restrict himself, however, to only this singular
image of war. Rather he painted other images of the wars contemporary to his own time including Massacre in Korea (1951, Musée
Picasso, Paris)(fig. 3).

Earlier Spanish artists depicted the horror of war as did Goya in
his Third of May (1808, Prado, Madrid)(fig. 4), and the destruction
of humanness and human sensibilities that resulted from such
wars, in his Saturn (1819–23, Prado, Madrid). In the somewhat
typical Spanish machismo characterized by an ambivalence toward Roman Catholicism—that is, of being simultaneously in
awe of its rituals and in disbelief of the magical power of its theology—Goya painted the Procession of the Flagellants (1794, Prado,
Madrid) and then attempted to debunk religious values in his depiction of The Witches Sabbath (1819–23, Prado, Madrid). Picasso
was heir to both Goya's images and that common Spanish male
ambivalence toward Roman Catholicism, if not toward all institu-
tionalized religions. In fact, throughout Picasso's oeuvre there is
both a fascination with and a rejection of Roman Catholicism
that visually correlates to the experience of being at the edge of
Søren Kierkegaard's abyss or Rudolf Otto's mysterrium tremen-
dum et fascinans. In Picasso's work, I find a myriad of images of

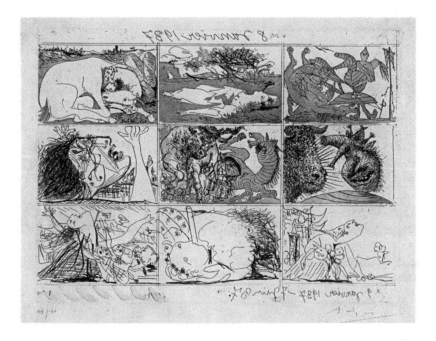

Fig. 2. Pablo Picasso, *Sueno y Mentira de Franco* (*Dreams and Lies of Franco*) (1937, Museum of Fine Arts, Boston). Etching and aquatint, 12¼ × 16¾ in. Courtesy, Museum of Fine Arts, Boston, Lee M. Friedman Fund [#1971.302]. The works of Pablo Picasso ©1996 S.P.A.D.E.M., Paris/A.R.S., New York.

the horrors of war such as in *Rape of the Sabine Women* (1963, Museum of Fine Arts, Boston)(fig. 5.) in which he again utilized the powerful image of the horse and rider, and the lamentation of the massacred innocents. In some way, all of these images relate to the power and uniqueness of *Guernica*.

I employ this reading of mythic iconoclasm to my iconographic and thematic study of *Guernica* to assist in the determination that the elemental mythological motifs that undergird those earlier images of war were those of the honor of the war and of the warrior. Picasso had been fascinated with three varied thematic approaches to an honorable but sacrificial form of death—the classical myth of the minotaur, the Spanish national ritual of the bullfight, and the Christian theology of sacrificial death and lamentation in the crucifixion of Jesus Christ. The common denominators among these myths were the image of the warrior and the

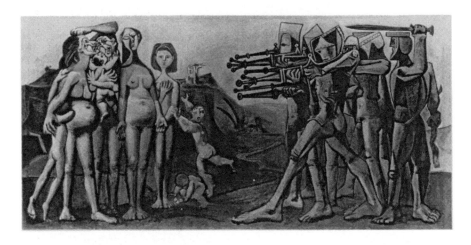

Fig. 3. Pablo Picasso, *Massacre in Korea* (1951, Musée Picasso, Paris).
Coutesy, Art Resource, New York. The works of Pablo Picasso ©1996
S.P.A.D.E.M., Paris/A.R.S., New York.

Fig. 4. Francisco de Goya, *Third of May* (1808, Museo del Prado, Madrid). Courtesy, Alinari / Art Resource, New York.

Fig. 5. Pablo Picasso, *Rape of the Sabine Women* (1963, Museum of Fine Arts, Boston). Oil on canvas, 195.4 × 131.0 cm (76⅞ × 51⅝ in.). Courtesy, Museum of Fine Arts, Boston. Julia Cheney Edwards Collection, Tompkins Collection, and Fanny P. Mason Fund in Memory of Alice Thevin [#64.709]. The works of Pablo Picasso ©1996 S.P.A.D.E.M., Paris/A.R.S., New York.

Fig. 6. Euxitheos (signed as potter) and Euphronios (signed as painter), *Death of Sarpedon*, Side A of calyx krater (c. 515, The Metropolitan Museum of Art, New York). Red-figured Attic vase, 18 in. high and 21¹¹⁄₁₆ in. diameter. Courtesy of The Metropolitan Museum of Art, New York. Purchase, Bequest of Joseph H. Durkee, Gift of Darius Ogden Mills and Gift of C. Ruxton Love, by exchange, 1972 [#1972.11.10]. All rights reserved, The Metropolitan Museum of Art [#1972.11.10].

Fig. 7. Pablo Picasso, *Minotauromachy* (*La Minotauromachie*), state seven (March 23, 1935) (New York: The Museum of Modern Art, New York). Etching and engraving on copper plate, printed in black, plate: 19½ × 27⅜ in. (49.6 × 69.6 cm). The Museum of Modern Art, New York. Abby Aldrich Rockefeller Fund. Photograph ©1996 The Museum of Modern Art, New York. The works of Pablo Picasso ©1996 S.P.A.D.E.M., Paris/A.R.S., New York.

Fig. 8. Pablo Picasso, *Le Taureau* (1945, Museum of Fine Arts, Boston). Lithograph, third state, 11⅜ × 16⅛ in. Courtesy, Museum of Fine Arts, Boston. Lee M. Friedman Fund [#1970.272]. The works of Pablo Picasso ©1996 S.P.A.D.E.M., Paris/A.R.S., New York.

image of voluntary sacrificial death. Without doubt, Picasso wove together these three major myths and two images in the *Guernica*—all, of course, through the figure of the male hero.

Picasso was familiar with artistic depictions of the classical hero in battle such as seen in Greco-Roman art including sarcophagi, temple pediments, and terra-cotta potteries. In many of these carved depictions on the sarcophagi or temple pediments, there is an overall composition of intersecting triangles within a rectangular frame. In both the relationship of forms and the compositional structure, Picasso was also aware of the classical iconography of the lamentation for the dead warrior and the repetition of the iconography of the horse and rider that were typical of terra-cotta potteries such as *Death of Sarpedon* (c. 515, The Metropolitan Museum of Art, New York)(fig. 6). More importantly, he was cognizant of the Greek visual and mythic tradition of the glory and honor of war, especially when the goddess Athena led the warriors into battle. The sculptural group from the west pediment of the Temple of Aphaia in Agina (fourth century B.C.E., Glyptothek, Munich) may prove crucial to an iconographic analysis of Picasso's *Guernica*. First, this group, a fragment of a larger whole, depicts one of the battles of the Trojan War—which had extraordinary influence on Mediterranean consciousness. Second, the heroes are exactly that—heroic and glorious—for this is a visual glorification of war, of the warrior's courage entering into battle, of the honor of war. Third, both this fragment and the whole image from the temple pediment are, of course, arranged in terms of pyramidal composition. Finally and accidently, these sculptures have been bleached white by the sun thereby raising our visual consciousness to a different level than the original images, which would have been vividly colored.

Guernica, of course, shares a visual and thematic history with these types of classical Greco-Roman art. There are common motifs such as the horse and rider, the horizontal and languid pose of the dead, the active posture of the male hero; such images, however, are fundamentally about the honor and glory of war, at least in Picasso's reading of them. Another common denominator between Picasso's paintings and Greco-Roman art is the pyramidal composition within a rectangular frame, and, with the temple sculptures, the common visual denominator of singular dependence on the simplicity of white. Yet the temple sculptures may have been bleached white, while Picasso's *Guernica* is intentionally black and white. The artist's selection of black and white instead of vivid or even muted colors for *Guernica* is an important element in the painting's powerful and enduring hold on its viewer's psyche.

Color makes an enormous difference, as evidenced by a comparison of Picasso's *Crucifixion* (1930, Musée Picasso, Paris) represented in black-and-white and in full color. Color is the painter's most powerful tool. Color sets the tone, the mood, the atmosphere, while highlighting some objects and hiding others. Color is provocative and evocative. For exactly those reasons, Picasso himself advised, "Color weakens."[17] Color takes away from our concentration on the composition and form of a painting by emphasizing our emotive response. Composition and form relate to our intellect. Picasso purposely chose to paint *Guernica* in black and white. In fact, he even stated that only in *Guernica* was "there a deliberate appeal to people, a deliberate sense of propaganda."[18] In restricting himself to black and white, Picasso also "played" with the then-common acceptance of photography, in reporting the news, of the Spanish Civil War.

So it seems that he has appropriated a series of recognizable elements and characteristics including contemporary photojournalism to communicate his message. It is not that simple, however—neither for Picasso nor for us. Clearly, he has taken traditional motifs and modes of visual imaging, but they are not represented or related in a traditional way. Rather, he has reordered the universe by breaking down the recognizable and forcing us to look at what he has done.

First, he has sought to intertwine the three mythological motifs of noble (read *heroic*) sacrificial death into one nontraditionally imagined—that is, abstract and nonrepresentational—traditional image. A favorite theme of Picasso, the *Minotaur* (1933: Museum of Fine Arts, Boston), appears and disappears throughout his work. Of course, the minotaur series of the 1930s that preceded *Guernica* was as much in response to the need for cover designs for *Le Minotaure* as to Picasso's fundamental fascination with his half-male, half-animal creature. In *Minotauromachy* (*La Minotauromachie*) (1935, The Museum of Modern Art, New York) (fig. 7), there are several motifs including the crushed horse, the young girl with upraised arm holding a light, and figures emerging from and disappearing into upper-story openings, which he would depict in *Guernica*. In *Minotaur and Dead Mare before a Grotto* (1936: Musée Picasso, Paris) (fig. 8), Picasso's introduction of colors, however muted, changes our experience of the minotaur who here explicitly relates to sacrificial death—if not as the sacrifice himself than as the sacrificer.

The image of the bull, whether fully or partially animal, obsessed Picasso. Single drawings of *Le Taureau* (1945, Museum of Fine Arts, Boston) (fig. 8) relate visually to both the minotaur series and to that second mythological motif of the Spanish national ritual—the bullfight. In *Corrida: The Death of the Torero* (1933, Musée Picasso, Paris) (fig. 9), there is once again the battle between the bull and the horse and rider. In this case, however, the rider loses. The sacrificial death is that of the toreador, not the bull. The ambiguity of the identity of the sacrifice is, of course, part of the fascination of this ritual for the audience.

As both a western European artist and a Roman Catholic, Picasso was familiar with the Christian myth of the sacrificial death of Jesus Christ.[19] The artist was, naturally, familiar with the tortured crucifixion and lamentation images found in traditional Spanish art such as those by Vélasquez and Zurbarán. In my study of Mathias Grünewald's influence on Picasso, I have noted that the iconography of the crucifixion haunted Picasso.[20] In fact, Picasso himself said, "There is no greater theme than the crucifixion exactly because it's been done for more than a thousand years millions of times."[21] The latter part of his sentence is extremely important—"exactly because it's been done for more than a thousand years millions of times." Thus, the ritual character of the repeated iconography of the crucifixion of Jesus Christ and the challenge to create an image of that crucifixion that would garner the attention of the audience. This was in fact Picasso's own challenge—to create images, no matter how banal or meretricious, that somehow through his reconfiguration of objects and human bodies stunned the viewer into seeing the world "as if for the first time."[22]

So I can suggest that in the development of *Guernica*, Picasso was dependent upon a series of traditional motifs and myths that somehow came together in a new way in his painting. For example, the painter had been awed by the exhibition at the Bibliothèque Nationale of eleventh-century illuminated manuscripts such as *The Flood, Apocalypse of Saint-Sever* [Ms. lat. 8878, fol. 85 recto] (11th century, Bibliothèque Nationale, Paris) (fig. 10), just before the bombing of Guernica. A survey of his oeuvre attests to his obsession with death imagery, as evidenced by his *Le Pichet Noir et la Tête de Mort* (1945, Museum of Fine Arts, Boston) (fig. 11), and his careful study of the traditional iconography

Fig. 9. Pablo Picasso, *Corrida: Death of the Torero* (1933, Musée Picasso, Paris). Courtesy, Giraudon / Art Resource, New York. The works of Pablo Picasso ©1996 S.P.A.D.E.M., Paris/A.R.S., New York.

Fig. 10. *The Flood, Apocalypse of Saint-Sever* [Ms.lat. 8878, fol. 85 recto] (11th century: Bibliothéque Nationale, Paris). Courtesy, Foto Marburg / Art Resource, New York.

Fig. 11. Pablo Picasso, *Le Pichet Noir et la Tête de Mort* (1945: Museum of Fine Arts, Boston). Lithograph, 12¾ × 17⅜ in. Courtesy, Museum of Fine Arts, Boston. Gift of Mrs. Frederick B. Deknatel [#1975.384]. The works of Pablo Picasso ©1996 S.P.A.D.E.M., Paris/ A.R.S., New York.

of death in western Christian art.[23] At least three years before the bombing and the painting of *Guernica*, Picasso was influenced by Grünewald's *Isenheim Altarpiece* (1515, Musée d'Unterlinden, Colmar) (fig. 12), particularly the central panel of the crucifixion.[24] In this most haptic presentation of the Christian theology of sacrificial death in western art, Picasso found particular empathy in the expressive power of human gesticulation.[25] He was moved by the black-and-white photographs Christian Zervos took of the *Isenheim Altarpiece* and later reproduced in a special issue of the *Editions "Cahiers d'Art"* (fig. 13) dedicated to Paul Eluard and Pablo Picasso. In my iconographic study of the visual relationship between *Guernica* and the *Isenheim Altarpiece*, I have noted how Picasso became obsessed with the figure of the lamenting Magdalene from Grünewald's polytych (fig. 14) and with the fundamental hapticity of the female body—two characteristic factors that would also play an important role in the development

Fig. 12. Mathias Grünewald, *The Isenheim Altarpiece* (closed showing *The Crucifixion*) (1515, Musée d'Unterlinden, Colmar). Courtesy, Giraudon / Art Resource, New York.

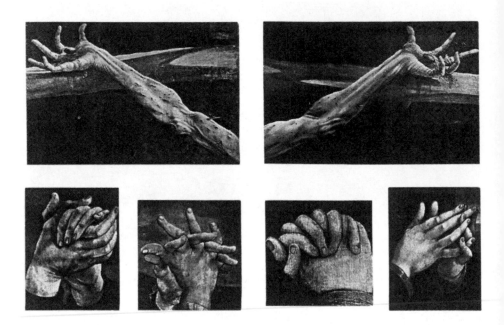

Fig. 13. Christian Zervos, pages 5 + 6 from *Mathias Grünewald: Le Retable d'Isenheim* (1937), special issue of *Cahiers d'Art*. Original photography by Christian Zervos. Photograph by David Hagen. Courtesy, *Cahiers d'Art*, Paris.

Fig. 14. Mathias Grünewald, *Mary Magdalene* detail from *The Isenheim Altarpiece* (1515, Musée d'Unterlinden, Colmar). Courtesy, Foto Marburg / Art Resource, New York.

Fig. 15. Pablo Picasso, *Woman Crying*, study for *Guernica* (1937, Centro de Arte Reina Sofia, Madrid). Courtesy, Giraudon / Art Resource, New York. The works of Pablo Picasso ©1996 S.P.A.D.E.M., Paris/ A.R.S., New York.

of *Guernica* and the later paintings such as *Woman Crying* (1937, Centro de Arte Reina Sofia, Paris) (fig. 15) that emerged from *Guernica*.[26]

Guernica, then, is a composite of mythological motifs and visual imagistic themes found throughout Picasso's oeuvre that are brought together into this particular canvas in a unique and singular way. He fuses the honor of war, the glory of the warrior, voluntary sacrificial death, and lamentation with his own Spanish male ambiguity toward Roman Catholicism. He builds upon artistic, mythological, and theological traditions. He breaks down the recognizable and reorganizes it in a new way. Picasso himself described the act of painting: "When you begin a picture, you often make some pretty discoveries. You must be on your guard against these. Destroy the thing, do it over several times. In each destroying of a beautiful discovery, the artist does not really suppress it, but rather transforms it, condenses it, makes it more substantial."[27] Like Eliade's description of the New Year rituals and my proposed methodology of mythic iconoclasm, Picasso understands that "one cannot 'repair' the world; one must annihilate it in order to re-create it."[28] A fundamental element to Picasso's mythic iconoclasm was societal as well as artistic—that is, the early twentieth-century artistic world of Paris, which nurtured this exiled artist's sense of vision.

Picasso moved to Paris at the early part of the century. Like other artists, writers, and philosophers living there, he became enamored of "le primitif"—especially of the power of so-called primitive art and ritual.[29] The opening of the Musée de l'Homme and the 1906 retrospective exhibition of the work of Paul Gauguin were important catalysts in the development not only of cubism but of modernism, Picasso being affiliated with both artistic movements. The modernists, even more so than the cubists, saw their roles as "artistes" as analogous to that of the shamans of so-called primitive religions. Like the shamans, they transformed objects, communicated with the sacred and had power—especially magical and sexual power. In his *Les Demoiselles d'Avignon* (1907, The Museum of Modern Art, New York) (fig. 16), we now see thanks to Leo Steinberg and William Rubin, Picasso's fascination with "le primitif," with sexuality, with power.[30] As a shaman, this artist has transformed the world he knew by breaking down traditional concepts of mass and volume, figure-ground relation, and form, and recreated a new world to shock us into a new way of seeing—an initiation, if you will, into the modern world.

Fig. 16. Pablo Picasso, *Les Demoiselles d'Avignon* (1907, The Museum of Modern Art, New York). Oil on canvas, 8 ft. × 7 ft. 8 in. (243.9 × 233.7 cm.). The Museum of Modern Art. Acquired through the Lillie P. Bliss Bequest. Photograph ©1996 The Museum of Modern Art, New York. The works of Pablo Picasso ©1996 S.P.A.D.E.M., Paris/A.R.S., New York.

What has Picasso recreated in *Guernica*? And what if anything has he shocked us into seeing? Perhaps Picasso's own response to a query as to whether art should be abstract offers the beginning of his answer: "No. Unaffected, simple, direct. It is like a bridge. What would be the best bridge? Well, the one which could be reduced to a thread, a line, without anything left over; which fulfilled strictly its function of uniting two separated distances."[31] The separated distances are not simply the twentieth-century world of *Guernica* and the classical world of the Trojan War but the totally different experiences of war they represent. For Picasso, Guernica signified neither the honor of the warrior nor the Christian theology of sacrificial death of Jesus Christ nor even the universal human experience of lamentation, although all those motifs were depicted in his *Guernica*. Rather, both the event and the painting signified the end to voluntary sacrificial death and began the "brutality and darkness"—Picasso's own terms for the bull in *Guernica*—of involuntary sacrificial death. This is a war with *no* honor. This is a war that needs a new mythology. Therefore, this is a war that can only be depicted in black and white— the visual equivalent of Eliade's *coincidentia oppositorum*.

In his visualization of the haptic agony of the destruction of the Basque town of Guernica, Picasso resorted to a retrieval of traditional visual connectors to classical mythology and Christian theology on the theme of sacrificial death and lamentation. Both the images that Picasso selected and his process of selection argue for mythic iconoclasm as an appropriate mode of interpretation and for the visual image as an appropriate vehicle for the establishment of modern mythic consciousness.

This Eliadean reading of *Guernica* as mythic iconoclasm has also raised larger interpretive issues of the relationship between the image and the word, iconoclasm as a visual mode of reinterpretation of myth, secular images as visual camouflages of the sacred, and art as ritual.[32] It may be a correct assumption in the history of religions that each religious tradition must make a decision between image and word. At the popular level of interpretation, it appears that western Christianity chose the word over the image. Yet I would argue that the visual image plays a primary role throughout the history of western Christianity. Even into the art of Picasso the visual persistence of crucifixion iconography and its intrinsic meaning plays a powerful—if not, primordial— role. This present study of Picasso's *Guernica* as a visualization of his so-called Secular-Century's fundamental myths clearly provides an example of the ritual dimensions of art for both the artist and the perceiver. The ostensible secular imagery present in *Guernica* reveals the latent (or camouflaged) visual presence of the sacred and its retrieval through references to both the classical and Christian traditions.[33] In this reconfiguration of the meaning of iconoclasm, I can suggest that it is an appropriate artistic mode for the retrieval and reinterpretation of a culture's fundamental mythology.

As a final word on my premise of the visual as the primal religious modality since *homo religiosus* is *homo aestheticus*, perhaps Picasso, as director of the Prado Museum himself said it best in his telephoned statement to the American Artists' Conference in 1937 following the bombing of Guernica. "It is my wish at this time to remind you that I have always believed, and still believe, that artists who live and work with spiritual values cannot and should not remain indifferent to a conflict in which the highest values of humanity and civilization are at stake."[34]

Notes

This essay was originally prepared for presentation at the History of Religions session, "The Problem of Myth in a Post-Eliadean Age" at the 1991 Annual Meeting of the American Academy of Religion. I am grateful to Laurie L. Patton who as chair of that session invited me to participate and who as co-editor of this volume supported a revision of my presentation for publication.

1. The *Guernica* bibliography is endless both in number of books, scholarly monographs, and articles and in the continuing interest in publication of them. The basic *Guernica* texts include Arnheim, *Genesis of a Painting*; Blunt, *Picasso's Guernica*; Chipp, *Picasso's Guernica*; Oppler, ed., *Picasso's Guernica*; Penrose, *Picasso*; and Rubin, ed. *Pablo Picasso*.
2. Read, "Guernica"; Tillich, "Existentialist Aspects of Modern Art" (1956), collected in his *On Art and Architechture*, 95; Campbell, *Masks of the Gods*, 4: 669. A favorite visual reference for Tillich, *Guernica* was also discussed by him in the same volume, in "The Demoniac in Art," 110 (unpub. 1956 lecture); "Protestantism and Artistic Style," 119, 124 (1957); "Contemporary Visual Arts," 136 (unpub. lecture n.d.); "Religious Dimensions of Contemporary Art," 179 (unpub. lecture n.d.); and "Theology and Architecture," (1955), 191.
3. For example, see the critiques in any of the following: Dudley, *Religion on Trial*; J. Z. Smith, *Imagining Religion*; Strenski, "Mircea Eliade"; Cave, *Mircea Eliade's Vision*, 79–80.
4. Strenski, *Four Theories*.
5. For a more in-depth discussion of Eliade's interpretation of the artist and the creative process than space can permit, see either my introductory essay, "Mircea Eliade," xi–xxi, esp. xi–xvi; or my "To Create a New Universe," 408–19.
6. Tracy, *Analogical Imagination*, 207.
7. Eliade, "Sacred in the Secular World," 110–11. Note that in this essay in

which Eliade provides his most in-depth analysis of Picasso's *Guernica* (as quoted here), the historian of religions indicates his dependence upon "Tillich and other specialists of culture" who enabled him "to discover the sacred character of the painting" (110–11).

8. Eliade, "Sacred and the Modern Artist," in *Symbolism, The Sacred, and the Arts,* 83; 1965 English translation of a 1964 French text. Eliade, "Crisis and Renewal," in *Quest,* 65–66.

9. Eliade, "Crisis and Renewal," 65.

10. Eliade, "Survivals and Camouflages" (1963), in *Symbolism, The Sacred, and the Arts,* 47–48.

11. For a survey of the history and varied meanings of "iconoclasm" in the art of world religions, see my "Iconoclasm."

12. Eliade, "Sacred and the Modern Artist," 83.

13. For both my initial explication (and elaboration) of the proposed methodology of mythic iconoclasm, as well as a critique of Eliade's singular application of it to modern art, see my "To Create a New Universe," esp. 414.

14. Eliade, "Eugene Ionesco and 'The Nostalgia for Paradise'" (1971), 164–70, esp. 166.

15. Many leading artists of all genres including Constantin Brancusi, Eugene Ionesco, and Isamu Noguchi, and Eliade himself serve as prime examples of this specialized category of the "nostalgia for paradise."

16. Whether Picasso's "nostalgia for paradise" can be viewed as having a positive or negative effect upon his art is open to debate. For a recent discussion of this "nostalgia for" the lost "paradise" of Picasso's childhood and its iconographic influence on his art, especially *Guernica,* see Miller, "Pablo Picasso," 3–18.

17. Ashton, *Picasso on Art,* 89.

18. Ibid., 140. From the now famous interview of Picasso in 1945 by American artist and soldier Jerome Seckler.

19. The term *western* is put in lowercase throughout this article. Although it is technically incorrect, I interpret it as a descriptive adjective that is beyond a geographic referent. In a similar situation, I would also lowercase the term *eastern* for the same reason.

20. See my "Essence of Agony," 31–48.

21. Ashton, *Picasso on Art,* 35.

22. Eliade, "Crisis and Renewal," 65.

23. For Picasso's fascination with death imagery, see Darr, "Images of Eros and Thanatos," 338–46. For the most recent interpretation of Picasso's knowledge of and representations of the traditional iconography of death in western Christian art, see Chipp, *Picasso's Guernica,* and my "Essence of Agony."

24. See my "Essence of Agony."

25. In my use of the term *haptic* throughout this essay, I have been influenced by Danz, *Personal Revolution and Picasso,* see esp. 6. Danz's retrieval of *hapticity* to signify the ability to express deeply felt and intuited emotional responses through the human body and gesticulation precedes the modern psychology of "body language." This understanding of the communication of ideas and feelings through the human body and gesticulation may be one of the fundamental powers of the arts. For the importance of gesticulation in the visual arts, see Barasch, *Giotto.* See also my "Essence of Agony."

26. See my "Essence of Agony."

27. Ashton, *Picasso on Art,* 9.

28. Eliade, "Sacred and the Modern Artist," 84.

29. In this use of the term *primitive,* I am being attentive to the actual language of artists like Picasso. Their use of the term reflects a particular moment in cultural (and intellectual) history and was in no way perceived or in-

tended as pejorative: rather, for them the term *primitive* intended an artistic and cultural superiority to what they perceived as the fragmentation of the modern world.
30. Steinberg, "Philosophical Brothel," 7–74; Rubin, "Picasso," 241–343.
31. Ashton, *Picasso on Art*, 65.
32. For a survey of the history and varied possibilities of art in world religions, see my "Religion and Art."
33. For an analysis of the latent (or camouflaged) sacred imagery in *Guernica* strictly in terms of Christian iconography, see my "The Essence of Agony."
34. Ashton, *Picasso on Art*, 145.

Works Cited

Apostolos-Cappadona, Diane. "To Create a New Universe: Mircea Eliade on Modern Art." *Cross Currents* 33 (1982/83): 408–19.

———. "The Essence of Agony: Grünewald's Influence on Picasso." *Artibus et Historiae* 26, no. 13 (1992): 31–48.

———. "Iconoclasm." *The Dictionary of Art.*

———. "Mircea Eliade: The Scholar as Artist, Critic, and Poet." In Mircea Eliade, *Symbolism, The Sacred, and the Arts*, edited by Diane Apostolos-Cappadona. New York: Continuum Publishing, 1992, xi–xxi.

———. "The Postmodern Presence of the Sacred: An Eliadean Reading of Postmodernist Art." *Atlanta Art Papers* 10, no. 6, (1986): 21–23.

———. "Religion and Art." *The Dictionary of Art.*

Arnheim, Rudolf. *The Genesis of a Painting: Picasso's Guernica.* Berkeley: University of California Press, 1973.

Ashton, Dore. *Picasso on Art: A Selection of Views.* New York: Viking Press, 1972.

Barasch, Moshe. *Giotto and the Language of Gesture.* New York: Cambridge University Press, 1988.

Blunt, Anthony. *Picasso's Guernica.* New York: Oxford University Press, 1969.

Bois, Yve-Alain. "Painting as Trauma." *Art in America* 76 (1988): 130–41.

Bozo, Dominique, Martin Friedman, Robert Rosenblum, and Roland Penrose. *Picasso from the Musée Picasso, Paris.* Exhibition catalogue. Minneapolis: Walker Art Center, 1980.

Breton, André. *Surrealism and Painting.* Translated by Simon Watson Taylor. New York: Harper and Row, 1972.

Campbell, Joseph. *The Masks of the Gods.* Vol. 4, *Creative Mythology.* New York: Penguin Books, 1983.

Cantelupe, Eugene B. "Picasso's *Guernica.*" *Art Journal* 31, no. 1, (1971): 18–21.

Cave, David. *Mircea Eliade's Vision for a New Humanism.* New York: Oxford University Press, 1993.

Chipp, Heschel. *Picasso's Guernica.* Berkeley: University of California Press, 1988.

Daix, Pierre. "Dread, Desire, and the Demoiselles." *Artnews* 87 (1988): 133–37, 172–73.

Danz, Louis. *Personal Revolution and Picasso.* New York: Longmans, Green, 1941.

Darr, William. "Images of Eros and Thanatos in Picasso's *Guernica.*" *Art Journal* 25 (1966): 338–46.

The Dictionary of Art. Macmillan. Forthcoming 1996.

Dillenberger, Jane. "Picasso's Transformations of Sacred Art." In her *Image and Spirit in Sacred and Secular Art,* edited by Diane Apostolos-Cappadona. New York: Crossroad Publishing, 1990, 166–89.

Dudley, Guilford, III. *Religion on Trial: Mircea Eliade and His Critics.* Philadelphia: Temple University Press, 1977.

Eliade, Mircea. *Autobiography, I: 1907–1937, Journey East, Journey West.* Translated by MacLinscott Ricketts. San Francisco: Harper and Row, 1981.

———. *Myth and Reality.* Translated by Willard R. Trask. New York: Harper and Row, 1964.

———. *No Souvenirs, Journal, 1957–1969.* Translated by Fred H. Johnson, Jr. New York: Harper and Row, 1977.

———. "The Sacred in the Secular World." *Cultural Hermeneutics* I (1973): 101–13.

———. *Symbolism, The Sacred, and the Arts.* Edited by Diane Apostolos-Cappadona. New York: Continuum Publishing, 1992.

———. *The Quest.* Chicago: University of Chicago Press, 1969.

Elsen, Albert. *Purposes of Art.* New York: Holt, Rinehart, and Winston, 1981.

Gottlieb, Carla. "The Meaning of Bull and Horse in *Guernica.*" *Art Journal* 24. (1964–65): 106–12.

Hlavachek, Lubos. "K Obsahovému Vykldu Picassova Obrazu *Guernica.*" *Umeni* 29 (1981): 543–66.

Inglott, Peter Serracino. "Picasso e il Crocifisso." *Arte Cristiana* 61 (1973): 121–28.

Kaufmann, Ruth. "Picasso's Crucifixion of 1930." *Burlington Magazine* 111 (1969): 553–61.

Miller, Alice. "Pablo Picasso: The Earthquake in Malaga and the Painter's Eye of a Child." In her *The Untouched Key.* New York: Doubleday, 1990, 3–18.

Oppler, Ellen C., ed. *Picasso's Guernica.* New York: W. W. Norton, 1988.

Penrose, Roland. *Picasso: His Life and Work.* New York: Harper and Row, 1973.

Penrose, Roland, John Golding, and Dominique Bozo. *Picasso's Picassos.* Exhibition catalogue. London: Arts Council of Great Britain, 1981.

Proweller, William. "Picasso's *Guernica:* A Study in Visual Metaphor." *Art Journal* 30 (1971): 240–48.

Read, Herbert. "Guernica: A Modern Calvary." *London Bulletin* 6 (1938): 6.

Rosenblum, Robert. "The Fatal Women of Picasso and DeKooning." *Artnews* 84, no. 8 (1985) 98–103.

Rubin, William, ed. *Pablo Picasso: A Retrospective.* Exhibition catalogue. New York: The Museum of Modern Art, 1980.

———. "Picasso." In *Primitivism in Modern Art,* edited by William Rubin. Exhibition catalogue. Vol. 1. New York: The Museum of Modern Art, 1984.

Russell, Frank D. *Picasso's Guernica: The Labyrinth of Narrative and Vision.* London: Thames and Hudson, 1980.

Smith, Jonathan Z. *Imagining Religion.* Chicago: University of Chicago Press, 1978.

Steinberg, Leo. "The Philosophical Brothel." *October* 44 (1988): 7–74. Rev. in *Art News* 71, nos. 9 and 10 (1972).

Strenski, Ivan. *Four Theories of Myth in the Twentieth Century.* Iowa City: University of Iowa Press, 1987.

———. "Mircea Eliade: Some Theoretical Problems." In *The Theory of Myth: Six Studies,* edited by Adrian Cunningham. London: Sheed and Ward, 1973.

Tillich, Paul. *On Art and Architecture.* Edited by John and Jane Dillenberger. New York: Crossroad Publishing, 1987.

Tracy, David. *The Analogical Imagination.* New York: Crossroad Publishing, 1981.

Wescher, Paul. "Picasso's *Guernica* and the Exchangeability of the Picture Parts." *Art Quarterly* 18 (1955): 341–50.

MARC MICHAEL EPSTEIN

HARNESSING THE DRAGON: A MYTHOS TRANSFORMED IN MEDIEVAL JEWISH LITERATURE AND ART

"Why is [the word *dragons* in Genesis 1:21] written *HaTani-nim* [plural] and not *HaTanin* [singular, since the Leviathan was reputed to have no mate]?—Lest one should say, 'It is a god,' as it says [Job 41:25].' When he raises himself up the mighty are afraid.'" *"The serpent corresponds to God."*

—R. Yehudah HeHasid

"'T'li' is a name for the *tanin,* and it is a symbol of the world of the intellect, because by this name are known those hidden things which are impossible to perceive with the senses."

—R. Yehudah HaLevi

Sylvain Lévi, the Anthologizers, and Jewish Mythophobia

Sylvain Lévi's Alsatian-Jewish identity may well have had a good deal to do with his distaste for the ritual-hating mythophilia that became a sine qua non of the Aryanist program, as Ivan Strenski argues in his essay in this volume. Contemporary Jewish scholars of Judaism avoided the term *myth,* in part, no doubt because they perceived in it a similar, often anti-Semitic, mythophilia. But more importantly, the idea of *myth* did not fit their post-Enlightenment conception of what Judaism should be. Scholars across the spectrum of observance strove to represent Judaism in the best and most universally honorable light. Liberal reformers and rationalist neoorthodox scholars alike believed that the essence of Judaism should be rational, not mythical or mystical. Most did not even acknowledge that such an entity as Jewish myth existed. Much like contemporary apologists for Christianity, they defensively contended that Judaism needed to cut itself free from the burdensome legacy of stultifying legalism and the ridiculous fantasies that were embarrassingly present in rabbinic literature. This would require a return to the pristine Hebrew Scriptures, which were deemed to represent the triumph of rational monotheism over the fearful and etiological world of pagan myth. It was a glorious moment for these self-perceived inheritors of the legacy of the Deuteronomist. It was as if once again, as in the time of Josiah, a long-sequestered book, this one inscribed *Ethical Monotheism*, had been rediscovered in the Temple, and with it all the accreted substrata of superstition—and myth— would be wiped away forever. God had triumphed over "the gods"; *sola Scriptura* was the byword of the moment. As for Scriptura herself, the divine authorship of the literal text having been dispensed with, the learned vied for the privilege of revealing that the uncomfortable and sometimes disconcerting mythic elements she bore in her very bosom were (to everyone's great relief) borrowed from the ancient Near East and, like the contemporary Yiddish edition of Shakespeare, "translated and improved."

Thus, scholars characterized the blatantly anthropomorphizing, richly iconic, and in fact deeply mythic texts they engaged as "legends," as folkloric elements, or as the old wives' tales of the rabbis. The great anthologists Jellinek, Wertheimer, Bialik, Ravnitsky, Eisenstein, and Ginzberg stripped the "legends" from the "legal material" in which they are often intimately intertwined in rabbinic texts, anthologizing them out of context. Having titrated the *legends*, they proceeded to philologically deconstruct or folkloristically motif-index them, depending on their inclinations. This entire process served to downplay the presence of truly mythic motifs found in rabbinic literature. The creators of the great anthologies evinced a philology-and-folklore–centered mythophobia as virulent as the Aryanists' ritual-hating mythophilia. Thus, the *legends of the Jews* came to be represented as existing apart from the central and pure monotheistic rationalism of the Jews, which they believed always to have been the essence of Judaism.

Unlike Lévi, who was a Sanskritist and later a scholar of Buddhism, the anthologizers of rabbinic legend could not respond to the mythophilic threat with a reassertion of the power of ritual. Lévi had the requisite distance for such a response. He had the luxury of being able to appreciate the ritual *sitz am leben* of "other people's myths," without the necessity of engaging its centrality in understanding the myths of his own people. Post-Enlightenment Jewish scholars working on Jewish topics could not reassert the power of ritual, since with the same zeal as they held fast to the ideal of an aniconic Judaism, the reformers were simultaneously battling what they perceived as the blind subservience of the ignorant Jewish masses to empty and outmoded ritual, and the neoorthodox were attempting to fit ritual into a dignified and rational framework. The time was not yet ripe for a reclamation of Jewish ritual as religiously empowering and the celebration of its intimate relationship with myth. That has only occurred among the inheritors of Gershom Scholem in the present generation of scholars, and mainly in the context of Kabbalah.

But Kabbalah is an obvious, and in some sense a relatively safe, area in which to acknowledge the existence of myth. Even before Scholem, its mythic nature was appreciated. Scholem's great contribution, in fact, was to demonstrate that Kabbalah was marginalized by Wissenschaft scholars precisely because it was so uncomfortably mythic in content. What is to be done about the fact that even in a post-ritual-phobic, Kabbalaphilic age, the position that Judaism is myth free has persevered, and done so considerably longer in the history of Jewish thought than it has almost anywhere else? Why is myth still a theologically dirty word for Jews?

It is time to acknowledge that not only legendary but truly mythic elements exist in, and coexist with, rabbinic culture both within and without the kabbalistic traditions. Certainly, some of those elements were what we might call "borrowings from Babylon," but when such so-called borrowings are still appearing in nineteenth-century texts and in twentieth-century oral folklore, it is time, perhaps, to notice that, origins aside, they have a life of their own and that the history of that life may be interesting and necessary to chronicle. The nineteenth-century mania for motif-indexing myths has proved difficult to overcome. The so-called Hebrew versions are still perceived as variants that add local color, while leaving unscathed the "universal core" of the myth, which is alleged to be inherently conservative and conventional. This is what makes the myth recognizable. In the case of the Hebrew versions, it is also what conveniently erases all taint of the arcane and particular. Even today, the most difficult part of gaining acceptance for an understanding of myth within Judaism and as part of the history of medieval Jewish *mentalités* is surmounting the common wisdom that "Hebrew myths" are universal gems presented in a Jewish setting, but that they have nothing particular to teach us about Jews.

What follows is an examination of the process of "harnessing myth" and turning it into a category of theological expression in Judaism. It uses as its example and central metaphor the harnessing of the dragon mythos by medieval Jews. I will examine various legends in rabbinic and medieval texts concerning dragons in which some of the rawer, riskier, more bothersome elements of the dragon mythos seem to have been maintained and transmitted. The ways in which ancient and medieval Jews attempt to "harness the dragon" in some ways directly parallel their attempts to harness myth, rather than to eradicate it, as we have observed their nineteenth-century descendants attempt to do. The theological method of the medievals, in turn, may point to certain ways in which we, as modern students of myth, ought to be carefully harnessing certain theories, rather than summarily jettisoning them. We will discern medieval Jews doing with myth, in other words, what the contributors to this volume have attempted to do with various theories of myth. We will observe them as they, in the words of the editors, "ask what they can salvage from [it] to bring forward into [their] new agendas."

I will focus inter alia upon several overlapping "harnessings," the literal image of the harnessing of the dragon in the service of God and the metaphorical implications of this image for the ways in which medieval people harnessed myth in the service of theology.

Before I do so, I want to explore two possibilities of harnessing in a theoretical framework: the possibility of harnessing certain nineteenth-century subjectivist tendencies in the service of the discourse of cultural particularism, not in a chauvinistic, but in a contextual sense, and the possibilities of harnessing Jung and Eliade, of rediscovering in particular traditions certain terms used by them in a universalizing sense.

Harnessing Subjectivist Chauvinism
and Universalist Archetypes

In the nineteenth century, the Hebrew versions of world legends
were deemed, by virtue of their translation into a "more highly
developed ethical monotheistic context," to have "improved" on
the benighted pagan versions because their moral and ethical fi-
ber content was higher. Scholars today would certainly deem this
a chauvinist and subjective value judgment. Yet there is a grain
of truth to it. Truthfully and objectively, at first glance "Hebrew
myths" do seem strikingly like universal gems presented in a Jewish setting. One can certainly find examples in Jewish lore of such
"universal motifs" as the primeval serpent or dragon or of the
world-encircling serpent or dragon, of the "cosmic serpent" or
dragon, even of the serpent or dragon who swallows the sun; but
that does not mean that they have nothing particular to teach us
about Jews. Simply because myths in Jewish sources look like
those of the surrounding culture, their underlying morals ought
not to be tacitly assumed to mirror non-Jewish versions exactly.
The biblical authors did transform myth in order to cause it to
reflect a specifically YHVHist point of view, and rabbinic culture
subsequently transformed myth as a forum for teaching Jewish
moral lessons. Thus, it would seem that we should not jettison
the nineteenth-century observation that the mythic strata are
transformed in the biblical and rabbinic tradition, but only the
chauvinistic hierarchy that their manner of presentation implies.
They were right to observe differences, but perhaps we ought not
to see them as deviations from or improvements over certain *archetypes* but merely as contextually related (and contextually revealing) variants.

The term *archetype* itself is one that needs to be harnessed. In
the light of the assumption of the essential universal nature and
merely Jewish flavor of Jewish myth, it would seem that the nascent field of the study of Jewish myth has no alternative but to
situate itself squarely in the camp of the deconstructionist and
New Historicist critics of Jung and Eliade. Such critics assert that
Jung and Eliade inherited the universalizing, motif-indexing
methodology of the nineteenth-century folkloristics and moved
it toward grander but ultimately objectionable conclusions. The
bitter fruit of this ancestral legacy, they assert, is painfully evident in the slipshod, free-associative free-for-all manifest in the
work of those who would wrest myth from the political, histori-

cal, and cultural milieus of the societies that produced it. Many seek, undoubtedly legitimately, to overthrow the Jungian conception of archetype as the Platonic form that lies beyond and dwarfs in importance the petty and particular manifestations of the myths of individual cultures, along with the expansive but ironically reductionist conclusion of such speculation—that these universal archetypes are the product of a metacultural Universal Mind. At the same time, it seems fascinating to consider that particular traditions themselves maintained concepts of archetypes in a pre-Jungian sense: primeval figures, paradigmatic creations, prototypical models. Thus, when I write of medieval texts discussing "the primordial serpent," I am literally translating a Hebrew term, *nahash hakadmoni*. One can reclaim an entire range of indigenously Jewish understandings of terms associated with primality, paradigm, and prototype, language so intimately connected with the work of Jung and Eliade that it is hard to remember how they were used before them. I would like to be able to use the term *archetype* in this internal context; hence I have coined the usage *indigenous archetype* to distinguish the idea from that of the universal Jungian archetypes.

In discussing the harnessing of the dragon, we ought to tread a sort of via media: while accepting the increasingly prevalent opinion that the idea of mythic archetypes ought no longer to be defended universally and uncritically, we should recognize nevertheless that this idea must not be eschewed summarily. Rather, we should seek such archetypes in the context of indigenous traditions, not as overarching inevitabilities but as fascinating examples of the ways in which native mythopoetic traditions order their internal world.

Harnessing the Dragon

To study the ways in which medieval Jews, building on the Talmudic and midrashic heritage, harnessed myth itself in the service of theology, transforming the near-mythic (or freshly demythologized) biblical image of the dragon in literature and art, one needs to begin with a survey of that image's development from the biblical transformations of the ancient Near Eastern dragon mythoi through the Talmudic periods, something that at first looks like conventional historical philology. But in its twists and turns this survey will reveal survivals of ancient and often disquieting elements of the dragon mythos in Judaism, specifically its signification of the tension and of the liminal arena be-

tween divine and demonic. Theologically speaking, those realms
have been noted as proximate; as we shall see, however, in terms
of Jewish textual and iconographic representation, they are more
than that; they are intermingled.

Dragons have held an almost irresistible fascination for every
human culture since the dawn of consciousness.[1] Medieval Jewish society was no exception. Dragons appear frequently in both
its literature and iconography. They have received little attention
because of the pervasive attitude that any startling, creative, or
unexpected element in the cultural production of medieval Jewry
must have originated in Christian culture and that in a Jewish
context it must serve a purely decorative or conventional function. That twentieth-century people are not used to thinking of
dragons as particularly *Jewish*, however, should not silence any
exploration of their iconographic significance in medieval Jewish
art and literature. On the contrary, we ought to examine the use
of dragons as manifestations of medieval Jewish creativity in the
realm of theology and symbolism. Representations of dragons in
art and literature are no mere survivals of a "universal mythic
consciousness," incompletely sublimated and subjugated. They
are played upon, they surface again and again, almost as if to
trouble the observer into theological self-examination. Medieval
kabbalah amplifies, reinterprets, and creatively manipulates
often-neglected symbols in the classical literature to create
indigenously medieval understandings. In the same way, medieval
Jewish authors and illuminators amplified, reinterpreted, and
creatively manipulated the ancient scriptural stratum of the
dragon mythos in accordance with the theological needs of their
indigenously medieval context.

The dragon is particularly interesting because it often seems to
serve as a metaphor for metaphysical things whose meaning is
veiled. Yehudah HaLevi, in *Sefer HaKuzari*, expresses it this way:
"The dragon is a symbol of the world of the intellect, because by
this name are known those hidden things which are impossible
to perceive with the senses."[2]

Harnessing the Dragon in the Hebrew Scriptures

Though they may point to hidden things, dragons are themselves
difficult to hide. They are conspicuous even in the Bible, where
they are the very first animals created by God in the first chapter
of Genesis, the first creation account, or the "P" source.[3] "God

said: 'Let the waters bring forth swarms of living creatures, and birds that fly above the earth across the expanse of the sky.' God created the great sea monsters (*HaTaninim HaGedolim*) and all the living creatures of every kind that creep, which the waters brought forth in swarms, and all the winged birds of every kind."[4]

All other creatures are mentioned generically by species: "the fish of the sea, the birds of the sky, the cattle . . . and all the creeping things."[5] But the dragons are identified by name; they are called *taninim*, (singular *tanin*)—dragons, or "great sea monsters." They are the only creatures that receive names before Adam is given the task of naming the animals.[6]

"P"'s conscious designation of the great dragons as the first of YHVH's creations certainly may be seen as an attempt to fashion an alternate mythology to those of the ancient Near East. The great *taninim* are undoubtedly the most impressive of the pre-Adamite creatures enumerated in Genesis. The balance of the Pentateuch, the Prophets and the Writings, paint a composite picture of the *taninim* as huge "fiery" or poisonous animals with the capacity to swallow a human being.[7] They were not coterminous with the Creator but were God's creatures, and hence never coregnant. The *tanin* frequently and fiercely conflicts with God, rising up from the Deep,[8] to attack the very Throne of God.[9] An analogue to the *tanin* is the Leviathan, the awe-inspiring "elusive" or "twisting serpent" mentioned in Isaiah, Job and Psalms. Like the *tanin*, its fate is ultimately to be subjugated by God, who either fights, vanquishes, or, interestingly, "sports with" it.[10] The dragon thus remains God's subject, and God's Throne, as we shall see, remains secure.

The unique, awesome, and threatening nature of the biblical sea monster made it an appropriate symbol for tyrannical human oppressors. God chose to transform Moses' staff into a *tanin* rather than into some other powerful beast because, as a figure of arrogance and power, the *tanin* was an appropriate symbol for pharaoh himself.[11] Ezekiel refers to the Egyptian pharaoh of his own time as the "mighty *tanin*, sprawling in its channels, who said, 'My Nile is my own; I made it for myself.'"[12] According to Exodus, Moses' *tanin* swallows up all the *taninim* created by the Egyptian magicians, symbolizing pharaoh's dominance over all of the lesser powers.[13] In both Exodus and Ezekiel, the *tanin* is ultimately vanquished: Moses' *tanin* is transformed back into a staff with the Name of God inscribed upon it,[14] and the *tanin* that represents pharaoh in Ezekiel is hauled up from its channels and flung into the desert.[15] This image of the vanquishing of the *tanin* finds parallels in other biblical texts and will prove crucial to an understanding of the dragon as a liminal symbol, situated upon the ambiguous dividing line between the divine and the demonic.[16]

The "J" source, or second creation account, in Genesis 2, mirrors the "P" source in introducing a prototypical reptilian figure.[17] The first animal "J" mentions by name is the *nahash*, the "primordial serpent" of the Garden of Eden (a dragonlike creature, as we shall see).[18] Like "P"s *taninim*, it is the only animal singled out for individual mention in this account. In fact, the primordial serpent is the first creature to which Scripture devotes a narrative. The image of the serpent as a crafty, evil tempter presented in that narrative, and its correlation with the *tanin*, figure prominently in the development of the image of the dragon.

Nahash is also the generic term for serpent in the Bible, but perhaps thanks to the powerful image of the serpent limned in Genesis 2, the *nahash* often attains dragonlike proportions and powers. But the interchangeability of the terms *nahash* and *tanin* is already clearly evident in Exodus, where on one occasion Moses' staff changes into a *tanin*, as I mentioned, but on another, into a *nahash*. Usually used in a metaphorical or natural historical context,[19] the very term *nahash* ("hissing" or "whispering") carries with it connotations of craftiness, poisonousness, and punishment.[20]

Harnessing the Dragon in Rabbinic Literature

Dragons are quite prominent in rabbinic literature, and the attitude of tannaitic and amoraic culture toward these creatures directly informs their manifestations in medieval texts and iconography. In the legends of the Talmud and in the midrashim both the serpent and the dragon embark upon their odyssey through the history of Jewish ideas as indigenous archetypes of evil and power.[21] In these sources, as in Exodus, the terms *nahash* and *tanin* are often interchangeable: a Talmudic source may refer to a *tanin*, and its midrashic retelling may refer to a *nahash* or vice-versa.[22] This interchangeability is used to bolster and corroborate the hints found in the biblical sources that the serpent is a reduced dragon.

The primordial serpent is cursed after it tempts Adam and Eve: "On your belly you shall crawl," God tells it, "and dirt shall you eat."[23] The fact that the serpent seems not always to have been a crawling beast leads the rabbis to conjecture that originally it "stood out distinguished and erect like a reed, and had legs . . . it was the size of a camel."[24] The midrashim elaborate upon the manner in which, after its crime, the serpent is brought to trial by God, and is punished with the loss of its legs and its stature.[25] Because the serpent "set its eyes on that which was not proper for it—sought what it was not granted," observes the Talmud, "what it possessed was taken away from it."[26] But the serpent's crime was not simple deception of Adam. It sought to have sexual relations with Eve, and, thus cuckolding Adam, to usurp his place as God's image and representative on earth.[27] This attempt to assume the place of Adam is, in effect, an attempt to usurp the place of God.[28]

The threat to Adam's supremacy posed by the serpent of the Garden of Eden in rabbinic legends amplifying the "J" account is implicitly paralleled by the threat to God's supremacy posed by the *tanin* in those elaborating upon the "P" account. In the latter, the *tanin* rallies the mysterious forces of "the Deep" to usurp the divine throne, and is subjugated by God.[29] Another aggadic parallel is the threat posed to God's supremacy by the fall of the unnamed angelic prince (Satanail-Lucifer), formerly the most favored in Heaven, when he becomes jealous of the first man and refuses to do homage to the "image of God." He is cast out from before the cosmic throne.[30]

The serpent of the Garden of Eden, the *Tanin*, and Satanail-Lucifer all receive similar punishments for their rebellions. They are, in each case, reduced from what they once were. The Edenic serpent was once essentially a dragon. Now it has become a mere snake. It must crawl on its belly and eat dust like a worm.[31]- Satanail-Lucifer, a prince of angels and favorite of God becomes *HaSatan*, the hinderer, God's tool and instrument. And the rabbis reduce the *tanin* by almost completely neglecting that fearsome and awful rebel of the *Urzeit* in favor of the Leviathan. The Leviathan is God's servant, but ultimately it is relegated by the rabbis to the *Endzeit*, where, though certainly a powerful beast from a human perspective, it is a divine plaything. For the amusement of the righteous who denied themselves the pleasures of the circus and of gladiatorial contests in this world, God arranges a battle between the Leviathan and its terrestrial counterpart, the monster Behemoth. The archangel Michael delivers the coup de grace, butchering both beasts for the delectation of the audience at an eschatological banquet.[32] Though the snake, the Leviathan, and Satan are each associated with wiliness, power, and cruelty, they are reductions of the Serpent, the *Tanin* and Satanail-Lucifer, which have been transformed from powerful rebels against God into servants whose power is harnessed and who do God's bidding.

Rabbinic tradition, following the lead of scripture, evinces a clear desire to vanquish and reduce the dragon, transforming it into a mere serpent or a blustering but ultimately subduable monster. Yet just as the modern-day snake retains the vestiges of the physiological infrastructure of its prehistoric legged ancestors, so does the serpent of rabbinic literature retain vestiges of the biblical dragon's tremendous and unchecked strength and power. In the rabbinic legend the serpent is often seen as an agent of fate.[33] Since it sealed the fate of human beings by being party to their fall, the serpent continues to serve as the agent of God in punishing them.[34] In a number of legends we learn that "the Divine Will is carried out through a serpent," as in the case of the Roman persecutor who is bitten by a snake as he relieves himself in a privy;[35] and that "a serpent never bites unless it is ordained."[36]

In some instances the serpent is not content merely to act as the agent of God in carrying out the fate of human beings. Indeed, it seems as if the serpent and its alter egos, the dragon and the Leviathan, begin to take on some divine characteristics themselves. For instance, the serpent seems to have tremendous power over life and death. In one source, planetary influence upon fate and "fate to be bitten by a snake" are mentioned together.[37] A snake is said to be the keeper of a miraculous stone which has dominion over life or death.[38] The Angel of Death himself is named Leviathan.[39]

In more dramatic illustrations of this phenomenon, rabbinic tradition not only attributes quasi-divine powers to the serpent, but, perhaps under the influence of or in response to Gnosticism, transforms the land-bound, dust-eating serpent into a cosmic figure. In a famous and exceedingly strange passage in Numbers, Moses is said to have made a serpent out of copper in order to remove a plague of "fiery serpents" from the Israelites in the desert.[40] He "mounted it on a standard," and all who gazed upon it were healed. The midrash understands the words *"sim oto al ness"*—"mounted it on a standard"—as "cast it up by a miracle," that is, he threw it up into the very vault of heaven, where it remained and was the determinant of the fate of the Israelites, for whosoever gazed up at it would live, and whosoever did not would die.[41] The so called *celestial* serpent, dragon, or Leviathan, is a powerful motif in rabbinic literature. The world is said to rest upon the fins of the Leviathan, or the Leviathan is seen as a serpent encircling the world.[42] A huge snake encircles the bier of a righteous person;[43] the righteous person surrounded by the snake is a microcosmic parallel to the world encompassed by the cosmic serpent, since *"zaddik yesod olam"*—"a righteous person is the foundation of the world."[44] A snake likewise encircles the machinery of Solomon's throne and by squeezing it sets it in motion.[45] This wondrous mechanical throne was a symbolic model in miniature of the universe, so the function of the snake that animates it is analogous to the function of the celestial serpent.[46]

The well-known ancient Near Eastern mythic motif of a serpent or a dragon of prodigious size becoming, in essence, the vault of heaven, forming the nexus of the sphere of the constellations, finds an echo in rabbinic sources, where it is theologically cleaned up and harnessed to the service of a monotheistic Rabbinic Judaism. In ancient Near Eastern mythology, after the battle between the god and goddess Kingu and Tiamat, the dragonlike Tiamat's upper body becomes the vault of the heavens. In rabbinic legend Behemoth and Leviathan, who are not gods or coregents but creatures, do battle, and the skin of the Leviathan forms a sparkling canopy over all the world.[47] Thus, it is not surprising that Jewish commentators, when discussing matters astronomical, saw the celestial dragon as the vault of heaven to which the signs of the zodiac are affixed. In that position it can assert its dominance over all powers in the universe, even to the extent of swallowing the sun.[48] By controlling the zodiac, as we shall see, this dragon can affect the course of fate.

Scripture itself is remarkably explicit that the serpent of copper was preserved and worshipped as a god until it was finally destroyed by King Hezekiah.[49] Some strata of rabbinic tradition have similarly few qualms about emphasizing the vestigial qualities of the snake that link it with the primordial serpent and the rebel dragons, depicting the snake as continuing its attempt to usurp the place of God as the one who determines fate. In the midrash God avers that humankind was ruled "yesterday by My will—but now by the will of the serpent."[50] The rabbis' response to this "threat to God" is not to repress such statements but to acknowledge the potential danger of the power of the serpent while attempting to limit it. The Talmud, for instance, admonishes that if one is praying and a snake winds round one's heel one should not stop the prayer but "concentrate upon one's Father in heaven."[51] Likewise, there is the assertion that "it is not the dragon (or serpent) that kills, but sin that kills."[52] It appears from the evidence in the Talmud and *midrashim* that there was indeed a conception of a cosmic serpent or dragon that controlled the fate of humankind in some unspecified way. This power was awesome, potentially impinging upon the sovereignty of God, and hence one finds statements that attempt to limit the dragon's influence. That influence is ultimately illusory and the texts emphasize the potential of each individual through the observance of the law of God to alter his or her fate.[53] Medieval texts, particularly mystical works and commentaries, attempt similarly to mitigate the power of the dragon.

Harnessing the Dragon in Medieval Jewish Texts

Shabbetai Donnolo, an Italian physician of the tenth century, commenting on *Sefer Yezirah*, a mystical text of the third century, brings the idea of the relationship between the dragon and fate into the medieval world. *Sefer Yezirah* states: "The t'li (dragon)[54] is in the universe like a king on his throne, the sphere (or cycle) is in the year like a king in his country, the heart is in a living being like a king in war."[55]

Donnolo's commentary, called *Ḥakhmoni*, describes how the heart gives moral order to the internal universe, the year gives order to time and the physical universe, and the dragon rules over the metaphysical, fated aspects of the universe such as the movements of the constellations, thus appearing to control all the other factors as well. For Donnolo and other kabbalists, the great twisted serpent is the axis upon which the fate of the universe, as determined by the constellations, is hung.[56] Some identify it with the constellation Draco.[57] The dominant paradigm of Donnolo's age depicted the heavens as comprising a celestial sphere in which the terrestrial one floated. It had a celestial equator situated directly above the terrestrial equator and a celestial Pole situated directly above the earth's North Pole. The heavens were stationary, but the sun moved through them from west to east over the course of the year. The circle traced upon the celestial sphere by the annual path of the sun as it moved through the heavens (or as moderns would express it, by the plane of the earth's orbit around the sun) is called the ecliptic, and the ecliptic has its own pole. The constellation Draco surrounds the ecliptic pole. In doing so, it winds through all the houses of the Zodiac, and all the stars appear to hang from it.[58] The *t'li* is also understood as the inclination between two celestial planes. In astronomical terms, this is the obliquity, the inclination separating the ecliptic and the celestial equator.

The commentators aver that it looks vaguely like the body of a huge fish, and hence is identified with the *t'li*. This furthers the association of the *t'li* with sea creatures such as the *tanin* and the Leviathan.[59] The two points, or "nodes" where the equator intercepts the ecliptic are the points of equinox. The vernal equinox is referred to as "the head of the dragon." The autumnal equinox is called "the tail of the dragon." These nodes are depicted as knots in the star charts.[60] Sa'adia, Al' Bargeloni and Maimonides refer to the *t'li* as *Al Jaz'har*, Persian for "knot" or "node."[61]

Other sources use the word *t'li* to designate the obliquity between the orbit of a planet or a satellite, such as the moon, and the ecliptic.[62] Like the points where the equator intercepts the ecliptic, the two points at which the orbit of a planet or satellite intersect with the ecliptic are called nodes. In this case, the "head of the dragon" is the ascending node (where the planet or satellite passes south to north); the "tail of the dragon" is the descending node (where the planet or satellite passes north to south).[63] The lunar nodes, the points at which the orbit of the moon passes through the ecliptic, are the points in the moon's orbit where an eclipse of the sun or the moon can occur. Hence, the midrashic image of the dragon who swallows the sun.[64] These nodes are deemed astrologically significant by R. Abraham Abulafia, who writes that the head of the *t'li* indicates merit, while the tail represents liability.[65]

According to some kabbalistic works, *T'li* is a place under the firmament called *Vilon*, inhabited by beings who are humanoid but behave like angels. These beings are imbued with divine wisdom, and have the power to impart it to human beings. *T'li* as cosmological locus rather than an animal of some sort thus serves as intermediary between the divine and the world in the same way that the Celestial Dragon does.[66]

One of the most startling identifications of the *t'li* is in *Sefer HaBahir:* "What is the *t'li?* It is the likeness before the Blessed Holy One. It is thus written, 'His locks are hanging.'"[67]

The literal sense of this seems to be that the *t'li* is the image that is most prominent before God because it is the largest constellation and is at the uppermost part of the celestial sphere. The *Bahir,* however, seems to imply that God is related to this "likeness" by more than a steady gaze: God and the *t'li* seem to mirror each other. The quote from the Song of Songs is about God Himself, in the guise of the Beloved. Just as his locks hang, so does the *t'li,* imitating God's appearance, as it were. The words likeness and before, which recall the Second Commandment,[68] in this context point out the danger of close equivalence between the "likeness" and the "Holy Blessed One." Idolatry directed at this image was certainly understood to be a possibility. Maimonides and others assert that the *t'li* was idolatrously worshipped in ancient times. R. Isaac of Acco identifies the *t'li* specifically with Baal.[69]

Thus, the commentaries on *Sefer Yezirah* and the astronomical-astrological texts paint the picture of the *t'li* as an enormous dragon that controls the constellations, has positive and negative astrological influences, can be related to the *tanin* and the Leviathan, and, possibly to God Himself, or, more accurately, to an idolatrous "challenger" to the divine throne.

According to Donnolo, the dragon only appears to rule over all. In fact, it was placed in its position by God, who has ultimate dominion over the universe and fate. And it is obvious that only through a relationship with God can one affect one's destiny. Donnolo extends this paradigm to the microcosm: he compares the function of the celestial dragon to that of the spinal chord in the human body, its head to the brain and its tail to the sexual organs.[70] By taming one's internal dragon, that is, by maintaining a proper balance between reason (represented by the brain) and instinct or emotion (represented by the sexual organs), one can theurgically affect the celestial dragon and alter one's fate. For Donnolo, the dragon represents not only power over good and evil in the world but the ability of human beings, by teaching their internal dragons proper behavior as it were, to control good and evil in the self and thus to affect their fate.

Donnolo's commentary was an important influence on the theology of the German Jewish pietists of the twelfth and thirteenth centuries known as *Hasidei Ashkenaz.* They, like Donnolo, manifested a desire to harmonize free will and determinism in their biblical commentaries as well as in their mystical tradition.[71]

The comments of Eleazar of Worms on the creation of the *taninim* (Genesis 1:21), are typical of this concern on the part of *Hasidei Ashkenaz* to limit the power of the dragon.

> *And God created:* Leviathan, upon whose fins the entire world rests. . . . And in the time to come God will command Michael and Gabriel to hunt him, and he will stand on his tail before them, and his head will reach the Throne of Glory. They will flee from him immediately, until he is destined to fall at the hands of Jonah. (Marginal note: This is the beast of which Job said, "And he is the ruler of all, the King of the children of pride" [Job 41:26], since even the proud angels fear him). And therefore, there is a hint here to "truth" (AMT) [in the final letters of the words] "And God created, (VaYivrA ElohiM eT)" for all the things which have been said regarding him are all true. And who will eat him? People of truth who are involved with the Torah of truth.

> *The taninim:* According to the plain sense they are great creatures, long and simple, and fire comes out of their mouths. Thus they live in water and pits (wells) and this is why it says (Psalms 148:7b) "*taninim* and all ocean depths." And it says in Isaiah (27:1) concerning the Leviathan "the Elusive Serpent," and . . . "the Twisting Serpent," and (it adds) "He will slay the *tanin* of the sea."

> Behold, the *tanin* is not the Leviathan, for it says "It was You who *crushed* the heads of Leviathan" (Psalms 74:14) but it says "It was You . . . who *smashed* the heads of the *taninim*," (Psalms 74:13b) distinguishing two types [of monsters]. Thus, it was necessary to add the particle *ET* to include the Leviathan. . . . "*Taninim*" in *gematria* equals "The Great Leviathan."[72]

Eleazar begins by making a distinction between the Leviathan and the *taninim*. The Leviathan is the beast upon whose body the world rests. In this sense the Leviathan is a parallel to the celestial serpent. The Leviathan will be hunted in the future, when "his head will reach the Throne of Glory," that is, when he attempts to claim the celestial realms and usurp the throne of God. The primeval *taninim*, on the other hand, have the appearance of conventional medieval dragons, serpentlike and fire-breathing.

The *taninim* were destroyed, but the Leviathan will be preserved until "the time to come"—the eschaton.

The end of the passage is more difficult. Eleazar seems to erase the distinction he has drawn between the Leviathan and the *taninim* by showing how the two are equivalent in *gematria*, the mystical hermeneutical process that substitutes number and number combinations for the letters of the Hebrew alphabet. *Equivalent* is indeed the operative term here: the mathematics of this equation do not work out exactly. TNNYM (*taninim*) (*sic*) = 550, whereas HLVYTN HGDVL (*HaLeviatan HaGadol*) = only 549. In the context of *gematria*, however, this does not negate the possibility of their conceptual equivalence. An imperfect numerical correspondence can indicate approximation rather than duplication of the terms whose numerology is being compared. Eleazar understood the force of the letters of the Hebrew alphabet and their power to create and destroy worlds.[73] He uses *gematria* to demonstrate the transformation of *taninim* into *HaLeviatan HaGadol* as a literary metaphor for the creative operations of God. In crushing the rebellion of the *taninim* during the creation, God had, as if recombining letters by *gematria*, reordered the factors of the primordial rebel-dragon's "personality." The dragon of eschatology was the Leviathan, which, while "great," was still ultimately a servant of God, thus allaying all fears of usurpation.

The great teacher of Eleazar of Worms, R. Yehudah HeHasid, is even more direct in explaining and allaying fears about the powerful dragon. On the same verse he remarks: "*HaTaninim:* "Why is [the word *dragons* in Genesis 1:21] written *HaTaninim* [plural] and not *HaTanin* [singular, since the Leviathan was reputed to have no mate]?—Lest one should say, 'It is a god,' as it says (Job 41:25). 'When he raises himself up the mighty are afraid.'" So it is written in the plural form, for the only truly singular One is the Blessed Holy One."[74]

The phrase "Lest one should say 'It is a god'" is quite startling. R. Yehudah here implies that the dragon assumes divine proportions and when it attempts to usurp the celestial throne, even the angels tremble. This is incontrovertible evidence that there was an awareness among the pietists that the mythic power of the dragon could grow out of proportion.

The celestial dragon also appears in the mystical literature of the pietists, once again in connection with the serpent of copper. In his biblical commentary Eleazar of Worms quotes the midrashic passage that Moses "threw the serpent up and it stood miraculously in the atmosphere of the world."[75] That this midrash was known in his circle and related to the celestial serpent is obvious from a passage in the mystical treatise *Sodei Razayya*, ascribed to Eleazar but most probably a work of his school.

The passage in question describes King Solomon's throne as an earthly parallel to the celestial throne. Connections between the prototypical and the actual and parallels between heaven and earth and macrocosm and microcosm (like those espoused by Donnolo) appealed to the pietists. They embraced the talmudic principle that "everything above is paralleled below."[76] Since one could not speak precisely about the awesome contents of God's abode, one would describe earthly parallels as a way of hinting at the celestial splendor.

As I mentioned, midrashic tradition describes how the machinery of Solomon's throne was set into motion by a giant serpent. This serpent is identified by the author of *Sodei Razayya*, who asserts that it was none other than "the serpent Moses made."[77] Moses' serpent, flung into heaven and the serpent on King Solomon's throne are one and the same. They both represent the celestial serpent affixed to the very throne of God. If this serpent performs a function on the divine throne analogous to the one it performs on Solomon's throne, it is powerful indeed, for then it would make the machinery of God's throne move—it would literally run the universe.

But this serpent of Moses, which moves the celestial throne, is not merely a serpent. Regarding it, Eleazar's teacher, R. Yehudah HeHassid, had said: "*The serpent* corresponds to God . . ."[78] [During the plague of serpents] God said, 'Make a *saraf*,' and Moses did not wish to, so God said, 'I will have mercy upon mine,' and thus it is written, 'and Moses made a serpent,'—corresponding to God."[79]

God commands Moses to make a *saraf*—a serpent. But *saraf* is also the term for fiery angel, and Moses fears that the people will worship it improperly. God is exasperated. "Very well, then," God thinks, "I *myself* will have mercy upon mine." The theologically careful Moses makes a serpent, and Moses and the people think that the image of the serpent curing the plague of serpents is a homeopathic remedy of sorts, the cure coming through the instrument of disease. But, R. Yehudah informs us, the image of the serpent corresponds to God's Self! Taken in conjunction with their other statements expressing fear that the *tanin* might be divinized, it seems that the major figures of *Hasidei Ashkenaz*

felt the ancient problem of the power of the celestial dragon still
to be a relevant one and expressed it in terms very much like
those of *Sefer HaBahir* and *Sefer Yezirah* and its commentaries.
How did they propose to contend with it?

One of the strangest and most interesting appearances of dragons in the literature of *Hasidei Ashkenaz* relates to this question.
The text is in the Bologna manuscript of *Sefer Hasidim:* "There
is a noxious beast (or demon) which is called Drakon in the Greek
language. If he is smote by a sword, he will not be damaged, but
if there should come against him (someone) born of a dragon, that
one can smite him. . . . The dragon who married the King's daughter said, 'I fear no one except the dragon born of the princess, and
he is in the prison-house.' The King said to the son of the princess, 'I will make you a free man and you will leave prison. Go
and take your father's sword and sit beneath the bed of the
Queen.'"[80] What happens next is very strange. The dragon comes
into the bedchamber and has sexual relations with the Queen,
whereupon the prince springs out from under the bed and destroys him. The text continues: "The Queen didn't tell anyone
that the dragon had had sex with her, for fear that if she said that
the dragon was her husband, her human husband would be dead
and she would have been [*sic*] poor and abject and without luck
all her days. Instead she said, 'He came in the guise of the King,
with the royal crown upon his head,' in the manner to which she
was accustomed." The text goes on to describe dragons who appear to women disguised as their husbands and how dangerous
these are. However, it concludes, these "noxious beasts do not
attack anyone except someone who has attacked them, or if he or
his ancestors wrote charms or callings-up or did magic or asked
dream questions. Therefore one should not do these things or say,
'I will do this to save a life'—do callings-up or charms, for this is
not wisdom. It shortens a person's life and the life of his descendants, and one shouldn't put a life in jeopardy in order to save a
life.[81] For it is written, (Deut. 18:13) 'You must be wholehearted
with *Lord* your God.' One shouldn't do anything except pray to
God for any illness and disease, or trouble, or problem."

In the literary context of *Hasidei Ashkenaz*, there is precedent
for understanding a dragon that disguises itself as a human being
in terms of a most powerful indigenous archetype: the "primordial serpent." The Bologna manuscript of *Sefer Hasidim* relates
how the primordial serpent "used to walk around on two feet and
looked a bit like a human being."[82] Moreover, the details of the

tale correspond with the midrashic elaborations on the account of the temptation of Adam and Eve by the serpent in Genesis 3. Seen from this perspective, the king in the tale represents God, or more accurately, his "image" and agent—Adam. The princess or queen, who copulates with the dragon, corresponds to Eve, who, according to the midrash, copulated with the primordial serpent. The son of the serpent and Eve is humankind, imprisoned in mortality but given a chance by God to earn freedom from it (*Olam HaBa*—the world to come) if he vanquishes evil.

The claim of the queen to have mistaken the serpent for the king is paralleled in legends which state that the serpent took the form of Adam when seducing Eve in order to prey on her credibility. To demonstrate that such a deception is possible, we have the description of the manner in which dragons can appear as husbands in order to deceive wives. The moral of the story appears to be that one should not be beguiled by dragons in human or divine clothing nor fear that one's spouse and protector (God) will die. One should not involve oneself in magical practices or shortcuts. One should not consort with the dragon, for it is God who is the arbiter of all fate; one must vanquish the dragon and abandon all practices except the pious worship of the true God.

This tale draws upon an eclectic variety of sources, both Jewish and non-Jewish.[83] In its final redaction it is in many ways a paradigm of the grapplings of *Hasidei Ashkenaz* with the issues of free will and determinism, their ambivalent relationship with magic, and their elaborate metaphysical speculation. For them, the dragon was real, and they understood the world as remaining very much within its coils. Yet they believed, in accord with the traditions of the Talmud, the midrashim, and the commentaries on *Sefer Yezirah*, that it is not the dragon itself but God, the master of the dragon, and of all other created beings who holds the power to alter fate. To God alone should prayer and supplication be addressed.

Harnessing the Dragon in Medieval Jewish Art

Medieval Jewish iconography is intimately linked with rabbinic and medieval texts. It may in fact be read as a text of sorts, as I have demonstrated elsewhere.[84] Jewish art emerging from the medieval milieu can certainly be said to express "the wishes, dreams and aspirations" of its creators, rather than strictly aesthetical goals.[85] It echoes and amplifies. It often gives voice to sentiments, political and theological, that it would have been difficult to make explicit in a medieval climate yet are implied in the texts it illustrates.

The important dragons and dragonlike creatures in Jewish literature appear only rarely in iconography; there are, for instance, no depictions of the primeval dragons in Jewish art.[86] When dragonlike creatures are illustrated, as in the case of the serpent of copper or the primordial serpent, there is nothing to distinguish them from their analogues in Christian manuscripts. The primordial serpent, for instance, may be depicted with a female human head, in direct conformity with Christian iconographic tradition.[87] Likewise, the serpent of copper is depicted as a winged dragon, which is one of the conventions for its appearance in Christian art.[88] The only inherently and explicitly *Jewish* dragon that appears in Jewish art is the Leviathan. It is generally depicted as a large fish alongside the Behemoth or engaged in the eschatological battle with that creature.[89] However, apropos of the function of the Leviathan as *ourabouros*, the serpent whose body forms the sky or is wrapped around the earth, and in accordance with its designation in Isaiah 27:1 as "the twisted serpent," the Leviathan is often depicted with its head touching its tail.[90] On Eastern European and Middle Eastern popular-style hallah covers for the Sabbath and on synagogue ceilings, the Leviathan is depicted enclosing other elements—the Behemoth, or the city of Jerusalem, a microcosm of the world as a whole. This motif may allude to the Messianic "day which is totally Sabbath," when peace will be spread over the city of Jerusalem and over the whole world, just as the Leviathan's skin will be spread as a canopy over the righteous.[91]

Most of the dragons that appear in medieval Jewish art are very similar in appearance to the grotesques found in the margins of medieval Christian manuscripts. This has led to their designation as purely decorative elements and to the neglect of their consideration as inherently Jewish symbols. This is odd, since, as I have demonstrated, the dragon is a powerful indigenous archetype in the ancient and medieval literature of the Jews. If one refrains from arbitrarily assuming that these dragons have no association with the textual context or with the iconographic context of the larger illustrations on a given page, one may begin to perceive some visual analogies between these illustrations of dragons and the more cosmological textual uses of the dragon as a fulcrum between the divine and the demonic.[92]

Threatening, demonic dragons and a protected Israel are a theme that pervades medieval Jewish art. The liturgical poem *Adon Imnani* for the first day of Shavuot is illustrated with dragons in nearly all its appearances in important Franco-German illuminated *mahzorim*, festival prayerbooks.[93] In a thirteenth-century example, dragons, some of which look very much like those on the facade of the cathedral of Troyes, seem to have been added merely for decoration, but if one observes their position, one notes that they are menacing the Israelites yet are unable to touch them as they receive the Torah and are sprinkled with the blood of purification by the priest at the altar.[94] This may again allude to the desire to have Jews focus on the law and worship of God rather than attempt to appease the cosmic dragon and to the belief that one will be protected from all such demonic creatures if one directs one's prayer to God alone.[95]

If the dragons were merely decorative, one might assume that they would be ubiquitous. Yet in the entire group of *mahzorim* surveyed by Gabrielle Sed-Rajna in her *La Mahzor Illuminee*,[96] this is one of the very few places such dragons do appear. Furthermore, they exhibit remarkable seriousness of purpose for grotesques—they do not double over on themselves or contort to fit the space; their attention is always fixed on the Israelites no matter which direction their bodies are facing. In some cases, they do more than merely threaten: they literally gnaw at the architectural foundations, symbolically attempting to destroy the foundations of Torah.

On the opening page of the book of Numbers in the Duke of Sussex Pentateuch (fol. 179v), there are four knights holding banners with the symbols of the major tribes camped around each of the four sides of the Tabernacle in the wilderness.[97] They are flanked by four hybrid grotesque dragons, three of which are winged, and by two smaller dragons of the two-legged variety, one of which is winged. These have been called "merely decorative" in the literature.[98] Yet their size and prominence, as well as the fact that the standard bearers are specifically depicted as knights, may hint that the artist intended the dragons as personifications of the difficulties the Israelites encounter in the saga of the book of Numbers. Perhaps they represent the fiery serpents in the desert. Or, as the human parts of the hybrids seem in some cases to correspond to caricatured ethnic types, perhaps they represent the occupants of the land of Canaan whom the Israelites would vanquish in battle. As the dragons rage outside, the knights stand

calmly within small golden aedicula lined with red. Thus the artist evokes a sense of divine protection commensurate with the
spirit of both the biblical verse "[God] led you through that great
and terrible wilderness in which there were venomous serpents"
(Deuteronomy 8:15) and the eschatological prophecy of Zechariah 2:9, "And I will be for you, says God, like a wall of fire around
you."[99] These hybrids are not "merely decorative" elements. If we
are to look at this iconography as a sort of text, how might we
read them? They serve as protagonists, introducing a narrative
tension into a static and hierarchical tableau. They convert the
whole scene from a mere diagram of the relative positions of the
Israelite tribes around the Tabernacle to a representation that
summarizes in iconographic shorthand the entire premise of the
book of Numbers—the various trials the Israelites faced in the
desert, and how God preserved them from these perils. It is appropriate that such a shorthand depiction of the predominant theme
of God's protection in the book of Numbers should appear with
the opening rubric of the book.

The iconographic tradition provides its own solution for the
problem of the threat to faith, Torah, and even divinity posed by
the dragon. When understood in the context of the texts they illustrate, some of the many images of dragons in Jewish manuscripts may represent the conquered t'li. In an Ashkenazic High
Holiday prayer book from the second half of the fourteenth century, there is an elaborate and lovely arch framing the words to
the Kol Nidrei prayer. There is a kneeling figure within this arch,
and all seems appropriate and right given the solemnity of the
liturgical context for which the text is intended. The entire lower
register of the page is dominated by two huge dragons with tails
intertwined who gnaw at the pillars of the arch within which the
words appear. What are such large grotesque dragons doing in
such a prominent place on such an important page? There is a
tradition that there are two intertwined t'lis—one male and one
female—corresponding to the plural taninim of Genesis and the
two serpents mentioned in Isaiah. Perhaps in this illumination
the blue dragon at the right represents the Pole or Draco (related
to the constellation and hence celestial blue), and the red dragon
at the left represents the Coiled Serpent, or the ecliptic (related
to the luminaries, hence fiery red). A red and a blue dragon, also
intertwined, illustrate a liturgical poem in the fifteenth-century
additions to the same manuscript. In this instance, the blue
dragon is depicted above the red dragon, corresponding accurately

to the relative positions of Draco and the ecliptic on the celestial sphere. In both of these illuminations, when related to the broader context of text and illustration, the dragons are symbolic of the reader and his congregation having conquered their belief in fate as read in the motion of the stars moved by the whim of the celestial dragon. The dragons illustrating the liturgical poem refer to the text "Happy is the nation for whom this is not so— from its God and redeemer it will garner a blessing." This is a play on the words of Psalm 144:15: "Happy is the people who have it so . . ." Thus, happy is the nation whose fate is not determined by the celestial dragon—from God alone will it receive its blessings. The dragons of the *Kol Nidrei* page relate to both the central illustration and the text. Though the apparently capricious and destructive forces of fate seem to gnaw at the underpinnings of faith (just as the threatening dragons discussed above were gnawing at the very foundations of Torah), the reader and his congregation realize that on Yom Kippur their fate is in the hands of God alone.

These illustrations acknowledge that the dragon exists, he is part of the universe, but he is a servant. His job is to uphold the structure of the constellations in their orbits—he is the foundation of the cosmos, but he is not its ruler, nor is he the arbiter of fate, for fate can be altered only by the power of *"Tshuvah, U'T'fillah, U'Z'dakah"*—repentance, prayer and charity.

Another example with a very similar message is found in an Ashkenazic manuscript of the fourteenth century. It is the illuminated catchword *Melekh* (King) beginning the liturgical poem *Melekh Amon Ma'amarkha MeRahok Muzav.*[100] This is a *piyyut* (liturgical poem) for the second day of Rosh HaShanah, a day upon which the poetic mood begins to shift from the celebration of the creation of humankind to the theme of Judgment as the cycle of the year moves toward Yom Kippur. The poem is based on *Pesikta Rabbati* 40,[101] which, in turn, is an excursus of several verses in Psalm 119: 89–96: "The LORD exists forever; Your word stands firm in heaven. Your faithfulness is for all generations. You have established the earth; it stands. They stand this day to [carry out] Your rulings, for all are Your servants . . . I am Yours; save me! For I have turned to Your precepts. The wicked hope to destroy me, but I ponder Your decrees. I have seen that all things have their limit, but Your commandment is broad beyond measure."

This Psalm asserts the primacy, the "firm foundation" of God's "word"—God's laws, as opposed to cosmic anarchy—in the heavens and on earth.[102] It forges a stern distinction between the divine laws and the servile and limited status of the heavenly bodies. The medieval Jewish commentators on this verse assert that it is God's will, rather than astrological conjunction, which orders the universe, and they celebrate the Psalmist's complete faith in God.[103]

Like the Psalm, *Pesikta Rabbati* 40 and the *piyyut* promulgate a theology which proclaims that, while God's justice is ordained of old, it is constantly tempered with mercy. "Your Merciful Name is exalted," writes the poet, "even as you sit in Judgment."[104] This context, with its image of a God who sits in judgment yet who always acts with mercy, recalls an aspect of the dragon that has not yet been discussed, and which is found in RaShI's interpretation of Lamentations 4:3, "Even the *tanin* offers the breast": "*Even the tanin* offers the breast and suckles its young: Even though it (the *tanin*) is cruel, it uncovers its breast."

The ambiguous image of a cruel dragon who cares for its young is a striking and important one, for it stands in answer to those who would assert that a God who is stern in judgment can have no mercy. This is the ultimate harnessed dragon, its mythology intact on the one hand but dramatically declawed and domesticated on the other, a figure of stern justice and yet, at the same time, of parental mercy. It is a far cry from the primordial rebel-dragon, but it seems appropriate for the illustration of a poem recited on a day that is the gateway to that day wherein Jews remind God that "we are Your children and You are our Parent."[105] The sources of the *piyyut*, with their emphases on the power of God over all the celestial and astrological powers, and the text of the *piyyut*, with its emphasis on mercy within judgment, are brought together by the image of the dragon. In the illumination of the initial word, a network of violet vines on a blue ground forms the well-hidden figures of dragons, like the powerful and ancient elements of the myth itself, the images of the dragons are hidden, subjugated by the sovereign power of God, represented by the word *Melekh*. Yet these domesticated dragons form a visual analogy with the idea of mercy within justice presented in the poem. This strongly corroborates the tensions that develop in the classical literature between the dragon as cosmic serpent and arbiter of fate, and divine law, which it always seems ready to overthrow. However, a new element is present here: just as in *Sefer HaBahir*, the dragon here is the mirror image, so to speak, of God. This is the mythic substratum that the rabbinic tradition has had to deal with all along—the powerful intermingling of the divine and the demonic that will simply not go away. The negative repercussions of what the *Bahir* calls this "likeness" are evident in many contexts. It was because of its divine likeness that the primordial serpent was able to deceive Eve, that the copper serpent became an object of idolatry, that the *tanin* was such a threat to God, that the serpent on God's throne has such power, and that the psalmist and the kabbalists must, each in their own way, assert God's dominance over the cosmic serpent. But here, finally, the disturbing mythos of the dragon is harnessed theologically.

The traditional Jewish morning liturgy praises God, "who forms light and creates darkness, who makes peace and creates everything." This is a paraphrase of Isaiah 45:7, which contains a theology so profoundly difficult and disturbing that if pronounced every morning it would make all but the most pious tremble and go back to bed. The original verse reads, "I am the *Lord* and there is none else, I form light and create darkness, I make peace and create evil." In many ways, the odyssey of this verse into the liturgy parallels the odyssey of the dragon mythos. Isaiah's words represent a biblical negation of the mythic consciousness which asserted that there were two (or more) powers in heaven. Even though the scriptural verse deconstructs and demythologizes that paradigm, the idea of praising a God who created evil was too much for the rabbinic creators of liturgy, and so they paraphrased it, employing "everything" as a euphemism for "evil." But to readers who know scripture, the subtext is still there. Such readers understand that God is the author of everything, including evil, and they are either troubled by that, or they take comfort in it—the choice is theirs. The biblical statement has been softened, but it still retains its original rebuke. A theological compromise has taken place.

A similar process takes place with the dragon. As we have observed, the dragon of scripture was originally a god in its own right but is transformed first into God's creature, then into a subjugated rebel against God. First in biblical, and later in rabbinic tradition, it is harnessed, but the harness does not hold. It is almost as if the dragon is constantly straining at the bit to escape, to get out and to attack God or to usurp God's place. Gradually, during the Middle Ages, a cold peace is struck with the underlying mythic elements of the image of the dragon. The dragon now becomes a theological metaphor for God's self, a positive image, but, almost sadly, a domesticated one.[106]

It is not only the harness of rabbinic tradition that can barely contain the dragon. The universalist archetypal harness will not hold him either. Symbols are forged not exclusively by Ur-passions but by specific historical contexts and, ultimately, often by compromises. And the study of myth itself is subject to historical change and development. Laurie Patton has asserted that if the native traditions and indigenous contexts are heeded, and the intellectual ancestors selectively applied, myth can be used to do good history. I would add that it can also be used to do good *histoire des mentalités*.

Yet it does not come easily. Readers who know myth as well as scripture understand that just as there is a fine line between, and often an intermingling of, the divine and the demonic, there is a fine line between Ur-passions and history, between art and text, and, in fact, between Jung and Eliade and us. They are either troubled by that, or they take comfort in it—the choice is theirs.

Notes

1. On the origin of the dragon concept, see Jonathan D. Evans in South, ed., *Mythical and Fabulous Creatures*, 26–58, esp. 30–31.
2. HaLevi, *Sefer HaKuzari*, bk. 4, chap. 24, 184.
3. Gen. 1–2:4a.
4. Gen. 1:20–21. The development of the depiction of dragons in postbiblical Jewish literature and art from sea creatures to creatures with both piscean and avian attributes is certainly due to the influence of the art and literature of the societies in which the Jews lived. But it may ultimately be precipitated by the fact that the "great *taninim*" were created on the fourth day of Creation, the day upon which both birds and fish are created.
5. Gen. 1:26.
6. Gen. 2:20.
7. Isa. 51:9; Job 7:12; Jer. 51:34; Deut. 32:33.
8. The *taninim* are equated with "the Depths" or "the Deep," with which they occasionally appear in poetic parallelism. Cf. Ps. 148:7, "Praise . . . *taninim* and all depths."
9. Cf. Job 41:25, and preceding note.
10. Isa. 27:1; Job 3:8 and 40:25; Ps. 104:26.
11. Exod. 7:9, 10, 12.
12. Ezek. 29:3, and see 32:2. This description, and all of Ezekiel's other pronouncements regarding the contemporary pharaoh, resonate with associations with the archetypical pharaoh, the pharaoh of Moses' time.
13. Another interpretation, and one that is most appropriate in terms of the final argument of this essay might be that the *tanin* of Moses' staff represents God, whose name is inscribed on the staff, and who subjugates all lesser powers. Both interpretations can coexist because of the intensely ambiguous and ambivalent relationship I hope to demonstrate exists between divine and demonic power.
14. Representing the ultimate dominance of God over the power of the dragon, which will be discussed further below.

15. Ezek. 29:4–5.
16. Ps. 91:3, 84:3.
17. Gen. 2:4b and following.
18. As mentioned above, the term *primordial serpent* is a direct translation of the Hebrew *naḥash hakadmoni*. See, for example *Bereshit Rabbah* 23:12.
19. Gen. 49:17; Ps. 58:5, 140:4. Deut. 8:15.
20. Eccles. 10:8. The *saraf* and the *tan* are two creatures which, due to confused etymologies and translations, are often mistakenly included among dragons in postbiblical literature. The *saraf*, whose name means "burning," in some contexts indicates one of the class of *serafim*, "fiery angels" (Isa. 6:2, 6). In other contexts, it implies a poisonous (burning, or literally fiery) snake (Num. 8:15, 21:6). The *tan* is a wild canine, probably a jackal. There is a difference of only a single letter between its plural form (*tanim*) and *tanin*. This is most notable in an instance in Lam. 4:3 where, although *tanim* is clearly meant (and is so amended in public reading—*kr'i*), the written text (*ktiv*) is retained as *tanin*. The Septuagint consistently translates *tanim* as *drakon*. Many later translators and commentators repeated its error, mistakenly bringing under the rubric of "dragon" a great number of references to a howling, solitary mammal of the wilderness and further confusing the issue of what exactly the term means.
21. In the Talmud and in the various *midrashim*, there are descriptions of the natural history of serpents, of the primordial serpent (BT *Sotah* 9b), and of the *tanin* as the primordial water dragon and the Leviathan as the eschatological plaything of God (BT *Bava Batra* 74b, *Bereshit Rabbah* 7:4 [ed. Mirkin, 47–48]). There are fantastic tales of serpents of prodigious size (BT *Nedarim* 28a, BT *Shevu'ot* 29a), and *halakhic* concerns regarding poisonous serpents whom it is feared will taint drinking water and wine (see, e.g. BT *Bava Kama* 115b). These last, *halakhic* serpents are the most numerous, but following closely behind are the many references to the serpent as the instrument of punishment by God and the serpent or dragon as a magical or cosmological arbiter of fate. It is clear that often when the text speaks of serpents, it can refer to dragons as well; *Drakon* is a Greek loanword and is rarely used. *Tanin* is usually used with specific reference to primordial water dragons, so the word for serpent is often used to refer to beasts conventionally regarded as dragons. *Naḥash*, (serpent) is by far the most common term.
22. Exod. 4:3, 7:15 *naḥash*/ Exod. 7:9, 7:10 *tanin*, in retelling of same story. This may occur even within the text of the Talmud itself. See BT *Berakhot* 33a and see RaShI on the biblical verses quoted. Such interchangeability is present in other languages and linguistic contexts as well, as for example in the case of the Old English "Wyrm," which means both snake and dragon.
23. Gen. 3:14.
24. *Bereshit Rabbah* 19:1 (ed. Mirkin I:134).
25. See, e.g., *Bereshit Rabbah* 20:4–5 (ed. Mirkin I:146–48).
26. BT *Sotah* 9b.
27. Ibid. obliquely, and see BT *Shabbat* 146a.
28. See *Bereshit Rabbah* 8:10 (ed. Mirkin, I:55–56). Cohen, "*Be fertile and increase*" is a comprehensive treatment of this theme.
29. See, e.g., Wakeman, *God's Battle*, and Day, *God's conflict*. The image of God as having "killed the *tanin* which is in the sea" (Isa. 27:1) is far less common than that of God's "crushing the heads of the *taninim* on the water" (Ps. 74:13, among other places). This is an ancient Near Eastern image of subjugation that has echoes in iconography. Many are the bas-reliefs of Egyptian or Assyrian kings placing a foot on the head—"crushing the head"— of a prostrate enemy, not killing, but subjugating him, making him, as it were, his plaything: "The Leviathan you have formed to sport

with" (Ps. 104:26). Thus, the pattern appears to be one of reduction which destroys rebelliousness but preserves power (albeit on a less awesome scale), and subjugation rather than eradication.

30. The earliest source for the fall of Satan is 2 Enoch 29:4–5: "One from the order of the archangels [identified as 'Satanail' in manuscript P] deviated, together with the division that was under his authority. He thought up an impossible idea, that he might place his throne higher than the clouds which are above the earth, and that he might become equal to my power. And I hurled him out of the height, together with his angels" (*Old Testament Pseudepigrapha*, ed. Charlesworth, 1:148). This angel was called Lucifer by the church fathers, due to a misapplication of Isa. 14:12. See Davidson, *Dictionary of Angels*, 176.

31. *Bereshit Rabbah* 19:1 (ed. Mirkin, I:134–35). One might extend the idea of reduction as a metaphor for what we are attempting to do methodologically with Jung's archetypes in transforming them into indigenous archetypes.

32. Cf. Eleazar Ben Kallir, *VeYipathu Sha'are Eden Gan*, trans. in Carmi, *Penguin Book*, 227–32.

33. Had humankind not fallen, the serpent would have been the servant of humanity (BT *Sanhedrin* 59b; *Bereshit Rabbah* 19:1 [ed. Mirkin, I:134–135]).

34. The "snake of the rabbis" punishes lawbreakers; for it there is no remedy (BT *Shabbat* 110a). One who gives a legal decision in the presence of his teacher (thus attempting to usurp the teacher's prerogative) "deserves to be bitten by a snake" (BT *Eruvin* 63a). A man encounters a series of troubles, but his meeting with a serpent is the culminating one that makes him forget all others (BT *Berakhot* 13a). Slanderers are punished by fiery serpents because the serpent was the archtypical slanderer (*Bamidbar Rabbah* 19:22 [ed. Mirkin, 10:237]).

35. *Kohelet Rabbah* 5:8, 15a.

36. *Kohelet Rabbah* 5:5, 27a. The serpent does not only punish evildoers: it may also despatch heroes to their death. In doing God's will in a way that seems to be part of the *natural order*, a serpent is sent to kill Bar Kokhba so that the Romans should not have the satisfaction of believing that they killed him (*Eykhah Rabbah* 2:2, 21a).

37. BT *Shabbat* 110a.

38. BT *Bava Batra* 74b.

39. BT *Bava Batra* 16a.

40. Num. 21:6–10.

41. *Bamidbar Rabbah* 19:23 (ed. Mirkin, 10:238).

42. This world-encircling serpent, which parallels the Greek *ourabouros*, finds an echo in various midrashic accounts. Cf. *Pirkei DeRabbi Eliezer* 9; *Midrash Aseret HaDibberot* 2 (Jellinek, *Beth HaMidrasch*, I:63).

43. BT *Bava Metsiah* 84b–85a.

44. Prov. 10:25.

45. Cf. *Midrash Kisseh VeIpodromin shel Shlomo HaMelekh* (Jellinek, *Beth HaMidrasch*, V:35).

46. Jellinek, *Beth HaMidrasch.*, II:83–85, and Gaster, *Exempla of the Rabbis*, 209, for a complete listing of sources, both Jewish and non-Jewish.

47. See Wakeman, *God's Battle*, 16–22, and *Midrash Hadar Zekenim* Gen. 3:21, 11.

48. BT *Avodah Zarah* 8a.

49. 2 Kings 18:4.

50. *Bereshit Rabbah*, 19:9 (ed. Mirkin, 1:141). In presenting the image of a servant whose power seems to threaten to eclipse that of his master, *midrashim* on the dragon invite comparison with those which present a similar image of Moses. If ever the reputation of a servant seemed to impinge on the power of his master even when that master was God, it was Moses,

called the "man of God," who was liable to be seen as a "man-God" (Cf. Ps. 90:1). Moses compares himself both to a serpent (*Shemot Rabbah* 3:12 [ed. Mirkin, 5:78–79]) and to the Leviathan (*Midrash Tanhuma [Shemot]*) as a servant of God, and in light of the traditions concerning the serpent and the Leviathan, this appears to be an apt comparison. For among all the prophets it was Moses who came closest to being considered quasi-divine. The rabbis, who need to establish their own authority, deal with the problem of the frightening power of Moses by playing up the very human side of his character and asserting that his gravesite was never revealed for fear it become a temple to his worship rather than to the worship of God (*Midrash Lekakh Tov, Deut.* 36:4 [ed. Buber, Vilna, 1884]).

51. BT *Berakhot* 30b.

52. BT *Berakhot* 33a.

53. The desire to limit the power of the serpent may shed light on the only actual occurrence of the word *dragon* in the entire Talmud. The discussion occurs in BY *Avodah Zarah* 42b. The Mishnah there teaches that the image of a dragon is grouped with the images of the sun and moon as a depiction that must be "cast into the salt sea" should it be found on a vessel, since it is considered idolatrous. A *baraita* (extracanonical mishnah) insists that all planets except the sun and moon are "permissible" as are all faces except the human face and all figures except the dragon. There is a further discussion of what exactly constitutes a dragon. Some say it is a creature with scales "between its joints." Some specify the joints of the neck, but the joins of the vertebrae seem to be the accepted placement. RaShI on this text comments that the dragon is "like a snake," and says that it has hair between its joints, perhaps still attempting to reconcile mammalian and reptilian characteristics.

   BT *Avodah Zarah* 42a mentions that if a dragon-shaped vessel is found and the head of the dragon has been removed, one my only use the vessel if it is certain that the head was removed by a non-Jew. Why should this be? It may be that Jews believed that they could take a magical shortcut to alter their fate by breaking the power of the cosmic dragon in effigy, rather than by the conventional path of piety. Such images were prohibited because they were suspect of having been employed for idolatrous purposes by Jews who clearly believed that it was the dragon and not sin that killed. While such idolatry was expected of non-Jews, resort to magical shortcuts by Jews was deemed inappropriate; or, perhaps, feared effective.

54. The word *t'li* seems to be related to the verb TLH—to hang. (Targum and RaShI to Gen. 27:3, 98). The word is *hapax legomenon* in the Bible. It occurs in the tale of Esau's hunt, when Jacob tells Esau, "Take your gear, your *t'li* and bow" (Gen. 27:3). The biblical word *t'li* has been interpreted as a "hanging" sword, a quiver, or a bola (a line with a ball which -hangs- from its end). In commentaries on *Sefer Yezirah*, *t'li* has been identified with the *Nahash bari'ah* of Job 26:16, 68; the *Nahash bari'ah* and *Nahash 'akalaton* of Isa. 27:1; as well as with the *Tanin* or Leviathan.

   For an enumeration of speculations on the nature of the *t'li* in the Bible and in commentaries on *Sefer Yezirah*, see A. Kaplan, *Sefer Yezirah*, 232 ff. For sources on the etymological bases of the word *t'li* and an exploration of the celestial dragon's astrological-astronomical significance, see Gefen, "*Teli*," 126–28; Harkavy, "*Tli Atalya*," 27–35; and Ish Shalom, "*Tanin, Livyatan Ve-nahash*," 79–101.

55. *Sefer Yezirah* 6:1, 118 par. 42. The triad of the dragon, the sphere or cycle, and the heart is the culmination of *Sefer Yezirah*. Note that this triad is remarkably similar to that mentioned in the Talmud as idolatrous (BT *Avodah Zarah* 42b).

56. See Gikatilla, *Ginat Egoz* part 2, 254; Cordovero, *Pardes Rimmonim* 21:8,

100a. See also *Zohar* I:125a, and Abraham b. Mordechai Azulai's *Or HaHamah* (a commentary on *Zohar Shemot*, part 2 of his *Kiryat Arba* (New York, Jewish Theological Seminary ms 2179), on that citation in the *Zohar*. For what follows on Donnolo the author is indebted substantially to Sharf, *Universe of Shabbetai Donnolo*.

57. *Sefer Raziel HaMalakh*, 18b; RaMbaM in standard editions of JT *Avodah Zarah* 3:3 (19a)—the constellation here, as in the commentary of R. Ovadiah M'Bertenoro and the Mordechai on Mishnah *Avodah Zarah* 3:3, represents an idolatrous deity.

58. Ptolemy, *Almagest*, chap. 7, 235. The *Almagest* is found in Hebrew translation (though Ptolemy's authorship was suppressed) as *Mishpetai HaMazalot*. A particularly striking illuminated example exists in Sassoon ms. 823 (astronomical tables by Jacob b. David b. Yom Tov Fu'al) (cf. D.S. Sassoon, *Ohel David* [Oxford, 1932], 2:1043; no. 823). See Langerman, Kunitzsch, and Fischer, "Hebrew Astronomical Codex ms. Sassoon 823," 253–92.

59. Dunash on *Sefer Yezirah*, 69); Saadia on *Sefer Yezirah*, 59–60); Bargeloni on *Sefer Yezirah*, 209.

60. In the aforementioned manuscript of *Mishpetai HaMazalot* (Sassoon ms. 823), for instance, Draco is depicted replete with its two nodes, on fol. 112, and with only one "knot" on fol. 118.

61. Sa'adia on *Sefer Yezirah* 59–60; Bargeloni on *Sefer Yezirah*. 209; Maimonides on JT *Avodah Zarah* 33 (19a).

62. *Baraita DeShmuel HaKatan* 2 (8a); *Sefer Tekhunah*, 101–4; Ibn Ezra Exod. 3:15, 25–34, particularly the end, and Job 28:3; and Moscato, *Kol Yehudah* on *Sefer HaKuzari* 4:23, 54a.

63. See, for example, the diagram in the Eleazar of Worms, *Perush HaRa MiGermayza le Sefer Yezirah*, 12b), where the ascending node is labeled "head of the dragon," and the descending node is called "tail of the dragon."

64. BT *Avodah Zarah* 8a.

65. *Or HaSekhel* 4:1 (New York, Jewish Theological Seminary ms 2320.11), fol. 41a.

66. See Vital *Ez HaHayyim*, chap. 8, 403.

67. *Sefer HaBahir*, par. 106, on Song of Songs 5:11.

68. Exod. 10:3–4: "You shall have no other Gods *before* Me. You shall not make for yourself a sculptured image or any *likeness* of what is in the heavens above, or on the earth below, or in the waters below the earth."

69. RaMBaM, *Mordechai* (840) to JT *Avodah Zarah* 3:3 (19a). Isaac of Acco, *Ozar Hayyim* (New York, Jewish Theological Seminary ms 1674.14), fol. 6a. See also JT *Shabbat* 9:1 (57b), *Avodah Zarah* 3:6 (22a), and RaMbaN on BT *Shabbat* 83b, "*Zeh*".

70. Donnolo, *Il Commento*, 20.

71. Both Donnolo's ideas and those of the Hasidim concerning free will and determinism sprung from the same Talmudic roots, "All is foreseen, but the right of choice is granted" (*Mishnah Avot*) 3:15.

72. *Perush HaRokeah Al'HaTorah*, Gen. 1:21.

73. Though it contains a great deal of astrological and astronomical information, Eleazar's commentary on *Sefer Yezirah* is especially and essentially concerned with the creative and destructive power of the Hebrew alphabet (Cf. *Sefer Yezirah* [ed. Shapiro, (Przemysl, 1888), 22 ff]).

74. *Perushei HaTorah LeRabbi Yehudah HeHasid*, Gen. 1:21.

75. *Perush HaRokeah Al'HaTorah*, Num. 21:8. Eleazar ascribes the plague of serpents in the desert to the fact that Israel "slandered their Creator, like the (primeval) serpent" (3:78).

76. *Shemot Rabbah* 33:4 (ed. Mirkin, 6:90–91), and see HeHasid, *Sefer Hasidim Parma* ms, 349; Bologna ms, ed. Margoliot, (Jerusalem, 1957), 205.

77. *Sodei Razzaya*, 24. The author quotes a midrash whose source is now lost.

78. ". . . and 'the *saraf*' to Moses."
79. *Perushei HaTorah LeRabbi Yehudah HeHasid*, Num. 21:8–9, 184.
80. *Sefer Hasidim*, 319, no. 469.
81. Ibid.
82. *Sefer Hasidim*, 579.
83. Such as the legend of the birth of Alexander, who was said to be the offspring of a queen and a dragon.
84. Epstein, *Dreams of Subversion* and "Elephant and Law," 465–78.
85. Berenson, *Aesthetics and History*, 180.
86. Though elemental dragons occasionally appear, as in an illustration of the earth opening up to swallow Sodom and Gommorah, as in the Miscellany presumed to be from Troyes, c. 1280. [London, British Library ms Additional 11639, fol. 740v], which is clearly based on contemporary Christian depictions of the mouth of Hell.
87. Miscellany, Troyes (?) c. 1280, fol. 520v. Yet in Spanish Haggadot, the serpent is depicted in a completely reptilian manner. (Cf. Golden Haggadah, Barcelona c. 1320, London, British Library ms Add. 27210, fol. 1v; Sarajevo Haggadah, North Spain c. 1350, Sarajevo, National Museum, fol. 3v; Sister Haggadah, Barcelona, mid–14th c., London, British Library, ms Or. 2884, fol. 2r.)
88. There are essentially two ways in which the serpent can be depicted in medieval Christian art. One is as a snake suspended or draped over a pole, which is overtly Christological. A famous example is the mid-twelfth-century walrus-ivory cross from Bury St. Edmunds, now in the Cloisters, N.Y., ill. in B. R. Jones, "Reconsideration." Significant later examples are to be found in the block-book editions of the Biblia Pauperum (see Schmidt, *Armenbibeln des XIV. Jahrhundert* , and the example of this scene with its typological companions, the Crucifixion and the Binding of Isaac in Avril, *Biblia Pauperum*, plate e]. The Cologne Bible of 1479 has a similar depiction, but the stick is not forked, and actually forms a Tau-cross. The other manner of depicting the copper serpent is as a dragon or winged snake upon a platform supported by a column or columns. Examples include the opening initial for the Book of Numbers in the Stavelot Bible (London, British Library Add. ms 28107, see Dynes *Illuminations*, plate 23], as well as the Bible Moralisce (see *La Bible Moralisee* [Paris, 1911], plate 81.]), and the Visconti Hours (see Meiss and Kirsch, *Visconti Hours*, plate 123). This depiction may go back to ancient prototypes such as the crowned, winged serpent depicted on the walls of a Pompeiian villa (see Hogarth and Clery, *Dragons*, 83). It is also the model which the sculptor of the famous Copper Serpent in the Basilica of St. Ambrose in Milan chose to use (see Bonnefoy and O'Flaherty, *Mythologies*, 2:682). The only depictions of the copper serpent in medieval Hebrew manuscript illumination follow this convention rather than that of the hanging serpent (Miscellany, Troyes (?) c. 1280, fols. 120v, 742v). Although this might lead to speculation that the tradition is originally even of Jewish origin, it is more likely that this mode of depiction, which may have ancient pagan roots (cf. Pompeii), may have been adapted because it is not Christological.
89. See Guttman, "Leviathan, Behemoth and Ziz." One of the more striking images is that of the Miscellany, Troyes (?) c. 1280, fol. 518v.
90. See the 13th-century depiction of the Messianic banquet in Biblioteca Ambroseana, Milan ms B30–31–32, 1236–1238 fol. 136r.
91. Cf. Leviathan enclosing Hebron (a parallel to the huge snake that encircles the bier of a righteous person [BT *Bava Meziah* 84b–85a]): Sabbath Cloth, Jerusalem, 1876 wool thread embroidered on cotton net, 81 X 78 cms. (Jerusalem, The Israel Museum. illus. in Ungerleider-Mayerson, *Jewish Folk Art*, 122 bottom right). Leviathan enclosing the Shor HaBar: print, Poland, nine-

teenth century (British Library, see Goldstein *Jewish Legends*, 117). Leviathan enclosing a city: dome of Gwodziec synagogue, 1640, see Davidovich, *Ziurei-Kir BeBatei Knesset BePolin*, plate 13. Davidovich identifies the city as Worms, presumably since Worms was depicted resting on a dragon (as a pun on its name, cf. Mogilev Synagogue, in Wischnitzer, *Architecture of the European Synagogue*, 142, plate 123.) But that image is not a dragon—it is clearly a fish. It is, furthermore, accompanied by the verses recited after the *'Aleynu* prayer, "You will not fear sudden terror, or the disaster that comes upon the wicked (Prov. 3:25) [if they] hatch a plot—it will be foiled; agree on action—it shall not succeed, for the LORD is with us (Isa. 8:10). Till you grow old, I will still be the same; when you turn gray, it is I who will carry; I was the maker, and I will be the Bearer; and I will carry and rescue [you] (Isa. 46:4)." These verses are certainly appropriate either in an aggadic context that describes the Leviathan as the "bearer" of the earth or the heavens or in an ethical-philosophical context that demands that one not fear "sudden terror or the disaster which comes upon the wicked" if these be the effects of the twisting and lashing of the servant or Leviathan, but to trust only in God, for "the LORD is with us."

92. It must be remembered however, that the cosmological understanding of the dragon, its association with God and with fate, was never completely explicit in any of the literature examined above. For instance, both the mystical text *Sefer Yezirah* and the opaque exegesis and legends of *Hasidei Ashkenaz* were intended only for initiates of elite groups adept at mining symbolism in search of secrets. It would follow, then, that when that symbolism was expressed in art, it might be done in a comparably opaque manner.

93. See, for example, the *Laud Mahzor* Ashkenaz, c. 1250–60. (Oxford, Bodleian Library ms Laud Or 32), fol. 127v, described in the text following; the "Esslingen" Mahzor, c. 1290. (Part 1: Dresden, Sachsische Landesbibliothek ms A 46 a; Part 2: Wroclaw, University Library, ms Or I,10), fol. 202v; and the Darmstadt Mahzor, Hammelburg, 1348. (Darmstadt, Lessische Landes-und-Hochshulbibliothek ms cod. Or. 13), fol. 126r, where the illustration is much simplified: Moses alone appears with the tablets, and the threatening dragons are accordingly simplified—a single dragon attacks a hare. See Epstein, *Dreams of Subversion*, Chapter 2, for a discussion of this hare as a symbolic representation of Israel.

94. Laud Mahzor fol. 127v.

95. The presence of dragons at Mt. Sinai is certainly also linked to the idea that though "the snake came to Eve and cast his filth upon her" (see BT *Shabbat* 146a; *Zohar* I:28b; I:122b; I:126a; I:145b among many other places), "When they stood at Mt. Sinai, Israel's filth was cleansed (literally 'ended'), [but] the nations which did not stand at Mt. Sinai, their filth was not cleansed" (See *Zohar* 1:26b; BT *Avodah Zarah* 22b, among many others). This has obvious parallels in the Christian doctrine of the Original Sin, which was exculpated by Mary in giving birth to Jesus. Iconographically, one would expect to see fleeing, rather than threatening, dragons if this were the context of the illuminations.

96. These are the Michael Mahzor, Ashkenaz 1285. (Oxford, Bodleian Library ms Michael 617 [no. 1033], 627 [no. 1035]; both volumes of the Worms Mahzor, Worms, 1272–90, (Jerusalem, JNUL Heb 4 781 I/II); the Leipzig Mahzor, Ashkenaz c. 1310. (Leipzig, University Library ms V 1102/I–II [1]); and the Tripartite Mahzor, Ashkenaz c. 1320, (Part I: Budapest, Academy of Science, ms a 384; Part II: London, British Library, ms Add. 22413; Part III: Oxford, Bodleian Library, ms Michael 619). Together with the Laud "Esslingen" and Darmstadt *mahzorim*, mentioned in note 93, these comprise all the important Ashkenazic *mahzorim* of the thirteenth-fourteenth centuries.

97. London, British Library, ms. Add. 15282.
98. Narkiss, *Hebrew Illuminated Manuscripts*, 104.
99. These verses are, in fact, linked together in *Shemot Rabbah* 24:4 (5:274), implying that the Israelites were protected by a wall of (supernatural) fire, just as appears to be the case in the illumination.
100. See Goldschmidt, *Mahzor L'Yamim HaNoraim* 1:47.
101. Ed. and trans. Braude (New Haven, 1959), 702.
102. See Ibn Ezra on this verse.
103. Ibn Ezra, on the verse "They stand as servants to do your will" emphasizes the adherence to God's laws to the [implied] exclusion of viewing the heavenly bodies as forces with independent power over fate. This is amplified by David Altschuler in the eighteenth-century commentary *Mezudat David* Psalm 119:89–91 (standard editions of the Hebrew Bible with commentaries): "Even if the heavenly bodies and their powers indicate that [things be] worse or better, behold, the decree of Your word is what stands in the heavens, and it nullifies their instruction. . . . Each day all the heavenly bodies and their powers arise to do Your bidding according to Your command—even if their instruction should [appear to be] the reverse [of Your will]—because they are all Your servants and are all compelled to perform the decree of the Omnipresent." A similar attitude may be found in the medieval commentators on the serpent of copper. They apologetically profess that it was not the serpent itself, but that when the Israelites gazed upwards they directed their hearts to their Father in Heaven, which was effective in stopping the plague. They desired to paint the experience of the Israelites with the serpent of copper in the desert as an eloquent testimony to the weakness of human beings in often idolizing the instrument, rather than the source of salvation. See RaShI, e.g. Num. 21:8, quoting BT *Rosh HaShanah* 29a, 470. The disjunction between these attitudes and those of kabbalists and philosophers may be due to the audiences for which the works were intended.
104. Literally, "Your Name," here referring to the Name HVYH, which represents God's mercy (Goldschmidt, *Mahzor* 47 n. 1).
105. Cf. *Ma'ariv*, Eve of Yom Kippur. See Davidson, *Ozar Hashirah* II:45. The origin of this *piyyut* is *Shir HaShirim Rabbah* 2:17.
106. The idea that God may be compared to a creature is an accepted one among exegetes. See RashI on Exod. 19:18, 241: "Scripture offers human beings a pattern which is well-known to them. . . . [Hosea 11:10:] 'As a lion He [God] does roar.' But who gave the lion power if not He, and yet Scripture compares Him [only] to a lion! But, [the reason is] that we describe Him by comparing Him to His creatures in order to make intelligible to the human ear as much as it can understand."

Works Cited

PRIMARY SOURCES

Avraham ibn Ezra. *Perush HaTorah*. Edited by Asher Vayzer. Jerusalem: Mossad HaRav Kook, 1976.

Babylonian Talmud. Vilna: Rom, 1880–83.

Bahir. Edited by Reuven Margoliot. Jerusalem: Mossad HaRav Kook, 1951.

Bahya ibn Paquda. *Hovot HaLevavot*. Edited and translated by Yosef Kapah. Jerusalem: Mossad HaRav Kook, 1973.

Cordovero, Moshe. *Pardes Rimmonim*. Munkacz, 1906.

David [ben] Amram HaAdeni. *Midrash HaGadol al hamishah humshe Torah*. Edited by Z. M. Rabinovits. Jerusalem: Mossad HaRav Kook, [1967].

Davidson, I. *Ozar HaShirah Veha Piyut: mi-zeman hatimat kitve Ha-Kodesh ad reshit tekufat HaHaskalah*. New York: Bet midrash HaRabanim de-Amerikah, [1924].

Donnolo, Shabbetai. *Il Commento di Sabbathai Donnolo sur Libro della Creazione*. edited by David Castelli. Florence: N.p., 1880.

Dunash ibn Tamim. *Sefer Yezirah im Perush Abusahul Dunash b. Tamim, hu R. Yizhak HaYisraeli*. Edited Menasheh Grossberg. London: N. p., 1902.

Eisenstein, J. D. *Ozar Midrashim*. New York: J. D. Eisenstein, 1915.

Eleazar of Worms [Ba'al HaRokeah]. *Perush HaRokeah Al'HaTorah*. Edited by Hayyim Konyevsky. Bnai Brak, New York: Y. ben A. Klugmann, 1978–86.

———. *Perush HaRa MiGermayza al Sefer Yezirah*. Edited by Zvi Elimelekh Shapiro of Dinov and Moshe Shapiro. Przemysl: H. A. Zupnik and H. Knoller, 1883.

———. *Sodei Razayya*. Edited Yisrael Kamelher. Bilgoray: N. p., 1936.

Gikatilla, Yossef. *Ginat Egoz*. Edited by M. Attia. Jerusalem: Yeshivat HaHayim VeHaShalom, 1989.

Goldschmidt, Daniel. *Mahzor L'Yamim HaNoraim*. Jerusalem: Koren, 1970.

HaLevi, Yehudah. *Sefer HaKuzari*. Edited by Y. Even Shmuel. Tel Aviv: Dvir, 1972.

Hizkiah bar Manoah. *Hizzkuni, Perushei HaTorah LeRabbenu Hizkiah bar Manoah*. Edited by Haim Dov Chavel. Jerusalem: Mossad HaRav Kook, 1988.

Jellinek, A., ed. *Beth HaMidrasch: Sammlung Kleiner Midraschim und vermischter Abhandlungen aus der Älteren jüdischen Literatur*. Vols. 1–4, Leipzig: Fridrikh Nies, 1853–1857. Vols. 5–6, Vienna: N. p., 1873–77.

Jerusalem Talmud. Krotoschin: N. p., 1886.

Midrash Hadar Zekenim. Bnai Brak, New York: Mahon LeHafazat Perushei Ba'alei HaTosafot 'al HaTorah, 1986.

Midrash Lekakh Tov. Edited by Shlomo Buber. Vilna: 1880.

Midrash Rabbah. Vilna: Rom, 1878.

Midrash Rabbah: meforash im peyrush mada'i hadash. Edited by M. A. Mirkin. 3d rev. ed. Tel Aviv: Yavne, 1977.

Midrash Tanaim al sefer Devarim. Edited by David Tsvi Hoffmann. Berlin: Ittskovski, [1909].

Midrash Tanhuma. Edited by Shlomo Buber. Vilna: Rom, 1885.

Midrash Tehillim. Edited by Shlomo Buber. Vilna: N. p., 1891.

Moscato, Yehudah. *Kol Yehudah* in Yehudah HaLevi *Sefer HaKuzari.* Zhitomir: Avraham Shalom Shadov, 1866.

Nahmanides. *Perush HaTorah.* Edited by Hayyim Dov Chavel. Jerusalem: Mossad HaRav Kook, 1959.

Pirkei DeRabbi Eliezer. Warsaw: N. p., 1852.

RaShI. *Perush HaTorah.* Edited by Hayyim Dov Chavel. Jerusalem: Mossad HaRav Kook, 1982.

Recanati, Menahem. *Perush 'al HaTorah.* Lemberg: N. p., 1840–41.

Saadia Gaon. *Perush Sefer Yezirah.* Edited by Yossef Kapah. Jerusalem: N. p., 1972, 59–60.

Sed-Rajna. *La Mahzor Illuminée.* Leiden: Brill, 1983.

Sefer Raziel HaMalakh. Warsaw: N. p., 1881.

Sefer Yezirah. Warsaw: N. p., 1884.

Sefer Yezirah, The Book of Creation. Edited and translated by Aryeh Kaplan. New York: Weiser, 1990.

Vital, Hayyim. *Ez HaHayyim.* Edited by Yehudah Zvi Brandwein. [Tel Aviv]: [HoZa'at Kitve Rabenu HaAri], 726 [1965/6], 403.

Yehudah ben Barzillai, al-Bargeloni. *Perush Sefer Yezirah.* Edited by Shlomo Zalman Hayyim Halberstam. Berlin: N. p., 1885.

Yehudah HeHasid. *Sefer Hasidim.* Edited by R. Margoliouth. Jerusalem: Mossad HaRav Kook, 1969.

———. *Perushei HaTorah LeRabbi Yehudah HeHasid.* Edited by Yizhak S. Lange. Jerusalem: N. p., 1974–75.

———. *Sefer Hasidim.* Edited by J. Wistinetski. [Jerusalem: Sifre Vahrman, 1969, reprint of Frankfurt A. M., N.p., 1924.

Zechariah b. Solomon Rofe. *Midrash HaHefez.* Edited by M. Havatselet. Jerusalem: Mossad HaRav Kook, 1981.

Zohar. Edited by Reuven Margoliot, Jerusalem: Mossad HaRav Kook, 1940–46.

PRIMARY SOURCES IN TRANSLATION

Abu'l Walid Marwan ibn JanaKh. *Sefer Shorashim: The Book of Hebrew Roots by Abu'l Walid Marwan ibn Janakh, called Rabbi Jonah, edited with an appendix containing extracts from other Hebrew-Arabic Dictionaries.* Edited by Adolf Neubauer and Wilhelm Bacher. Oxford: Clarendon Press, 1875.

Carmi, T. *The Penguin Book of Hebrew Verse.* New York: Penguin Books, 1981.

Charlesworth, James H., ed. *The Old Testament Pseudepigrapha.* Garden City, N.Y.: Doubleday, 1983.

Midrash Tehillim. The Midrash on Psalms. Translated from the Hebrew and Aramaic by William G. Braude. New Haven: Yale University Press, 1959.

Ptolemy. *The Almagest, by Ptolemy.* [Translated by R. Catesby Taliaferro.] Great Books. Chicago: Encyclopaedia Britannica [1955].

Tanakh: A New Translation of the Holy Scriptures according to the Traditional Hebrew Text. Philadelphia: Jewish Publication Society, 1985.

SECONDARY SOURCES

Avril, Henry. *Biblia Pauperum: A Facsimile and Edition.* Ithaca, N.Y.: Cornell University Press, 1987.

Berenson, Bernard. *Aesthetics and History.* Garden City, N. Y.: Doubleday, 1954.

Bodenheimer, F. S. *Animal and Man in Bible Lands.* Leiden: Brill, 1960.

Bonnefoy, Yves, and Wendy Doniger O'Flaherty. *Mythologies.* Chicago: University of Chicago Press, 1991.

Cohen, Jeremy. *"Be Fertile and Increase, Fill the Earth and Master It": The Ancient and Medieval Career of a Biblical Text.* Ithaca, N.Y.: Cornell University Press, 1989.

Davidovich, David. *Ziurei-Kir BeBatei Knesset BePolin.* Jerusalem: Mossad Bialik, 1968.

Davidson, G. *A Dictionary of Angels.* New York: Free Press, 1967.

Day, John. *God's Conflict with the Dragon and the Sea: Echoes of a Canaanite Myth in the Old Testament.* Cambridge: Cambridge University Press, 1985.

Dynes, Wayne. *The Illuminations of the Stavelot Bible.* New York: Garland, 1978.

Epstein, Marc M. "The Elephant and the Law: Adoption and Adaption of a Medieval Christian Motif in the Art of the Jewish Minority." *Art Bulletin,* September 1994, 465–78.

———. *Dreams of Subversion: Medieval Jewish Art and Literature.* University Park: Penn State Press, 1996.

Gaster, Moses. *Exempla of the Rabbis.* New York: Ktav, 1968.

Gefen, Shemtov. "Teli." *Sefer Zikaron la-yovel ha-shivim shel Aleksander Ziskind Rabinovits: mukdash le-hakirot be-sifrut uvesafah.* [Tel Aviv]: Defus HaPoel HaZair, 1924, 126–28.

Goldstein, B. *The Astronomy of Levi ben Gerson (1288–1344), Critical Edition of Chapters 1–20 with Translation and Commentary.* New York: Springer-Verlag, 1985.

Goldstein, David. *Jewish Legends.* New York: Peter Bedrick Books, 1987.

Guttman, J. *Hebrew Manuscript Illumination.* New York: Braziller, 1978.

———. "Leviathan, Behemoth and Ziz: Jewish Messianic Symbols in Art." *Hebrew Union College Annual* 39 (1968): 219–30.

Harkavy, A. E. "*Tli Atalya.*" *Ben Ami,* January 1887, 27–35.

Hogarth, Peter, and Val Clery. *Dragons.* London: Allen Lane, 1979.

Ish-Shalom, B. "*Tanin, Leviatan VeNahash—L'Peshro shel Motiv Aggadi.*" (Hebrew). *Da'at* 19 (1986–87): 79–101.

Jones, Bernice R. "A Reconsideration of the Cloisters Ivory Cross with the Caiaphas Plaque Restored to Its Base." *Gesta* 30 (1991): 65–88.

Langerman, Y. Z., P. Kunitzsch, and K. A. F. Fischer. "The Hebrew Astronomical Codex MS. Sassoon 823." *JQR,* n. s. 78, no. 3–4 (1988): 253–92.

Meiss, Millard, and Edith Kirsch. *The Visconti Hours.* New York: Braziller, 1972.

Narkiss, B. *Hebrew Illuminated Manuscripts.* Jerusalem: Keter, 1969.

Sassoon, D. S. *Ohel David.* Oxford: Clarendon Press, 1932.

Schmidt, Gerhard. *Die Armenbibeln des XIV. Jahrhundert.* Gratz: N. p., 1959.

Sharf, A. *The Universe of Shabbetai Donnolo.* New York: Ktav, 1976.

South, Malcolm, ed. *Mythical and Fabulous Creatures: A Sourcebook and Research Guide.* New York: Peter Bedrick, 1988.

Ungerleider-Mayerson, Joy. *Jewish Folk Art from Biblical Days to Modern Times.* New York: Summit, 1986.

Wakeman, M. K. *God's Battle with the Monster: A Study in Biblical Imagery.* Leiden: Brill, 1973.

Wischnitzer, Rachel. *The Architecture of the European Synagogue.* Philadelphia: Jewish Publication Society, 1964.

LAURIE L. PATTON

AFTERWORD

In the American Academy of Religion's 1996 announcements, the "History of the Study of Religion" section called for papers on "Mircea Eliade in the U.S.A., and the history of his academic reception, including discussions of his life, contributions, and influence." Clearly the issues of myth, method, and our intellectual ancestors are not dead, or even moribund. The discussion at this point has taken on a life of its own; the ancestors no longer provide us with tools, but have themselves become the objects of study in the field of mythology. This brief afterword will suggest some possible new directions for future discussion about myth and method. Its purpose is not to attempt an overview of the voluminous current literature (one hopes much of that has been provided by the articles themselves) but rather to suggest some of the theoretical and procedural implications of the articles in this volume.

These essays have implied that the making of and the theorizing about myth are mutually influential enterprises—at times, even the same enterprise. As a result of this perspective we can argue that, even as we make our ancestors the objects of study in their own right, we are at the same time creating a radically new kind of lineage. As Douglas suggests, F. Max Müller stands as the inheritor, not the examiner, of the quasi-fictive Indo-European mythological tradition; as Strenski demonstrates, Sylvain Lévi acts not only as the analyzer, but as the transmitter of an anti-mythological ritual tradition; as Segal argues, Jung becomes the translator of the Gnostic tradition; and, as Ziolkowski demonstrates, Frazer is the grand reteller both of the story of the priest of Nemi and of all of its literary variants. If mythologists make this argument, then it is incumbent upon them to accept and declare their own role, not only within the scholarly enterprise, but in the transmission of narrative itself—even if that role is only to be a transporter of myth into the language of the academy.

A weaker form of this argument about myth and method can also be made: Even if the boundaries between myth and the study of myth are to be kept intact at some level, they are still accepted as mutually implicating activities. Thus, scholars are still bound to consider the effects, either positive or negative, that their study must have on mythological traditions. Conversely, they are also accountable for the effects that the mythological traditions might have had on them. Some mythologists may not be persuaded by either strong or weak forms of the argument but believe instead that such mutual effects are impossible. The authors of this volume would argue that, at the very least, it is important for such mythologists to respond to the critique made in these essays. At the very least, such mythologists are bound to describe the relationship of distance they establish between themselves and their objects of study.

Does this critique mean that the study of mythology is open to endless self-examining prolegomena of confessions—a kind of eternal regress of intellectual inertia? Not in the least; it only means that the predispositions, as well as the effects, of mythological study must be admitted and noted before the mythologist proceeds further. The study of anthropology has wrestled with this challenge for decades; it is time that the textual tradition, too, see itself as a kind of culture that is shaped and molded by, and in turn shapes and molds, those who venture into its fields. To put it another way, if in fact our intellectual ancestors were mythmakers, then so are we. And as such, we must be clear about the traditions to which we are accountable—how and to whom we wish to retell our narratives.

Other scholarly venues also open up from this radical new lineage. If the boundaries between the myths and the mythmakers are blurred, then it might be possible to examine the fruitfulness of methods that were traditionally applied to myth, and apply them to theory, and vice-versa. We might, for instance, take Dundes's arguments in this volume one step further and perform a Stith-Thompson motivic analysis upon Freud's *Totem and Taboo;* or study the uses of etymology, such as that performed on Indo-European myths, on twentieth-century theorists of Indo-European myths. How would the Freudian motif of patricide and punishment fare in comparison to other Stith-Thompson taletypes? When does Dumézil himself use etymology, and what do such etymological moments say about his attitude toward language?

This new lineage suggests that we might also take myths seriously as theories in their own right, juxtaposing their propositions and analyzing their modes of reasoning—not, as some might have it, in order to add to the index of possible theoretical models of the world, but to evaluate them as forms of narrative reasoning equal to our own. This perspective has begun to develop in the fields of theology, philosophy, and anthropology. The juxtaposition of the worldviews of Lévi-Strauss and a Theravada monk has been attempted by Ivan Strenski; those of Kant and the Maori by Gregory Schrempp; those of Durkheim and Xunzi by Robert Campany—all with intriguing results.[1]

The study of mythology has a unique contribution to make to such studies in that it emphasizes the primacy of narrative structure and has the philological and historical tools at its disposal to make the most of those structures. This kind of study can be deepened and expanded by mythologists who want to examine the relative merits of master narratives in any number of cases. For instance, one might ask with new theoretical seriousness why and how a Malinowskian master narrative might be considered better to tell than a Trobriand one, and vice-versa. This indeed was the question of colonized peoples when there was no possibility of their having a voice in the discussion, and yet now it can be asked again with new vigor.

In a related vein, it should be clear that these essays yield important fruit for comparative study. We must begin with a caution: If, as Doniger argues, our awareness of the limits of comparative study is now being replaced by our awareness of the limits of contextual study, then the commonsense approach in both cases is to practice both with a certain degree of prudence. Yet the mythologist's tone of moderation need not be so somber; it can also be creative. Mythologists can take advantage of our forebears' historical positions: possibilities for responsible comparison are opening up precisely because the twentieth century has introduced new points of historical contact between actual mythological traditions. If we were studying the myths of the ancient world, for example, we would be justified in comparing a Greek and a Celtic myth because they were brought together in the writings of Strabo, who facilitated contact between the two cultures. So too, in this century and earlier, previously unrelated narrative traditions have been brought together in history in the very persons of our intellectual forebears—the anthropologists, sociologists, mythologists, and literary critics who began to tell these narratives differently because of their positions between two cultures. Comparative work can take advantage of this perspective just as it does that of Strabo or Herodotus.

We might imagine, for instance, something beyond the simple exposé of a Christian missionary perspective within the study of mythology. We might instead consider a comparative study of the narrative attempts of different missionaries to retell myths from a Christian perspective. The same comparative approach would be fruitful, mutatis mutandis, for analyzing the narrative strategies of collectors, folklorists, anthropologists, psychologists, and sociologists—all of whose political, social, and philosophical motivations in a particular narrative tradition might be usefully compared to one another.

Moreover, as Lincoln, Grottanelli, and Doniger all suggest, comparative work is not necessarily incompatible with history, despite the recent (and empirically reasonable) trend to link comparative mythology with ahistorical, totalitarian systems, and by extension, fascism. Yet this conclusion also need not take on the tone of bland moderation. The essays of this volume join an emerging body of inquiry that holds out the possibility of conducting comparative work with resistant, even subversive political concerns, and one can and should be even more creative in pursuing this possibility. A comparative study of fascisms themselves, and their uses of mythology, should be the interest and domain not only of political studies but also of comparative mythologists who insist on resisting such totalitarian impulses. Relatedly, as Bantly's article implies, the self-conscious manipulation by political systems of personal, political, and mythical identities needs to be examined on a comparative scale as well as from an area-studies point of view.

At a more theoretical level, one might also ask—from a comparative perspective again—how and why history has become such an important part of the story that must be told about mythology. As Benjamin Ray's essay suggests, the call to historicize is frequently made without serious reference to historiographical writing or consideration of whether such a move will in fact more adequately represent multiple interpretations of a mythological text. We might examine, then, what other narrative and rhetorical purposes such pleas have for mythologists who make them and what sorts of cultural effects might be intended. Are these purposes the same, for example, as Lévi-Strauss's hopes for structuralism's therapeutic effects on society? How do they compare with the hopes of a thorough critique of modernity embodied in Eliade's early association with the Iron Guard and later association with American liberal thinkers?

The question of the cultural participation of mythologists leads naturally to the possibilities raised by essays in this volume concerning art, literature, and mythology. As all of them suggest in various ways, it is no longer an issue simply of the camouflage of ancient myth by modern and postmodern art and the recovery of mythic forms in the modern and postmodern environment. It is instead a question of interruption and reconfiguration of art by myth and myth by art—whether it be Epstein's medieval dragon or Apostolos-Cappadona's Picasso. This view, again, suggests that competing narratives about the relationship between myth and art are at stake, and several possibilities for research emerge from such a perspective.

First, the camouflage might well be treated as a form of myth-making in its own right. If Frazer's *The Golden Bough* has attained the status of a myth itself, then mythologists might examine its impact upon twentieth-century culture in the same way that one traced the trail of the priest of Nemi. Picasso's *Guernica* has, along with its iconoclastic effects, taken on a life of its own and represents a certain master-narrative, despite its original status as a reconfiguration of other mythological and artistic motifs. The dragon will be yet again harnessed by Jewish exegetes, and its twentieth-century formulations will not simply be reconfigurations of the medieval but some new thing that constitutes yet another kind of original starting point for future generations. Bruno Bettelheim's Little Red Riding Hood may have a different kind of cultural force in the West from that of the brothers Grimm in Germany, which, in turn, had a different cultural impact from that of its counterpart in rural France.

These twentieth-century myths, however, also exist in an age of mechanical reproduction; thus the retelling of myths may take the form of mass dissemination, and not that of the fireside performance or even the local political rally. In her essay, Mary Douglas suggests that myths can be forcibly narrativized out of their ritual contexts and pleads for the reconnection of the relationship between a narrative and the circumstances of its production. So, too, the field of mythology needs to combine its analyses with examinations of the developing technologies of publishing and mass-marketing throughout the twentieth century. An Internet version of Little Red Riding Hood or an e-mail storytelling collective would have yet again another kind of cultural impact, one that mythologists would do well to begin to imagine.

In addition to the challenges of technologies, the West exists in an increasingly attenuated environment of challenge to the arts by religious orthodoxies of various kinds. The world of artistic production, whether it be the plastic or the literary, can provide some answer to that challenge by articulating its own master narrative, such as that attempted by Wendy Steiner for liberalism in her recent book *Scandal of Pleasure*.[2] Mythologists might study debates between artists and religious groups with such issues in mind. What competing master narratives are at stake, for instance, in the study of Bible as literature in Western college curricula? What kinds of master narratives emerge from the analysis of Andres Serrano's *Piss Christ* in the Paula Cooper Gallery in New York City? Is iconoclasm itself a regular, standard feature of the Western artist's master narrative—one whose properties are not simply to resist other mythic formulations but also to stand alongside them with its own potential hegemonic force?

If, indeed, the presence of mythological motifs in a work of art or literature implies both disruption and continuity, mythologists might take advantage of the recent trend in literary analysis toward an analysis of "the fragment." We might look again at the notion of the mythological fragment, not as some of our forebears have done, as building blocks toward some cognitive or ontological deep structure, but as forms in themselves. There may indeed be artistic or literary remnants of myths that are not simply parts of some lost whole but whose very nature it is to be fragmentary and whose function might be disruptive in order effectively to reconfigure and challenge previously accepted meaning.

We return, then, to the question of lineage with altogether different lessons to learn from our ancestors than we had thought. Our critique of them as involved in the production and extinction of myth forces us at the same time to join them, insofar as we ourselves are at risk for committing the same errors. As they make the transition from thinkers we emulate to historical objects we study, our ancestors earn the quiet, albeit disbelieving respect that any historical object can and should have. And even though we might repudiate their myths and their methods, we acknowledge the force of the unintended lessons they still have to teach us.

Notes

1. See Ivan Strenski, "Lévi-Strauss and the Buddhists," in *Religion in Relation*, 110–32; Gregory Schrempp, "Antinomy and Cosmology: Kant among the Maori," in *Myth and Philosophy*, 151–80; and Robert F. Campany, "Xunzi and Durkheim as Theorists of Ritual Practice," in *Discourse and Practice*, 197–232.
2. See in particular her essays "The Literalism of the Left" and "Fetish or Fatwa," in *The Scandal of Pleasure*, 60–127.

Works Cited

Campany, Robert F. "Xunzi and Durkheim as Theorists of Ritual Practice." In *Discourse and Practice*, ed. Frank Reynolds and David Tracy. Albany: State University of New York Press, 1992, 197–232.

Schrempp, Gregory. "Antinomy and Cosmology: Kant among the Maori." In *Myth and Philosophy*, ed. Frank Reynolds and David Tracy. Albany: State University of New York Press, 1990, 151–80.

Steiner, Wendy. *The Scandal of Pleasure.* Chicago: University of Chicago Press, 1995.

Strenski, Ivan. *Religion in Relation: Method, Application, and Moral Location.* Columbia: University of South Carolina Press, 1993.

CONTRIBUTORS

INDEX

CONTRIBUTORS

DIANE APOSTOLOS-CAPPADONA is Research Associate at the Center for Muslim-Christian Understanding at Georgetown University. In addition to numerous articles for scholarly journals in religion and the arts, she is the author of the *Encyclopedia of Women in Religious Art* (1996); *Dictionary of Christian Art* (1994); and *The Spirit and the Visions: The Influence of Christian Romanticism on the Development of 19th-century American Art* (1994). Her most recent edited works include: *Isamu Noguchi: Essays and Conversations* (1994); and *Symbolism, The Sacred and the Arts*, by Mircea Eliade (1985).

FRANCISCA CHO BANTLY is assistant professor of religion at Georgetown University. In addition to numerous articles in scholarly journals on the topics of Buddhist fiction and philosophy in China and Korea, she is author of *Embracing Illusion: Truth and Fiction in the Dream of the Nine Clouds*.

MARY DOUGLAS retired from University College London in 1977, and, after teaching in the United States, is now retired in London. An anthropologist with Africanist experience and interests, Mary Douglas is particularly interested in methodology in the social sciences, avoiding an ethnocentric basis for social thought, the politicization of nature, rival representations of danger, and rival theories of psyche and justice. Her current research is on pollution ideas, with special reference to the priestly books of the Bible. Her publications include *Purity and Danger* (1966); *Natural Symbols* (1970); *Essays in the Sociology of Perception* (1982); *Risk and Culture* (1982); *Risk Acceptability* (1985); *How Institutions Think* (1986); *Risk and Blame* (1992); *In the Wilderness: The Doctrine of Defilement in the Book of Numbers* (1993); and *Thought Styles* (1996).

WENDY DONIGER is Mircea Eliade Professor of the History of Religions at the University of Chicago. Among her many books are three translations for Penguin Classics: *Hindu Myths, The Rig Veda* and the *Laws of Manu* (with Brian K. Smith). She is the author of several books on Indian mythology and the comparative study of mythology, including *Śiva: The Erotic Ascetic; Dreams, Illusion, and Other Realities; Women, Androgynes, and Other Mythical Beasts;* and *Other Peoples' Myths.* Her most recent edited work includes *Mythologies,* an English-language edition of Yves Bonnefoy's *Dictionnaire des Mythologies,* and *Purāna Perennis: Reciprocity and Transformation in Hindu and Jaina Texts.*

ALAN DUNDES is a professor of anthropology and folklore at the University of California, Berkeley. A folklorist who advocates the application of psychoanalytic theory to myth and other genres of folklore, he is the author of numerous books on folklore, including *La Terra in Piazza: An Interpretation of the Palio of Siena* (1975). His edited work includes *Sacred Narrative: Readings in the Theory of Myth* (1984).

MARC MICHAEL EPSTEIN is Director of Jewish Studies at Vassar College. He writes and speaks on aspects of the interior landscape of the medieval Jewish minority and is the author of several publications on Jewish art and symbolism, including *Dreams of Subversion in Medieval Jewish Art and Literature* (1996). He received the Ph.D. from Yale University and has been a Lady Davis Fellow at Hebrew University. He was director of the Books and Manuscripts Division of the Judaica Department of Sotheby's New York, and serves as Consulting Curator to the Bernard Museum of Judaiea, New York City.

CRISTIANO GROTTANELLI is professor of Storia delle Religioni, University of Pisa, Italy. He is author of *Ideologie Miti Massacri: Indoeuropei di Georges Dumézil* (1993), and *Kings and Prophets* (forthcoming). He is also editor of *Soprannaturale e potere nel mondo antico e nelle società tradizionali* (with M. F. Fales, 1985); *Sacrificio e societa nel mondo antico* (with N. Parise, 1994); *Gli Occhi di Alessandro: Potere sovrano e sacralità del-corpo da Alessandro Magno a Ceausescu* (with S. Bertelli, 1990); and *Anathema: Regime delle offerte e vita dei santuari nel Mediterraneo antico* (with G. Bartoloni e G. Colonna, 1990).

BRUCE LINCOLN is professor of the history of religions and an associate member of the Departments of Anthropology and Classics at the University of Chicago. He is the author of numerous books and articles on the construction of social authority, Indo-European society, and ritual roles for women. His recent work includes *Discourse and the Construction of Society* (1989); *Death, War, and Sacrifice: Studies in Ideology and Practice* (1991); and *Authority: Construction and Corrosion* (1994).

LAURIE L. PATTON is assistant professor of early Indian religions at Emory University. From 1991-1996 she taught at Bard College and and acted as research associate at the Southern Asian Institute, Columbia University. In addition to journal articles on the topics of early India religions, comparative mythology, and theory in the study of religion, she is the author of *Myth as Argument: The Bṛhaddevatā as Canonical Commentary* (1996). Her most recent edited work is *Authority, Anxiety, and Canon: Essays in Vedic Interpretation* (1994). She is currently completing a book on magic and commentary in late Vedic India.

BENJAMIN CALEB RAY is professor of religious studies at the University of Virginia. His primary field of teaching and research is sub-Saharan African religions, a subject on which he has written two books: *African Religions* (1976) and *Myth, Ritual and Kingship* (1991) and numerous articles in journals and encyclopedias. As adjunct curator of African Art at the Bayly Museum of the University of Virginia, he has produced several exhibitions of Africa art on the World Wide Web: "African Art: Aesthetics and Meaning"; "Art of the African Mask"; and "Images of Ancestors: Ties that Bind." He has also written on the ritual aspects of Stonehenge, bear rituals, and shamanism among hunter-gatherers.

ROBERT A. SEGAL is Reader in Theory of Religion in the Department of Religious Studies, University of Lancaster, England. He has previously taught at Reed College, Stanford University, the University of Pittsburgh, Louisiana State University, and Tulane University. He is the author of *The Poimandres as Myth* (1986); *Joseph Campbell* (1987, 1990); *Religion and the Social Sciences* (1989); and *Explaining and Interpreting Religion* (1992). He is the editor of *In Quest of the Hero* (1990); *The Gnostic Jung* (1992); and *The Allure of Gnosticism* (1995). He is completing a book surveying modern theories of myth for the Indiana University Press Folkloristics Series.

IVAN STRENSKI has recently completed two manuscripts: *Durkheim and the Jews of France* (forthcoming from University of Chicago Press, 1997), an inquiry into the question of the "Jewishness" of Durkheim's thought, and *The Time of Sacrifice*, a history of ideologies and theories of ritual and civic sacrifice in fin-de-siècle France. He is the author of *Four Theories of Myth in the Twentieth Century: Cassirer, Eliade, Lévi-Strauss, and Malinowski*, and *Religion in Relation* (1993). He serves currently as the Holstein Family Community Professor of Religious Studies, University of California, Riverside, and as the North American editor of *Religion*.

ERIC J. ZIOLKOWSKI, associate professor in the Religion Department at Lafayette College, writes and teaches in the area of religion and literature. He is the author of *The Sanctification of Don Quixote: From Hidalgo to Priest* (1991) and editor of *A Museum of Faiths: Histories and Legacies of the 1983 World's Parliament of Religions* (1993). In addition to a number of essays which he has contributed to edited volumes, his articles have appeared in professional journals published in the United States, Great Britain, and Japan.

INDEX

Numbers in *italics* refer to illustrations.

Lightning Source UK Ltd.
Milton Keynes UK
UKOW051701200412

191184UK00001B/38/P